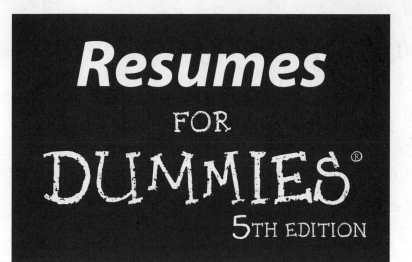

Resumes
FOR
DUMMIES®
5TH EDITION

Resumes FOR DUMMIES®

5TH EDITION

by Joyce Lain Kennedy

BICENTENNIAL
1807
WILEY
2007
BICENTENNIAL

Wiley Publishing, Inc.

Resumes For Dummies®, 5th Edition

Published by
Wiley Publishing, Inc.
111 River St.
Hoboken, NJ 07030-5774
www.wiley.com

Copyright © 2007 by Joyce Lain Kennedy

Published by Wiley Publishing, Inc., Indianapolis, Indiana

Published simultaneously in Canada

WILEY

About the Author

Joyce Lain Kennedy is America's first nationally syndicated careers columnist. Her twice-weekly column, CAREERS NOW, appears in newspapers and Web sites across the land. In her four decades of advising readers — young, senior, and in-between — Joyce has received millions of letters inquiring about career moves and job search and has answered countless numbers of them in print.

Joyce is the author of seven career books, including *Joyce Lain Kennedy's Career Book* (McGraw-Hill), and *Electronic Job Search Revolution, Electronic Resume Revolution*, and *Hook Up, Get Hired! The Internet Job Search Revolution* (the last three published by Wiley). *Resumes For Dummies* is one of a trio of job market books published under Wiley's wildly popular For Dummies branded imprint. The others are *Cover Letters For Dummies* and *Job Interviews For Dummies*.

Writing from a San Diego suburb, the country's best-known careers columnist is a graduate of Washington University in St. Louis. Contact Joyce at jlk@sunfeatures.com.

About the Technical Reviewer

James M. Lemke has earned a reputation as a leader in talent strategies and processes. He is director of organizational development for Opportunity International. Previously, Jim spent 15 years as a human resources consultant. His client list included: Real Networks, Southern California Metropolitan Water District, Northrop Grumman, Southwest Airlines, Jet Propulsion Laboratory, United Arab Emirates University, and the White House. Jim has held executive positions with Wachovia Bank, TRW, UCLA, Walt Disney Imagineering, and Raytheon. He resides in Mesa, Arizona. Contact Jim at jmlemke@aol.com.

Dedication

To **Kathleen Mikol Cox,** a remarkable editor who once helped a grateful careers columnist crack the Dummies code — and again and again, ten books in all.

Author's Acknowledgments

Any book is a collaborative effort and I owe applause to a variety of people who guided me through a challenging process. Please clap your hands together and give enormous recognition to these individuals:

Kathryn Kraemer Troutman, whose firm, The Resume Place, Inc. (www. resume-place.com), created the 48 sample resumes in this book. Troutman and her team, led by **Sarah Blazucki,** produced groundbreaking illustrations that topped my high expectations.

James M. Lemke, the world's greatest technical reviewer whose cutting-edge knowledge is indispensable to my work. Jim's globe-trotting job keeps him awake and online in airports around the world.

John S. Gill, a college student and my technical associate who knows everything I don't about conducting computer analysis, and who gets my vote for Most Likely to Succeed at whatever he goes after.

Traci Cumbay, this book's talented, conscientious and insightful project editor pulled excellent rabbits out of sometimes so-so hats. A strong editor's focused oversight on an ambitious work makes all the difference.

Kelly James, a high school student and my editorial associate whose eagle-eyes never met a typo she invited to stick around, and who provided helpful online research assistance.

Gail Ross, my literary agent-attorney and friend who continues to help me find new chapters to write about.

Robert N. Weinreb, M.D. and **J. Rigby Slight, M.D.,** eminent vision authorities who kept my eyes alive all the way to the finish line.

And cartloads of thanks to the following very special experts for a wide range of editorial contributions:

Richard H. Beatty	**Paul Hawkinson**
Tony Beshara	**Ron Krannich, Ph.D.**
Joel Cheesman	**Kay Luo**
Gerry Crispin	**Mark Mehler**
Jason Goldberg	**John Sumser**

Publisher's Acknowledgments

We're proud of this book; please send us your comments through our Dummies online registration form located at www.dummies.com/register/.

Some of the people who helped bring this book to market include the following:

Acquisitions, Editorial, and Media Development

Project Editor: Traci Cumbay

    (Previous Edition: Kathleen A. Dobie)

Acquisitions Editor: Lindsay Sandman Lefevere

    (Previous Editions: Kathy Cox)

Assistant Editor: Courtney Allen

Copy Editor: Traci Cumbay

Editorial Program Coordinator: Hanna K. Scott

Technical Editor: James M. Lemke

Editorial Manager: Michelle Hacker

Editorial Supervisor and Reprint Editor:
Carmen Krikorian

Editorial Assistant: Erin Calligan, David Lutton

Cartoons: Rich Tennant (www.the5thwave.com)

Composition Services

Project Coordinator: Erin Smith

Layout and Graphics: Brooke Graczyk, Denny Hager, Stephanie D. Jumper, Barbara Moore, Barry Offringa, Heather Ryan

Proofreaders: Jessica Kramer, Techbooks

Indexer: Techbooks

Publishing and Editorial for Consumer Dummies

    Diane Graves Steele, Vice President and Publisher, Consumer Dummies

    Joyce Pepple, Acquisitions Director, Consumer Dummies

    Kristin A. Cocks, Product Development Director, Consumer Dummies

    Michael Spring, Vice President and Publisher, Travel

    Kelly Regan, Editorial Director, Travel

Publishing for Technology Dummies

    Andy Cummings, Vice President and Publisher, Dummies Technology/General User

Composition Services

    Gerry Fahey, Vice President of Production Services

    Debbie Stailey, Director of Composition Services

Contents at a Glance

Introduction 1

Part 1: Pitching Your Resumes
in a New Era Job Market 7

Chapter 1: The All-Purpose Resume Is So Five Minutes Ago 9
Chapter 2: New Quick Ways to Find the Right Jobs 29
Chapter 3: Spotlight Your Resume in a Web 2.0 World 45
Chapter 4: Familiar Search Tools That Haven't Gone Away 59

Part 11: Resume Basics That Wow 'Em Every Time 73

Chapter 5: Creating Your Best Resume 75
Chapter 6: Content Makes the OnTarget Difference 103
Chapter 7: Wow Words Work Wonders 123
Chapter 8: Refine Your Design for Great Looks 141
Chapter 9: Passages: Resumes for Your Life's Changing Phases 151
Chapter 10: Successful Solutions to Resume Problems 175

Part 111: Bringing It All Together:
Sample OnTarget Resumes 197

Chapter 11: A Sampling of OnTarget Resumes by Industry and Career Field 199
Chapter 12: A Sampling of OnTarget Resumes by Experience Level and Age 219
Chapter 13: A Sampling of OnTarget Resumes for Special Circumstances 239
Chapter 14: A Sampling of Extreme Resume Makeovers 259

Part IV: You've Sent Your Wow. What to Do Now 279

Chapter 15: References Safeguard Your Resume 281
Chapter 16: Twisting in the Wind? Follow Up! 289
Chapter 17: Almost Got the Interview Date? Read This First 305

Part V: The Part of Tens 309

Chapter 18: Ten (×3) Ways to Prove Your Claims 311
Chapter 19: Ten Ways to Improve Your Resume 315
Chapter 20: Ten Tips on Choosing Professional Resume Help 319
Chapter 21: Ten Pet Peeves of Recruiters 325
Chapter 22: Your Ten-Point Resume Checklist 331

Index 337

Table of Contents

Introduction 1

About This Book..1
Conventions Used in This Book 2
Foolish Assumptions 3
How This Book Is Organized..3
 Part I: Pitching Your Resumes in a New Era Job Market 3
 Part II: Resume Basics That Wow 'Em Every Time......................4
 Part III: Bringing It All Together: Sample OnTarget Resumes 4
 Part IV: You've Sent Your Wow. What to Do Now 4
 Part V: The Part of Tens...4
Icons Used in This Book..5
Where to Go from Here..5

Part 1: Pitching Your Resumes in a New Era Job Market.. 7

Chapter 1: The All-Purpose Resume Is So Five Minutes Ago 9

In a New Era, the Targeted Resume Rules....................................9
Market Forces Zap Unqualified Resumes 10
Game-Changing Government Rules Impact Resumes....................12
 Navigating the regulations 14
 Sign of the times 15
Three Steps to Writing a Targeted Resume..................................15
 Step 1: Prepare your core resume 16
 Step 2: Research requirements of job 16
 Step 3: Customize each spinoff resume................................16
Sample Core Resume and Spinoffs...16
 The back story on Lauren L. Simpson 17
 Lauren's core resume 17
 Lauren's spinoff resume A...17
 Lauren's spinoff resume B...22
In a New Era, the OnTarget Resume Brings You So Up to Date................25

Chapter 2: New Quick Ways to Find the Right Jobs **29**

The Young Giants: Vertical Job Search Engines 30
    Using a vertical: The generic basics 32
    Meet the verticals...33
        SimplyHired.com..33
        Indeed.com...33
        Jobster.com..34
        GetTheJob.com..35
        Yahoo! HotJobs 36
Job Boards Rising..36
    Finding job boards 37
    Using job board resources 38
The Continuing Power of Newspapers 39
    But here's the rest of the story...40
    A new wind is blowing on newspapers 41
Hunting on Company Web Sites 41
Seeking and Finding Is Easier than Ever......................................43

Chapter 3: Spotlight Your Resume in a Web 2.0 World **45**

Online Employee Referral 46
    What it is...47
    Getting started 47
    Finding more info..48
Online Social Networking...48
    What it is...48
    Getting started 49
    Finding more info..50
Blogs 51
    What it is...51
    Getting started 52
    Finding more info..53
Really Simple Syndication (RSS) 53
    What it is...53
    Getting started 54
    Finding more info..54
Instant Messaging 54
    What it is...55
    Getting started 56
    Finding more info..56

Podcasts 56
    What it is..57
    Getting started 57
    Finding more info...58
Web 2.0 Is a Work in Progress 58

Chapter 4: Familiar Search Tools That Haven't Gone Away **59**
Scannable Resumes: Same as Ever 60
Plain Text Resumes: A Long Last Gasp.......................61
E-Forms: Fill in the Blankety-Blanks..........................64
Yippee! The Fully Designed, Handsome Resume Is Back!.......................66
From Identity Theft to Recruiter Turnoff:
    Why Resume Blasting Is a Bad Idea 67
    Privacy and identity theft problems 67
    Risks in your workplace 68
    Overexposure to recruiters...............................69
Online Screening Keeps On Keepin' On 69
    Sample components of online screening............70
    Pros and cons of online screening 71
    Can your resume be turned away?......................72
Match Your Resumes to the Jobs................................72

Part II: Resume Basics That Wow 'Em Every Time 73

Chapter 5: Creating Your Best Resume **75**
"Telling It" Mutes; "Selling It" Sings 75
Focus Your Resume..77
Resume Formats Make a Difference............................80
Reverse Chronological Format 81
    Strengths and weaknesses 81
    Who should use this format and who should think twice 82
    Creating a reverse chronological resume...........84
Functional Format..84
    Strengths and weaknesses 84
    Who should use this format and who should think twice 85
    Creating a functional resume 85

Hybrid Format 87
     Strengths and weaknesses 87
     Who should use this format and who should think twice 87
     Creating a hybrid resume 87
Professional Format 89
     Strengths and weaknesses 89
     Who should use this format and who should think twice 89
     Creating a professional resume 89
Academic Curriculum Vitae 91
     Strengths and weaknesses 91
     Who should use this format and who should think twice 91
     Creating an academic curriculum vitae..................................94
International Curriculum Vitae Format 94
     Strengths and weaknesses 94
     Who should use this format and who should think twice 94
     Creating an international curriculum vitae..............................97
Other Resume Presentations...97
     Variations on a theme 97
          Accomplishment format 98
          Linear format 98
          Keyword format 98
     Resume letters 99
     Portfolios 99
     Video resumes 100
     Web resumes 101
     Multimedia resumes 101
Choose What Works for You 101

Chapter 6: Content Makes the OnTarget Difference 103
The Parts of Your Resume 103
Leading with Contact Information 104
Hooking the Reader with a Summary or Objective 106
     Choosing an objective 107
          When to use an objective 107
          Advantages of an objective 107
          Disadvantages of an objective 108
     Opting for a summary...108
          When to use a summary 108
          Advantages of a summary 110
          Disadvantages of a summary 110

Making Education, Experience, Skills, and
  Competencies Work for You..110
    Education 110
    Experience..111
    Skills 111
    Competencies 113
    A few examples of core competencies 114
    Including competencies in your resumes 116
Gaining Extra Points 117
    Activities...117
    Organizations 118
    Honors and awards 118
    Licenses and samples of your work..118
    Testimonials 119
Shaping Your Content on Application Forms 119
Content to Omit: Your Salary Story 120
Accomplishments Are Your Content Aces....................................121

Chapter 7: Wow Words Work Wonders **123**
Wow Words Can Bring Good News 124
    Wow words for administration and management 124
    Wow words for communications and creativity...........................125
    Wow words for sales and persuasion 125
    Wow words for technical ability..126
    Wow words for office support 127
    Wow words for teaching 128
    Wow words for research and analysis 128
    Wow words for helping and caregiving 129
    Wow words for financial management....................................130
    Wow words for many skills 131
Keywords Are Key to Finding You...131
    Keywords for administration/management 132
    Keywords for banking...133
    Keywords for customer service 133
    Keywords for information technology.....................................134
    Keywords for manufacturing 134
    Keywords for human resources 134
Where to Find Keywords..135
Get a Grip on Grammar 136
A Few Words about Spelling 137
Words Sell Your Story..139

Chapter 8: Refine Your Design for Great Looks **141**

Resumes That Resonate 142
   Word processing 142
   Printing 142
   Paper selection 142
   Consistency, consistency, consistency 143
   When three's not a crowd 143
   Come on, break it up! 143
   Open spaces 144
   Typefaces and fonts 145
   A few more tips on appearance 146
Choosing between Two Resume Layouts 146
Design That Gets the Word Out 150

Chapter 9: Passages: Resumes for Your Life's Changing Phases . . .**151**

Scoring Big as a Recent Graduate 152
   Quick take: Rookie strengths 152
   Quick take: Rookie soft spots 152
   Tips for recent graduates 153
      Beef up your sales pitch 153
      Clarify your aim 154
      Ditch unhelpful information 154
      Data-mine your college experience 154
   Gaffes common to new graduates 155
      Falling short of image standards 155
      Omitting heavy-hitter points 155
      Overcompensating with gimmicky language 157
      Making employers guess 157
      Leveling the experience field 157
      Stopping with bare bones 157
      Hiding hot information 157
      Highlighting the immaterial 158
      Ignoring employers' needs 158
      Writing boastfully 158
Grabbing Good Jobs as a Baby Boomer 158
   Quick take: Boomer strengths 158
   Quick take: Boomer soft spots......................................159

Tips for baby boomers 160
Match your target job description 160
Shorten your resume..161
Focus your resume 161
Show that you're a tower of strength....................................161
Demonstrate political correctness...161
Distribute your resume online 161
Murder ancient education dates..162
Trim your resume to fighting weight 162
Use appropriate headings 162
Taking a lower-level job...162
Gaffes common to boomers 163
Choosing the wrong focus 163
Using old resume standards..164
Lacking a summary 164
Revealing age negatively...165
Appearing low-tech 165
Not supplementing a high school education 165
Winning Interviews as a New Civilian...165
Quick take: Transitioning military strengths 166
Quick take: Transitioning military soft spots 166
Tips for new civilians..167
Advertise what you're selling...167
Consider your best format 167
Zero in on job fairs 168
Protect your identity from theft 168
Be a resource collector 168
Visit key Web sites..170
Get the message about milspeak..170
Changing Course with an OnTarget Resume 172

Chapter 10: Successful Solutions to Resume Problems 175

Too Much Experience..176
Too many qualifications or ageism? 176
Too much experience in one job..178
Divide your job into modules..178
Deal honestly with job titles..178
Tackle deadly perceptions head-on 179
Highlight the issue..179

Too Long Gone: For Women Only 180
    Sift through your past 182
    Use professional terms 182
    Know the score 182
Job Seekers with Disabilities 183
    Deciding whether to disclose a disability 184
    Explaining gaps in work history 184
    Asking for special equipment 185
When Demotion Strikes..185
Gaps in Your Record 187
Too Many Layoffs That Aren't Your Fault 189
Explaining Mergers and Acquisitions 189
Here a Job, There a Job, Everywhere a Job, Job 190
    Overcoming a job-hopping image 190
    Cleaning out your job closet 192
When Substance Abuse Is the Problem...192
A Bad Credit Rap 193
Ex-Offenders Job Hunting 194
    Know that negative information is dangerous.....................194
    Avoid the chronological format..194
    Present your prison experience in nonprison terms...................195
    Get help with your resume and job search 195
Look for Ways to Scoot Past Resume Blocks..................................195

Part III: Bringing It All Together: Sample OnTarget Resumes 197

Chapter 11: A Sampling of OnTarget Resumes by Industry and Career Field 199

Chapter 12: A Sampling of OnTarget Resumes by Experience Level and Age 219

Chapter 13: A Sampling of OnTarget Resumes for Special Circumstances 239

Chapter 14: A Sampling of Extreme Resume Makeovers 259

Part IV: You've Sent Your Wow. What to Do Now 279

Chapter 15: References Safeguard Your Resume 281
The Harm Caused by a So-So Reference 281
Seven Things You Should Do about References...........................282
  Ban references from your resume.......................................282
  Expect employers to check references..................................283
  Choose references with thought 283
  Help references help you..284
  Cover your bases with a reference folder 284
  Stamp out bad references 286
  Thank everyone..287
Finding References without Shedding Your Cloak of Secrecy 287
Allow Enough Time for Skillful Reference Management 288

Chapter 16: Twisting in the Wind? Follow Up! 289
Why Follow-Up Efforts Are Essential Today 290
Questions to Ask Yourself Before Following Up...........................291
  Should I phone or e-mail my follow-up? 292
  What if the ad says "no phone calls"? 292
  What is the most powerful opening statement I can make?.........293
  What are other compelling opening statements? 293
  How much information can I find out
    from a central phone operator?.....................................294
  What are some tips to get past screeners, a.k.a. gatekeepers?....294
  What can I do if I keep getting booted to voicemail? 296
  Why shouldn't I leave a message asking
    the target to call me back? 297
  How can I keep track of all my calls, e-mails,
    and contacts as I follow up?.......................................298
  When is it time to throw in the towel and move on?...................298
Monitoring Your Follow-up Efforts..299
  Using the Follow-Up Matrix..299
    Factors on the Follow-Up Matrix 300
    The Values Key...301
  Checking out a sample Matrix 303
Fast-Tracking Your Successful Follow-Up 303

Chapter 17: Almost Got the Interview Date? Read This First **305**

  When Your Job Conflicts with an Interview Date 305
  Face-to-Face Beats Ear-to-Ear 306
  Going Overboard on Ardor Can Cost You Money 307
  When the Interview Is Out of Town 307
  Making the Most of Your Moment...308
  Little Things Do Mean a Lot 308

Part V: The Part of Tens *309*

Chapter 18: Ten (×3) Ways to Prove Your Claims **311**

  Say It with Numbers..312
  Say It with Percentages 312
  Say It with Dollar Amounts 313

Chapter 19: Ten Ways to Improve Your Resume **315**

  Match Your Resume to the Job 315
  Use Bulleted Style for Easy Reading 315
  Discover Art of Lost Articles 315
  Sell, Don't Tell 316
  Show Off Your Assets..316
  Make Sure Your Words Play Well Together 316
  Reach Out with Strength 317
  Trash a Wimpy Objective..317
  Check the Horse's Mouth 318
  Erase the "Leave-Outs" 318

Chapter 20: Ten Tips on Choosing Professional Resume Help **319**

  Choose a Resume Writing Service, Not a Clerical Service....................320
  Ask Around for a Great Resume Pro 320
  Request a Free Initial Consultation...321
  Watch Out for Overuse of Forms...321
  Look for a Fair Price..321
  Check Out Samples 322
  Take Aim 322
  Consider a Certified Resume Writer 323
  Remember That Design Counts..323
  Know That a Poor Resume Is No Bargain 324

Chapter 21: Ten Pet Peeves of Recruiters 325

Resume-Free Pitches...325
Major Mismatches...325
E-Stalking..326
Caps and Taps and Typos 328
Too Much Information..328
Date Grate 328
Guess Who 329
File Style 329
Useless and Uninformative 330
Probable Prevarication..330

Chapter 22: Your Ten-Point Resume Checklist 331

Tit for Tat 331
Format and Style 331
Focus and Image...332
Achievements and Skills...332
Language and Expressions..332
Content and Omissions 332
Length and Common Sense 333
Appearance: Online Attached and Paper Resumes 333
Sticky Points and Sugarcoating 333
Tap the Power of OnTarget Resumes 335

Index...337

Introduction

When the editors and I first talked about updating this book from the 4th edition, which was published four years ago, we were thinking, well, "revision."

The result, after six intense months of research and writing, is quite different. *Resumes For Dummies,* 5th Edition, is about 85 percent new content, and all the sample resumes in Chapters 11 to 14 are new.

Necessity was the engine driving the radical makeover. From reinvented recruiting technology, to unmanageable millions of resumes choking employer databases, to government mandates in the name of diversity fairness, a sea change has occurred in the recruiting space over the past several years.

All this change demands a fresh look at how you write and market your resumes. A minor revision just wouldn't cut it; you deserve to know the ropes and rules for a New Era in recruiting and job finding.

About This Book

Resumes For Dummies, 5th Edition, is a playbook showing you how to tap the power of amazing new technology to write and use your resumes in search of a good job.

Technology came to resumes in the early part of a time period — roughly 1994 to 2005 — now called *Web 1.0.* In 1995, when writing the debut edition of this work, I explained that resumes were being scanned and read by job computers, and — imagine this — transmitted over the Internet! The fasten-your-seatbelt bumps and wonders happening in Web 1.0 were nothing less than a revolution in the traditional employment process.

Fast forward to right now. Refasten your seat belts and expect surprise after surprise as *Web 2.0* replaces Web 1.0. What we're dealing with today is a kind of revolution of a revolution.

The second Web phase is again bulldozing the traditional job market with an array of ambitious ideas and software aimed at solving recruiting-industry problems and meeting the needs of employers. But a number of developments lighten the load for job seekers, adding high-octane fuel for successful searches. What's the big difference between the first and second Web phases?

Web 1.0 is characterized by static, rigid formats and job boards. Web 2.0 moves toward richer, more interactive resources (see Chapter 3).

The advancing technology of Web 2.0 is why *Resumes For Dummies,* 5th Edition, pinpoints the best ways to distribute your resume, as well as create it.

There's one more notable difference between the beginning days of Web 1.0 and Web 2.0: In Web 1.0, everyone wanted to know how to *get on* the Web; in Web 2.0, everyone wants to know how to *get noticed* on the Web.

In these pages I tell you how to get noticed by creating an OnTarget resume (see Chapter 1) and distributing it wisely.

Conventions Used in This Book

To help you navigate this book, I've established the following conventions:

- ✔ *Italic* is used for emphasis and to highlight new words or terms that are defined.
- ✔ `Monofont` is used for Web addresses.
- ✔ Sidebars, which are shaded boxes of text, consist of information that's interesting but not necessarily critical to your understanding of the topic.

Further, in the sample resumes throughout the book, I substitute a reminder to add the relevant dates in your resume with the word "dates" enclosed in editorial brackets — [dates] — instead of actual years to keep your attention focused on key resume concepts.

Watch out also for the numbering system I use in the sample resumes in Chapter 1 and Chapters 11 to 14. I put cross-matching numbers there to guide you through important aspects of each resume, but you don't want to stick numbers in yours.

Foolish Assumptions

I assume you picked up this book for one of the following reasons:

- ✔ You've never written a resume and want an experienced, friendly hand on your shoulder.

- ✔ You have written a resume — it got you where you are today — and you want to do better next time.

- ✔ You like where you are today but want more from life than blooming where you're planted. To move to the next level, your experience tells you that it's time for a resume makeover.

- ✔ You need a new resume for that great job you heard about but worry that too many competitors will submit virtually the same cookie-cutter document pirated from somewhere. To stop looking like a human photocopy machine, you want to understand resume writing from the ground up.

- ✔ You've heard about sweeping technology-based changes in the way people and jobs find each other. A realist, you know that technology can't be uninvented. You want to be sure your resume is in sync with the very latest updates.

I further assume that you are someone who likes information that cuts to the chase, sometimes with a smile.

How This Book Is Organized

Getting through the job interview door depends on much more than just being a great candidate. This book takes you through everything you need to know about creating your best resumes, getting them into the right hands, and landing interviews. Here's where you can find all the legs of the adventure.

Part 1: Pitching Your Resumes in a New Era Job Market

This part covers the Web 2.0 changes that are streaming into recruiting offices. You can also review here the technology of the 1990s still in use. Plus, here's where you discover how to move your OnTarget resumes to the right eyes.

Part II: Resume Basics That Wow 'Em Every Time

Format, content, words, design, savvy handling of special considerations and problems — all these factors impact the quality of your resume. Find out how best to highlight your good points and downplay the not-so-good ones here. And how to do it all with grace, clarity, and readable style.

Part III: Bringing It All Together: Sample OnTarget Resumes

What does an OnTarget resume look like? Turn to this part to find out. Here you get to take a long look at resumes that make use of the strategies I describe in this book. I show you resumes from new grads and baby boomers, from nurses and business analysts, and from people who've moved straight up in a career and those who've had a few stumbles. I also show you some startling resume makeovers.

Part IV: You've Sent Your Wow. What to Do Now

Because of intense competition for better jobs (which especially affects mid-career and baby-boomer candidates), the follow-up tips of earlier times may be too tentative to be effective. This part includes creative new moves that keep you from waiting all alone by your cell phone for calls that never come.

Part V: The Part of Tens

In these short chapters, I give you quick bits of information on yet more resume topics. I offer guidance on proving your resume claims, avoiding unnecessary mistakes, choosing professional resume help, recognizing the big peeves of recruiters, and, finally, using a resume checklist that won't take half a day to complete.

Icons Used in This Book

For Dummies signature icons are the little round pictures you see in the margins of the book. I use them to laser-guide your attention to key bits of information. Here's a list of the icons you find in this book and what they mean.

This icon directs your attention to techniques that cause readers to lavish praise and respect on your resume and then move it to the "you betcha" file.

No move achieves the resume–interview connection every single time. This icon reminds you to think through an issue and try to make the best choice for your situation.

Some points in these pages are so useful that I hope you'll keep them in mind as you read. I make a big deal out of these ideas with this icon.

Advice and information that can spark a difference in the outcome of your resume-led job search are flagged with this icon.

Watch out for deep waters filled with things that bite. This icon signals there could be trouble ahead if you don't make a good decision.

Where to Go from Here

Most *For Dummies* books are set up so that you can flip to the section of the book that meets your present needs. You can do that in this book, too. I tell you where to find the information you might need when I refer to a concept, and I define terms as they arise to enable you to feel at home no matter where you open the book.

But this book breaks new ground in resume creation and distribution. To get ahead and stay ahead, start by reading Chapters 1 through 4. They provide the foundation you need to come through a Web 2.0 job search with the interview invitations that lead to employment offers.

P.S. The good news is that you need not be a techie to make sense out of Web 2.0 innovations and to bend them to your will as a job seeker. Using a new e-tool is like owning a stylish automobile: You don't have to know how to repair its engine to get *ooohs* and *ahhhs* as you drive it smartly down the street.

Part I
Pitching Your Resumes in a New Era Job Market

The 5th Wave   By Rich Tennant

In this part . . .

Changes aplenty make the current Web climate different from that of just a couple years ago, and this part gets you up to date. I also show you how to sift through the myriad online job boards and how to get your resume into the hands that can get you the interview.

Chapter 1

The All-Purpose Resume Is So Five Minutes Ago

. . . .

In This Chapter

▶ Understanding the radical change overtaking recruitment and resumes

▶ Responding to the pull of market forces and the push of government regulations

▶ Writing targeted resumes, from a core document to spinoff communications

▶ Fighting back when technology isn't your friend and your resumes go missing

. . . .

*H*ey there! Is your job search stalling out after you submit a resume but before you are offered an interview?

If your answer is *yes,* this book can open significant new insights for you with a quick update on how to thrive in a landscape where recruiting processes have turned digital but resume practices are stuck in analog.

In a New Era, the Targeted Resume Rules

Job seekers, brace yourselves. Trolling the job market is getting trickier and requires more effort than the last time you baited your resume hook. Even if you were job hunting fairly recently, resumes and related techniques that were revolutionary in the savvy job seeker's toolkit a mere dozen years ago are headed for history. *The all-purpose resume is at the top of the list of job search tools gliding to irrelevance or extinction.*

You probably have an all-purpose resume lying around in a desk drawer somewhere. What you and legions of job seekers everywhere like about the all-purpose resume is that it casts a wide net to snag the attention of many employers — and it saves time for those of us who are too busy getting through the day to keep writing different resumes for different jobs. I appreciate that. But, sorry to say, your one-size-fits-all work of art is obsolete, and it's going to get lost in more and more recruiting black holes.

Of friends and resumes

"The number one way to use your OnTarget resume is to find a friend to walk it into the hiring manager's or recruiter's office with the friend's stamp of approval," advises Mark Mehler, cofounder and principal of CareerXroads and a long-time Internet job-hunting expert. He says his firm's annual survey of how people get hired at major corporations shows that one out of three openings is filled this way.

The all-purpose, or generic, resume is being replaced by the targeted resume (which I refer to in this book as OnTarget), a resume that is tailor-made for a specific employment goal.

An OnTarget resume is a marketing tool that convinces the reader your work will benefit a specific employer and that you should make the cut of candidates invited in for a closer look. An OnTarget resume

- ✔ Addresses a given opportunity, making it easy to see how your qualifications are a close match to a job's requirements.
- ✔ Uses powerful words to persuade and clean design to attract interest.
- ✔ Plays up strengths and downplays any factor that undermines your bid for an interview.

In previous editions of this book, I said that when you want to be picked out of a crowd and invited to a job interview, nothing beats a perfect or near-perfect match between a job order and your resume. What was solid advice in earlier years has become critical advice in this New Era. I repeat: _Targeting your resume for each job is becoming necessary, not just smart._

Hurried along and killed off by technology advances, the demise of the generic resume is driven by two factors: the pull of market forces and the push of government mandate. I explain both factors in the next two segments.

Market Forces Zap Unqualified Resumes

The word got out, slowly at first. And then — whoosh! — millions of job seekers found out how easy it is to instantly put a resume in the hands of employers across the country as well as across town.

Post and pray became the job seekers' mantra as they learned how to manipulate online resumes and click them into the digital world as quickly as fast-shuffling dealers lay down cards at casino poker tables.

Are resumes outdated?

Every few years for as long as I can remember, an employment "thought leader" announces that resumes are old hat and unnecessary, advising that you, as a job seeker, forgo resumes and talk your way into an interview.

The problem with this advice is that it's impractical — it doesn't work for most people. Very few of us are extroverted and glib enough to carry the entire weight of an employment marketing presentation without supporting materials before or during face-to-face meetings.

Now a new resume attack has surfaced. This time it turns on technology. Industry consultants observe that companies are weary of sifting through too many resumes and instead will substitute structured e-profiles, screening questions via the Web, and assessment instruments (tests) in deciding who gets offered a job interview.

As my crystal ball is in the repair shop, I don't know *whether, when,* or *how widely* technology will erase resumes. But this is what I believe:

At some point in a hunt for better employment, everyone needs market-driven job search communications. That is, everyone needs a resume or something very much like a resume that tells the buyer (employer) such critical facts as these:

- Why you are an excellent match for the job
- What skills you bring to the organization
- Why you are worth the money you hope to earn
- Your capacity for doing the work better than other candidates
- Your ability to solve company or industry problems

The resume rush began back in the first phase of the World Wide Web, which retroactively is termed *Web 1.0,* a time frame of about 1994 to 2005.

But the Net's resume sludge got yuckier and more frustrating as commercial resume-blasting services appeared on the scene. Almost overnight, it seemed, anyone willing to pay the price could splatter resume confetti everywhere an online address could be found.

The consequences of resume spamming for employers were staggering: Despite their use of the Web 1.0 era's best recruiting selection software, employers were overrun with unsolicited, disorganized generic resumes containing everything but the kitchen sink.

And what about the job seekers who sent all those all-purpose, unstructured resumes? They were left to wonder in disappointment why they never got a callback.

It's all in the numbers. A job advertised by a major company in the era before Web 1.0 might have attracted hundreds or even thousands of responses, but the same ad posted online creates a feeding frenzy of many thousands of resumes. A few super-sized companies report that they receive millions of unsolicited resumes each year. No wonder the Web is falling-down-drunk with billions of resumes that overwhelm both technology and eyeballs. No wonder employment databases are hammered with such mismatches as sales clerks and sports trainers applying for jobs as scientists and senior managers, and vice versa.

Fast-forward to 2005 when digital curtains went up on a second Internet phase. It's called *Web 2.0,* a term suggesting a host of new ideas and amazing software that has leapt onto the world recruiting stage. Web 2.0 is fueled by the desire of companies to eliminate resume fatigue and, at the same time, to ace out the competition in acquiring top talent. And, of course, employers universally want to do it better-faster-cheaper.

Briefly, the Web-based services of Web 2.0 are characterized by their movement away from static, rigid Web sites merely listing jobs and links to apply for them and toward richer, more interactive and socially inclusive methods. (To read more about Web 2.0 services, check out Chapters 2 and 3.)

As employers hope to use Web 2.0 solutions to dry out the resume deluge created by Web 1.0 innovation, job seekers have updated aspirations as well.

In Web 1.0, job seekers wanted to know how to *get on* the Internet. In Web 2.0, job seekers want to know how to *get noticed* on the Internet.

Market forces, the term describing the interaction of supply and demand that shapes a market economy, are pulling companies toward targeted resumes by rewarding them with less unnecessary work to wade through. And market forces are pulling job seekers toward targeted resumes by showing them how to get noticed on the Internet.

Game-Changing Government Rules Impact Resumes

As market forces pull toward targeted resumes, the federal government pushes.

The government didn't set out to establish resume targeting as a newly essential job-market skill. But that's what happened as a result of the government's official guidelines mandated in 2006 by the Office of Federal Contract Compliance Programs (OFCCP), the agency established to track the diversity hiring record of those applying for positions with federal contractors.

The rationale for the government's interest in employment practices is that federal tax dollars should not support discrimination in the workplace. The agency's new guidelines are intended to encourage hiring fairness toward those who work for federal contractors. Accurate record keeping is required for gender, race, and ethnicity. (Strangely, age isn't included in the OFCCP protected classes.) While the diversity issue was already in place before 2006, it effectively was on the back burner and probably would have stayed there except that the Internet came along and made it so easy for everyone to apply for every job under the sun.

How likely are you to be covered by the new OFCCP rules? Perhaps more likely than you think. It's surprising how many businesses are subject to "federal contractors or subcontractors" mandates. Estimates range from a conservative 20,000 companies in the United States to nearly 200,000 facilities and companies worldwide, of which half are reported to be construction firms. One in five American workers is thought to be employed by federal contractors. (Official government figures aren't available at this writing but may be in the future following the establishment of a federal contractor database required by 2006 legislation.)

Even if you postal mail, fax, or hand deliver your resume to someone at a friend's backyard barbeque and never, ever send it online, you still may be classified as an Internet applicant if the contractor accepts some applications for a specific position via the Internet; all applicants for that position must now be considered Internet applicants, according to the rules.

The OFCCP action to deal with Internet record keeping started with a question: Who is an "Internet applicant" and who is a looky-lou?

Why does anyone care? Think about it this way: If 50,000 individuals send a contractor unsolicited and unqualified resumes, should those people, for diversity counts, be considered applicants? The OFCCP says *no*. The agency believes that their inclusion would muddy the database used for official audits and lawsuits based on bias claims.

Using a transportation metaphor, the OFCCP guidelines identify people who should be counted as Internet applicants because they have a specific destination in mind and drive straight for that destination. By contrast, people who should not be counted aimlessly cruise traffic-jammed streets hoping to get lucky and find an acceptable destination. Policy makers insist that the government must know who is and who isn't an Internet applicant to measure hiring fairness when dealing with the otherwise unmanageable hoards of online resumes.

Gain competitive advantage as you distribute your resumes by bearing in mind the official criteria for your being validated as an Internet applicant:

- You express your interest for a particular position.
- The employer considers you for employment in a particular position.
- You have the basic qualifications for the particular position.
- Prior to receiving a job offer for the particular position, you don't drop out of consideration for the job — by taking other employment, for example, or saying you're no longer interested in the particular position.

JUDGMENT CALL

To clone or not to clone: Mirroring ad language

Must you use the exact words in the job ad? Two schools of thought exist on this question. Some authorities advise that you should state your qualifications in the identical language used in the ad to which you respond. The ditto contingent points out that computer selection software awards rating points to a resume based on how closely your words mirror those in the job ad: Get closer to the ad, get more points.

Others disagree, saying that modern recruiting software is sophisticated enough to grasp your qualifications even though you use synonyms and related terms and not the exact same words.

Career advisers won't have a definitive answer on the same words-or-synonym question until enough time has passed to give us more experience with the new OFCCP mandate.

I agree with the latter view — that synonyms and related terms are acceptable — and largely have taken that approach in this book. But if you're worried that a company is using older, limited software, go with the ditto school. The important thing is to play matchmaker with each resume you submit.

Navigating the regulations

Because the OFCCP rules are new to most of us, the following recommendations for resume success with federal contractors are crucial. Most of the tips come from CareerXroads (www.careerxroads.com) co-founder and principal Gerry Crispin, who is way out in front on Internet applicant expertise. Crispin advises that you

- ✔ **Follow the company's instructions.** Do exactly as the company instructs you on how to apply. One way to make it easy for employers to consider you for a specific job is to clone a portion of the job description to your resume for each job you target.

- ✔ **Clearly spell out your matching qualifications.** Make a list of basic requirements and check item by item to be sure you have included your qualification for each one. If you're missing a requirement-qualification match, your resume will gather dust unless no one else qualifies and the company is desperate. (I talk more about matching qualifications to requirements in the section "Three Steps to Writing a Targeted Resume," and illustrate targeting throughout sample resumes in Chapters 11 to 14.)

- ✔ **Send multiple resumes to the same company.** Monitor your preferred company's Web sites and submit a new targeted resume for each position that interests you.

- ✔ **Keep your resume current.** Do you remember the classic tip to stay at the top of a list of candidates by changing a word or two in your resume and reposting to job boards frequently? Well, that tip is alive and well. "OFCCP rules allow companies to pick a random pool of applicants by searching the job boards for 'most recent' qualified applicants," Crispin observes. "In those cases, no one will even look at a resume that is more than two or three weeks old."

Sign of the times

Although there are enough federal contractor jobs to justify your paying attention to the OFCCP guidelines, the new rules appear to be spreading into job search quarters across America, starting at the largest companies, says Gerry Crispin, whose CareerXroads consulting firm arranges scholarly conferences where staffing professionals at major corporations share their best practices.

Additionally, the buzz among recruiting-industry insiders is that the Equal Employment Opportunity Commission will soon extend similar, if not identical, guidelines to all U.S. companies with more than 50 employees. Whether the EEOC drops the other diversity-protection shoe in the near future or not, Crispin believes the targeted resume is gaining mainstream status in the United States.

"More and more companies are accepting the OFCCP definition of Internet applicants — individuals who continue to express interest, who are being considered for a specific position, and who meet the position's basic qualifications," Crispin says. "The move toward targeted resumes ensures that job seekers who willy-nilly apply for every job that is even close will be wasting their time."

Three Steps to Writing a Targeted Resume

When you begin to think seriously about greener grass, the race is on! You already need 36-hour days to accomplish all the responsibilities you carry on your shoulders. And then you see a job that you hope has your name on it but can't carve out the time to write from scratch a targeted resume that will show an employer why you're the one to interview.

Your answer is to begin building a core resume before the pressure hits, using it as a base to spin off targeted editions when you must move quickly. Constructing a targeted resume is easier when you follow this game plan.

Step 1: Prepare your core resume

Probe your memory to jot down every factor in your background that you could use to customize a resume, from experience, competencies, and skills to education. This is your working model, a resume you will never submit to an employer but a rich well you will draw from time and time again. Use as many pages as you need. (To get pointers on content, go to Chapter 6.)

Step 2: Research requirements of job

If you're responding to a specific advertised job, jot down the requirements that the ad lists. Don't confuse the job duties and the stated requirements. Deal first with the requirements and then see how you can show experience or education that matches the most important job duties.

When you're not responding to a specific advertised job but are posting your resume in an online database, attempt to attract interest in your candidacy by researching the most commonly requested qualifications for a given occupation or career field. You can do this by studying many job ads.

Step 3: Customize each spinoff resume

After compiling the requirements you must satisfy in a tailor-made resume, scour your core resume to see whether you can add secondary items mentioned in the ad that further improve your chances and start writing.

Resume professional Kathryn Troutman suggests a way to cut down on your time and effort customizing each resume. Constructing a two-page resume, customize the first page and, whenever possible, keep the second page the same each time. Freezing the second page isn't always possible, Troutman says, but the concept is a good starting point.

Sample Core Resume and Spinoffs

Look over the following examples for Lauren L. Simpson created by Resume-Place.com CEO Kathryn Troutman. (For privacy reasons, names and other identifying data have been changed.) You'll see how attention to details can make all the difference in getting your resume noticed, first by computers and then by humans.

The back story on Lauren L. Simpson

Lauren grew up on the Mid-Atlantic seaboard (Baltimore, Washington, D.C., and Northern Virginia). After graduating from high school, Lauren worked for a year as an administrative assistant at a health insurance company in Northern Virginia. Deciding she didn't want to continue in administrative work, Lauren landed a job as a sales associate at a nationwide women's wear chain.

Lauren was good at retailing, and after six months the clothing chain offered her a managerial traineeship at one of the chain's stores in Texas. Once there, Lauren enrolled in the retailing program of a well-regarded school of business at the state university. While working and studying, Lauren was promoted to assistant manager.

After graduation from college, another retailer recruited Lauren, who spent several years at the new company. Although successful there, Lauren had a change of mind and began to feel that she'd gotten off on the wrong foot. Retailing isn't really what she wants to do for the rest of her life and she's looking around for another way to learn a livelihood.

Although going back to school and retooling for another career field is an option Lauren is considering, she isn't anxious to incur student debt. Before doing that, she's checking out how she can adapt her hard-earned education to related but different types of work.

Lauren's core resume

Using a reverse chronological time frame (see Chapter 5), Lauren writes a comprehensive document, highlighting her competencies, skills, and accomplishments. (See Figure 1-1) Your core document can run as many pages as you need to include *all* your qualifications. No one but you will see it.

She creates distinct units that she can add and subtract as needed when she targets a specific position.

Lauren's spinoff resume A

Spotting a job ad in a trade publication for a sales position with a cosmetics company that markets products through beauty salons, Lauren takes note of the employer's requirements (which are listed in a mission statement in the box atop spinoff resume A; see Figure 1-2.)

Lauren makes sure she addresses each of the cosmetics company requirements in her targeted resume.

Lauren L. Simpson

19 First Avenue, Austin, Texas, 76746
lauren@email.com, (512) 555-1212

PROFESSIONAL EXPERIENCE

Brilliant Buyers Inc.   [dates]
Austin, Texas
Company is a specialty airport retailer selling 10 brands in 67 stores in major airports throughout U.S.

Merchandising Coordinator
- Buyer's right hand in selecting merchandise for 67 stores. Set up new vendors, create SKUs, place and expedite orders.

- Responsible for product launches in four separate concepts: Silver, Gold, Playful Kids and DogTown. Use strong communications skills to make product presentations to store personnel.

- Supervise implementation of products into stores. Give work direction and supervise employee set-ups of new product lines.

- Problem solving 24/7: Communicate with vendors, manufacturers, and receivers to resolve shipment problems; for example, product out of stock, wrong product, or shipment to wrong location.

- Created model for quarterly human resources newsletter distributed to all employees, explaining merchandising policies and highlighting new products.

- Organize and conduct quarterly schedule of Webcasts for all store managers, in which managers have opportunity to ask questions of buyer and receive answers. Conduct conference calls intermittently as needed. The agenda for both Webcasts and conference calls include new product assortment, floor sets, markdowns, and sales and promotions.

- Competent with paperwork: Review and approve all tickets and receivers for hundreds of purchase orders going to 67 stores weekly.

- Assist in merging data from old point-of-sale system to new Celerant System; changed thousands of SKUs from old system to convert correctly into new system.

- Meet weekly with buyers and merchandising assistants to discuss sales, budgets, and airport news—terminal closures and construction or strikes—impacting company sales.

Accomplishments
- In a commendation to my personnel file, HR Director complimented me on creating the model for a quarterly human resurfaces newsletter, complimenting me on my "professionalism, creativity, and presentation of company values." Additionally, the director praised my "marketing presentation approach to the newsletter, which 'made all the difference in readability.' "

- After six months of assisting buyer in making product presentations to store personnel, buy has since sent me solo to 35 stores, expressing confidence in my "gifted marketing and sales abilities."

- Product returns from airport stores are down 12 percent since my involvement in selecting merchandise.

Figure 1-1: A core resume is a comprehensive document.

LouAnn's

Based in Denver, LouAnn's is a division of Outwear, FAS, with apparel marketed to professional middle-to-upper income women in 220 stores across the U.S.

Assistant Manager, Barton Creek Square, Austin, Texas   [dates]
Sales Associate & Manager-In-Training, Barton Creek Square, Austin, Texas   [dates]
Sales Associate, Tysons Corner Center, McLean, Va.   [dates]

Sales & Business Analysis
- Maximized merchandise visibility by analyzing customer traffic patterns before floor sets.
- Set effective work schedules by analyzing each employee's sales as well as store sales.

Customer Relationship Management
- Developed 16 high-spending regular customers by building and cultivating supportive relationships with new customers.
- Sold by appointment whenever possible.

Management
- Communicated via phone and email with corporate management multiple times daily.
- Met national goals and competed with stores across the U.S. for daily sales results, as well as comparable percentages over the previous year.
- Supervised two to three part-time sales reps per shift.
- Trained employees how best to utilize the preferred corporate selling system and industry standards for up-selling.
- Worked with floor plans to display merchandise for maximum attraction and sales.
- Met daily management responsibilities: maintaining sales floor, inventory, shipping, ordering and record-keeping. Keyboard 40 WPM, competent use of Microsoft Suite, including Word, Excel, Outlook and PowerPoint.

Accomplishments
- Personally delivered one-third of overall store revenues by closing $30,000 to $40,000 sales per month in store with 7 staff (3 full time, 4 part time).
- Consistently maximized income through commissions earned.
- In three months [dates], averaged $15,000 per month sales from regular customers.

OTHER EXPERIENCE

Blue Circle/Blue Badge of Virginia   [dates]
McLean, Va.
State office of health insurance company.

Administrative Assistant
- After high school, worked one year in administration for government marketing department.
- Compiled marketing analysis, and supported cross-company project teams.

EDUCATION

Bachelor of Science, McCombs School of Business   [date]
Retail Merchandising
University of Texas, Austin

Cosmetic Sales To Salons. Sales Specialist. Reverse Chronological. Retailer seeks to become manufacturer's sales agent to retail outlets. Requirements: Strong sales ability[1], Strong communication and presentation skills[2], Computer skills: Word, Excel, Outlook and comfort with new program[3], college degree[4], min. 3 yrs in relationship based sales[5].

Lauren L. Simpson
19 First Avenue, Austin, Texas, 76746
lauren@email.com, (512) 555-1212

Objective
Seeking field sales position with Beauty Beckons Inc. Wish to be responsible for developing sales and relationships with assigned salons, as well as to develop new business relationships with salons in my territory.

Offering closely related experience/skills for this position

- 3.5 Years in relationship based sales [1]
- Reliable and proven sales ability
- Tested communications ability with groups and individuals
- Support of salon management: sales, business plans, product selection, & inventory management
- Leadership of new product launches, special event management, high quality product presentations
- Deliverance of training for salon employees; review sales production
- Support of new business development—marketing, brand promotion
- Monitoring of business development budgets, merchandise & special promotions
- Appropriate appearance and grooming for quality cosmetic products

Professional Experience

Brilliant Buyers Inc.   [dates]
Austin, Texas
Company is a specialty airport retailer selling 10 brands in 67 stores in major airports throughout U.S.

Merchandising Coordinator
- Buyer's right hand in selecting merchandise for 67 stores. Set up new vendors, create SKUs, place and expedite orders.
- Responsible for product launches in four separate concepts: Silver, Gold, Playful Kids and DogTown. Use strong communications skills to make product presentations to store personnel.[2]
- Supervise implementation of products into stores. Give work direction and supervise employee set-ups of new product lines.
- Problem solving 24/7: Communicate with vendors, manufacturers, and receivers to resolve shipment problems; for example, product out of stock, wrong product, or shipment to wrong location.
- Created model for quarterly human resources newsletter distributed to all employees, explaining merchandising policies and highlighting new products.
- Organize and conduct quarterly schedule of Webcasts for all store managers, in which managers have opportunity to ask questions of buyer and receive answers. Conduct conference calls intermittently as needed. The agenda for both Webcasts and conference calls include new product assortment, floor sets, markdowns, and sales and promotions.
- Competent with paperwork: Review and approve all tickets and receivers for hundreds of purchase orders going to 67 stores weekly.
- Meet weekly with buyers and merchandising assistants to discuss sales, budgets, and airport news—terminal closures and construction or strikes—impacting company sales.

Figure 1-2: Spinoff A addresses each of the ad's requirements.

Lauren L. Simpson   Page 2

Accomplishments
- In a commendation to my personnel file, HR Director complimented me on creating the model for a quarterly human resurfaces newsletter, complimenting me on my "professionalism, creativity, and presentation of company values." Additionally, the director praised my "marketing presentation approach to the newsletter, which 'made all the difference in readability.' "
- After six months of assisting buyer in making product presentations to store personnel, buy has since sent me solo to 35 stores, expressing confidence in my "gifted marketing and sales abilities."
- Product returns from airport stores are down 12 percent since my involvement in selecting merchandise.

LouAnn's
Based in Denver, LouAnn's is a division of Outwear, FAS, with apparel marketed to professional middle-to-upper income women in 220 stores across the U.S.

Assistant Manager, Barton Creek Square, Austin, Texas   [dates]
Sales Associate & Manager-In-Training, Barton Creek Square, Austin, Texas [dates]
Sales Associate, Tysons Corner Center, McLean, Va.   [dates]

Sales & Business Analysis
- Maximized merchandise visibility by analyzing customer traffic patterns before floor sets.
- Set effective work schedules by analyzing each employee's sales as well as store sales.

Customer Relationship Management[5]
- Developed 16 high-spending regular customers by building and cultivating supportive relationships with new customers.
- Sold by appointment whenever possible.

Management
- Communicated via phone and email with corporate management multiple times daily.
- Met national goals and competed with stores across the U.S. for daily sales results, as well as comparable percentages over the previous year.
- Supervised two to three part-time sales reps per shift.
- Trained employees how best to utilize the preferred corporate selling system and industry standards for up-selling.[1]
- Worked with floor plans to display merchandise for maximum attraction and sales.
- Met daily management responsibilities: maintaining sales floor, inventory, shipping, ordering and record-keeping. Keyboard 40 WPM, competent useof Microsoft Suite, including Word, Excel, Outlook and PowerPoint.[3]

Accomplishments
- Personally delivered one-third of overall store revenues by closing $30,000 to $40,000 sales per month in store with 7 staff (3 full time, 4 part time).
- Consistently maximized income through commissions earned.
- In three months [dates], averaged $15,000 per month sales from regular customers.[5]

Education
Bachelor of Science, McCombs School of Business[4]   [date]
Retail Merchandising
University of Texas, Austin

To illustrate the concept of targeting, I have added numbers and cross-matched them between the cosmetic company's requirements and Lauren's qualifications. The numbers on this sample resume are for illustration purposes only. Do not put numbers on your own actual resumes.

Here's how Lauren addresses each of the cosmetics company's requirements:

- ✔ Requirement 1 shows up in the skills summary and under management duties at LouAnn's.
- ✔ Requirement 2 is addressed by her merchandising coordinator duty at Brilliant Buyers Inc.
- ✔ Requirement 3 appears as a management skill at LouAnn's.
- ✔ Requirement 4 is met under the education segment. Note that Lauren spells out her retail merchandising studies because the salon job requires a familiarity with what retail customers will buy.
- ✔ Requirement 5 is noted in two places. The first is a subhead titled "Customer Relationship Management" at LouAnn's. The second is also at LouAnn's, within the accomplishments segment.

Lauren purposely did not include certain information, such as her job right after high school as an administrative assistant at a health insurance company because it isn't relevant to the position she seeks.

Lauren's spinoff resume B

Lauren took note of an online job posting for a marketing position advertised by a health insurance company. She printed out the job posting, which included the basic qualifications, and echoed the posting in her objective, almost word for word. (The basic qualifications are described in a mission statement in the box atop spinoff resume B; see Figure 1-3.) Lauren takes care to address each of the health insurance company's requirements in her targeted resume.

To illustrate the concept of targeting, I have added numbers and cross-matched them between the health insurance company's requirements and Lauren's qualifications. The numbers on this sample resume are for illustration purposes only. Don't put numbers on your own actual resumes.

Here's how Lauren address the requirements from the ad placed by the health insurance company:

- ✔ Lauren meets requirement 1 in the education segment. Because the health insurance marketing job is not on the retail level, Lauren selects a few different facts from her core resume than those she chose for Spinoff Resume A. Lauren truthfully writes that she has a business degree and doesn't mention retail merchandising, a study that is within the school of business she attended.

Retail To Health Insurance Marketing. Retailer seeks healthcare marketing position. Reverse Chronological. Requirements: Bachelor's degree in business or marketing[1], min. 5 years' experience in marketing, or in education/marketing mix[2], knowledge of healthcare industry[3], Leadership in collaborative work environment[4].

Lauren L. Simpson
19 First Avenue, Austin, Texas, 76746
lauren@email.com, (512) 555-1212

Objective: Marketing Planning Specialist – for health care insurance company to coordinate marketing of government program segments, including Medicare, Public Programs, and Federal Employee Programs; to work with corporate communications and outside vendors in development of marketing collateral, direct mail and advertising; and to assist Market Segment Manager.

Summary Of Qualifications:
- Five years' marketing/education experience [2]
- Liaison with corporate communications and vendors
- Develop effective marketing materials, direct mailprojects
- Coordinate marketing campaigns for new and existing products
- Assist Market Segment Manager with market analysis, strategy, planning and reporting
- Assist with marketing plans to grow enrollment programs
- Coordinate new product introductions
- Lead teams for collaborative marketing projects [4]
- Expert in Excel, Word, PowerPoint skills
- Skilled oral communicator, competent writer and editor

Professional Experience:

Brilliant Buyers Inc. [2]   [dates]
Austin, Texas
Company is a specialty airport retailer selling 10 brands in 67 stores in major airports throughout U.S.

Merchandising Coordinator
- Buyer's right hand in selecting and marketing merchandise for 67 stores. Set up new vendors, create SKUs, place and expedite orders.
- Responsible for product launches in four separate concepts: Silver, Gold, Playful Kids and DogTown. Use strong communications skills to make product presentations to store personnel.
- Supervise implementation of products into stores. Give work direction and supervise employee set-ups of new product lines.
- Problem solving 24/7: Communicate with vendors, manufacturers, and receivers to resolve shipment problems; for example, product out of stock, wrong product, or shipment to wrong location.
- Created model for quarterly human resources newsletter distributed to all employees, explaining merchandising policies and highlighting new products.
- Organize and conduct quarterly schedule of Webcasts for all store managers, in which managers have opportunity to ask questions of buyer and receive answers. Conduct conference calls intermittently as needed. The agenda for both Webcasts and conference calls include new product assortment, floor sets, markdowns, and sales and promotions.
- Competent with paperwork: Review and approve all tickets and receivers for hundreds of purchase orders going to 67 stores weekly.
- Meet weekly with buyers and merchandising assistants to discuss sales, budgets, and airport news—terminal closures and construction or strikes—impacting company sales.

Figure 1-3: Spinoff B was adapted to apply for a marketing position.

Lauren L. Simpson   Page 2

Accomplishments

- In a commendation to my personnel file, HR Director complimented me on creating the model for a quarterly human resurfaces newsletter, complimenting me on my "professionalism, creativity, and presentation of company values." Additionally, the director praised my "marketing presentation approach to the newsletter, which 'made all the difference in readability.' "

- After six months of assisting buyer in making product presentations to store personnel, buy has since sent me solo to 35 stores, expressing confidence in my "gifted marketing and sales abilities."

- Product returns from stores down 12 percent since my involvement in marketing merchandise.

LouAnn's

Based in Denver, LouAnn's is a division of Outwear, FAS, with apparel marketed to professional middle-to-upper income women in 220 stores across the U.S.

Assistant Manager, Barton Creek Square, Austin, Texas   [dates]
Sales Associate & Manager-In-Training, Barton Creek Square, Austin, Texas   [dates]
Sales Associate, Tysons Corner Center, McLean, Va.   [dates]

Marketing Management

- Met national goals and competed with stores acrossthe U.S. for daily sales results, as well as comparable percentages over the previous year.

- Supervised two to three part-time sales reps per shift.

- Trained employees how best to utilize the preferred corporate selling system and industry standards for up-selling.

- Met daily management responsibilities: maintaining sales floor, inventory, shipping, ordering and record-keeping. Keyboard 40 WPM, competent use of Microsoft Suite, including Word, Excel, Outlook and PowerPoint.

Accomplishments

- Personally delivered one-third of overall store revenues by closing $30,000 to $40,000 sales per month in store with 7 staff (3 full time, 4 part time).

- Consistently maximized income through commissions earned.

- In three months [dates], averaged $15,000 per month sales from regular customers.

Other Experience:

Blue Circle/Blue Badge of Virginia [3]   [dates]
McLean, Va.
State office of health insurance company.

Administrative Assistant

- After high school, worked one year in administration for government marketing department.

- Compiled marketing analysis, and supported cross-company project teams.

Education:

Bachelor of Science, McCombs School of Business [1]   [date]
University of Texas, Austin

If during an interview Lauren is asked about her studies in retail merchandising, Lauren will finesse the issue, briefly pointing out the plus factors in learning retail merchandising, and then moving onto her marketing and business coursework and her experience-based accomplishments.

✔ Lauren responds to requirement 2 with her marketing experience at Brilliant Buyers.

✔ Requirement 3, knowledge of the health care industry, was more difficult to match than the other requirements but Lauren puts on her game face and reaches back to the health insurance company she worked for right after high school.

✔ Lauren addresses requirement 4 in her opening summary of qualifications. A reading of her resume backs up her claims regarding leadership in a collaborative environment.

In a New Era, the OnTarget Resume Brings You So Up to Date

The pace of globalization today is faster and more sweeping than at any time in world history, says Federal Reserve Chairman Ben Bernanke.

In a recent speech before Federal Reserve leaders, the central banking chief went on to explain that few lands are left out of the globalization of the planet: "The emergence of China, India, and the former communist-bloc countries implies that the greater part of the Earth's population is now engaged, at least potentially, in the global economy."

Few argue Bernanke's conclusion — even if they don't like it. But another aspect of globalization not often mentioned is that in economic terms, capital (money) is chasing cheap labor all over the globe: Jobs are shipped to low-wage countries and educated and skilled workers migrate to developed nations with good jobs on offer.

The pursuit of cheap labor creates growing worldwide competition and directly impacts your resume — now and in the years ahead.

Never forget the resume–job interview connection. To nab one of the better jobs and to move up the rewards chain, your targeted resume has to attract a decision maker who will invite you to an interview to further explain how you will give that employer precisely what his or her organization says it wants and needs to succeed.

When technology fails: The human antidote

The job market is made up of A-list candidates and B-list candidates (and many candidates who are perceived to be further down the alphabetic scale).

If you're a seasoned worker, have you ever noticed that A-list candidates are typically younger than you and have recently done the very job the employer is trying to fill?

On the other hand, when you're a rookie, does it seem as though those on the A-list are typically older than you and have recently done the very job the employer is trying to fill?

The definition of frustration is when you are treated like an ant at a picnic because you're not perceived as an A- or B-list candidate.

Unfortunately, your exclusion rate from interview offers may be high when the employer uses online recruiting tools.

An answer to your dilemma: When technology kicks you to the curb, consider back-to-the-future strategies that are most advantageous to you. Play on your turf. Get personal:

✔ Develop your own job leads by doing substantial research and targeting your resume for a direct application.

✔ Network to a referral-chain, asking each of 20 or more people whom you call daily: "Who else should I be talking to?"

✔ Follow up on job ads, but to diffuse the crushing competition attempt to figure out who the hiring manager is and contact that decision maker directly (see Chapter 2). You can even write a resume letter (see Chapter 5) to that person, but do not mention the job ad. Your approach is that you've been researching companies where your excellent qualifications might be a good fit. Even if this "happy coincidence" causes the hiring manager to send your resume to the HR department, now it arrives from an important executive and will likely be examined.

✔ Remember that the vast majority of jobs are found in small businesses. Many aren't yet using modern job-search tools and will value your person-to-person approach.

When you write your targeted resume, remember the magic formula:

Employer wants	*You offer*
A	A
B	B
C	C
D	D

To accomplish this custom-fit hiring, make your self-marketing document an OnTarget resume that convinces a single employer that your *value proposition* (a buzzword meaning reason for hire) is a perfect fit for the job, not a *maybe* fit for the job.

That is, meet as many of the employer's requirements as you truthfully can. Admittedly, doing so isn't a walk on the beach. Expect to do some head scratching and creative thinking from time to time in a world growing not only more global but more complex as the clock ticks.

Chapter 2

New Quick Ways to Find the Right Jobs

In This Chapter

▶ Using new gorilla job search engines

▶ Revisiting vigorous job boards

▶ Reviewing media job ads

▶ Going directly to company Web sites

This book shows you how to master the New Era art of peppering each resume with persuasive marketing facts that target a job's requirements. Chapter 1 explains why the matchup between job requirements and your qualifications has become critical and occupies much of this work. But your efforts will go down the drain if you can't put your marketing facts before people who can hire you.

The Internet makes it easier than ever to uncover hoards of job opportunities; the trick is to find the right ones for you. In this chapter, I discuss the online tools you can use to reach the right eyes without stumbling around and wasting time. First, examine the really new tools and then take an updated look at familiar resources.

One important note: The history of the past decade proves that recruiting technology can turn on a dime. That's why I cover this chapter's online job-hunt destinations as a digest, using relatively few examples to illustrate the concepts you want to know.

The Young Giants: Vertical Job Search Engines

Vertical search engines — also called *verticals* or *VJSEs* or *aggregators* — are the job seeker's new best friends, and they're changing the online recruitment game in dramatic ways. You can think of VJSEs as "Google for jobs." That is, the verticals work like Google or other search engines, except they search only for job listings.

Verticals represent the next level in job search and they have arrived in the nick of time for harried job seekers who can use the services without cost.

In days of yore (before early 2005), you could grow old and gray wasting weeks trudging through job listing after job listing on various job boards. One informed guesstimate says there are 50,000 job boards around the world! By contrast to this crowded cybermart where you board-hop from one site to another and on and on, the cutting-edge job verticals offer one-stop job shopping.

Modern day hunter-gatherers, the verticals do the collection work for you, making it possible to go to one place and see virtually all the jobs that fit your personal criteria on the Internet. They give you the options to slice and dice your search results, based on what you want, such as full or part time, large companies or small, and so forth. And they reveal when each job was posted. Some verticals even show you where the jobs are clustered on a map.

How do the verticals do it? Specialized search engines scrape (crawl) the Web to find and haul in job content. That is, they use automated programs (software) called *spiders* or *robots*. The *'bots* go sleuthing on the Web, compiling a vast array of listings from newspaper classified ads, job boards, corporate sites, and industry associations.

The verticals also receive *online feeds* (direct communications) from job boards that want their listings included in a VJSE's inventory of jobs.

Based on the keywords you supply, you can bring all relevant listings to your computer in one search by using a vertical job search site.

The vertical sites usually don't engage in job transactions themselves but pass users along to the source of the information. The verticals can point you to specialty job boards you've never heard of but that are opportunity rich for your occupation or industry.

TIP

Four signs of hot verticals

Even though VJSEs are gifts from the technology gods who know how busy you are, they're not all created the same. Whether you experiment with one vertical at a time, or arrange for relevant job listings to your computer from several verticals simultaneously and watch them compete for jobs that match your criteria, bear in mind the four basic requirements for a great experience. They are:

✔ A search-and-match technology that works correctly

✔ Wide coverage of available jobs with dates of postings

✔ Easy-to-use delivery options (e-mail or RSS feeds; see Chapter 3)

✔ Tools for saving and managing saved searches

I don't comment on how verticals score on each criterion because, like auto model redesigns, each year brings changes for the young verticals. Judge for yourself. You may be able to get expert comments from the Job Search Engine Guide (www.rmwilsonconsulting.typepad.com), as well as Joel Cheesman's blog (www.cheezhead.com).

While it's true that some of the material that vertical engines come up with also appears on large search engines (such as Google, Yahoo, MSN, or Ask.com), the general-purpose engines lack the vertical engines' *relevancy* (the degree to which a job matches what you specified, or the ability to *filter* (sort out unwanted search results).

By contrast, job seekers using VJSEs can filter search results using a wealth of criteria. You may, for example, want to look at jobs at companies with annual revenues of more than $100 million, or within 25 miles of a ZIP code, or only those jobs based on another criterion that you choose.

The biggest potential fly in the VJSE soup is what could happen when the new vertical giants do not have contractual agreements with the original publishers of job ads. Some verticals are attempting to index and post for free all the job openings in the universe, including those that employers paid to place on job boards, in print, and through other media. Whether potential legal squabbles eventually cut into your one-stop convenience by shrinking the number of job postings you can shop on a VJSE is unknown. But for now and the foreseeable future, vertical job search sites are the hot new bloodhounds to help you sniff out the jobs you want.

Using a vertical: The generic basics

While each vertical search engine includes specific instructions on the best way to use it, you can expect certain basic information to apply across the board. Here are the general steps you're likely to follow when using a vertical search engine:

1. **Create a personal account.**

   Register with one or several verticals. Many job listings will appear on all the verticals because, with exceptions, they pull their inventory from the same places.

2. **Decide how to receive the jobs.**

   You may prefer daily or weekly job alerts. Or you may choose an RSS (real simple syndication) feed (Chapter 3) to have job ads sent as they are posted directly to your computer or handheld device.

3. **Set preferences.**

   Use the preferences setting to select the jobs you want to show on your results page. You may select to show results based only on location (ZIP codes) or timeliness, for example.

4. **Become familiar with related options on the vertical site.**

   Options vary by vertical but may include such extras as a map of the job's location, salary market information, company research, or potential contacts inside the target company.

5. **Narrow your search.** Drill down through the job listings to be as specific as possible to get to the jobs you want.

   Quality — not quantity — counts most. Look for freshness of the listing and those jobs that are relevant to your preferences. Search on skills, interests, and location.

6. **Track and save your searches.**

   Each vertical allows you to save your searches on its site. Doing so enables you to manage the most current and desirable listings.

7. **Upgrade to advanced search, if you need it.**

   If you're drowning in job listings or seem to be missing the mark, try using the vertical's advanced search feature. You can search by such criteria as keywords, words in job title, company, type of job, and location.

Alison Doyle's book, *The About.com Guide to Job Searching: Tools and Tactics to Help You Get the Job You Want* (Adams Media, 2006) provides more information on using vertical job search engines to scout job leads.

Meet the verticals

Here's a thumbnail sketch of each of the best-known verticals, those that offer the most amenities and draw from thousands of sources. Expect the details of any or all of these sites to change from time to time.

SimplyHired.com

Simply Hired is an award-winning site that says it's building the largest online database of jobs on the planet and recently announced more than five million job listings indexed from large and small job boards, newspaper and classified listings, government and association Web sites, and company Web sites.

The site's personable founders are dog lovers who enjoy a good joke: The site once ran a contest for the best true I-was-fired tale on its sister site, Simply Fired (www.simplyfired.com). Dog owners can search for jobs at dog-friendly companies all over the country and find a job that welcomes best four-pawed friends in the office. But if that doesn't make you barking happy, the company offers a host of other filters including family- and minority-friendly employers.

What about the power of who-you-know? Simply Hired's business network partner LinkedIn offers a referral job network that aims to connect job applicants with hiring managers. Simply Hired's "Who Do I Know" button displays after each job listing to help you discover whether you have an "inside friend" whom you can tap for referrals or information. The service has a similar partnership with the social networking site, MySpace (careers.myspace.com). The result is a splashy pairing of business or social networking with vertical search.

On Simply Hired, you can save and simultaneously post a resume on a number of carefully chosen job sites. Additionally, you can use any computer to visit your account.

Indeed.com

In one simple search, Indeed gives job seekers free access to millions of jobs from thousands of Web sites. All the job listings from major job boards, newspaper classifieds, associations, and company career pages are included .

The company says that more than one million new jobs are added weekly. To keep your opportunities fresh, Indeed automatically removes all jobs after 30 days.

With the familiar look and feel of general search engines, the popular Indeed makes it easy to drill down by keyword and location to jobs that fit your requirements. You can quick-search from the Indeed home page. Just type keywords into the "What" box describing the kind of job you want, and enter a city, state or ZIP code in the "Where" box. Then click the "Find Jobs" button or hit the Enter key on your keyboard.

You can put search results on your plate in several different ways. For example, you can

- ✔ View results ranked by relevance (how close the job comes to what you want).
- ✔ View results ranked by date, with newest jobs appearing first.
- ✔ View results by distance of your potential commute to work.

Indeed's "Advanced Job Search" allows for more sophisticated filtering: You can specify exact phrases, exclude jobs that contain certain keywords, exclude jobs from recruiters, and limit results to jobs published today or within the last week.

There's more. When you want to research a company, investigate salaries for that kind of job, see who you may know at the company through networking sites like LinkedIn and Ryze, or view the job's location on Google maps, click on the "more actions" link next to each job search result.

Jobster.com

The hip, youth-oriented Jobster site seems headed toward cyberwall-to-cyberwall coverage of online recruiting functions — from gathering employee referrals to social networking. More than a leading vertical online recruiting service, Jobster lets users search for jobs either nationwide or within a particular region from its massive inventory of jobs.

For instance, a job seeker curious about the working environment at a particular company may be able to read spirited postings from people who already work there in a Jobster-run workers' online social network (see Chapter 3).

Additionally, you can receive two types of e-mail alerts, which you can customize to your job interests and delivery preference. *Job alerts* give you a heads-up about new jobs on the Internet that match your interests. *Insider alerts* notify you about new jobs that you can be referred to (by someone you know inside the hiring company) and be recommended for by Jobster. It's kind of like getting prequalified for a mortgage when buying a house.

You don't need to submit a resume through Jobster's system but if you do, remember that it handles only plain text (ASCII) versions.

Where are verticals headed?

"Verticals are going gangbusters," says search engine expert Joel Cheesman. The head of HRSEO, a search engine optimization firm specializing in recruitment, and the author of Cheezhead, an award-winning blog about online search, Cheesman thinks that information overload has created the right environment for vertical search to thrive. A veteran recruitment-industry authority, Cheesman answers my questions.

Why are we so hooked on search engines?

The human brain has to digest between 3,000 and 10,000 ad messages every day, according to various studies. Makes your eyes glaze over, doesn't it? The rise in acclaim of search engines like Google is due, in large part, to helping people cut through the tremendous clutter. Simply stated, search engines help people find what they want when they want it. Figure out a few keywords for your specific need and Google is typically there with a good answer.

When did verticals come along to create specific categories?

Although an early model of job verticals first turned up in 1997 to help users search for specific information categories, such as images, news, or even product information, the extension of using ever more sophisticated search to find jobs was a natural development and makes a lot of sense.

Although not an entirely new phenomenon, sites that send out spiders to aggregate job content from sites like CareerBuilder, association portals, and corporate Web sites have gained momentum just in the past few years.

How about breaking-news developments?

The vertical job search game looks to stay hot for the foreseeable future. As of this writing, Monster is beta testing a vertical offering under its FlipDog brand. Net-Temps, a stalwart in the staffing industry, has launched a vertical named Searchjobs.com.

If success breeds competition, the current landscape of vertical job search will show robust growth. As the great 20th Century comedian Jimmy Durante often sang: "Everybody wants to get inna de act."

Receiving a Jobster e-mail gives you a direct connection to a company's hiring team, and that helps you stand out from others.

GetTheJob.com

GetTheJob.com gathers job postings from more than 150,000 corporate Web sites and presents them to job seekers in a searchable database. At this writing, the site holds about 2.3 million job listings. The inventory of job openings is directly collected only from companies that are hiring; no third-party recruiters are allowed to post openings. The database of jobs represents the hidden (or hard-to-find) job market because 50 percent to 60 percent of the postings can't be found on commercial job boards.

GetTheJob's "Direct Connect" technology links job seekers to each posting on the hiring company's Web site. This allows you to read the entire job description and deadhead for the job, without middle-people standing in your way.

Another reason to pounce on GetTheJob.com is that it's free of Internet job scams and "too good to be true" hype about jobs that don't really exist.

GetTheJob.com is a newcomer in the ranks of job search verticals, but its operators say the company is hot on the trail of some new features that will "vastly improve" the job-seeker experience.

Yahoo! HotJobs

In addition to providing advertised job listings on the Yahoo! HotJobs site (`hotjobs.yahoo.com`), the company uses its sophisticated search technology to crawl the Internet. It offers job seekers listings from other employer and job-related sites. This means you can inspect jobs in both employer-paid and crawled job listings — all at no cost to you.

Besides actively searching for jobs, you can upload your resume so that employers can find you when they search the company's database for candidates.

Additionally, you can sign up for personal job search agents where you enter your job criteria, such as industry, location, experience level, salary, and so forth. You receive new job postings that match your criteria e-mailed to you directly when a suitable job is in the database. Yahoo! HotJobs also has tools to help you find a job and also manage your career — everything from a job recommendation engine to a salary calculator to advice on networking and interviewing.

Job Boards Rising

Since 1994, when job boards effectively began operating in the then new recruiting terrain, it has seemed as though another one appears daily, leading one observer to announce: "Holy resume, Batman — another job board launches!" Today, as noted earlier in this chapter, estimates put the number of job boards operating globally as high as 50,000.

If you've been in the job market during the past 15 years or so, you probably know that a job board is a Web site where you can look for a job. Employers pay job boards to post their open positions. Job seekers typically view their jobs for free.

You can apply through a job board for specific positions, or you can post your resume in the board's resume database. When you mouse aboard a job board, you can search for job listings by career field, occupation, job title, location, and job detail keywords. The emphasis is on local job markets because most people won't move for a job unless they have little choice.

Job boards have not been frozen in time. They often add user-friendly enhancements, including privacy-sensitive features and fast-forward matching of job situation and job seeker.

You find job boards in two basic flavors:

- ✔ **General job boards,** such as CareerBuilder and Monster, cover all kinds of jobs.
- ✔ **Specialty (or *niche*) job boards** cover a specific group of jobs, according to factors like industry (EducationAmerica.net), geography (Atlanta Recruiter.com) or job-seeker qualifications (MBACareers.com).

Job boards are established hunting grounds for vertical job search engines. You can, of course, skip the verticals if you prefer and go straight to a job board. Many people do.

Finding job boards

The only constant in Internet job search is change, but I want to give you a sense of where to find some high-traffic job boards. As of this writing, the following are the top three sites (according to traffic) in six commonly sought categories.

Go to TopJobSites.com (www.topjobsites.com) to get the latest site rankings, which are published monthly.

General	*College*
Monster.com	GraduateProspects
CareerBuilder.com	CollegeGrad.com
HotJobs.com	eRecruiting

Executive	*Niche*
The Ladders.com	Dice.com
CareerJournal.com	Jobsinthemoney.com
6FigureJobs.com	eFinancialCareers.com
Diversity	***International (English)***
LatPro	Naukri.com
Hispanic.com	JobsDB.com
DiversityWorking.com	JobStreet.com

Using job board resources

The most comprehensive, searchable listing of job boards is published online by AIRS, a respected training and technology company that helps recruiters round up candidates.

Revised annually, the listing is called *AIRS Job Board and Recruiting Technology Directory.* It is available for downloading to anyone for free, says AIRS chief executive officer Chris Forman. The total number of job boards listed is in the thousands, and the directory runs about 100 pages. Each year's edition appears at the end of the previous year.

This valuable resource includes job sites for virtually every niche and is organized in a "yellow pages" style: employment hubs, industry, business function, government, financial services, healthcare, diversity, technical, college and alumni, and contractors, both part time and hourly. Find the directory at www.airsdirectory.com.

 The Guide to Internet Job Searching, 2006–2007 edition, by Margaret F. Dikel and Frances E. Roehm (McGraw-Hill, 2006), is a terrific book that includes the listing of some 700 job boards and career information sites, compiled and checked by two pros who have specialized in online job search since it was invented in the early 1990s. The sites are divided by topic and job area. The book also includes basic information on how to search online.

Additionally, you can Google to locate specific job boards, using relevant search terms, such as "job board marketing Nashville" to find a job board in the Nashville, Tennessee, area that specializes in marketing jobs.

BEWARE

Watch out for the black hole at major job boards

Recruiter Mary Nurrenbrock doesn't sugarcoat it when describing her view of the practice of responding to jobs advertised on the major job boards:

"When you respond to openings directly through job boards, your resume usually ends up in a black hole, a passive database. If you're responding right from the board, it's going to HR. Bad move. These guys are up to their eyeballs and usually don't even really know what the hiring manager is looking for. That is, if the HR person even sees the resume in the passive database.

"You need to get to the hiring manager, not HR. How? When you visit a job board and see a job that looks like it's a fit (you notice I didn't say that it looks interesting), go to that company's Web site and get a name. Most of the corporate sites have profiles. Get the name of the VP Marketing, CEO, CMO — whomever the open position is likely to report to.

"Figuring out the address isn't hard. Look under the press releases where you'll usually find a company contact e-mail address. Use the same format — john_doe@, john.doe@, jdoe@ — to send your resume. If it bounces back, try a different format. If that doesn't work, try to wrangle the address from the company receptionist. If all else fails, snail mail it.

"What usually happens next is that the hiring manager sends your resume to HR. But we're trying to avoid that, right? No, we're trying to avoid the black hole. Now the HR person is looking at a resume that came to her from an internal source. Big difference!"

Job Central National Labor Exchange (www.jobcentral.com) is in a class by itself — a nonprofit Web site owned by 200 major employers through their membership in Direct Employers Association. JobCentral's search engine takes you directly to the careers page of member corporations advertising open jobs you may spy and want to make a run at.

The Continuing Power of Newspapers

"The dead tree industry is done for and all the job ads are online."

I've seen and heard versions of that requiem for classified print ads in newspapers and in specialized publications during the past dozen years or so. The truth is, it's not true.

As breathless — and later debunked — press releases from online recruiting vendors roll into my message box, I am reminded of the joke about the tabloid editor's instant message to his on-the-spot reporter: "Send all details. Never mind facts."

Speaking of facts, job ads certainly are trending online, especially with readers under 35. There's no debate about that. And my guess is that online recruiting usage will break even with print or slightly overtake it within the next couple of years.

But here's the rest of the story

The latest (December 2005; updates are expected to be issued annually) reliable study says that newspaper job ads are still licking the new digital kids on the block.

The study, issued by The Conference Board (a major business research organization), reports that despite the proliferation of online job boards, *three out of four job seekers still use newspapers to look for jobs*.

The Internet was not far behind, with *three out of five job seekers using the 'Net*.

In other words, 75 percent of U.S. job seekers are turning the pages with a red Sharpie in hand, while 60 percent of job seekers are firing up their computers with a mouse at the ready.

Conventional wisdom contends that print classified advertising is valuable mainly for hourly and lower-wage jobs. That point, too, is addressed by The Conference Board study, which states that newspapers are still the most common method of looking for a job in three of the four major regions across the United States (The Western region is the exception), and in all but the top income group (households with incomes of $50,000 and over).

More than 75 percent in the highest group reported using the Internet in their job search, while roughly 70 percent used newspapers. Those with household incomes below $25,000 were more likely to search newspapers (80 percent) than the Internet (50 percent).

The net result of The Conference Board finding is that job seekers are working both sides of the media market. "Job seekers are combining newspaper ads and checking Internet job postings as part of their job search efforts," according to The Conference Board's research director, Linda Barrington. "It is a minority that only uses the Internet."

A new wind is blowing on newspapers

Even that minority may be reading online job postings that began life as a print newspaper job ad. Most help-wanted sections have found second homes online, so that you can search for jobs in the touch-and-feel comfort of the pages in your own familiar newspaper or on your favorite newspaper's Web site. Moreover, employers who advertise with print ads often request that you send your resume online to them.

Job finding has become too complex and too challenging to ignore either medium. As I explain in Chapter 1, you're hunting in a New Era.

Search success is based not on where you find a job opening but on whether your responding resume sparks an interview, and what happens during that interview.

Hunting on Company Web Sites

No one has hard numbers on the number of company (also called corporate) Web sites today; suffice it to say there are so many you can't possible look at all of them for your job hunt (see GetTheJob.com and other vertical job search engines in the segment above).

Critics accuse many corporate Web sites of being dated. Old school. Flat. Dull. So what? Does having the latest and greatest matter when you're hopping on a company Web site to see whether it offers a job you want? One viewpoint: A company with a modern Web site is likely to offer other innovations as well, such as new equipment and state-of-the-art training. Another viewpoint: It makes little difference whether a company site looks and functions like a relic; the big question is, does it inventory the kinds of job you want?

Whichever viewpoint you adopt, here are things to bear in mind about submitting your resume through a corporate Web site.

Unlike general job sites, such as Monster.com and Career Builder, the universe of company Web sites is decentralized. Unless you're using a vertical job search engine, exploring that universe is time consuming. You can easily spend two hours taking the measure of just a couple of corporate career sites, picking up details you should know to maximize opportunity.

As you scan a company site, back up to the home page and click to press releases, annual report, and general areas for any edge you can use to enhance your application when you move to the careers area.

Susan Joyce, the talent behind Job-Hunt.org, reminds you: "In addition to visiting the employer's Web site to see what the company does, also check the company out on Yahoo Finance, BusinessWire.com, Hoover's, and so forth to discover the latest news about the employer's industry. Don't be the last person hired before layoffs begin."

When you reach the careers area and begin submitting your resume in earnest, remember to pay close attention to each requirement of the position and customize your resume to show that your qualifications are a bull's eye for those requirements.

Don't bother sending a hard copy to the company's human resources department; it's unnecessary and will likely be tossed. You can, of course, send a hard copy to a hiring manager, as Mary Nurrenbrock discusses in the sidebar in this chapter, "Watch out for the black hole at major job boards."

Pay attention to specific instructions on each company's site. And don't be surprised if you're asked to take online pre-employment tests or respond to screening questions.

Some corporate sites won't accept anonymous candidates who cloak their identity. Some candidates use anonymous resumes to maintain their privacy and stay out of trouble with their current employer. An anonymous resume is stripped of the resume subject's name and contact information. Former employers may not be identified by name but described generically (ABC Tools becomes Mid-Sized Tool Company, for instance). Anonymous resumes are distributed by job sites or third-party employment services but employers often consider them to be too much trouble to bother with.

If you aren't comfortable or experienced in applying through corporate Web sites, visit a few of the best-of-the-best company sites for job seekers, as determined for 2006 by consultants Gerry Crispin and Mark Mehler, principals of CareerXroads.com. Crispin and Mehler are definitive authorities on Fortune 500 recruiting practices. Each year they review corporate sites' ability to "target, engage, inform, and respect the job seeker."

In alphabetical order, the CareerXRoads' top 25 sites for staffing pages follow:

- Agilent (www.jobs.agilent.com)
- Bank of America (www.bankofamerica.com)
- Bell South (www.bellsouth.com)
- C. H. Robinson (www.chrjobs.com)
- Capital One (www.capitalone.com)
- Federated (www.federated-fds.com)
- Ford (www.mycareer.ford.com)

✔ GE (www.gecareers.com)

✔ General Mills (www.generalmills.com)

✔ Goldman Sachs (www.gs.com)

✔ HCA (www.hcahealthcare.com)

✔ Intel (www.intel.com)

✔ Kodak (www.kodak.com)

✔ Lilly (lilly.com)

✔ Merck (www.merck.com)

✔ Microsoft (members.microsoft.com)

✔ Morgan Stanley (www.morganstanley.com)

✔ P&G (pg.com)

✔ Sherwin Williams (www.sherwin-williams.com)

✔ Southwest Airlines (www.southwest.com)

✔ Starbucks (www.starbucks.com)

✔ Target (target.com)

✔ Texas Instruments (www.ti.com)

✔ Whirlpool (www.whirlpoolcareers.com)

✔ Xerox (www.xerox.com)

Seeking and Finding Is Easier than Ever

As you launch your job-finding campaign, I recommend that you start with vertical job search engines as a destination for your OnTarget resumes; if you don't seem to be scoring winners, add general and niche job boards, as well as company Web sites.

As modern tools assist your job hunt, be glad that you can find job leads today much faster than ever before. But while the Web is indisputably the engine driving change in the job market, Southern California career coach Mark James (www.hireconsultant.com) puts its value for most people in perspective:

A recipe for unemployment: Click and send, cross your fingers, and hope the phone rings. A recipe for employment: Press a full-bore campaign that includes human networking and researching job leads from all media.

Chapter 3

Spotlight Your Resume in a Web 2.0 World

In This Chapter

▶ Discovering tech-driven ways to meet your future boss

▶ Flying in on the magic coattails of employees and others

▶ Using online social networking services to get noticed

▶ Blogging your way to a job by reading or writing

▶ Being aware of the dark side of Internet empowerment

*W*eb 2.0 technologies — the new matchmakers in the job market — are adding opportunities for you to connect with employers. (I explain Web 2.0 and its forerunner, Web 1.0, in Chapter 1.)

Web 2.0 sites are online services you visit to make something happen, usually with other people. The new wave of start-up hubs typically depends not on traditional top-down communication from the site's management but on bottom-up data flow from you and me and, well, everyone who wants to contribute content. Techies refer to the new services by the geeky phrase "user-contributed content."

You probably recognize the names of some recently popular everyone-is-smarter-than-anyone ventures. From the youth-attracting hangout at MySpace to the video-sharing site YouTube to the grass-roots online encyclopedia Wikipedia, they all encourage interconnection and input. Jump on in; the cyber-water's fine, they say. The services provide the technology, and the rest of us provide the substance.

These Web 2.0 services are finding their way into the job world. Many are free, drawing an income stream from ads; others charge fees. You can check out ways to use your resumes to snag interviews on any of them. The only way to understand this newfangled stuff is to use it. With a little practice, it's easy.

Whether you're a job seeker with a streak of ambition a mile wide or a person who just wants to go with the flow but keep an escape hatch handy if your job starts to sink, now's the time to bone up on the rudiments of how technology can serve you in the job market.

I describe the following carousel of job search tools with a broad brush because technology at the leading edge changes rapidly. Some observers estimate the average lifespan for much current technology is about 24 months. Whatever the time frame of change, its warp speed renders many details quickly obsolete in a book. Not only does technology move forward, but companies using it come and go.

This chapter is intended to inform you, not to serve as a short-lived directory of Web 2.0 services. Instead, these pages are designed to start you off well by pointing you in newer directions.

Note that I describe the following Web 2.0 technologies separately for clarity, but in practice, they often work side by side or join together. For example, the job search site Jobster (`www.jobster.com`) has gathered together most Web 2.0 features that you can imagine under its umbrella. Simply Hired (`www.simplyhired.com`), Indeed (`www.indeed.com`), and JobCentral National Labor Exchange (`www.jobcentral.com`) are additional examples of sites that combine a number of Web 2.0 technologies described in this chapter.

What follows is a nonexhaustive list of nuggets from the Web 2.0 world.

Online Employee Referral

You've probably heard this adage: Birds of a feather flock together. The recruiting industry translates that to mean good people tend to know other good people. In a nutshell, that's the central argument behind online employee referral services.

Because employers tend to rely on referrals as a way to spot great candidates, job seekers can increase their odds of being interviewed and hired by getting employees and other "connectors" (individuals who bring people together) to sing their praises.

What it is

An online referral service is an e-mail job distribution method paid for by employers. As a job seeker, an online employee referral service helps you identify which of your contacts may know people at the companies where you want to work. A referral service may also help you request a direct referral to some employers' hiring teams. And the service may enable you to keep tabs on jobs that you can get referred for via the people you know and the people they know.

A number of services pay a fee to referrers — company employees or trusted outsiders acting as amateur recruiters — when a hire is made. The typical fee is $500 to $3,000 or more. The size of the reward varies widely but generally is a much smaller fee than the 20 to 30 percent of the new hire's first-year salary paid to professional third-party recruiters. Some online recruiting services pay no fees to referrers.

The industry leaders, according to the Electronic Recruiting News in Email publisher John Sumser, are Jobster (`www.jobster.com`) and H3 (`www.h3.com`), both of which are free for job seekers.

"Lots of companies and organizations have an internal (private label) online referral program," Sumser says. "Associations, trade groups, and other shared interest organizations also have them."

Getting started

Get out your Christmas-card list and directories of any group of which you're a member — alumni, church, professional organization, environmental activist group, bowling league, and so forth. Familiarize yourself with online recruiting services that refer people to companies. Read the site's FAQ (Frequently Asked Questions) and follow directions.

The basic process of getting inside the loop of a referral system works like this:

1. When you spot a company where you'd like to work, check your personal contact lists for the name of anyone you know who works at that company. Ask your contact for a referral to the job.

2. After you have been referred, you can inquire about jobs, refer your friends, and get alerts by e-mail about jobs that interest you.

Finding more info

Online employee referral programs often work in tandem with online social networking technology. The programs themselves are the best information source.

Online Social Networking

How do you feel about posting your persona on an e-billboard for virtually anyone to see? (Yes, social networking services insist that passwords and other privacy guards are in place, but they're far from foolproof.)

Job seekers and employers worldwide are beginning to take a page from youth-oriented MySpace (www.myspace.com), Facebook (www.facebook.com), and other social nets as they turn to business-oriented services where people post career profiles and recruiters search for prospective employees.

What it is

Online networking services offer you help in three ways:

- ✔ Enabling you to locate contacts, who, working inside a company you covet, are a potential source of referrals, names of managers, tips on company culture, hiring mode, and other useful information. You may have to hop from one person's profile to another to another and so forth until you reach your objective.

- ✔ Helping find managers in a company to whom you can send your unsolicited resume (after breaking the ice with an exchange of e-mail; a resume sent out of the blue likely will be considered spam mail and deleted).

- ✔ Introducing you to recruiters, who can see your profile in a virtual networking service and contact you.

LinkedIn (www.linkedin.com) is the best known of the business-oriented virtual networks. Others with a business focus include Jobster's (www.jobster.com) network, Ryze (www.ryze.com), Ecademy (www.ecademy.com), and ExecuNet (www.exeunet.com).

Eons (www.eons.com) is a virtual network for Americans aged 50 plus, with a broad content that sometimes includes job suggestions. Classmates.com (www.classmates.com) is more for "that old gang of mine" connections but sports a work-and-career section where you can look for acquaintances by company. Zoominfo (www.zoominfo.com) is not a virtual network, but can deliver some of the same results for job seekers in that it is a search engine for discovering people, companies, and relationships.

Some sites are free of charge; others charge fees for contacting other members and certain other services. A few are fee only.

Indiscreet postings on a social network can mean really big trouble for job seekers. Many employers review profiles on social networking sites when considering candidates for jobs. Surprisingly, the hard lessons learned aren't always acquired by the young and the wireless flouting photos from drunken parties, stories of sexual escapades, profanity-laced comments, and similar projections of less-than-businesslike behavior.

Experienced professionals old enough to know better can make unintended strategy errors too. A California woman called in sick so that she could join friends on a rafting trip. The woman's job hit the fan when her boss, checking entries on the boss's teen-aged daughter's vertical network, stumbled across a dated photo of the fibbing professional employee enjoying white-water fun on the very day she was supposedly ill. Big oops.

The safest bet is to assume future employers will read everything you post, including extreme political or religious views and rants on any controversial topic. Here's an easy guideline to stay out of job market trouble: Treat every online profile with the respect you give a resume.

Getting started

Think about online networking as comfortable connectivity. Instead of dealing with faceless strangers whom you wouldn't know if you tripped over them, you deal with individuals you now or soon will know, and whose faces you can see and identify.

The essential process to hook up with an online social network follows this pattern:

1. Someone who's already in the network invites you to join. You may also be able to join without an invite — most virtual networks also let users join on their own.

Does your online profile do more harm than good?

Employers want to hire people whose qualifications are a good fit for the job's requirements. Recruiters often try to "source" these candidates from scratch by identifying relevant candidates through online social networks and blogs.

The bright side to online profile sourcing is that the more information in your profile and the more sites where it's posted, the more recruiters who can find you and the more they can know about you to incite their interest.

The dark side to online profile sourcing is that you risk typecasting yourself if you are a person who could be considered for several different career roles (school admissions officer, health plan coordinator, computer sales representative, and so on.) Pigeonholing yourself limits the range of your opportunities.

In another scenario, employers are willing to spend time checking you out online only if they're already very interested because of a referral, or successful interview, or well-done resume. An inappropriate fact on a canned profile could cause reconsideration of your value.

Put your best face forward

A problem with some profiles is the tendency to share insider stuff that seems okay when you're speaking to friends but may not be perceived favorably by potential employers. One job seeker wrote that she rides a motorcycle with her husband, which could raise questions about risk taking and health insurance costs. Her revelation would have been positive had she been applying for a job marketing Hogs or as a stunt double, but, alas, she wanted to be a court reporter.

Another job seeker led off his profile with the news that he is a cancer survivor. Health insurance costs? Reliable attendance? Longevity on the job?

The litmus test for revealing personal data in an online profile is the same as that for a resume: *Does including this information enhance my perceived qualifications for the type of job I seek?* If not, out it goes! Image is everything. Remember the workplace is not a confessional. Celebrate marketable abilities, skip private spice, and gag motormouth tendencies.

---

2. After selecting a virtual network that appears to include your kind of people, register, create a password and fill in a career profile. (For privacy and safety, do *not* include your street address in your profile.)

3. Explore the range of other network members who have registered with the service.

4. Make contacts as appropriate to your job search.

Finding more info

The job referral sites themselves are your best source of additional information.

Blogs

Blogs are more plentiful than bubbles in champagne. Millions and millions of them effervesce around the globe — and even from outer space. In 2006, the space tourist and American businesswoman Anousheh Ansari wrote of everyday life on the International Space Station, commenting in her blog that space smells like a "burned almond cookie."

Earlier blogs (Web logs in the 1990s) were online personal journals filled with trivia and aimless reflections of a blogger's day. It's an understatement to say that times have changed — and at broadband speed.

The usefulness of blogs to job seekers is gathering attention — and, some say, momentum — helped along by the morphing of those early personal journals into sleek Web sites that showcase content posted by one or several authors, and which welcome comments from visitors on these posts. A small but growing number of employment-related blogs are capturing audience and advertising to become media stars and influences in the job market.

What it is

You can write blogs today that show your expertise in any career field. Although rare, one woman went a step further and blogged her way into a job. Carolynn Duncan, hearing about a job opening from a friend, created a blog specifically to convince the hiring executive at Provo Labs Consulting in Provo, Utah, that she was the right person for the job. She called her blog "Why Provo Labs Wants to Hire Carolynn Duncan" and posted it on Blogger (www.blogger.com). After reading her words and calling her in for an interview, the hiring executive offered Duncan the position, adding "I often scour a candidate's resume, e-mail address, and Web site for anything resembling a blog."

Company blogs are not quite as common as crab grass but plenty of them are up and running. At Microsoft, for instance, employees write blogs about topics pertinent to their work; now Microsoft is using those blogs to develop a dialogue with potential hires. An example is Heather Hamilton's blog, "Marketing and Finance at Microsoft" (blogs.msdn.com/heatherleigh).

The vast majority of Americans won't create a blog but will settle for reading blogs and perhaps making a comment now and then. Researchers for the trade publication *Advertising Age* say that about 35 million workers in the United States visit blogs and spend an average of 40 minutes a day reading them (office goof-off time?). The researchers speculate that one out of four blog visits could be considered job related.

Blogs are the ultimate Web insider's clubhouse. They attract loyal, everyday readers who hold an avid interest in a blog's topic. Recruiters understand that to hire the right people, you have to go where the right people hang out. That's why recruiters cruise career-field-related blogs, looking for top talent in a specific occupation — or for experts who can steer them to top talent.

In a recent development, job ads are beginning to appear on blogs. Joel Cheesman (www.cheezhead.com), a leading consultant in online recruiting technology, agrees that niche targeting by employers through blogs is growing: "Blogs are exceptional ways for employers to reach the eyeballs of top talent to fill their job openings," Cheesman says. "As a result, an increasing number of blogs are providing the ability to post jobs. We're at the start of the blog niche targeting trend."

The nascent blog-meets-job-board move is beginning in the information technology sector, which is where traditional boards also started. A couple of examples of blogs with jobs as this book went to press: Crunchboard (www.crunchboard.com) and 37Signals (www.37signals.com).

Getting started

Finding blogs that you want to read regularly takes a bit of shopping around. Try these suggestions to kick off your hunt:

1. Find the right blogs for you. One option is to use your browser. Enter a topic and add "blog" to the search term. For example, "employment blog" brings up a zillion possibilities, from George's Employment Blawg (www.employmentblawg.com) and Labor Employment Law Blog (www.laboremploymentlawblog.com) to The Self-Employed Business Owners Blog (www.passionforbusiness.com/blogs) and Employment Digest (www.employmentdigest.com).

   Don't forget to look for blogs in your career field. For instance, searching for "nurse blog" results in a long roster of nursing blogs. One, Med Blogopathy (www.mediblogopathy.blogspot.com) is packed with more human interest text than jobs but the site is a good place to get the feel for content and the types of comments you eventually may want to make.

   You can also turn to a blog search engine for blogs, such as Search4Blogs (www.search4blogs.com).

2. When you find a blog you like, check out the site's *blogroll* (links of blogs on similar topics). George's Employment Blawg, for example, lists several pages of other employment and recruiting blogs. The same is true for Med Blogopathy.

3. Time manage your chosen blogs by reading from a free news aggregator, such as Bloglines (www.bloglines.com). Once you've registered and selected the blogs you want to track, you can quickly monitor what's been posted since you last read them because new information appears in boldface. If you're tracking only one or two blogs, you can skip the news aggregator.

To establish your own blog, find a host site that offers free service for beginning bloggers — such as Blogger (www.blogger.com), BlogEasy (www.blogeasy.com), or Typepad (www.typepad.com) — and start writing.

Finding more info

In addition to the tips above, to keep up with blog-based job ads, visit Blogs with Jobs (www.blogswithjobs.com).

Really Simple Syndication (RSS)

The evolution of technology that is designed to give you a heads-up when a job you want becomes available reminds me of the difference between periodic television network news programming and all-news cable television. Instead of having to watch the news at 6 p.m. or 11 p.m., you can watch late-breaking news on your timetable 24/7.

Familiar free online job search agents at major job boards periodically send you e-mail alerts about jobs that meet your specific search criteria. But the modern and also free Really Simple Syndication (RSS) technology whisks *live feeds* to your computer or handheld devices around the clock with the latest jobs from thousands of employers and job sites.

What it is

RSS is a rapidly growing platform for the immediate distribution of online content, in this case, job postings.

How does RSS beat the older e-mail job agents? Three ways: efficiency, relevance, and timeliness. Here's how it works:

- Sending RSS job feeds to your RSS reader prevents e-mail job alerts from clogging your in-box.

> ✔ RSS feeds are said to more closely target your stated requirements. Like an advanced search, you get a closer match to what you want. For example, if you're an accountant and you want a job in Milwaukee, an e-mail search agent might return everything with the term "accountant" or its variations, such as accounting for lost automobiles in Milwaukee. RSS job feeds are programmed to mirror your wishes.
>
> RSS job feeds are a wonderful way to get the first word when a new job is posted. And the feeds can be programmed to also include breaking news in industry concerns, information that could put you at the head of the line in job interviews.

Getting started

How do you read RSS feeds? You can receive RSS feeds in a few different ways. You can download a news reader program, many of which are free; use your Web browser to search for "free newsreader program." Alternatively, some browsers and Web sites offer similar news-reader ability already built in. Vertical job search engines described in Chapter 2 give simple instructions on how to add their live job feeds to your computer or mobile devices. And if you're really unsure, again use your Web browser to search for "install an RSS reader."

Finding more info

When the die-hard techie hunger in you needs more nourishment, look up RSS (file format) on Wikipedia, the free encyclopedia at `en.wikipedia.org/wiki/RSS_feeds`.

Instant Messaging

And you thought instant messaging (IM) was just for those under arthritic age. The quicker-than-e-mail alternative for online communication is moving rapidly to mainstream America. A recent online post from Ray Geide, the publisher of the free online newsletter "Ray's Computer Tips," says his wife introduced him to IM when he was on a trip to Russia. "She didn't want to put up with the slowness of sending e-mails back and forth," Geide says.

"With instant messaging, we could see when the other was on the Internet and communicate back and forth in real time," Geide explains. "It was like talking on the telephone except that instead of talking we typed and instead of using telephones we used our computers connected to the Internet. As talking on a telephone happens in real time, so instant messaging happens in real time. As soon as the person you are messaging with types a message and sends it, you see it and can respond by sending a message back which that person sees at that time."

What it is

Instant messaging services are yet another new tool you can use to receive real-time or near real-time job postings. An IM service allows you to send messages and resumes to any of the people on your *buddy list* or *contact list* (the IM version of an address book), as long as that person is online.

Examples of IM messages you might send to your buddy list include these:

- *I'm looking for a sales job. Not retail. Here's resume. Can anyone push it around?*
- *I'm trying to get hired in accounting by XYZ corp. Know anyone inside who could walk my resume to HR or acct. mgr?*
- *Have you seen any great job postings for insurance claims adjusters? Pls advise.*
- *Hey, 300 pals, who'll rehearse me for big job interview?*
- *Who just interviewed for job you don't want? Maybe I do. Try me.*

 Posting a profile online creates privacy issues, but if you want to do so and to use IM in your job campaign, you need to add your IM information to your job search account at job sites and social or business networks and job referral services that support the technology.

 Alison Doyle, About.com (www.about.com) job searching guide, cautions you to adopt a professional-sounding IM screen name. If you've already got a goofy IM screen name (like nocrapola, 60isnew40, or girlgonewild), set up a new IM account used only for job searching with a no-nonsense moniker.

Hacking is a dark side of computer security problems of worms, viruses, and other Internet ills that already plague e-mail. The number of "poisoned" instant messages is exploding, in part because of trust expectations.

Although smart computer users know not to open suspicious e-mail, they're more trusting of a message sent from someone on their IM buddy list. Solution: Install antivirus software designed specifically for IM programs.

Getting started

Ready, aim, download an instant messaging program like this:

1. **Choose one or more from the biggest players in the free public IM space.**

   Working from most prominent down, they are

   - AOL Instant Messenger (www.aim.com)

   - MSN Messenger (get.live.com)

   - Yahoo! Messenger (messenger.yahoo.com)

   - ICQ (www.icq.com)

   - Google Talk (talk.google.com)

   - Internet Relay Chat (www.mirc.com)

   The more technically minded IMer who wants to be in several IM spaces at once can use free or inexpensive software, such as Trillian (www.ceruleanstudios.com) or Gaim (gaim.sourceforge.net) to help you keep it all straight.

2. **Add buddies to your buddy list. For job search purposes, the more the merrier.**

3. **Begin chatting away and building your network.**

Finding more info

The free public instant messaging programs give you more details about what's under their hoods.

Podcasts

As a job seeker, you can use a podcast the same way you can use a blog to spotlight your achievements and experience — to differentiate yourself from those with whom you are competing.

"Just having a podcast will set you apart from others and positions you as being on the cutting edge," says communications strategist Catherine Kaputa, author of *U R a Brand!: How Smart People Brand Themselves for Business Success* (Davies-Black, 2006). "You can turn an industry presentation, talk or panel discussion into a podcast to underscore your leadership and presentation skills."

Podcasting isn't yet mainstream, but based on reports that podcast feeds increased tenfold in six months in 2006, they may be headed in that direction. If you want to try podcasting as a way to get noticed in a Web 2.0 world, Kaputa recommends that for the highest impact, you do it while podcasting is still novel.

What it is

Podcasting is a way to distribute audio and video feeds (information or music over the Internet), rather than text alone. To make a podcast, you need a computer, microphone, Internet access and recording software, such as Roxio Easy Media Creator (`www.roxio.com`) or Audacity (`audacity.sourceforge.net`) a free audio editor.

To listen to a podcast on a mobile device (iPod, Blackberry, MP3 player, or cell phone) or a computer, you need Internet access.

An employer may use a podcast as a recruiting tool to help spread a branding message that explains why the company is a good place to work and to bolster communications with candidates the company hopes one day to hire.

When a podcast is offered on a Web site, the sponsors make it easy for you with an invitation to "sign up here" and click.

Getting started

You can find a tutorial on How do I make a podcast?" on Boutell.com (`www.boutell.com/newfaq/creating/makepodcast.html`). Or, if you're the sort of person who'd rather make reservations than dinner, consider using the commercial Feedburner service (`www.feedburner.com/fb/a/podcasts`).

Finding more info

Vendors, professional associations, and affinity Web sites present a regular stream of podcasts. Listen and watch a few podcasts to form your own opinions.

Web 2.0 Is a Work in Progress

"Web 2.0: The New Guy at Work" shouts a headline in a recent *BusinessWeek* article. The article's subhead continues the thought with a powerful claim: "As they seep into corporate offices, Web Services will change how you do business." Take that to include how you do resume business.

The capsules of Web services in this chapter describe those that are first out of the gate, but others are standing by, not yet slick enough to make a run for the winner's circle.

As a single example of advances that, at this writing, are not quite ready for prime time, mobile job search is a promising technology under development. Imagine seeing a text message of "Job match! We have a job for you." as you check your mobile phone while at the mall, watching your kid's baseball game or even walking along the seashore. Mobile job search technology can deliver job search result summaries to mobile phones and other handheld devices. But for now, the technology doesn't allow candidates to apply for a position with a handheld device. Instead, candidates must use e-mail to respond to a job alert or to send a new resume. Those challenges will be worked out, probably in the near future.

Technology is always evolving. Stay tuned, and make it work for you.

It never hurts to make friends with nerds and geeks.

Chapter 4

Familiar Search Tools That Haven't Gone Away

In This Chapter:

▶ Revisiting scannable resumes and fax machines

▶ Eyeing fading plain text versus handsome resumes

▶ Foiling identity theft and coping with spam filters

▶ Understanding online screening techniques

*N*ot all Web technology tools have held up under the rigors of time and progress.

Certain familiar, day-to-day job search tools — job boards and company Web sites, for instance — retain star status in determining where to send your resumes. (See Chapter 2 for a discussion of job boards and company Web sites.)

The handsome and fully formatted word-processed resume is another earlier tool that remains on job seekers' hit parade. The handsome resume reappeared about five years ago as an improvement to the drab plain text (ASCII) resume that was in vogue during the 1990s when it was the only form that older computer-scanning technology could electronically read.

But other search tools from the 1990s — such as scannable and plain text resumes — are showing their age.

In this chapter, I examine the current state of selected first-born electronic technology tools used in the job market — and give you the lowdown on how they can shape your employment chances.

Scannable Resumes: Same as Ever

A *scannable resume* is a resume that a recipient, usually a clerk in an employment office, scans into a computer as an image. Because computers read resumes differently than people do, you have to follow certain inconvenient rules, which I describe in this section, to be fairly sure that your scannable resume will be read as you intended.

A scannable resume may start life as a paper resume that you can postal mail, hand deliver, or fax on a fax machine; the employer uses a scanning machine to enter a hard copy resume into a candidate database. More often these days, you create a scannable resume on your computer and e-mail it to an employer, who electronically enters it directly into a database.

After an employer has your scannable resume, computer software extracts from it a summary of basic information, pulling out factors like your name, contact information, skills, work history, years of experience, and education. Scanned resumes and their extracted summaries sleep peacefully until an HR specialist or recruiter searches the summaries by keywords to retrieve candidates who match the requirements of a job opening. The technology ranks candidates, from the most qualified to the least qualified. The relevant resumes get a wake-up call and pop to the recruiting screen, where human eyes take over the recruiting tasks.

The once-desirable scannable resumes are on their way out, joining MS DOS (operating software) in computer museums. Recruiters now prefer the newer intake systems that allow resumes to travel smoothly online and move straight into an electronic resume-management database without the need to conform to scanning rules.

Even so, don't trash your scannable resume just yet. If an employer or job site directs you to send a resume that can be scanned, do it. And do it well, so that your resume doesn't go AWOL in a database. Take the following steps to prevent scanning errors from putting you on the sidelines:

✔ **Use type that's clear and readable.** Don't use a condensed typeface. White space separates letters; no space smushes them together. Letters must be distinctively clear with crisp, unbroken edges. Avoid arty, decorative typefaces.

✔ **Avoid these bad-scan elements:**

 - Italics or script

 - Underlining

 - Reverse printing (white letters on a black field)

 - Shadows or shading

 - Hollow bullets (they read like the letter *o*)

TIP

The old/new fax trick

Sometimes you may find it advantageous to go back to the future when your online resumes never seem to result in a callback. If you can learn the name and fax number of the hiring manager for a job you want, try sending the manager your scannable resume by fax.

Sending scannable resumes by postal mail is another option, especially effective with older, conservative managers and company owners.

- Number signs (#) for bullets (the computer may read it as a phone number)

- Boxes (computers try to read them like letters)

- Two-column formats or designs that look like newspapers

- Symbols, such as a logo

- Vertical lines (computers read them like the letter *l*)

- Vertical dates (use horizontal dates: 2006–2010)

✔ **Feel free to use larger fonts for section headings and your name.** A font size of 14 to 16 points is good. Larger headings look better on the electronic image of your resume when humans read it (which they don't always do). I recommend you format the body of your resume in a 12-point font size, the section headings in 14-point, and the name in 16-point.

✔ **Do keep your scannable resume simple in design and straightforward.** Recruiters call this approach "plain vanilla," and they like it because it doesn't confuse computers.

✔ **Do send your paper resume without staples.** Paper clips are okay. Follow this tip for all resumes that you mail or hand deliver because staples are a pain to pull out before feeding a scanner one page at a time.

Plain Text Resumes: A Long Last Gasp

The plain text resume (also known as an ASCII resume) is an online document constructed without formatting in plain text file format. It is most often sent by e-mail, but can be sent by fax, postal mail, or courier.

The main characteristic about this resume is its looks (or lack of same). It's so ugly only a computer could love it. See Figure 4-1 for an example of a plain text resume.

```
Plain Text Resume


        Della Hutchings
        890 Spruce Ave.
        Las Vegas, NV 22222
        945-804-9999
          E-mail: dellah@aol.com
        Admin Assist, 4 yrs exp, 6 software pgms, time mgt skills

        SUMMARY
        ======================================================================
        Word. WordPerfect. Lotus. Excel. PageMaker. QuickBooks
        Bilingual: Spanish. Time management. Budgeting. Organizational
        skills.

        EMPLOYMENT
        ======================================================================
        University of Upper Carolina                            [dates]
        Church Knoll, NC


        ASSISTANT TO DIRECTOR OF ACADEMIC TECHNOLOGY
        Use and support a wide variety of computer applications
        Work with both Macs and Dell computers
        Communicate with clients in South America
        Apply troubleshooting and problem solving skills
        Maintain complex scheduling for employer, staff, self
        Responsible for dept. budget administration; 100% balanced

        Mothers for Wildlife Inc.                               [dates]
        ADMINISTRATIVE ASSISTANT

        Edited/wrote newsletter
        Organized rallies and letter-writing campaigns
        Maintained mailing lists
        Saved organization $5,000 changing equipment

        EDUCATION
        ======================================================================
        University of Upper Carolina at Chapel Hill, NC         [dates]
        BA with honors in International Studies

        Won Gil award for best honors thesis on Latin America
        GPA in Major: 3.8/4.0

        AFFILIATIONS
        ======================================================================
        Carolina Hispanic Students Association
        Amnesty International
        Concept of Colors (Multicultural modeling group)

        HOBBIES
        ======================================================================
        Like details: Writing and Web design

        AWARDS
        ======================================================================
        On present job: Administrative Assistant of month four times   [dates]
        Recognized for productivity, organization, attention to detail
        and interpersonal skills
```

Figure 4-1: Plain Text (ASCII) Resume. This sample resume for Della Hutching is included solely to illustrate the appearance of a plain text resume. It is not intended to convey strong content.

Although plain text resumes are heading into the sunset, until the recruiting world is totally living large with handsomely formatted e-resumes, you may be stuck with the plain-Jane look. So here's the drill. Create your resume in your favorite word-processing program, save it, and then convert it to plain text (ASCII) like this:

1. **Click Edit → Select All.**

2. **Click Edit → Copy.**

3. **Open notepad. To get there click Start → Programs → Accessories → Notepad.**

4. **Click Edit → Paste.**

5. **Turn on the "Word-wrap" feature in the "Format" drop-down menu.**

6. **Save the resume as "yourname.txt" (for example, "JohnGill.txt").**

Don't forget to spell check *before* you save your resume as an ASCII file.

Because your resume now has ASCII for brains, it won't recognize the formatting commands that your word-processing program uses.

Don't use any characters that aren't on your keyboard, such as "smart quotes" (those tasteful, curly quotation marks that you see in this book) or mathematical symbols. They don't convert correctly, and your resume will need fumigating to rid itself of squiggles and capital *U*'s.

You know that you're off in the wrong direction if you have to change the preferences setting in your word processor or otherwise go to a lot of trouble to get a certain character to print. Remember that you can use dashes and asterisks (they're on the keyboard), but you can't use bullets (they're *not* on the keyboard).

Although you can't use bullets, bold, or underlined text in a plain text document, you can use plus signs (+) at the beginning of lines to draw attention to part of your document. You can also use a series of dashes to separate sections and capital letters to substitute for boldface. When you don't know what else to use to sharpen your ASCII effort, you can always turn to Old Reliable — white space.

Be on guard against other common ASCII landmines:

✔ **Typeface/fonts:** You can't control the typeface or font size in your ASCII resume. The text appears in the typeface and size that the recipient's computer is set for. This means that boldface, italics, or different font sizes don't appear in the online plain text version. Use all caps for words that need special emphasis.

- ✔ **Word wrap:** Don't use the word wrap feature when writing your resume because it will look as weird as a serial letter *E* running vertically down a page. Odd-looking word wrapping is one of the cardinal sins of online resumes. Set your margins at 0 and 65, or set the right margin at 6.5 inches. Then end each line after 65 characters with hard carriage returns (press the Enter key) to insert line breaks.

- ✔ **Proportional typefaces:** Don't use proportional typefaces that have different widths for different characters (such as Times Roman). Instead, use a fixed-width typeface (such as Courier) so that you have a true 65-character line. For example, if you compose and send your resume in Courier 12 and it's received in the Arial typeface, it should still work well with most e-mail programs, surviving transport with a close resemblance to the original line length.

- ✔ **Tabs:** Don't use tabs; they get wiped out in the conversion to ASCII. Use your spacebar instead.

- ✔ **Alignment:** Your ASCII resume is automatically left-justified. If you need to indent a line or center a heading, use the spacebar.

- ✔ **Page numbers:** Omit page numbers. You can't be certain where the page breaks will fall, and your name and page number could end up halfway south on a page.

When you send your ASCII resume, paste it with a cover note (a very brief cover letter) into the body of your e-mail.

E-Forms: Fill in the Blankety-Blanks

The e-form is just a shorter version of the plain text resume, and you usually find it on company Web sites. The company encourages you to apply by setting your plain text into designated fields of the forms on the site.

The e-form is almost like an application form, except that it lacks the legal document status an application form acquires when you sign it, certifying that all facts are true.

Follow the on-screen instructions given by each employer to cut and paste the requested information into the site's template. You're basically just filling in the blanks with your contact information that's supplemented by data lifted from your plain text resume.

The subject line online

Whether you're sending a scannable, plain text, or handsome word-processed resume online, the subject line of your e-mail can bring you front and center to a recruiter's attention.

✔ When you respond to an advertised job, use the job title. If none is listed, use the reference number.

✔ When you send an unsolicited resume, write a short "sales" headline. For example: Bilingual teacher, soc studies/6 yrs' exp. Or, Programmer, experienced, top skills: Java, C++.

Never just say *Bilingual teacher* or *Programmer*. Sell yourself! Keep rewriting until you've crammed as many sales points as possible into your "marquee."

Should you show a "cc" for "copy sent" on your resume? If you're e-mailing a hiring manager (such as the accounting manager), copy the human resources department manager; that saves the hiring manager from having to forward your resume to human resources and is more likely to result in your landing in the company's resume database to be considered for any number of jobs.

Remember that e-forms can't spell check, so cutting and pasting your resume into the e-form body, instead of typing it in manually, is your best bet. Because you spell checked your resume before converting it to ASCII (of course you did!), at least you know that everything is likely to be spelled correctly.

Virtually all company Web sites now encourage you to apply online through their applicant portals. You're asked to fill out an online form, upload, or cut and paste your resume. Most companies ask you to answer demographic questions about race, gender, and so forth as a way of collecting data for the *Equal Employment Opportunity Commission* (EEOC). You aren't required to include this information to be considered for employment. Nevertheless, women and minorities are well advised to oblige the demographics request. What if you're a white male? Your call.

E-forms work well for job seekers in high-demand occupations, such as nursing, but they don't work so well for job seekers who need to document motivation, good attitude, and other personal characteristics and achievements that computers don't search for. When you rely on an e-form to get an employer's attention, you're playing 100 percent on the employer's turf.

Ed's attachment etiquette

Ed Struzik knows what recruiters want. Struzik, president of BEKS Data Services, Inc. (www.beksdata.com), speaks from the vantage point of a dozen years' experience in providing outsourced resume-processing services and applicant-tracking system consulting to numerous Fortune 100 companies. Here are a few pitfalls he says resume senders need to avoid when e-mailing attachments:

✔ *Do not* attach EXE files. An Executable file could contain a virus, and no one will chance having the hard drive or network infected.

✔ *Do not* attach ZIP files. Who's to say the ZIP file doesn't contain an infected Executable? And besides, can your resume be so large that you have to ZIP it?

✔ *Do not* attach password-protected documents. How would you expect someone or something to open it without the password?

Yippee! The Fully Designed, Handsome Resume Is Back!

Before electronic and online resumes came along, the good-looking paper resume was the gold standard. The best sported a number of compelling embellishments: attractive formatting, appealing typefaces and fonts, bold-faced headings, italics, bullets, and underlining. The embellishments, tastefully done, were refreshing to read until technology all but killed them off more than a decade ago in favor of the electronically correct but truly blah plain text resumes I describe in the section "Plain Text Resumes: A Long Last Gasp."

The handsome resume was wonderful and was sorely missed by resume readers who grew bleary-eyed looking at pure text the whole long day.

That's in the past. Smart technology has brought back the good-lookers we gave up in the '90s to make sure our resumes arrived intact over the Internet.

Now you can usually attach your resume as a fully formatted, handsome dog of a document in a word-processing program, usually MS Word or WordPerfect. Check out Chapter 8 to find out how to make yours good-looking enough to be voted the Resume with Which You Are Most Likely to Succeed.

TIP

Stop and ask directions

Although scannable and plain text resumes are headed the way of carbon paper, and the vast majority of resume readers prefer to cast their eyes on the handsome resume, make a reality check. You job hunt in a time of transitioning technology, including an explosion of filters that will not accept word attachments. The attachments are refused as a way to avoid viruses and to keep out spam (including resume spam).

This means that you can never be 100 percent sure what technology is being used where you want to send your resume. The solution is to ask by telephone or by e-mail the company human resource department or the company receptionist the following question:

> *I want to be sure I'm using your preferred technology to submit my resume. Can I send it as an attachment, say in MS Word or WordPerfect?*

Alternatively, if you don't have a clue, you can send your resume within the body of your e-mail as plain text and also attach it as a word-processed document.

From Identity Theft to Recruiter Turnoff: Why Resume Blasting Is a Bad Idea

Resume blasting services (also jokingly known as resume spamming services) advertise their willingness to save you time and trouble by "blasting" your resume to thousands of recruiters and hiring managers all over the Internet — for a fee, of course. The pitches are tempting, but should you avail yourself of this miraculous service? Just say no! Resume blasting can bring you big trouble, from making identity theft easier for crooks, to irritating your boss, to making you an "untouchable" for recruiters.

Privacy and identity theft problems

Concerning identity theft issues, privacy expert Pam Dixon advises being cautious with your resume's information. On her nonprofit World Privacy Forum (www.worldprivacyforum.org), she continually updates a must-read report titled "Job Seeker's Guide to Resumes: Twelve Resume Posting Truths."

Truth Number One says this: "If you're going to post a resume online, post your resume privately. Most job sites offer anonymous posting that lets you mask your contact information and e-mail address when you post a resume.

This resume posting option allows you to decide who sees your real information, such as your home address. Masking this information is perhaps the single most important step job seekers who want to post a resume online can take to protect themselves."

Is Pam Dixon overreacting? No. The media has been full of horror stories of identity theft for some years.

Admittedly, merely being careful about releasing your resume information online won't keep you safe from identity theft in these days when the guard rails on privacy are coming down in so many ways in so many places. But do be stingy with your private information.

Identity theft may be the worst-case scenario, but it isn't the only life-altering problem that can arise when you put your business on e-street.

Risks in your workplace

Use a resume-blasting service while you're employed, and you might lose your current job. "Many employers do search for their employees' resumes in job site resume databases and search engines," explains Susan Joyce, CEO of Job-Hunt.org, who tracks the privacy issue.

Get your resume past spam gatekeepers

You may not know whether your resume becomes cyber-litter because a spam or virus filter deletes it unread. Susan Joyce, who operates Job-Hunt.org (www.job-hunt.org) offers these tips for getting your resume where you want it to go:

✔ Do send e-mail to only one company at a time. If your ISP (Internet Service Provider) suspects you're sending out a battalion of messages, its computers may kill your work. On the receiving end, filters may see a large number of addressees as incoming spam and eliminate your resume.

✔ Do look at the junk mail you get and avoid using subject lines with exclamation points, all capitals, or spam buzzwords, such as "free," "trial," "cash," or "great offer." Even appropriate phrases like "increased sales $10,000 a month," can trigger spam filters, thanks to junk pitches such as "Make $10,000 a month from home working part time." When you're in doubt, try spelling out dollar amounts.

✔ Don't use too many numbers in your e-mail address, such as jobseeker12635@yahoo.com. Filter software may think the numbers are a spammer's tracking code.

✔ Send your resume to yourself and see whether it lands in your junk filter bin. One software expert runs every resume and cover note through three spam filters on his computer before e-mailing them.

"When employees' resumes are found grazing in someone else's pasture before noon," says CareerXroads' Mark Mehler, who consults with countless company managers, "they may be on the street by the end of that same day."

Overexposure to recruiters

One more reason not to spread your resume all over the map: When you're targeting the fast track to the best jobs, nothing beats being brought to an employer's notice by an important third person — and an independent recruiter qualifies as an important third person.

Employers are becoming resistant to paying independent recruiters big fees to search the Web when they theoretically can save money by hiring in-house corporate recruiters to do it. That's why recruiting agencies need fresh inventory that employers can't find elsewhere. If you want a third-party recruiter to represent you, think carefully before pinning cyber-wings on your resume.

In addition to losing control of your resume, its wide availability can cause squabbles among contingency recruiters over who should be paid for finding you. An employer caught in the conflict of receiving a resume from multiple sources, including internal resume databases, will often pass over a potential employee rather than become involved in deciding which source, if any, should be paid.

Online Screening Keeps On Keepin' On

Your OnTarget resume may never be read if an employer's online screening program decides in advance that you aren't qualified for the position's stated — or unstated — requirements. In essence, screening software has the first word about who is admitted for a closer look and who isn't.

Online screening is an automated process of creating a blueprint of known requirements for a given job and then collecting information from each applicant in a standardized manner to see whether the applicant matches the blueprint. The outcomes are sent to recruiters and hiring managers.

Online screening is known by various terms — *prescreening* and *pre-employment screening,* to mention two. By any name, the purpose of online screening is to verify that you are, in fact, a good fit for the position and that you haven't lied about your background. Employers use online screening tools (tests, assessment instruments, questionnaires, and so forth) to reduce and sort applicants against criteria and competencies that are important to their organizations.

If you apply online through major job sites or many company Web site career portals, you may be asked to respond yes or no to job-related questions, such as:

- ✔ Do you have the required college degree?

- ✔ Do you have experience with (specific job requirement)?

- ✔ Are you willing to relocate?

- ✔ Do you have two or more years' experience managing a corporate communications department?

- ✔ Is your salary requirement between $55,000–$60,000/year?

Answering "no" to any of these kinds of questions disqualifies you for the listed position, an automated decision that helps the recruiters thin the herd of resumes more quickly but that could be a distinct disadvantage to you, the job searcher. (Without human interaction, you may not show enough of the stated qualifications, but you may have compensatory qualifications that a machine won't allow you to communicate.)

On the other hand, professionals in shortage categories will benefit by a quick response, such as nursing. Example: *Are you an RN?* If the answer is "yes," the immediate response, according to a recruiter's joke, is "When can you start?"

Sample components of online screening

The following examples of online screening aren't exhaustive, but they are illustrations of the most commonly encountered upfront filtering techniques.

- ✔ **Basic evaluation:** The system automatically evaluates the match between a resume's content (job seeker's qualifications) and a job's requirement and ranks the most qualified resumes at the top.

- ✔ **Skills and knowledge testing:** The system uses tests that require applicants to prove their knowledge and skills in a specific area of expertise. Online skills and knowledge testing is especially prevalent in information technology jobs where dealing with given computer programs is basic to job performance. Like the old-time typing tests in an HR office, there's nothing subjective about this type of quiz: You know the answers, or you don't.

- ✔ **Personality assessment:** Attempts to measure work-related personality traits to predict job success is one of the more controversial types of online testing. Dr. Wendell Williams, a leading testing expert based in the Atlanta area, says that personality tests expressly designed for hiring are in a totally different league than tests designed to measure things like communication style or personality type: "Job-related personality testing is highly job specific and tends to change with both task and job," he says. "If you are taking a generic personality test, a good rule is to either pick answers that fall in the middle of the scale or ones you think best fit the job description. This is not deception. Employers rarely conduct studies of personality test scores versus job performance and so it really does not make much difference."

✔ **Behavioral assessment:** The system asks questions aimed at uncovering your past experience applying core competencies the organization requires (such as fostering teamwork, managing change) and position-specific competencies (such as persuasion for sales, attention to detail for accountants). I further describe competencies in Chapter 6.

✔ **Managerial assessments:** The system presents applicants with typical managerial scenarios and asks them to react. Proponents say that managerial assessments are effective for predicting performance on competencies, such as interpersonal skills, business acumen, and decision making. Dr. Williams identifies the many forms these assessments can take:

- **In-basket exercises** where the applicant is given an in-basket full of problems and told to solve them.

- **Analysis case studies** where the applicant is asked to read a problem and recommend a solution.

- **Planning case studies** where the applicant is asked to read about a problem and recommend a step-by-step solution.

- **Interaction simulations** where the applicant is asked to work out a problem with a skilled role player.

- **Presentation exercises** where the applicant is asked to prepare, deliver, and defend a presentation.

- **Integrity tests** measure your honesty with a series of questions. You can probably spot the best answers without too much trouble.

Pros and cons of online screening

Here's a snapshot of the advantages and disadvantages of online screening, from the job seeker's perspective:

✔ **Advantages:** In theory, a perfect online screening is totally job-based and fair to all people with equal skills. Your resume would survive the first cut based only on your ability to do well in the job. You also are screened out of consideration for any job you may not be able to do, saving yourself stress and keeping your track record free of false starts.

✔ **Disadvantages:** The creation of an online process is vulnerable to human misjudgment; I'm still looking for an example of the perfect online screening system. Moreover, you have no chance to "make up"

Level playing field for salaries

When employers demand your salary requirements before they'll schedule an interview, you are at a disadvantage in negotiating strength. But with hundreds of Web sites broadcasting the compensation information supplied by a trio of salary calculator services — Salary.com (`www.salary.com`), Salary Expert (`www.salaryexpert.com`), and PayScale (`www.payscale.com`) — the tables are turning.

You can, with a few clicks, get a free ball-park estimate of your market worth. For a fee under $100, you can order a detailed report from these salary-calculator services that pinpoint your market value. Now, you become a more informed and more equal partner in the negotiation. If your market rate is $75,000/year and you answer the question earlier in this section "Is your salary requirement between $55,000 and $60,000 per year?" you can answer "no" and keep looking.

missing competencies or skills. (An analogy: You can read music, but you don't know how to play a specific song. You can learn it quickly, but there's no space to write "quick learner.")

Can your resume be turned away?

What if you get low grades on answering the screening questions — can the employer's system tell you to take your resume and get lost? No, not legally. Anyone can leave a resume, but if they don't pass the screening, the resume will be ranked at the bottom of the list in the database.

The bottom line is that if you don't score well in screening questions, your resume will be exiled to an electronic no-hire zone even if it isn't physically turned away.

Match Your Resumes to the Jobs

Part I covers new Web 2.0 and surviving Web 1.0 online job search tools. Knowing both the latest and the traditional methods is critical to move your resumes along cyberways and byways that lead to interview offers.

But never forget that to get past software filters, your resumes must spell out your qualifications for the jobs' requirements. If you're parking your resumes in an online database rather than responding to a specific job ad, make sure they specify that you possess the most commonly requested requirements in a given career field.

Part II

Resume Basics That Wow 'Em Every Time

The 5th Wave   By Rich Tennant

"Frankly? I'd stay away from using 'plucky' as a keyword unless you're looking for a job at a chicken processing plant."

In this part . . .

How do you show off your strengths and shine the best light on your not-so-strengths? This part shows you how to handle a whole slew of less-than-ideal work histories or situations — from too much experience to too little. In this part, I also explain how to give your content the zing it needs and how to make sure it's a looker.

Chapter 5

Creating Your Best Resume

- -

In This Chapter

▶ Selling your value to people you want to work for

▶ Focusing your resume like a high-powered laser

▶ Selecting the format that champions your image

▶ Comparing format features in case you're not sure

▶ Sampling uncommon formats

- -

*H*ow much are you worth to employers? Your resume inspires their first best guess, so you want to make sure it's a compelling portrait of your strengths and skills. Paint yourself in murky colors on a stained canvas, and you're likely never to get in the door. This chapter shows you how to structure your resume so that you come off as a masterpiece.

As you kick off a personal marketing campaign with you as the product, build your main job search communication on a solid foundation and put it in lights with the right shade of persuasive promotion.

The time has come for seeker to meet substance: 3-2-1 begin!

"Telling It" Mutes; "Selling It" Sings

Pretend you're in the market for replacement windows in your home. Which of the following two messages would better tweak your interest in taking a closer look at the company?

The Turner Group has been in existence replacing windows for 30+ years at the same easy-to-find showroom. We offer 25 different models and window sizes — a choice to fit every home and budget.

The Turner Group has been assisting homeowners to protect their home values with 25 models of high-quality replacement windows at discount prices — and in all sizes — since the mid-1970s.

The first statement is an example of telling it; the message is "look at us!" The second statement is an example of selling it, and its message is "here's what we can do for you."

OnTarget resumes don't tell it — they sell it! Dry, dull descriptions of what you did on a job is as boring as video of a friend's childhood birthday parties.

Instill excitement! List your background facts but make sure you position them as end-user (employer) benefits.

One way to sell your value and your benefits to an employer who has the power to hire you is to get specific. Communicate the importance of what you've done by using details — numbers, names, achievements, outcomes, volume of sales or savings, and size of contracts, for example.

Remember, when you sell it, you breathe life into a rigid, dreary, boring, and generally coma-inducing document. Here are several examples of the sell-it strategy for resumes.

Tell it	*Sell it*
Supervisor of HR generalist and recruiting functions for 10 years at company headquarters.	Supervisor with 10 years' successful management of 6 HR generalists and 3 recruiters for regional company with 3 administrative offices and 8 manufacturing plants.
Worked as network administrator with responsibility for administration and troubleshooting.	As network administrator, created in excess of 750 user scripts, installed 16 workstations, administered security codes to 350 clients, supervised installation of company-wide Microsoft XP Pro, and regularly solved stress-causing malfunctions in operating system and software.
Leading sales rep for new homes in prestigious development in year when housing market began to cool.	In a cooling housing market (off 11% from previous year), became number-one sales rep, selling $7,800,000 in 12 months — 13 homes at $600,000 floor.

Other chapters of this book clue you in on more techniques of approaching your resume with a sell-it mindset, the starting gate of today's high-stakes resume derby. In the classic film *Butch Cassidy and the Sundance Kid,* Butch Cassidy tells Sundance: "You have vision but the rest of the world wears bifocals." Help employers see not only what you were responsible for but how well you did it and why it mattered.

Focus Your Resume

Too many jobs in your background threaten your focus. *Unfocused* is an ugly word in job-search circles, one that indicates you lack commitment, that you're perpetually at a fork in the road. It's a reason *not* to hire you.

When your resume looks as though it will collapse under the weight of a mishmash of jobs unconnected to your present target, eliminate your previous trivial pursuits. Group the consequential jobs under a heading that says *Relevant Work Experience Summary.* What if this approach solves one problem — the busy resume — but creates another, such as a huge, gaping black hole where you removed inconsequential jobs? Create a second work history section that covers those holes, labeling it *Other Experience.* Figure 5-1 shows an example.

Dealing with an unfocused career pattern on paper is easier when it's done under the banner of a temporary service company. The treatment in this case lists the temporary services company as the employer. You choose one job title that covers most of your assignments. Under that umbrella title, identify specific assignments. Give the dates in years next to the temporary services firm, skipping dates for each assignment. Figure 5-2 shows an example.

What if you work for several temporary services at the same time? The simple answer is that you use the same technique of dating your work history for the temporary service firms, not for the individual assignments. This dating technique is a statement of fact; you legally are an employee of the temporary services firm, not of the company that pays for your temporary services.

When excess jobs or focus isn't a problem, you may choose an alternative presentation for a series of short-term jobs, as I show you in Chapter 4. The alternative doesn't mention the staffing firm(s) but only the names of the companies where you worked.

Impacted Resume with Focus

Professional Experience

UNITECH, Hamburg, Germany
Computer Laboratory Assistant, [dates]
> Manage and troubleshoot hardware and software systems. Recover data, create programming architecture, and install parts and software. Assist a team of 18 engineers.

TECHNIK TECH, Hamburg, Germany
Assistant to System Analysts, [dates]
> Participated in construction, repair, and installation of systems at local businesses. Diagnosed faulty systems and reported to senior analysts, decreasing their workload by 25%.

TRADE NET, Berlin, Germany
Applications and Network Specialist, [dates]
> Set up and monitored a Windows-based BBS, including installation, structure, security, and graphics. Authored installation scripts for Trade Net, licensing U.S. software use in Europe.

Other Experience

AMERICAN TOY STORE, Berlin, Germany, Sales Representative, [dates]
Arranged and inventoried merchandise, directed sales and customer relations. Developed strong interpersonal skills and gained knowledge of retail industry.

CAMP INTERNATIONAL, Oslo, Germany, Activities Director, [dates]
Organized daily activities for more than 300 children from English-speaking countries, including sports, recreation, and day classes. Supervised 10 counselors and kitchen staff of five, developing responsible and effective management skills.

Figure 5-1: Solving the black-hole problem in a jobs-impacted resume by creating a focus plus a second work history section.

Focusing with Temp Jobs

Professional Experience

Relia-Temps [dates]

Executive Secretary

- North Western Banking Group
Perform all clerical and administrative responsibilities for 10-partner investment and loan firm, assisting each partner in drafting contracts, reviewing proposals, and desiging various financial programs. Supervise 7 staff members. Introduced 50% more efficient filing system, reducing client reviews from 4 to 3 hours.

Administrative Assistant

- Mosaic Advertising
Supervised 3 receptionists and 4 clerical specialists, reporting directly to president. Administered daily operations of all accounting and communication transactions. Using extensive computer savvy, upgraded company computer networks withWindows 98.

- Blakeslee Environmental, Inc.
Assisted 8 attorneys at interstate environmental protection agency, scheduling meetings and conferences, maintaining files, and updating database records. Redesigned office procedures and methods of communication, superior organizational skills.

Figure 5-2: Listing your temporary job assignments without looking unfocused.

Resume Formats Make a Difference

Resume format refers not to the design or look of your resume but to how you organize and emphasize your information. Different format styles flatter different histories.

At root, formats come in three family trees:

- ✔ The *reverse chronological* lists all employment and education, beginning with the most recent and working backward.
- ✔ The *skills-based functional* shouts what you can do instead of relaying what you've done and where you did it.
- ✔ The *hybrid* or *combination* is a marriage of both formats.

Note: The narrative format is an outdated chronological format that starts with the oldest facts and works forward to the newest facts. A pretentious variation of the narrative format uses the third person as though you were writing a biography. I don't bother to even discuss them, and I strongly suggest that you don't use either one.

These basic styles have spawned a variety of other formats, the best known of which are these:

- ✔ Professional
- ✔ Academic curriculum vitae
- ✔ International curriculum vitae

Table 5-1 gives you a breakdown of which format to use when.

Table 5-1	Your Best Resume Formats at a Glance
Your Situation	*Suggested Formats*
Perfect career pattern	Reverse Chronological
Rookie or ex-military	Functional, Hybrid, Accomplishment, Linear
Seasoned ace	Functional, Hybrid, Accomplishment
Business	Reverse Chronological, Accomplishment
Technical	Accomplishment, Reverse Chronological, Hybrid
Professional	Professional, Academic Curriculum Vitae, Portfolio

Your Situation	Suggested Formats
Government	Reverse Chronological, Professional
Arts/teaching	Professional, Portfolio, Academic Curriculum Vitae
Job history gaps	Functional, Hybrid
Multitrack job history	Functional, Hybrid
Career change	Functional
International job seeker	International Curriculum Vitae
Special issues	Functional, Hybrid

The following sections explore each type of resume format so that you can choose the style best for you and your skills.

Reverse Chronological Format

The *reverse chronological* (RC) format, shown in Figure 5-3, is straightforward: It cites your employments from the most recent back, showing dates as well as employers and educational institutions (college, vocational-technical schools, and career-oriented programs and courses). You accent a steady work history with a clear pattern of upward or lateral mobility.

Strengths and weaknesses

Check to see whether the reverse chronological resume's strengths are yours:

- ✔ This upfront format is by far the most popular with employers and recruiters because it is so, well, upfront.

- ✔ RC links employment dates, underscoring continuity. The weight of your experience confirms that you're a specialist in a specific career field (social service or technology, for example).

- ✔ RC positions you for the next upward career step.

- ✔ As the most traditional of formats, RC fits traditional industries (such as banking, education, and accounting).

Take the weaknesses of the reverse chronological format into account:

- ✔ When your previous job titles are substantially different from your target position, this format doesn't support your objective. Without careful management, the RC reveals everything, including inconsequential jobs and negative factors.

- ✔ RC can spotlight periods of unemployment or brief job tenure.

- ✔ Without careful management, RC reveals your age.

- ✔ Without careful management, RC may suggest that you were plateaued in a job too long.

Who should use this format and who should think twice

Use the reverse chronological if you fall into any of these categories:

- ✔ You have a steady school and work record reflecting constant growth or lateral movement.

- ✔ Your most recent employer is a respected name in the industry, and the name may ease your entry into a new position.

- ✔ Your most recent job titles are impressive stepping stones.

- ✔ You're a savvy writer who knows how to manage potential negative factors, such as inconsequential jobs, too few jobs, too many temporary jobs, too many years at the same job, or too many years of age.

Think twice about using the RC under these circumstances:

- ✔ You have a lean employment history. Listing a stray student job or two is not persuasive, even when you open with superb educational credentials enhanced with internships and co-op experiences.

  With careful attention, you can do a credible job on an RC by extracting from your extracurricular activities every shred of skills, which you present as abilities to do work with extraordinary commitment and a head for quick learning.

- ✔ You have work-history or employability problems — gaps, demotions, stagnation in a single position, job hopping (four jobs in three years, for example), reentering the workforce after a break to raise a family.

  Exercise very careful management to truthfully modify stark realities. However, you may find that other formats can serve you better.

Reverse Chronological Format

YOUR NAME
Home Address
City, State, Zip Code
Home and Cell Phones
E-mail

Objective:
A position that uses your skills.

SUMMARY
- Years of work experience, paid and unpaid, relevant to target position's requirements
- Achievement that proves you can handle the target
- Another achievement that proves you can handle the target
- Skills, competencies, characteristics — facts that further your ability to handle target job
- Education and training relating to the target (if unrelated, bury in resume body)

PROFESSIONAL EXPERIENCE AND ACCOMPLISHMENTS

[dates]   **Job Title**   Employer, Employer's Location
A brief synopsis of your purpose in the company, detailing essential functions, products and customer base you managed.
- An achievement in this position relevant to objective (do not repeat summary)
- A second achievement in this position relevant to current objective
- More accomplishments, i.e., awards, recognition, promotion, raise, praise, training

[dates]   **Job Title**   Employer, Employer's Location
Detailed as above.

[dates]   **Job Title**   Employer, Employer's Location
A briefer synopsis of your purpose in the company, overviewing functions, products, customer base.
- An achievement made during this position relevant to current objective
- More accomplishments, i.e., awards, recognition, promotion, raise, praise, training

[dates]   **Job Title**   Employer, Employer's Location
An even briefer synopsis of your purpose in the company, overviewing functions, products, customer base.
- An achievement made during this position that's relevant to current objective

EDUCATION AND PROFESSIONAL TRAINING

Degree(s), classes, seminars, educational awards and honors
Credentials, clearances, licenses

Figure 5-3: The tried-and-true, basic reverse chronological format.

Creating a reverse chronological resume

To create an OnTarget RC resume, remember to

- Focus on areas of specific relevance to your target position.
- List all pertinent places you've worked, including for each the name of the employer and the city in which you worked, the years you were there, your title, your responsibilities, and your measurable achievements.

To handle problems such as unrelated experience, you can group unrelated jobs in a second work history section under a heading of Other Experience, or Previous Experience, or Related Experience. I tell you more about handling special circumstances in Chapter 9.

Functional Format

The *functional format*, shown in Figure 5-4, is a resume of ability-focused topics — portable skills or functional areas. It ignores chronological order. In its purest form, the functional style omits dates, employers, and job titles. But, employers don't like it when you leave out the particulars, so contemporary functional resumes list employers, job titles, and sometimes even dates — but still downplay this information by briefly listing it at the bottom of the resume. The functional format is oriented toward what the job seeker can do for the employer instead of narrating history.

Strengths and weaknesses

The following are the strengths of the functional format:

- A functional resume directs a reader's eyes to what you want him or her to notice. It helps a reader visualize what you can do instead of when and where you learned to do it. Functional resumes salute the future rather than embalm the past.
- The functional format — written after researching the target company — serves up the precise functions or skills that the employer wants. It's like saying, "You want budget control and turnaround skills — I have budget control and turnaround skills." The skills sell is a magnet to reader eyes!

> ✔ It uses unpaid and nonwork experience to your best advantage.
>
> ✔ It allows you to eliminate or subordinate work history that doesn't support your current objective.

Weaknesses of the functional format include the following:

> ✔ Because recruiters and employers are more accustomed to RC formats, departing from the norm may raise suspicion that you're not the cream of the crop of applicants. Readers may assume that you're trying to hide inadequate experience, educational deficits, or who knows what.
>
> ✔ Functional styles may leave unclear which skills grew from which jobs or experiences.
>
> ✔ This style doesn't make a clear career path obvious.
>
> ✔ This format doesn't maximize recent coups in the job market.

Who should use this format and who should think twice

This resume is heaven-sent for career changers, new graduates, ex-military personnel, seasoned aces, and individuals with multitrack job histories, work-history gaps, or special-issue problems.

Job seekers with blue-ribbon backgrounds and managers and professionals who are often tapped by executive recruiters should avoid this format.

Creating a functional resume

Choose areas of expertise acquired during the course of your career, including education and unpaid activities. These areas become skill and functional headings, which vary by the target position or career field. Note any achievements below each heading. A few examples of headings are: *Management, Sales, Budget Control, Cost Cutting, Project Implementation,* and *Turnaround Successes.*

List the headings in the order of importance and follow each heading with a series of short statements of your skills (shown in Figure 5-4). Turn your statements into power hitters with measurable achievements.

Functional Format

YOUR NAME
Address, City, State, Zip Code
Home and Cell Phones
E-mail

Job Title You Desire

More than (# years paid and unpaid) work experience, in target area, contributing to an (achievement/result/high ranking in industry/top 5% of performance reviews). Add accomplishments, strengths, proficiencies, characteristics, education, brief testimonial — anything that supports your target job title.

PROFESSIONAL EXPERIENCE AND ACCOMPLISHMENTS

A TOP SKILL (Pertinent to objective and job requirements)
 • An achievement illustrating this skill, and the location/employer of this skill*
 • A second achievement illustrating this skill, and the location/employer of this skill*

A SECOND TOP SKILL (Pertinent to objective and job requirements)
 • An achievement illustrating this skill, and the location/employer of this skill*
 • A second achievement illustrating this skill, and the location/employer of this skill*

A THIRD TOP SKILL (Pertinent to objective and job requirements)
 • An achievement illustrating this skill, and the location/employer of this skill*
 • A second achievement illustrating this skill, and the location/employer of this skill*

A FOURTH SKILL (Optional — must relate to objective and job requirements)
 • Detailed as above

A UNIQUE AREA OF PROFICIENCY (Pertinent to objective and job requirements)
 • An achievement testifying to this proficiency, including the location/employer*
 • A list of equipment, processes, software, or terms you know that reflect your familiarity with this area of proficiency
 • A list of training experiences that document your qualifications and proficiency

EMPLOYMENT HISTORY

[dates]	**Job Title**	Employer, Location
[dates]	**Job Title**	Employer, Location
[dates]	**Job Title**	Employer, Location
[dates]	**Job Title**	Employer, Location

PROFESSIONAL TRAINING AND EDUCATION
Degrees, credentials, clearances, licenses, classes, seminars, training

* Omit locations/employers if your work history is obviously lacking in lockstep upward mobility

Figure 5-4: No experience? Use the functional resume format.

Hybrid Format

The *hybrid*, a combination of reverse chronological and functional formats, satisfies demands for timelines as well as showcases your marketable skills and impressive accomplishments. Many people find the hybrid to be the most attractive of all formats.

Essentially, in a hybrid, a functional summary tops a reverse chronological presentation of dates, employers, and capsules of each position's duties. Figure 5-5 gives you a template for this format.

Strengths and weaknesses

A hybrid format combines the strengths of both the reverse chronological and functional formats, so check out those earlier sections. Its weakness is that, like a functional resume, it departs from the straightforward reverse chronological format that a very conservative employer may prefer.

Who should use this format and who should think twice

The hybrid is a wise choice for rookies, ex-military personnel, seasoned aces, those with job history gaps or a multitrack job history, and individuals with special-issue problems.

The hybrid style is similar to the contemporary functional format — so much so that making a case for distinction is sometimes difficult.

Career changers or job seekers needing more appropriate formats, such as the functional, should skip the hybrid.

Creating a hybrid resume

Build a functional format of ability-focused topics and add employment documentation — employers, locations, dates, and duties.

Hybrid Format

YOUR NAME
Address, City, State, Zip Code
Home and Cell Phones
E-mail

Objective: Position as_____using your____ (#) years of experience in skills key to target.

SUMMARY OF QUALIFICATIONS
Number of years in area of target position
Related education, training and accreditation
An achievement pertinent to objective
Qualifications that reinforce your candidacy for this position
Other accomplishments, characteristics, proficiencies

SUMMARY OF SKILLS
• Technical skills   • Processes   • Computer software

ACCOMPLISHMENTS AND EXPERIENCE

Job Title, Top Qualifications Used   Employer, Location   [dates]

   A Top Skill (Pertinent to objective/requirements)
   • Accomplishments made while in this position
   • Several apt achievements from position, pertinent to this skill and the objective
   Another Skill (Pertinent to objective)
   • Several achievements pertinent to this skill and the objective

Job Title, Top Qualifications Used   Employer, Location   [dates]

   A Top Skill (Pertinent to objective/requirements)
   • Accomplishments made while in this position, even more detailed
   • Several apt achievements from this position, similar to above
   Another Skill (Pertinent to objective)
   • Several achievements pertinent to this skill and the objective

Job Title, Top Qualifications Used   Employer, Location   [dates]

   A Top Skill (Pertinent to objective/requirements)
   • Accomplishments made while in this position
   • Several apt achievements from position, pertinent to this skill and the objective
   Another Skill (Pertinent to objective)
   • Several achievements pertinent to this skill and the objective

PROFESSIONAL TRAINING AND EDUCATION
Degrees, accreditations, licenses, clearances, courses

Figure 5-5: The hybrid format — the best of both worlds.

Professional Format

A professional format, also called a *professional vitae* or *professional CV* is slightly long winded (say, three to five pages) but factual. It emphasizes professional qualifications and activities. This format, shown in Figure 5-6, is essentially a shortened academic curriculum vitae.

Strengths and weaknesses

The professional resume is mandatory for certain kinds of positions; your choice is whether to send this type or go all the way and send an academic curriculum vitae.

But be aware that professional resumes are reviewed under a microscope; every deficiency stands out. Adding a portfolio that shows your experience-based work skills may compensate for missing chunks of formal requirements. Just make sure that any unsolicited samples you send are high quality and need no explanation.

Who should use this format and who should think twice

Professionals in medicine, science, and law should use this format. Also use it when common sense of convention makes it the logical choice, as when you're applying for a leadership civil service appointment in government.

For most nonprofessionals, especially managers, the professional format is tedious.

Creating a professional resume

Begin with education, professional training, and an objective. Follow with a summary of the main points you want the reader to absorb. Follow that information with details of your professional experience and accomplishments.

Professional Format

YOUR NAME
Address, City, State, Zip Code
Home and Cell Phones
E-mail

EDUCATION AND PROFESSIONAL TRAINING

Degrees, credentials, awards, achievements, honors, seminars, clearances, licenses.

OBJECTIVE: A position that uses your talents, with an emphasis on your special skills.

SUMMARY

- Number of years of work experience, paid and unpaid, relevant to target

- Accomplishment(s) that prove your unique candidacy for this position

- Qualifications geared for the objective position or company requirements

- Other things the employer will like to know — proficiencies, characteristics, achievements, training, credentials and education

PROFESSIONAL EXPERIENCE AND ACCOMPLISHMENTS

[dates]   **Job Title**   Employer, Employer's Location

A brief synopsis of your purpose in the company, detailing essential functions and products you managed, and your customer base.

- An achievement made during position pertinent to target

- A second achievement made during position also pertinent to target

- More achievements — awards, recognition, promotion, raise, praise, training

[dates]   **Job Title**   Employer, Employer's Location

An even briefer synopsis of your purpose in the company, overviewing functions, products, customer base.

- An achievement made during this position that is applicable to target

- More achievements — awards, recognition, promotion, raise, praise, training

* *List three previous jobs with the same detail as above; divide jobs according to job title, not employer.*

Figure 5-6: The long but effective professional format is perfect for certain careers.

Follow the template in Figure 5-6, paying attention to accomplishments. Just because you present yourself in a low-key, authoritative manner doesn't mean that you can forget to say how good you are.

Academic Curriculum Vitae

The academic *curriculum vitae* (CV) is a comprehensive biographical statement, typically three to ten pages, emphasizing professional qualifications and activities. A CV of six to eight pages, ten at the most, is recommended for a veteran professional; two to four pages is appropriate for a young professional just starting out (see the "Professional Format" section earlier in this chapter).

If your CV is more than four pages long, show mercy and save eyesight by attaching an *executive summary* page to the top. An executive summary gives a brief overview of your qualifications and experience.

Among various possible organizations, the template in Figure 5-7 (a variation of the hybrid format but with exhaustive coverage) illustrates a lineup of your contact information, objective, qualifications summary, skills summary, and professional background.

Strengths and weaknesses

A CV presents all the best of you, which is good, but for people with aging eyes, a CV may be too reading-intensive. More important, weaknesses in any area of your professional credentials are relatively easy to spot.

Who should use this format and who should think twice

Anyone working in a PhD-driven environment, such as higher education, think tanks, science, and elite research and development groups needs to use this format.

Anyone who can avoid using it should do so.

Academic Curriculum Vitae Format

YOUR NAME
Curriculum Vitae
Address, City, State, Zip Code
Home and Cell Phones
E-mail

Objective (optional): Position as_____(title of position employer offers) using ___ (#) years of experience in _____ (qualifications essential and specialized to the position).

SUMMARY OF QUALIFICATIONS

- A summary of your education, proficiencies, and career pertinent to target
- Number of years in objective area, explaining similarities to job and its responsibilities
- Related education, training, and accreditation, reflecting employer's goals/priorities
- An achievement directly related to target
- Traits reinforcing your candidacy for this position, specifically those asked for by the employer and those generally in demand in the field
- Other accomplishments, characteristics, knowledge either rare or prized in the field

SUMMARY OF SKILLS

•Topics of specialty or innovation within field •Areas of particular familiarity •Software equipment •Processes •Terminology relevant to target •Languages

PROFESSIONAL BACKGROUND
EDUCATION
Degrees:
    Ph.D., institution, date of degree (or anticipated date), specialization
    M.A./M.S., institution, date of degree, major, minor, emphasis, concentration
    B.A./B.S., institution, date of degree, major, minor
Courses: Those taken, honors, seminars, number of units, G.P.A. (if a recent graduate)
Other Accreditations: Licenses, clearances
Academic Achievements: Appointments, nominations, leaderships, scholarships, grants, awards, praise, scores, recognitions, accomplishments
Affiliations: Societies, associations, clubs, fraternities, sororities, leagues, memberships

PH.D. DISSERTATION
    Title, advisor, director
    Abstract summary (4-5 sentences) discussing content and methodology

HONORS, AWARDS, AND ACHIEVEMENTS
Appointments, nominations, leaderships, awards, praise, scores, recognitions, accomplishments, high scores, grades, G.P.A.s, fellowships, scholarships, grants, (including B.A./B.S.)

Figure 5-7: Brevity definitely isn't a feature of the academic CV (this continues on the next page).

TEACHING EXPERIENCE

Job Title, Top Qualifications Used   Employer, Location   **[dates]**

A Top Responsibility (Relevant to objective)
• Accomplishments made in this position targeting the employer's priorities/mission
• Several other achievements from this position, pertinent to objective
Another Skill (Appropriate to objective)
• Several achievements from this position, pertinent to objective

* *Repeat above pattern for each position.*

RESEARCH EXPERIENCE
Positions, locations, dates, descriptions of research in pertinence to target position

TEACHING INTERESTS
Discipline, certification

RESEARCH INTERESTS
Areas of inquiry

PUBLICATIONS
* List all those you are willing to show the search committee
* Include work in progress or pending
* Cite works as follows:

•**"Title of work,"** Name of publication/publisher (*Newsletter, Newspaper, Magazine, Journal, Book*), location of publisher (state & city or major city), date of publication, volume number (v.##), issue number (#.#), series number (#.#.#), page numbers (# - #) (type quotes around the title of your article).

PRESENTATIONS AND PUBLIC APPEARANCES
* Include conference papers and research reports
* List as follows:

•**"Title of presentation,"** location of presentation (City, State), [dates]; optional synopsis of content and/or purpose of presentation, audience, results, etc.

PROFESSIONAL AFFILIATIONS
A society, association, league, or club with which you associate, position held, [dates]
A society, association, league, or club with which you associate, position held, [dates]
A society, association, league, or club with which you associate, position held, [dates]

RECOMMENDATIONS
Names and contact information of 3-4 references willing to write recommendation letters

CREDENTIALS

Creating an academic curriculum vitae

Create a comprehensive summary of your professional employment and accomplishments: education, positions, affiliations, honors, memberships, credentials, dissertation title, fields in which comprehensive examinations were passed, full citations of publications and presentations, awards, discoveries, inventions, patents, seminar leadership, foreign languages, courses taught — whatever is valued in your field.

International Curriculum Vitae Format

The *international CV* is *not* the same document as an academic CV. Think of an international CV as a six- to eight-page excruciatingly detailed resume (Figure 5-8 gives you a template). Although it solicits private information that's outlawed in the United States, such as your health status, the international CV is favored in some nations as a kind of global ticket to employment.

The international CV is usually a reverse chronological format that includes your contact information, qualifications summary, professional background, education, and personal information. Some European countries prefer the chronological format, which lists education and work experience from the farthest back to the present.

Americans should remember that when working overseas for a native employer, they are not protected by Equal Employment Opportunity laws.

Strengths and weaknesses

International employment experts say that if you don't use this format, foreign recruiters may think you're hiding something. But keep in mind that the international CV format intrudes into private areas of your life.

Who should use this format and who should think twice

Use this format if you're seeking an overseas job and don't object to revealing information that may subject you to discriminatory hiring practices.

Individuals who feel strongly about invasions of privacy or fear or identity theft or who aren't willing to be rejected out of hand because of gender, religion, race, age, or marital status should avoid this format.

International Curriculum Vitae Format

YOUR NAME
Curriculum Vitae
Home Address, City, State, Country, Province, Zip Code
Include international codes:
Home and Cell Phones
E-mail
Objective (optional): Position as_____(title of position employer offers) using
your___ (#) years of experience in _____ (skills essential and specialized to the position).

SUMMARY OF QUALIFICATIONS

- A summary of your education, proficiencies, and career pertinent to target
- Number of years in area of objective, explaining similarities to it/its responsibilities
- Related education, training, and accreditation, reflecting employer's goals/priorities
- An achievement directly related to target, that the employer needs
- Traits reinforcing your candidacy for this position, specifically those asked for by the employer and those generally in demand in the field
- Other accomplishments, characteristics, knowledge either rare or prized in the field
- Traveling in field, countries visited, improvements made, distinctions, and so forth

SUMMARY OF SKILLS
- Topics of specialty or innovation within field • Areas of particular familiarity
- Software equipment • Processes • Terminology relevant to target • Languages

PROFESSIONAL BACKGROUND

EMPLOYMENT

Job Title   Employer, Location   **[dates]**
Present
A Top Responsibility (Relevant to objective)
- Accomplishments made in this position targeting the employer's priorities/mission
- Several other achievements from this position, pertinent to objective
Another Skill (Appropriate to objective)
- Several achievements from this position, pertinent to objective

   * *Repeat above pattern for all jobs.*

PROFESSIONAL HONORS
All honorary positions, awards, recognitions, or titles, with locations, [dates]

PUBLICATIONS
•**"Title of work,"** Name of publication/publisher (*Newsletter, Newspaper, Magazine, Journal*), location of publisher (country, languages, state & city or major city), date of publication, volume number (v.##), issue number (#.#), series number (#.#.#), page numbers (# - #)

   * *Repeat above citation for all publications.*

Figure 5-8: The international CV is an option when applying for jobs outside your home country. It's continued on the next page.

PRESENTATIONS AND PUBLIC APPEARANCES

•**"Title of presentation,"** location of presentation (Country, City, State, Province, Language), Date; optional synopsis of content and/or purpose of presentation, audience, results, etc.

* Repeat above citation for all presentations.

PROFESSIONAL AFFILIATIONS

All societies, associations, leagues, or clubs, positions held, locations, [dates]

EDUCATION

Degrees: Ph.D., institution, date of degree (or anticipated date), specialization
M.A./M.S., institution, date of degree, major, minor, concentration
B.A./B.S., institution, date of degree, major, minor
* Give equivalents of these degrees in other countries
Courses: Those taken, honors, seminars, number of units, G.P.A. (if a recent graduate)
Other Accreditations: Licenses, clearances
Academic Achievements: Appointments, nominations, leaderships, scholarships, grants, awards, praise, scores, recognitions, accomplishments
Affiliations: Societies, associations, clubs, fraternities, sororities, leagues, memberships

DOCTORAL DISSERTATION

Title, advisor, director
Abstract summary (4-5 sentences) discussing content and methodology

HONORS, AWARDS AND ACHIEVEMENTS

Appointments, nominations, leaderships, awards, praise, scores, recognitions, accomplishments, high scores, grades, G.P.A.s, fellowships, scholarships, grants, (including B.A./B.S/equivalents)

PERSONAL INFORMATION

• A sentence or so that describes personal attributes pertinent to employer's interests. Think positively, omit negatives, and highlight goal-oriented, functional characteristics that promise of a good worker-employer relationship and reliably good work product. Present specific work-related examples of these personality highlights and explain how they are significant to the employer. Without exaggerating, accentuate the positive, and include all favorable quotes from employers and co-workers, members of the clergy, and public service, volunteer organization, nonprofit organization and political officials
• Age, Marital Status (Single, Engaged, Married)
• Hobbies and leisure activities (travel, clubs, sports, athletics, collections, subscriptions)
• Volunteer service, public service

Of course, if you want an overseas job and you don't use this format, you may be out of luck unless you're working through an American recruiter. The recruiter can interpret your concerns and negotiate for a bare minimum of personal information. Nationals of countries other than the United States can also use this technique.

Creating an international curriculum vitae

Formality prevails with the international CV. England has a suggested CV form, which is more like the American resume than not.

- ✔ If you're applying in a non-English-speaking country, have your CV translated into the appropriate foreign language. Send both the English and the native-language version.

- ✔ Unless it's untrue, mention in the personal section that you have excellent health.

- ✔ Suggest by appropriate hobbies and personal interests that you'll easily adapt to an overseas environment.

- ✔ If you're submitting your international CV on paper, handwrite the cover letter that goes with it — Europeans use handwriting analysis as a screening device. If your handwriting is iffy, enclose a word-processed version as well.

In addition, make sure that your cover letter shows a sincere desire to be in the country of choice.

Other Resume Presentations

A few adventuresome job seekers are using newer resume formats, developing distribution technology and imaginative styles of communication. Take a quick look at possibilities that can't be classified as mainstream methods but may be just the vehicle you need to find the job you want.

Variations on a theme

Among mutations of the three basic formats (reverse chronological, functional, and hybrid) are the following.

Accomplishment format

A variation of the hybrid resume, the accomplishment format shows both qualifications and accomplishments. One sequencing frequently used by executives in mobile industries — such as advertising, communications, and publishing — data starts with name and contact information, followed by an objective. This is followed by bullet points under headings of qualifications, skills, and accomplishments. The resume concludes with professional experience and education.

The accomplishment format is a popular favorite of job seekers returning to payroll status after a period of self-employment.

Linear format

A linear format flows one line at a time. It relates achievements, winning moves, and star points in short, quick spurts and is designed to attract and tease the eyes of busy readers (which means most businesspeople). The linear hallmarks: very little detail, super attention to sizzle (hyped but provable achievements), not much depth, and lots and lots of white space. The linear format doesn't use an objective but opens with a skills summary. It showcases a robust career progression and in a skilled writer's hands can be very effective.

Keyword format

All formats should be heavily sprinkled with *keywords* — nouns identifying your qualifications that employers use to search resume databases (see Chapter 7).

Until the turn of the century, keyword resume formats were popular. This format placed a profile of keywords (really a skills summary) at the top of a document. The keywords were front-loaded because the resume-reading software of the time could absorb only a fixed amount of information, and resume writers wanted to get their keyword licks in before the software hit its limit. Today the software has much improved and can pick up keywords *anywhere* in a resume. (See Chapter 7 to find out about keywords.)

When you use industry abbreviations (for example, "ROI"), spell out the term at least once in your resume. Even though many systems are smarter than they used to be, a lot of older technology products out there won't "get it" unless you spell out "return on investment."

Resume letters

When you're doing a targeted mailing campaign, a resume letter attracts attention because it reads more like a story than a document. The resume letter is a combination of cover letter and resume; often it is two pages. It typically opens with a variation of the question: "Are you looking for a professional who can leap high buildings in a single bound?" A resume letter opening might look a little something like this:

> *Should you be in the market for an accomplished, congenial senior human resources specialist who has earned an excellent reputation for successful HR technology acquisition analysis and management, this letter will be of interest to you.*

The letter continues on to give a basic overview of a job seeker's strengths, including previous employers, achievements, skills and competencies, as they would apply to the recipient company.

 Even though you'll use postal mail to send a resume letter and have no way of knowing whether you fall under Internet Candidate rules (see Chapter 1), take care to discover the key qualifications most often required for the position you seek. Targeting is a no-lose strategy even for cold mailings.

Your strengths message may be in paragraph form or in bulleted statements. The resume letter format can be especially useful for a professional with an abundance of experience. But don't substitute a resume letter when you're responding to a job advertisement that asks for a resume. The employer calls the shots.

One of the most amazing placements I've ever heard about was the case of the chemist who at age 50 left the profession to take a fling dealing cards at a casino. Five years later, at age 55, he wanted to return to the chemistry workplace. A cold mailing of a well-written resume letter to owners of small chemical companies turned up a caretaker CEO job while the owner took an extended two-year trip out of the country.

Portfolios

Samples of your work, gathered in a portfolio, have long been valuable to fields such as design, graphics, photography, architecture, advertising, public relations, marketing, education, and contracting.

Often, you deliver your portfolio as part of the job interview. Some highly motivated job seekers include a brief version of a career portfolio when sending their resumes, although recruiters say that they want fewer, not more, resume parts to deal with. If you must include work samples to back up your claims, send only a few of your very best. The portfolio is a showcase for documenting a far more complete picture of what you offer employers than is possible with a resume of one or two pages. Getting recruiters to read it is the problem. When you determine that a portfolio is your best bet, take it to job interviews. Put your portfolio in a three-ring binder with a table of contents and tabs separating its various parts. Mix and match the following categories:

- **Career goals** (if you're a new graduate or career changer): A brief statement of less than one page is plenty.

- **Your resume:** Use a fully formatted version in MS Word.

- **Samples of your work:** Include easily understandable examples of problem solving and competencies.

- **Proof of performance:** Insert awards, honors, testimonials and letters of commendation, and flattering performance reviews. Don't forget to add praise from employers, people who reported to you, and customers.

- **Proof of recognition:** Here's where you attach certifications, transcripts, degrees, licenses, and printed material listing you as the leader of seminars and workshops. Omit those that you merely attended unless the attendance proves something.

- **Military connections:** The U.S. military provides exceptionally good training, and many employers know it. List military records, awards, and badges.

Make at least two copies of your portfolio in case potential employers decide to hold on to your samples or fail to return them.

Your portfolio should document only the skills that you want to apply on a job. Begin by identifying those skills, and then determine which materials prove your claims of competency.

Video resumes

A *video resume* (or *video podcast*) actually is a canned video interview in which a candidate speaks about her qualifications, goals, and strengths. Employers shy away from video resumes because they fear a candidate's image and sound could bring discrimination charges against them by old, minority, fat, or ugly candidates.

Web resumes

Web resumes (or *e-portfolio* or *HTML resumes*) are electronic documents that you post on a personal Web site. The format may simply display credentials, or it may go glamorous with links to sound and graphics of your work samples. Job seekers in cutting-edge technology fields, theater, marketing, and design are attracted to the presentation.

Multimedia resumes

Multimedia resumes are similar to Web resumes, but they're on a disk that can be sent by postal mail. An attention-getting novelty in the 1990s, they're rarely used today.

Choose What Works for You

The big closing question to ask yourself when you've settled on a format is:

Does this format maximize my qualifications for the job I want?

If the format you've chosen doesn't promote your top qualifications, take another look at the choices in this chapter to select a format that helps you paint a sparkling self-portrait.

Chapter 6

Content Makes the OnTarget Difference

· ·

In This Chapter

▶ Understanding the parts of your resume

▶ Dumping content that doesn't open interview doors

▶ Deciding whether to use an objective or summary

▶ Using good judgment on salary requests

▶ Shaping your content in application forms

· ·

A prospective employer makes a leap of faith investing money in you as a new and untried employee. Are you really a good match for the position and the company? A resume's content is the first step toward answering that question.

How important is content? In comparing a position's requirements to your qualifications (see Chapter 1), what your resume says is mission-critical.

The Parts of Your Resume

To make your contents easy to access, organize the facts into various categories. Here are the essential parts that make up a resume:

- ✔ Contact information
- ✔ Objective or summary statement
- ✔ Education and training
- ✔ Experience

- Skills
- Competencies
- Activities
- Organizations
- Honors and awards

You may also include:

- Licenses
- Work samples
- Testimonials

To increase the likelihood that your resume will position you for an interview, take the time to understand the purpose of the different resume parts, which I explain in the following sections.

No more than you want to carry around 30 pounds of extra weight do you want fat in your resume — family, early education, favorite things, and so forth. Trim it! The rule for including data on a resume is simple: *If the data doesn't support your objective to be invited for an interview, leave it out.*

Leading with Contact Information

Include on your resume the following information, in the following order:

- **Name:** No matter which format you choose, place your name first on your resume. If your name isn't first, a job computer may mistake Excellent Sales Representative for your name and file you away as Ms. Representative. You may want to display your name in slightly larger type than the rest of the contact information and in boldface.

- **Mailing address:** Some resume advisers say the need to give a street address is no longer valid. The theory is that stating city and state is adequate in view of today's concerns about personal privacy and identity theft. At first thought, the omission of a street address seems reasonable. Why not save the space for information that markets you?

  Not so fast. This book's technical reviewer, Jim Lemke, points out that if you apply to a company career site and are asked to upload or paste your resume in a window, the odds are 99 percent that you're being entered into an *applicant tracking system,* also called a candidate management system or applicant management system. By any name, an ATS is a software application designed to help a company recruit employees more efficiently. At minimum, an ATS usually includes features to post job openings online, screen resumes, acknowledge receipt of resumes, and generate interview requests by e-mail to potential hires.

ATS systems check your e-mail address and sometimes your physical address to look for duplicates. If you leave off your physical address, the system may not accept your resume, or if it does, you may not receive an acknowledgment if the company sends acknowledgment communications by postal mail.

Unless there's a reason to hide your physical location, which you could do with a mail box address, continue to give a street name with the unit number, city, state, and zip code.

If you're a college student or member of the military who'll be returning home, give both addresses, labeled *Current Address* and *Permanent Address.* You can add operational dates for each address, but don't forget to delete a date after it's passed. Otherwise, you look like a product whose shelf date has passed.

✔ **Valid telephone number:** Use a personal phone number, including the area code, where you can be reached or where the recruiter can leave a message.

Don't allow children to answer this line. Don't record a clever message — play it straight. If you must share a telephone with kids, emphasize the need for them to answer the phone professionally and to keep their calls short. In addition to — or instead of — a landline, give your mobile (cell) telephone number.

✔ **Other contact media:** Also give your e-mail address, and, if you have one, your Web page address.

What about using company resources? Should you ever use your employer's e-mail address or letterhead? Many employers see an employee's use of company resources to find another job as small-time theft.

In certain situations, however, you can use your company's help. For example, when a company is downsizing, it's expected to provide resource support for outplacement. Contract employment is another exception: When you're ending the project for which you were hired, your employer may encourage you to use company resources. Indicate permission to use them in your resume's cover letter: *The project for which I was hired is finishing ahead of schedule; my grateful employer is cooperating in my new search.*

Is it okay to list your work telephone number on your resume? In a decade when employers have been tossing workers out without remorse, it's a tough world and you need speedy communications. The practical answer is to list your work number if you have a direct line and voice mail or a mobile phone. To show that you're an ethical person, limit calls to a couple minutes — just long enough to arrange a meeting or an evening callback. Avoid the issue by carrying your personal mobile phone to work and calling back on breaks.

Hooking the Reader with a Summary or Objective

Your OnTarget resume needs a hook to grab attention. The hook immediately follows your name and contact information and is expressed as an *objective* or as a *summary*.

A summary is known by many names. Among the most popular are skills summary, highlights summary, asset statement, power summary, career highlights, career summary, career profile, career focus, summary of qualifications, and accomplishments profile.

The two types of hooks — objective and summary — differ in emphasis. The objective is self-centered, stating *what you want;* the summary is work-centered, stating *what you offer.* Sometimes the job objective and summary are combined. Here are examples of the various approaches:

> *Objective:* Assistant to Executive

> *Summary:* Over 14 years of progressively responsible office support experience, including superior computer skills, with an earned reputation for priority-setting and teamwork.

And here's how an unlabeled combined objective and summary might look:

> Assistant to Executive, to keep operations under firmer control, using computer skills, contemporary office procedures, and pleasant manner with people.

However you fashion it, the hook tells the recruiter what you want to do and/ or what you're qualified to do.

Debate rages among career pros over the topic of objective versus summary.

> ✔ Objective backers say that readers don't want to slog through a document, trying to guess the type of position you want and how you'd fit into the organization.

✔ Summary advocates argue that a thumbnail sketch of your skills and other competencies allows your qualifications to be evaluated for jobs you may not know about specifically, or offers an easy way to itemize your matching qualifications for a specific job's requirements. This factor is a serious consideration in a New Era of resume database searches.

Focus (Chapter 5) will speed your resume to the eyes of people who can hire you, whether you style it as a job objective or as a summary — or as an unlabeled combination of both.

Choosing an objective

Your objective states what you want to do and the direction in which you're heading. It gives immediate focus to your resume and is the hub around which all the other information in your document relates.

When to use an objective

The time is right to use an objective under these conditions:

✔ You know the position being offered; make that job title your job objective.

✔ You have a greatly diversified background that may perplex some employers.

✔ You're a new graduate, a career changer, a service member exiting the military, a member of the clergy switching to the secular job market, an educator seeking another career field, or a homemaker reentering the paid workforce. A job objective says what you're looking for.

Advantages of an objective

Most studies show that employers prefer objectives for quick identification purposes. They like to see the name of their job openings at the top of a resume. Because you cite those qualifying achievements that support your objective and forget random experiences, the finished product (when done well) shows that you and the desired job appear to be a well-matched pair.

If you're responding to an advertised job, remember to match the basic qualifications it requires in the body of your resume (Chapter 1) even if the job seeks a "window pane technician" and your objective says "window pane technician." An objective that echoes the job title in the job ad is merely a first step in showing that you're a great match.

Being objective about objectives

The debate over job objective or a variant of a skills summary continues unabated. I overheard these snatches of recruiters' opinions at a recruiting forum.

✔ "By including their desired job title in the online objective statement, job seekers increase the chances that their resume will match an employer's search string."

✔ "I prefer to see 'Career Summary' in place of 'Objective'. If the objective doesn't match an employer's idea of the job, the resume will probably be discarded. By putting a one-paragraph 'commercial' as the very first thing the employer sees, you know that an overview of your qualifications is read."

✔ "As an in-house [corporate] recruiter, any resume I receive without an objective tells me the applicant is either a desperate jack-of-all trades who will take any job offered, or has not thought about his career enough to know what he wants. Both are huge red flags. I think an objective is essential."

✔ "We advise candidates to leave off the objective or we may remove it before sending to a client. Use the objective space to include more information on accomplishments and experience."

Disadvantages of an objective

Ideally, you will write a customized resume for each position (or career field) for which you apply. You may even write a customized resume for each position for which you apply at the *same* company. The downside to a narrow job objective is that you may not be considered by the same employer for other open positions that you didn't know about. But if the objective is too broadly focused, your objective statement becomes meaningless.

Opting for a summary

If you choose to begin your resume with a summary, you can still target it to specific positions with the mix of strengths, skills, accomplishments, and other background elements that you include.

When to use a summary

The time is right to use a summary under these conditions:

✔ You're a person with widely applicable skills. Recruiters especially like a skills summary atop a reverse chronological resume because it lets them creatively consider you for jobs that you may not know exist.

✔ You're in a career field with pathways to multiple occupations or industries (an administrative assistant, for example).

✔ You know that your resume is headed to an e-database. Because you want to be considered for multiple related positions — which may have the same or similar requirements — you try to design your summary broadly enough to accomplish this goal without sounding as though you're a jack-of-all-trades.

Soar with a summary

Accomplishments are the patron saints of OnTarget resumes. Part III contains sample resumes that illustrate a variety of effective *summaries.* But here's a quick peek at a top-rated summary by Jan Melnik in *Executive's Pocket Guide to ROI Resumes and Job Search* by Louise Kursmrak and Jan Melnik (JIST Publishing).

Senior Marketing Executive

Providing Consistent Market Leadership to Leverage Exceptional Marketing & Sales Results

Outstanding record of highly focused, strategic marketing and sales leadership. Exceptional executive-leadership skills with talent for establishing and communicating vision, developing strategy, executing tactical plans, and motivating and empowering teams and individuals to achieve remarkable, sustainable results.

- Achieved rapid speed-to-market in successful product launches through hands-on leadership of brand and product development, strategic planning, packaging, marketing, and innovative distribution channels.
- Reputation for consistently creating value and delivering strong sales results.
- Precision focus on identifying and capitalizing on new business opportunities to generate profitable and sustainable growth.

Demonstrated Strengths...

• Profit & Performance Improvement	• Team Leadership/Motivation	• Strategic Planning
• Sales & Marketing Strategy/Execution	• Collaboration/Teamwork	• Results Orientation
• New Business Development	• Customer/Channel Expertise	• Brand Repositioning

---

A summary typically contains the three to five skills and competencies — sometimes more — that best support your job aspiration. The data in your statement need not be proven with examples in this brief section; for now it stands alone as assertions. In effect, you're saying, "Here's who I am. Here's what I can do for you." The summary is a tease, encouraging the reader to hang in there for proof of what the opening claims.

An exciting summary can revive a fading job achievement. Suppose you have an achievement that took place four or five years ago and is now needed to qualify you for a job. In a focused summary, the golden oldie achievement still sells for you as though it happened yesterday.

> # What's first — education or experience?
>
> The general rule in resume writing is to lead with your most qualifying factor.
>
> With certain exceptions (such as law, where your choice of alma mater can dog you throughout life), lead off with experience when you've been in the workforce for at least one year. When you're loaded with experience but low on credentials, list your school days at the end — and perhaps even omit them entirely if you didn't graduate.

Advantages of a summary

Recruiters believe that what you're prepared to do next should be pretty evident from what you've already done. Another argument is premised on psychology: Employers aren't known for being overly concerned with what you want *from* them until they're sure of what you can do *for* them.

Summaries offer an easy way to identify the qualifications you have that match a particular job's requirements. Or identify qualifications that position you for related positions unknown to you in a given career field.

Disadvantages of a summary

A summary doesn't explicitly say what you want and why the employer would want you. The summary resume can backfire if it claims everything from soup to nuts yet misses the targets identified by employers for specific positions.

Making Education, Experience, Skills, and Competencies Work for You

When you begin drafting your core resume (see Chapter 1), carefully consider the following four categories of essential information.

Education

List your highest degree first — type of degree, major, college name, and date awarded.

✔ New graduates give far more detail on course work than do graduates who've held at least one post-graduation job for one year or more.

✔ Omit high school or prep school if you have a college degree.

✔ If you have a vocational-technical school certificate or diploma that required less than a year to obtain, list your high school as well.

✔ Note continuing education, including seminars related to your work.

✔ If you fall short of the mark on the job's educational requirements, try to compensate by expanding the continuing education section. Give the list a name, such as *Professional Development Highlights,* and list every impressive course, seminar, workshop, and conference that you've attended.

Experience

Describe — with quantified achievements — your present and previous positions in reverse chronological order. Include specific job titles, company names and locations, and dates of employment. Show progression and promotions within an organization, especially if you've been with one employer for eons.

Consider using more than one *Experience* heading. Try headings such as *Accounting and Finance-Related Experience, General Business Experience,* and *Healthcare and Administration Experience.* Doing so is yet another way of reinforcing your qualifications for the job you seek.

Skills

Skills today are the heart and soul of job finding and, as such, encompass a variety of experiences. These are skills:

> Collaborating, editing, fundraising, interviewing, managing, blogging (Internet), researching, systematizing, teaching

And these are skills:

> Administering social programs, analyzing insurance facts, advising homeless people, allocating forestry resources, desktop publishing, coordinating association events, designing home furnishing ads, marine expedition problem-solving, writing police reports, updating Web sites

Top accomplishments

The accomplishments that most interest employers include:

- ✔ Increased revenues
- ✔ Saved money
- ✔ Increased efficiency
- ✔ Cut overhead
- ✔ Increased sales
- ✔ Improved workplace safety

- ✔ Purchasing accomplishments
- ✔ New products/new lines
- ✔ Improved record-keeping process
- ✔ Increased productivity
- ✔ Successful advertising campaign
- ✔ Effective budgeting

And these are also skills:

> Dependable, sense of humor, commitment, leadership, persistence, crisis-resilient, adaptable, quick, results-driven

And these are still more skills:

> Brochures, Java, five years, 100% quota, telemarketing, senior management, spreadsheet, MBA, major accounting firm. Skills used to be thought of in the classic meaning of general and industry-specific abilities. Recruiting industry professionals expand the term to include personal characteristics as well as past employers, special knowledge, achievements, and products.

A *skill,* in job-search terms, is any identifiable ability or fact that employers value and will pay for. That means that "five years" is a skill, just as "word processing" is a skill; employers pay for experience.

Where do skills belong on your resume? Everywhere. Season every statement with skills. Skills are indispensable. Whether you use an e-resume or a traditional paper resume, you must name your skills or be left behind.

What's the easiest way to name your skills? You can ask at a library for books with comprehensive skills information suitable for adults, such as *Career Success: A Step-By-Step Workbook for Students, Job Seekers and Lifelong Learners,* by Urban Whitaker (O'Brien and Whitaker Publishers). Additionally, you can use Google (www.google.com) to find free online presentations of skills. Search on terms such as *transferable skills checklist, job skills list,* and *uncovering your skills.*

Skills are one part of the concept of *competencies,* which I discuss next.

Competencies

Controversy swirls around the concept of competency-based hiring models used in employee selection.

A *competency-based approach* is a method that focuses on the skills and talents needed to be able to perform a particular task to a certain standard. The method uses a series of assessment tools (tests) that identify not only the *technical skills* a candidate possesses, but the candidate's *behavioral* competencies as well. Competency-based models can be broken down into two categories:

- ✔ **Work-based competencies.** These include the job-specific characteristics, skills, and abilities, such as fluency in the Spanish language or the ability to work with Microsoft Word.
- ✔ **Behavior-based competencies.** These are personal characteristics, such as interpersonal skills, attitudes, and motivation.

Although competency-based hiring models became popular in the United States a decade ago, they are in use chiefly by larger, sophisticated employers. Not everyone is on board with the same concept. In fact, competencies are known by a variety of terms, such as *key characteristics that it takes to be successful, success factors, attributes,* and so on.

Viewpoints also differ about whether the competency-based hiring model has crashed and burned and is headed behind yesterday's hill along with no-longer-popular concepts, such as quality circles. One noted employment researcher says, "Almost every major competency project we have witnessed has ended in failure, usually right around the three-year mark at a cost of millions of dollars."

Other employment experts say that's crazy Mark Twain talk — the author famously said, "The reports of my death have been greatly exaggerated." Competency advocates insist that key characteristics live and thrive. As one recruiting leader said: "Look at evidence all around us. Read a few job listings on major job boards and you'll see that most companies still reference specific behavioral competencies as being important to job success and to the selection of high-performing candidates."

Competencies vs. keywords

Don't confuse competencies with typical keywords employers use to search through databases for suitable candidates. Developing competencies for your target position and field (Chapter 1) makes sense because it concentrates your mind on the position you seek.

Competencies statements don't make good keywords, and the company won't uncover your resume based on your behavioral competencies. So why do it? Accomplishment and skill keywords initially snag the interviewer's attention, but when he or she keeps reading and sees that you've also included competencies statements, the interviewer will note that there's no moss hanging from your hair and that you understand the competency model. This sophistication will be a plus for interviewing purposes.

My take: If you're aiming for a job with a large employer, bone up on competency policy at each company. You can call the company's human resource department and ask, "Do you use a competencies model in recruiting?" If so, ask whether you can obtain a lexicon of the company's *core competencies* and the *role competencies* for the target position. Sometimes, the HR specialist will reveal the competencies and sometimes not. But you're missing a bet if you don't ask.

If the company uses the competencies model, note your measurable accomplishments, and then add your personal behavioral competencies that made them possible.

A few examples of core competencies

A competency is a set of characteristics that produces superior performance. It includes knowledge, the things we know. It includes skills, the things we can do. It includes attitudes, how we do things. Each of us has multiple competencies; each job requires multiple competencies.

Competencies do not come in a handy-dandy, one-size-fits-all package. They vary from industry to industry, and from company to company.

The following very simple illustration of four competencies illustrates those a company might use for a technical sales representative.

Product knowledge	*Planning & organization*
Displays knowledge of products	Prioritizes and plans work activities
Explains product features and benefits	Uses time efficiently
Understands financial terminology	Plans for additional resources
Researches competitors' products	Integrates changes smoothly
	Sets goals and objectives
	Works in an organized manner
Technology usage	*Sales skills*
Demonstrates required skills	Achieves sales goals
Adapts to new technologies	Overcomes objections
Troubleshoots technological problems	Initiates new contacts
Uses technology to increase productivity	Maintains customer satisfaction
Keeps technical skills up to date	Maintains and promptly submits records

Competencies in the animal kingdom

Animals have core competencies, too. Consider the story of the cat that thought it was a squirrel and applied for employment on the food production line at a huge acorn silo. The silo management thought that, based on its ability to leap from tree to tree, the cat would do an equally good job as the squirrels on its workforce.

Unfortunately, that assumption didn't prove true. Management hadn't factored into the hiring decision the knowledge and behavioral components of the cat's competency package.

At first, the cat dazzled management with its spectacular leaps, branch-to-branch, tree-to-tree. But the cat's productivity rating soon began to plummet. The cat that thought it was a squirrel brought home only a few acorns a week and was just exhausted at the end of each day. Puzzled, management investigated, watching the cat for a full week.

What management discovered was that you could put into a thimble the cat's knowledge of acorn gathering. The cat spent most of its day swiping at nimble-winged birds that kept flying away from the cat's enthusiastic pounces. Outmaneuvered, weary, and desperate, the cat did its best to gather the paltry few acorns it could find in the few minutes before quitting time. Clearly, the cat lacked natural ability to gather acorns, and its behavior rankled bird lovers throughout management.

Too bad, management said, issuing the cat a pink slip. The cat just doesn't have the native "nut-gathering tree smarts" that squirrels use by instinct to do a bang-up job of squirreling away a winter's feast. And as for behavior, management explained that it wanted a high producer, not an avian predator.

Coworker squirrels, watching from the sidelines, wondered whether the feline's competency failure in acorning while leaping may have inspired the familiar phrase, "What a cat don't know, a cat don't know."

TIP Where can you find lists of more competencies? In addition to company Web sites and books (*Competency-Based Resumes* (2005) and *Competency-Based Interviews* (2006), both by Robin Keesler and Linda Strasburg; Career Press), look at competitors' job ads and professional association Web sites.

Including competencies in your resumes

 REMEMBER Most good resumes focus on knowledge, skills, and accomplishments. They only hint at competencies required to do the work. To capture behavioral competencies on a resume, you must show how your accomplishments confirm your competencies. Or to turn it around, you must show how your competencies made it possible for you to rack up home runs.

To connect your behaviors with your accomplishments, you might say:

> **Product development:** *Created new midmarket segment supporting an annual growth rate of 20% in a flat industry, demonstrating high energy and business acumen.*

In the above example, the verb "demonstrating" connects the accomplishment (Created new mid-market segment supporting an annual growth rate of 20% in a flat industry) with competencies (high energy and business acumen). Other verbs you can use to bridge the two types of information include:

- Confirming
- Displaying
- Exhibiting
- Illustrating
- Manifesting
- Proving
- Revealing
- Verifying

Gaining Extra Points

You covered the meat and potatoes of your resume content. What can you add that will strengthen your image? You could, for instance, draw from your activities to show that you've got the right stuff. John Gill of Carlsbad, California, paid his own expenses to spend his college spring break building houses for the poor in Mexico. That act of sacrifice shows Gill's character, that he goes out of his way to do important things for others. That's good resume content.

What's in your diary and how will it strengthen your image? Here are a few thoughts on the nitty-gritty of buffing your image.

Activities

Activities can be anything from hobbies and sports to campus extracurricular participation. The trick is to analyze how each activity is relevant to the target job; discuss skills, knowledge, or other competencies developed; and list all achievements. Make sure that this section doesn't become meaningless filler.

In addition, avoid potentially controversial activities: Stating that you're a moose hunter won't endear you to animal-loving recruiters. If you've been able to research the reader and have found that you two have a common interest, list it on your resume so that it can become an icebreaker topic during an interview.

Organizations

Give yourself even more credentials with professional and civic affiliations. Mention all important offices held. Relate these affiliations to your reader in terms of marketable skills, knowledge, and achievements. A high profile in the community is particularly important for sales jobs.

Just as you should be careful about which activities you identify, so too should you be sensitive to booby traps in organization memberships:

- ✔ Listing too many organizations may make the reader wonder when you'd have time to do the job.

- ✔ Noting that you belong to one minority group organization may work in your favor, but reporting your membership in five minority group organizations may raise red flags. The recruiter may worry that you're a trouble-making activist.

- ✔ And, of course, you know better than to list your membership in religious or political organizations (unless you're applying for a job that requires such membership). They don't apply to your ability to do the job, and some readers may use them to keep you out of the running.

Honors and awards

List most of the achievements for which you were recognized. If the achievement had zero to do with work or doesn't show you in a professional light, don't take up white space with it; for example, you probably wouldn't list a Chili Cook-Off award unless you're applying for a job as a chef.

Licenses and samples of your work

If you're in the legal, certified accounting, engineering, or medical profession, add to your resume the appropriate license, certifications, and other identifications required for the position. For a professional resume or CV, you may also list descriptions or titles of specific work that you've done or include samples of your work along with your resume. If asked to include samples of your work, be selective about what you send.

Testimonials

After citing an achievement, you can follow up with a short, flattering quote from your boss or a client:

- For an information systems technician: Bob Boss told the entire office that "I am thrilled that Charlie Pitman cut Internet access and telephone costs by 80% [date]."

- For a sales rep at a copy shop. "Jennifer Robertson's resourcefulness in getting inside the SoapSuds account and expanding it by 15% after others had tried for months is truly impressive," said Barbara Boss, my direct supervisor in [date].

Testimonials work, or advertisers wouldn't spend billions of dollars to use them. Be sure to check with your source before adding a quote to your resume.

Shaping Your Content on Application Forms

Application forms (paper or online) aren't resume content, but they're kissing cousins. Filling out these forms requires a shift in what you say because you have to sign them, *making the application form a legal document.* Lies can come back to bite you. Stick to the facts as you follow these rules:

- If you can, take the application home where you won't be rushed and can spend adequate time polishing your application to get it just right. Photocopy the application form before you begin in case you find errors on the original (or spill coffee on it) and need a clean copy.

- Verify all dates of employment and salaries to the letter.

- Enter the full name and last known address of former employers. If former employers are no longer available, don't substitute coworkers.

- If asked for salary history, give your base salary (or add commission and bonuses), omitting benefits.

- Give a complete employment history in months and years, including trivial three-week jobs that you wisely left off the resume. If you don't tell the whole story, you leave a loophole of withholding information that later can be used against you if the employer decides that you're excess.

- Unless you have a condition directly affecting your ability to do the job for which you're applying, you need not elaborate on any disability.

- ✔ Divulge any criminal record unless your records are sealed; consult a lawyer about the possibility of expungement before job hunting.

- ✔ Be honest about having collected unemployment benefits (but remember that repeaters are frowned on); if you're caught lying about it later, practice your farewell speech.

- ✔ Autograph the application; you've been honest — why worry?

Content to Omit: Your Salary Story

Never mention salary on your resume. Period.

Sometimes a job ad asks for your salary history or salary requirements. Realize that revealing dollar figures in advance puts you at a disadvantage. This is especially true if you've been working for low pay — or if you've been paid above market.

In addition to job ads, profile forms on job Web sites and online personal agent programs almost always ask for your salary information. If you decide to participate, state your expectations in a range ($xxx to $xxx), and include the value of all perks (benefits, bonuses), not just salary, in your salary history.

When you choose to disclose your salary history or requirements online, make a distinction between general information forms and formal signed applications (legal documents). Include benefits (total compensation) on general information forms, but omit benefits on formal signed applications that ask for "salary history."

Make sure you do these two things before you provide salary information:

- ✔ Research the market rate for someone with your skills and experience. Start with the Web sites Salary.com (www.salary.com), Salary Expert (www.salaryexpert.com), and PayScale (www.payscale.com).

- ✔ Find out why the smart money advises against being too quick to pipe up with hard figures on the money you've made and the money you want. What can you expect in return for revealing salary information, job unseen? You get a chance to name your price and hope you find takers, many of whom will want to talk your price down. Get advice by reading articles by Jack Chapman on JobStar (www.jobstar.org). Absorb all you can — salary negotiation is as complex as buying a house.

Putting your content in online resume builders

How much do the free online resume builders offered at virtually all substantial job boards and some company Web sites help you "sell to it rather than tell it?"

Many automated resume builders benefit the recruiting side of the employment industry, not the job-seeking side. Their builder software, aiming for efficiency, tries to standardize data — to compare apples to apples. Such builder software limits you to a synopsis of bare bones information. That is, they offer space for the essentials — your contact information, last three jobs, and education, for example. But they may not provide space for humanizing experiences, such as volunteerism, honors, and awards.

If you use specific resume builder software program to construct your online resume, notice whether it (a) favors the recruiter, or (b) surprise!, favors the job seeker.

If you want to use an online resume builder with a job board or a company Web site, remember to think for yourself and not assume the technology will bring to light your most marketable qualities, which this book shows you how to emphasize.

Exception to my salary silence advice: Tell recruiters with whom you have a serious interest in working how much you've earned and how much it will cost an employer to hire you. Otherwise, know that recruiters don't want to waste time playing games and are likely to fold up their interest and wave goodbye.

Accomplishments Are Your Content Aces

Chapter 5 speaks of selling, not telling, your worth. Citing your earned accomplishments and achievements are how you make that happen. To capture the best job, you know that you can't simply add the latest job description and recalculate the same old resume with updated data.

Focus on your best content and present it forcefully. Because you have very few words to work with, choose precisely the correct words; Chapter 7 takes you to the word desk. Don't rush the construction of your resume: If you build it right, the interviews will come.

Chapter 7

Wow Words Work Wonders

In This Chapter

▶ Wow words: Action verbs that sell you

▶ Keywords: Nouns that sell you

▶ Resume grammar: Simple rules that sell you

▶ Resume spelling: Simple tips that sell you

*W*ords: How powerful they are. It doesn't take many of them to change the world: The Lord's Prayer has 66 words, Lincoln's Gettysburg address numbers just 286 words, and the U.S. Declaration of Independence contains but 1,322 words.

Winston Churchill needed only two words to bind Russia to the *Iron Curtain*. A brief four words memorialized Martin Luther King's vision: *I have a dream*. And in a single sentence, John F. Kennedy set the challenge for a generation: *Ask not what your country can do for you, but what you can do for your country.*

Words are powerful — big words like *motherland* and *environmentalism* and small words like *peace* and *war* or *dawn, family, hope, love,* and *home.*

Words are pegs to hang your qualifications on. Words are the power that lifts you above the faceless crowd and sets you in Good Fortune's way. The right words can change your life.

Begin your hunt for the right words to build an OnTarget resume, from action verbs and keyword nouns, to grammar and spelling tips.

Wow words are action verbs describing your strengths: *improve, upgrade, schedule.* Keywords are usually nouns demonstrating essential skills: *technology transfers, PhD organic chemistry, multinational marketing.* A smattering of both can make your resume stand up and sing. An absence of either can make your resume sit down and shut up.

Wow Words Can Bring Good News

Use power-play verbs to communicate your abilities and accomplishments. A punch-zip delivery keeps these achievement-oriented verbs campaigning for you. The important thing is to choose words of substance and power that zero in on your abilities and achievements.

Try not to use the same word twice on your resume — the thesaurus in a word-processing program can give you more possibilities.

Take a look at the Wow words that follow and check off those words that work for you:

Wow words for administration and management

advised	initiated	prioritized
approved	inspired	processed
authorized	installed	promoted
chaired	instituted	recommended
consolidated	instructed	redirected
counseled	integrated	referred
delegated	launched	reorganized
determined	lectured	represented
developed	listened	responded
diagnosed	managed	reviewed
directed	mediated	revitalized
disseminated	mentored	routed
enforced	moderated	sponsored
ensured	monitored	streamlined
examined	motivated	strengthened
explained	negotiated	supervised
governed	originated	taught
guided	oversaw	trained
headed	pioneered	trimmed
influenced	presided	validated

Wow words for communications and creativity

acted	edited	proofread
addressed	enabled	publicized
arranged	facilitated	published
assessed	fashioned	realized
authored	formulated	reconciled
briefed	influenced	recruited
built	initiated	rectified
clarified	interpreted	remodeled
composed	interviewed	reported
conducted	introduced	revitalized
constructed	invented	scheduled
corresponded	launched	screened
costumed	lectured	shaped
created	modernized	stimulated
critiqued	performed	summarized
demonstrated	planned	taught
designed	presented	trained
developed	produced	translated
directed	projected	wrote

Wow words for sales and persuasion

arbitrated	judged	purchased
catalogued	launched	realized
centralized	lectured	recruited
consulted	led	reduced
dissuaded	liaised	reported
documented	maintained	repositioned
educated	manipulated	researched
established	marketed	resolved

expedited	mediated	restored
familiarized	moderated	reviewed
identified	negotiated	routed
implemented	obtained	saved
improved	ordered	served
increased	performed	set goals
influenced	planned	sold
inspired	processed	solved
installed	produced	stimulated
integrated	promoted	summarized
interpreted	proposed	surveyed
investigated	publicized	translated

Wow words for technical ability

analyzed	expedited	operated
broadened	fabricated	packaged
charted	facilitated	pioneered
classified	forecast	prepared
communicated	formed	processed
compiled	generated	programmed
computed	improved	published
conceived	increased	reconstructed
conducted	inspected	networked
coordinated	installed	reduced
designed	instituted	researched
detected	integrated	restored
developed	interfaced	revamped
devised	launched	streamlined

drafted	lectured	supplemented
edited	maintained	surveyed
educated	marketed	systematized
eliminated	mastered	trained
excelled	modified	upgraded
expanded	molded	wrote

Wow words for office support

adhered	distributed	managed
administered	documented	operated
allocated	drafted	ordered
applied	enacted	organized
appropriated	enlarged	packaged
assisted	evaluated	planned
assured	examined	prepared
attained	executed	prescribed
awarded	followed up	processed
balanced	formalized	provided
budgeted	formulated	recorded
built	hired	repaired
charted	identified	reshaped
completed	implemented	resolved
contributed	improved	scheduled
coordinated	installed	screened
cut	instituted	searched
defined	justified	secured
determined	liaised	solved
dispensed	maintained	started

Wow words for teaching

acquainted	designed	influenced
adapted	developed	informed
advised	directed	initiated
answered	dispensed	innovated
apprised	distributed	installed
augmented	educated	instituted
briefed	effected	instructed
built	empowered	integrated
certified	enabled	lectured
chaired	enacted	listened
charted	enlarged	originated
clarified	expanded	persuaded
coached	facilitated	presented
collaborated	fomented	responded
communicated	formulated	revolutionized
conducted	generated	set goals
coordinated	grouped	stimulated
delegated	guided	summarized
delivered	harmonized	trained
demonstrated	implemented	translated

Wow words for research and analysis

administered	detected	interviewed
amplified	determined	invented
analyzed	discovered	investigated
applied	documented	located
articulated	drafted	measured

assessed	edited	obtained
audited	evaluated	organized
augmented	examined	pinpointed
balanced	exhibited	planned
calculated	experimented	prepared
charted	explored	processed
collected	extracted	proofread
compared	focused	researched
compiled	forecast	reviewed
composed	found	riveted
concentrated	generated	screened
conducted	grouped	summarized
constructed	identified	surveyed
consulted	integrated	systematized
critiqued	interpreted	unearthed

Wow words for helping and caregiving

advanced	encouraged	reassured
advised	expedited	reclaimed
aided	facilitated	rectified
arbitrated	familiarized	redeemed
assisted	fostered	reeducated
attended	furthered	referred
augmented	guided	reformed
backed	helped	rehabilitated
balanced	instilled	repaired
boosted	liaised	represented
braced	mentored	served
clarified	ministered	settled

collaborated	negotiated	supplied
comforted	nourished	supported
consoled	nursed	stabilized
consulted	nurtured	streamlined
contributed	obliged	translated
counseled	optimized	treated
demonstrated	promoted	tutored
diagnosed	provided	unified

Wow words for financial management

adjusted	economized	reported
administered	eliminated	researched
allocated	exceeded	reshaped
analyzed	financed	retailed
appraised	forecast	returned
audited	funded	saved
balanced	gained	shopped
bought	generated	secured
budgeted	increased	sold
calculated	invested	solicited
computed	maintained	sourced
conciliated	managed	specified
cut	marketed	supplemented
decreased	merchandised	systematized
developed	planned	tested
disbursed	projected	tripled
dispensed	purchased	underwrote
distributed	quadrupled	upgraded
doubled	reconciled	upsized
downsized	reduced	vended

Wow words for many skills

accomplished	evaluated	overhauled
achieved	executed	performed
adapted	facilitated	prioritized
adhered	forecast	promoted
allocated	founded	proposed
appraised	governed	reconciled
arbitrated	guided	rectified
arranged	illustrated	remodeled
articulated	improved	repaired
assured	increased	reshaped
augmented	initiated	retrieved
collected	integrated	solved
communicated	interpreted	stimulated
composed	invented	streamlined
conceptualized	launched	strengthened
conserved	led	trained
contributed	navigated	upgraded
coordinated	optimized	validated
demonstrated	organized	won
dispensed	originated	wrote

The last word on Wow words: Little words never devalue a big idea.

Keywords Are Key to Finding You

Recruiters and employers use keywords to search and retrieve e-resumes in databases for available positions. "Keywords are what employers search for when trying to fill a position: the essential hard skills and knowledge needed to do the job," explains this book's technical reviewer, James M. Lemke. Keywords are chiefly nouns and short phrases. That's your take-home message. But once in a while, keywords can be adjectives and action verbs. Employers choose their own list of keywords — that's why no list is universal.

In computerized job searches, keywords describe not only your knowledge base and skills but also such things as well-known companies, big-name colleges and universities, degrees, licensure, and professional affiliations.

Keywords identify your experience and education in these categories:

- Skills
- Technical and professional areas of expertise
- Achievements
- Professional licenses and certifications
- Other distinguishing features of your work history
- Prestigious schools or former employers

Employers identify keywords, often including industry jargon, that they think represent essential qualifications necessary for high performance in a given position. They specify those keywords when they search a resume database.

Rather than stopping with action verbs, connect your achievements. You managed *what?* You organized *what?* You developed *what?* Job computers look for the *whats,* and the whats are usually nouns.

The new emphasis on defining Internet applicants (see Chapter 1) which requires that job seekers offer each job qualification listed for a specific position, makes it more important than ever to use the qualifying keywords. Otherwise, you'll be overlooked for that particular job.

Keywords are arbitrary and specific to the employer and each employer search. So the keywords (qualifications) in each job ad are the place to start as you customize your resume for the position. But you need to make educated guesses when you're responding not to advertised jobs but merely warehousing your resume online. The following lists provide a few examples of keywords for selected career fields and industries.

Keywords for administration/management

administrative processes	facilities management
bachelor's degree	front office operations
back office operations	office manager
benchmarking	operations manager
budget administration	policy and procedure

change management

crisis communications

data analysis

document management

production schedule

project planning

records management

regulatory reporting

Keywords for banking

branch manager

branch operations

commercial banking

construction loans

credit guidelines

debt financing

FILO (First In, Last Out)

financial management

investment management

investor relations

loan management

loan recovery

portfolio management

retail lending

ROE (Return On Equity)

ROI (Return On Investment)

trust services

turnaround management

Uniform Commercial Code Filing

workout

Keywords for customer service

account representative

call center

customer communications

customer focus groups

customer loyalty

customer needs assessment

customer retention

customer retention innovations

customer service manager

customer surveys

field service operation

Help desk

key account manager

order fulfillment

order processing

product response clerk

records management

sales administration

sales support administrator

service quality

telemarketing operations

telemarketing representative

Keywords for information technology

automated voice response (AVR)

chief information officer

client/server architecture

cross-functional team

data center manager

director of end user computing

disaster recovery

end user support

global systems support

help desk

multimedia technology

network development analyst

project lifecycle

systems configuration

technology rightsizing

vendor partnerships

Keywords for manufacturing

asset management

assistant operations manager

automated manufacturing

capacity planning

cell manufacturing

cost reductions

distribution management

environmental health and safety

inventory control

just-in-time (JIT)

logistics manager

manufacturing engineer

materials coordinator

on-time delivery

outsourcing

shipping and receiving operation

spares and repairs management

union negotiations

warehousing operations

workflow optimization

Keywords for human resources

Bachelor of Science, Business Administration (BSBA)

college recruitment

compensation surveys

cross-cultural communications

diversity training

organizational development (OD)

recruiter

regulatory affairs

sourcing

staffing

grievance proceedings	succession planning
job task analysis	team leadership
labor contract negotiations	training specialist
leadership development	wage and salary administration

Keywords are the magnets that draw nonhuman eyes to your talents.

Where to Find Keywords

How can you find keywords for your occupation or career field? Use a highlighter to pluck keywords from these resources.

- ✓ **Online and printed help-wanted ads:** Highlight the job skills, competencies, experience, education, and other nouns that employers ask for.

- ✓ **Job descriptions:** Ask employers for them, check at libraries for books or software with job descriptions, or search online. To find them online, just enter such terms as "job descriptions" or "job descriptions trainer" or "job descriptions electrical engineer" on a search engine, such as Google (www.google.com).

- ✓ The *Occupational Outlook Handbook* and *Dictionary of Occupational Titles* (both published by the U.S. Department of Labor): Both books are at schools and libraries; the Handbook is online at www.bls.gov/oco.

- ✓ **Your core resume:** Look through to highlight nouns that identify job skills, competencies, experience, and education.

- ✓ **Trade magazine news stories:** Text about your career field or occupation should be ripe with keywords.

- ✓ Online or printed **annual reports of companies in your field:** The company descriptions of key personnel and departmental achievements should offer strong keyword clues.

- ✓ **Programs for industry conferences and events:** Speaker topics address current industry issues, a rich source of keywords.

- ✓ **Internet search engine:** Plug in a targeted company's name and search the site that comes up. Look closely at the careers portal and read current press releases.

  You can also use Internet search engines to scout out industry-specific directories, glossaries, and dictionaries.

Mining for keywords in job descriptions

The excerpts below of two job descriptions posted on Business.com (www.business.com; search on job descriptions) illustrate how you can find keywords almost everywhere. In these examples, the keywords are italicized.

Auto Dismantler:

✔ Knowledge of proper operation of *lifts, fork-lifts, torches, power wrenches,* etc.

✔ Knowledge of *warehouse, core,* and *stack locations.*

✔ Skill to move *vehicles* without damaging vehicle, other vehicles or personnel.

✔ Skill to remove *body* and *mechanical parts* without damage to part, self, or others.

✔ Ability to read a *Dismantler report* and assess *stock levels.*

✔ Ability to accurately assess condition of *parts* to be inventoried.

Budget Assistant:

✔ Reviews *monthly expense statements,* monitors *monthly expenditures,* and gathers supporting *documentation* for supervisor review and approval.

✔ Performs basic *arithmetic operations* to calculate and/or verify *expense totals* and *account balances.*

✔ Operates *computer* to enter data into *spreadsheet* and/or *database.* Types routine *correspondence* and *reports.*

✔ Operates office equipment such as *photocopier, fax machine,* and *calculator.*

Get a Grip on Grammar

Resume language differs from normal speech in several ways. In general, keep the language tight and the tone professional, avoiding the following:

✔ **First-person pronouns (I, we):** Your name is at the top of each resume page, so the recruiter knows it's about *you.* Eliminate first-person pronouns. Also, don't use third-person pronouns (he, she) when referring to yourself — the narrative technique makes you seem pompous. Simply start with a verb.

✔ **Articles (the, a, an):** Articles crowd sentences and don't clarify meaning. Substitute *retrained staff* for *retrained the staff.*

✔ **Helping verbs (have, had, may, might):** Helping verbs weaken claims and credibility — implying that your time has passed and portraying you as a job-hunting weakling. Say *managed* instead of *have managed.*

✔ **"Being" verbs (am, is, are, was, were):** Being verbs suggest a state of existence rather than a state of motion. Try *monitored requisitions* instead of *requisitions were monitored.* The active voice gives a stronger, more confident delivery.

✔ **Shifts in tense:** Use the present tense for a job you're still in and the past tense for jobs you've left. But, among the jobs you've left, don't switch back and forth between tenses. Another big mistake: dating a job as though you're still employed (2008–Present) and then describing it in the past tense.

✔ **Complex sentences:** Unless you keep your sentences lean and clean, readers won't take time to decipher them. Process this mind-stumper:

Reduced hospital costs by 67% by creating a patient-independence program, where they make their own beds, and as noted by hospital finance department, costs of nails and wood totaled $300 less per patient than work hours of maintenance staff.

Eliminate complex sentences by dividing ideas into sentences of their own and getting rid of extraneous details:

Reduced hospital costs by 67%. Originated patient independence program that decreased per-patient expense by $300 each.

✔ **Overwriting:** Use your own voice; don't say *expeditious* when you want to say *swift.*

✔ **Abbreviations:** Abbreviations are informal and not universal — even when they're career-specific. Use *Internet* instead of *Net.*

The exception is industry jargon — use it, especially in digital resumes. Knowledge and use of industry jargon adds to your credibility to be able to correctly and casually use terms common to the industry in which you're seeking employment.

A Few Words about Spelling

What is the name of a resume self-defense manual for job seekers? The dictionary!

Of all the reasons causing recruiters and hiring managers to shoot down resumes, carelessness with spelling, grammar, and choice of words rank close to the top. Even when the real reason for rejection is bias or something else entirely, as in "I just don't like that dude," the use of misspelled words is a convenient justification. Who can quarrel with the adage "Garbage in, garbage out"?

Goofy spelling

You don't have to win a spelling bee but, if you're like me (someone who has been known to make some *humongus spelling miztakes*), you need to be on Code Red alert when you're putting words down for the world to read. Here is a sampling of frequently misspelled words. Add your personal goofy spellings to the list.

accommodate	guarantee	personnel
address	immediate	recommend
all right	independent	referred
bureau	its/it's	reference
calendar	judgment	relevant
category	maintenance	schedule
column	millennium	sergeant
committed	miscellaneous	their/they're/there
conscientious	misspell	truly
definitely	nuclear	until
experience	occasionally	your/you're
government	occurrence	weather/whether

Employers especially recoil from impaired spelling when the job seeker botches the interviewer's or the organization's name. (You can Google your way to the company's Web site to spell the organization's name; you can call to confirm the spelling of the interviewer's name.) Here's the take-away message:

Know thy computer spell checker. Know thy dictionary, in print or online at dictionary.com. And know a human being who can carefully proofread your resumes to pick up grammar mistakes or misused words.

BEWARE

Avoid poison words

Recruiters advise staying away from the following words on your resume:

✔ **Responsibilities included:** Make your resume accomplishment-driven, not responsibilities-driven. Job-descriptions language tells, not sells, in a resume.

✔ **Salary:** Money talk doesn't belong on a resume, period. Spilling your financial beans limits your options because you may be priced too high or too low, If you absolutely must deal with salary history or salary requirements before the interview, discuss dollars in a cover letter.

✔ **Fired:** Don't let this word slip into your resume if you want it to escape being lost in a database. *Laid-off* or *reduction in force* generally aren't good terms either, but you can use them when circumstances make it sound as though you were fired. A *lay-off* or *a reduction in force* implies the action was no fault of yours, but *fired* suggests that you screwed up. The basic rule: Don't state why you left a position; save the explanation for an interview.

✔ **References available upon request:** References are assumed. Save the space for more important information.

✔ **Social Security number:** Never make yourself vulnerable in this era of identity theft. The exception to this rule is when you apply for a federal government position; in that case, you're required to submit your SSN.

✔ **Assisted with, worked with, helped with:** Did you really just assist or help someone else? Were you standing by watching someone else do the work? Use action verbs to describe how you contributed to each achievement.

✔ **Also:** The word is unnecessary. (for example, Manage budget of $1 million. *Also* interface with consultants.) Write tightly. Eliminate *also, an, the,* and *and* wherever you can. Use the saved space to pack more punch, and the resume won't lose meaning.

Words Sell Your Story

Remember, when your words speak for you, you need to be sure to use words that everyone can understand and that relate to the job at hand. Value your words. Each one is a tool to your future.

Chapter 8

Refine Your Design for Great Looks

. . . .

In This Chapter

▶ Keeping paper resumes clean-cut

▶ Considering design factors in digital resumes

▶ Giving your qualifications room to breathe

▶ Unstuffing an overstuffed resume

. . . .

*G*ood design is always about more than simply looking good. Good resume design means making your document both appealing and accessible for prospective employers. Making it relevant. Making it feel right for the job you seek and appropriate for someone in your shoes. There's no reason why handsome physical design cannot be — and every reason why it should be — applied to the resume information so important to your journey ahead.

As I mention in Chapter 4, most modern recruiting software can now handle fully formatted resumes in a word-processing attachment (usually MS Word or Corel WordPerfect). This means that all the design tips for paper resumes in this chapter work fine for attached online resumes.

Although handsome resumes are back in vogue, there will be times when it is still necessary to send your word-processed resume in plain text, also called ASCII. In fact, you may as well create an ASCII version at the start of your job search and store it on your computer. Doing so allows you to conveniently and repeatedly copy and paste it, without reformatting each time.

You will, of course, still need to make the customizing changes to the position or career field now effectively required by market forces and government rules (see Chapter 1). For ASCII tips, see Chapter 4.

Resumes That Resonate

Although the market is moving away from paper resumes toward digital resumes, tree-and-ink products will be around for the foreseeable future — if for no other reason than for distribution at career fairs, for circulation throughout your network, and to bring to job interviews. Here are suggestions on how to make the first cut in the employment screening process.

Word processing

Use a computer equipped with word-processing software to produce your resume. Typewritten copies are still okay, but it's hard to produce clean, crisp copy on a typewriter.

Printing

Today's standard is a sharp-looking resume printed on a laser or inkjet printer. Old-fashioned dot matrix printers lack the ability to crank out high-quality work.

Paper selection

In a digital era, how good should your paper be? Although you're using paper only for hand-to-hand delivery, the standards haven't changed. For professional, technical, managerial, and executive jobs, the stock for a paper resume should be quality paper that contains rag content of perhaps 25 percent, as well as a watermark (a faint image ingrained in the paper). For lower-level positions, any decent-looking paper will do.

What color should you choose? Stick to white or off-white, eggshell, or the palest of gray. Print on only one side of the sheet.

What about theme papers — musical notes for musicians, tree leaves for environmental jobs, and the like? Although the use of theme paper for resumes has grown over the past decade, my preference is for plain stock unless you're in a highly creative field. Most employers still prefer the no-frills look in paper.

Consistency, consistency, consistency

Make reading easy on employers by deciding on a style and sticking to it. You detract from your words — and your image — when you do the following things:

- ✔ Mix differently spaced tabs and indentations.

- ✔ Make a habit of mixing bullet styles. You can mix bullets and checkmarks if the result is tasteful and doesn't look cluttered.

- ✔ Use different spacing between lines. Keep your line spaces the same between headings and the body text for each data point. You're going for a finished look, which means no fanciful visual additions.

When three's not a crowd

Certain groupings are just more pleasing to the eye, so many resume pros use the rule of threes: three skills groups, three accomplishments, three sentences on a topic, and so forth. A grouping of five is also attractive.

But avoiding even numbers is not a hard-and-fast rule — groups of two and four are equally acceptable. Look for examples of odd-number groupings in the sample resumes in Part III. Ask a friend with artistic good taste to look at your final draft and give you a review of your design technique.

Come on, break it up!

How often have you tried to read a solid block of text and given up because it makes you want to run for the eye drops? Employers and recruiters reading resume after resume also space out on dense text, especially in small type. The answer is to break it up, to segment your data points in related groups.

Too blocky and dense

Great Eastern Bank, Princeton, NJ
2003-2008
Second Vice President – Global Markets Project Manager
• Developed, outlined, and scheduled 98 conferences covering spectrum of financial risk management issues

- Launched 53-page quarterly newsletter on new products and fluctuations Researched and edited copy from technical specialists and regulatory agencies
- Expanded circulation of client newsletter more than 500% in three years
- Managed $1.2 million budget and monitored department expenses
- Provided marketing management support for Senior Vice President
- Traveled to Hong Kong, Singapore, and London delivering educational seminars on derivative products and uses
- Administered 17 bank personnel policies for seven staff members
- Directed office closure due to outsourcing.

Just right

Great Eastern Bank, Princeton, NJ
2003-2008
Second Vice President – Global Markets Project Manager

Communicator:
- Developed, outlined, and scheduled 98 conferences covering spectrum of financial risk management issues
- Launched 3-page quarterly newsletter on new products and fluctuations
- Researched and edited copy from technical specialists and regulatory agencies
- Expanded circulation of client newsletter more than 500% in three years

Manager:
- Managed $1.2 million budget and monitored department expenses
- Provided marketing management support for Senior Vice President
- Administered 17 bank personnel policies for seven staff members
- Directed office closure due to outsourcing

Business Traveler:
- Traveled to Hong Kong, Singapore, and London delivering educational seminars on derivative products and uses

Open spaces

White space is the master graphic attention-getter; it makes recruiters *want* to read a resume. Too often, job seekers hearing that they must not exceed one page (untrue), try to cram too much information in too little space.

A ratio of about one-quarter white space to text is about right. Line spacing between items is vital. Although some resume pros advise that you right-justify the text (aligning it down the right side of the page), there's no hard-and-fast rule on whether it's best to leave the right-hand margins ragged or justified. I prefer ragged margins because right justification creates awkward white spaces.

Whichever you choose, be clear that an overcrowded page almost guarantees that your resume won't be read by younger recruiters and hiring managers who grew up in an age of television and quick-reading stories in newspapers, magazines, and Web content. And older eyes won't take the wear and tear of too many words jammed into a small space.

Typefaces and fonts

A *typeface* is a family of characters — letters, numbers and symbols. A *font* is a specific size of a typeface. For example, Helvetica is a typeface; Helvetica 10-point bold, Helvetica 12-point bold, and Helvetica 14-point bold are three different fonts.

No more than two typefaces should appear on one resume, but if you don't have an eye for good design, stick to one typeface. Times New Roman, Arial, Verdana, or Helvetica used alone is a fine choice for your resume.

If you want to mix two typefaces, I like Helvetica for the headings and Times New Roman for the text and lesser headings. Printing your name in small capital letters can be pleasing. Using larger type (12, 14, or 16 pt.) or boldface for headings can give them necessary prominence. Use italics sparingly; you don't want to overdo emphasis, and italicized words lose readability in blocks of text.

Professional resume writers use many tricks of the trade to put more information in a resume without making it seem overstuffed. They condense type, use a smaller-size font, and manipulate vertical spacing. Most amateur resume writers don't want to get into this depth of detail, but if you do, a good resource is Susan Britton Whitcomb's *Resume Magic: Trade Secrets of a Professional Resume Writer* (JIST Publishing).

A few more tips on appearance

When wrapping up the fair face of your resume, bear these factors in mind:

- ✔ Your name and contact information can be flush left, centered, or flush right. Look at examples in Chapter 12.

- ✔ Important information jumps in the recruiter's face when set off by bullets, asterisks, and dashes.

- ✔ Typos and spelling errors are attention killers. They are seen as carelessness or as a lack of professionalism. Even when your resume is a customized point-by-point match for the job being filled, a spelling mistake or poor grammar impacts its overall impression and may well sink your chances.

  Use your computer's spell-check feature, read your finished resume carefully, and ask a friend who is a good proofreader to read it also.

- ✔ Don't staple together a two- or three-page resume or put it in a folder or plastic insert. The resume may be photocopied and distributed, or it may be — *gasp,* shades of old technology! — scanned into a database.

  To minimize the risk of a page becoming an orphan, put a simple header or footer atop each page after the first with your name and page number. In a multiple-page resume, you may want to indicate the total number of pages (for example, Page 1 of 2).

Choosing between Two Resume Layouts

Using a simple, cleanly designed layout is fundamental. It may be the difference between your resume being read or passed over.

Take a look at what I mean: Figure 8-1 shows you the *before* version of the resume of Bruce Begovic, who holds a new master's degree in biology. It's nothing but a "design dump" in which Bruce's data is merely unloaded onto a single page without giving thought to layout refinements. Pass the eyewash!

Bruce's *after* version, Figure 8-2, opens up the design structure, adds balance and expands the resume into one-and-a-half pages. It is simple, makes use of a smart typeface, and limits boldface, all of which permits emphasis on the really important qualifications for his biotech career field: education, lab experience, research experience, teaching experience, and an excellent graduate GPA.

Bruce Begovic
* 760-431-9999 *
* 9999 Veranda Ct. Carlsbad CA 92010 * bbegovic@gmail.com *

Offering solid competencies and proven track record documented by Master's degree in Biology and targeted Bachelor's degree, paired with eight years' part time work experience in biotech, communications and teaching/tutoring fields

Education

Master of Science, Biology -California State University San Marcos, [date]
- Graduate thesis project entailed locating and classifying full length-retrotransposable element through probing of genomic library and PCR-mediated genome walking

Bachelor of Science, Biology with Cellular and Molecular Biology Concentration
California State University, San Marcos, [date]
- Coursework: Molecular Cell Biology, Animal Physiology, Genetics, Microbiology, Immunology, Virology, Neurobiology, Viral Evasion, Biochemistry, Research Mathods
- Hazardous Communications and Laboratory Safety trained and certified, [date]
- Radioactive Materials Handling and Safety trained and certified, [date]
- Instructional qualifications include California Basic Education Skills Test certification

Skills

- RDA
- PCR, QPCR
- mass spectrometry
- gel electrophoresis
- SDS-PAGE
- Cloning
- restriction digests
- southern blotting
- plasmid prep
- cell culture
- bioinformatics
- probe design
- DNA extraction
- DNA, RNA isolation
- radiolabeling
- protein purification
- MS Word, Excel, PowerPoint

Work Experience

Graduate Lab Research Associate   [dates]
California State University, San Marcos
- Project leader in a representational difference analysis to determine somatic cell genomic rearrangements between healthy and virally infected species
- Responsible for training and supervision of undergraduate students

Teaching Associate   [dates]
California State University, San Marcos
- Supplemental Instruction course leader for Principles of Genetics class
- Instructor for Intro to Cell/Molecular Biology lab, General Education Science lab
- Teaching Assistant for Genetics Lab

Biology Department Lab Technician   [dates]
California State University, San Marcos
- Prepared graduate/undergraduate lab exercises for classes including: Genetics, Cellular Biotechnology, Microbiology, and Animal Physiology
- Responsible for media /solution preparation, cell culture and all other aspects of lab component preparation
- Supervised undergraduate assistants

Primary Science/Math Tutor   [dates]
Tutoring Pros Educational Services
- Tutored high school students in science and math, including Advanced Placement Biology, Chemistry, Calculus, Statistics and Physics courses

Editorial Associate   [dates]
Sun Features, Inc.
- Research online, copy edit and fact check a wide range of topics for nationally syndicated columnist Joyce Lain Kennedy
- Provided content evaluation and technical direction for several of Kennedy's *For Dummies* books

Accomplishments

- 3.9 GPA in graduate courses
- Presenter, Plant and Animal Genome Conference, [date]
- Presenter, Society for Molecular Biology and Evolution Conference, [date]
- Financed 100% of education through concurrent part-time employment and University grants

Figure 8-1: Bruce's initial thrown-together resume looks like he wrote it in 10 minutes on the fly. Yawn.

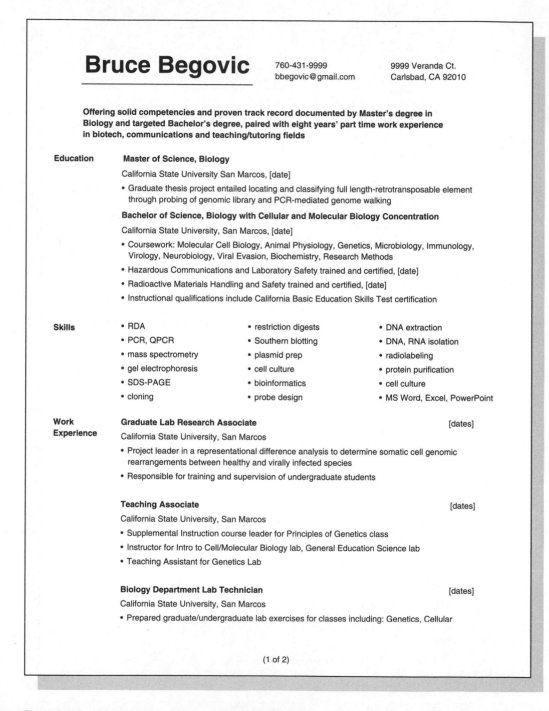

Bruce Begovic

760-431-9999
bbegovic@gmail.com

9999 Veranda Ct.
Carlsbad, CA 92010

Offering solid competencies and proven track record documented by Master's degree in Biology and targeted Bachelor's degree, paired with eight years' part time work experience in biotech, communications and teaching/tutoring fields

Education

Master of Science, Biology

California State University San Marcos, [date]

- Graduate thesis project entailed locating and classifying full length-retrotransposable element through probing of genomic library and PCR-mediated genome walking

Bachelor of Science, Biology with Cellular and Molecular Biology Concentration

California State University, San Marcos, [date]

- Coursework: Molecular Cell Biology, Animal Physiology, Genetics, Microbiology, Immunology, Virology, Neurobiology, Viral Evasion, Biochemistry, Research Methods
- Hazardous Communications and Laboratory Safety trained and certified, [date]
- Radioactive Materials Handling and Safety trained and certified, [date]
- Instructional qualifications include California Basic Education Skills Test certification

Skills

- RDA
- PCR, QPCR
- mass spectrometry
- gel electrophoresis
- SDS-PAGE
- cloning

- restriction digests
- Southern blotting
- plasmid prep
- cell culture
- bioinformatics
- probe design

- DNA extraction
- DNA, RNA isolation
- radiolabeling
- protein purification
- cell culture
- MS Word, Excel, PowerPoint

Work Experience

Graduate Lab Research Associate [dates]

California State University, San Marcos

- Project leader in a representational difference analysis to determine somatic cell genomic rearrangements between healthy and virally infected species
- Responsible for training and supervision of undergraduate students

Teaching Associate [dates]

California State University, San Marcos

- Supplemental Instruction course leader for Principles of Genetics class
- Instructor for Intro to Cell/Molecular Biology lab, General Education Science lab
- Teaching Assistant for Genetics Lab

Biology Department Lab Technician [dates]

California State University, San Marcos

- Prepared graduate/undergraduate lab exercises for classes including: Genetics, Cellular

(1 of 2)

Figure 8-2: Bruce's revised resume dramatically improves his resume's appearance and projects an image that reinforces his value.

Biotechnology, Microbiology, and Animal Physiology

- Responsible for media /solution preparation, cell culture and all other aspects of lab component preparation
- Supervised undergraduate assistants

Primary Science/Math Tutor [dates]

Tutoring Pros Educational Services

- Tutored high school students in science and math, including Advanced Placement Biology, Chemistry, Calculus, Statistics and Physics courses

Editorial Associate [dates]

Sun Features, Inc.

- Research online, copy edit and fact check a wide range of topics for nationally syndicated columnist Joyce Lain Kennedy
- Provided content evaluation and technical direction for several of Kennedy's For Dummies books

Accomplishments
- 3.9 GPA in graduate courses
- Presenter, Plant and Animal Genome Conference, [date]
- Presenter, Society for Molecular Biology and Evolution Conference, [date]
- Financed 100% of education through concurrent part-time employment and University grants

(Bruce Begovic 2 of 2)

Which version would you rather read — the tight one-pager, or the clean, open design on the two-pager?

Design That Gets the Word Out

Because you're counting on your resume to get you through the interview door, pay attention to its appearance as well as its content. Readers should easily and quickly grasp your targeted resume's elements that show you're a strong match for the job. If you're choosing between "easily read" or "overdesigned," go for easily read.

As a busy recruiter says: "The resume design makes a great deal of difference. Most of us don't have time to search through a resume looking for information. If it's not easy to spot, the resume will go into the 'do not call' pile. The better the design of the resume, the more likely we are to interview."

Chapter 9

Passages: Resumes for Your Life's Changing Phases

In This Chapter

▶ Recent graduates: How to start your career well

▶ Baby boomers: How to successfully continue your career

▶ Returning military members: How to get back in civilian clover

▶ Upscale and federal hopefuls: A few pointers on how to ace moves to new turf

At several points in the flow of your life, you're likely to find yourself in a "just passing through" stage where you're temporarily required to come up with new solutions to employment roadblocks. At such stages, you're temporarily required to think differently about how to put your best foot forward.

Often the techniques you've used before — or that you may use in the future — just aren't delivering the goods for you in this life phase. When you hit a passages wall, step back and ask yourself, "How can I fix this problem for this particular stage in my life?"

In changing from one style of life or workplace to another, refresh your resumes with strategies and techniques that will ease the transition. When faced with a new situation, remind yourself to sell solutions, not histories.

This chapter shows you how to do just that and tackles the passages issue for three main times of transition: recent graduates, baby boomers, and returning military members. I briefly touch on two other related situations: aspiring to move into or within the executive ranks, and aiming to enter or leave federal employment.

Scoring Big as a Recent Graduate

If you've just walked the cap-and-gown line, here's a primer on the strengths and weaknesses packaged with your individual situation.

Quick take: Rookie strengths

As a recent graduate, you have three main selling points and various minor ones:

- ✔ You're energetic and fired up to tackle assigned tasks. With no kids, you're more likely to smile when asked to work long hours than are older employees who have family obligations.

- ✔ You're more current in technical skills than older competitors.

- ✔ You're available for the right price. You cost much less than what an older, experienced person expects. Maybe half as much.

Throw in assertions that you are a fast learner, are untarnished by earlier workplace habits that may be anathema to new employers, and that, as a rookie, you are prime material to be developed in concert with a prospective employer's viewpoints. Provide real-life examples of each claim or you'll be devalued as a windbag who has merely memorized slick talking points.

Quick take: Rookie soft spots

Weaknesses you have to wrestle include the stereotyping by employers of recent graduates as inept greenhorns who can't find their butts with both hands. In fact, multiple and recent surveys raise the decibel level on what many employers have long suspected or complained about: Most college students lack marketable skills.

One respectable study (American Institutes for Research) conducted in 2006 alleges that more than half of students at four-year schools and more than 75 percent at two-year colleges lack the skills to perform complex literacy tasks. Yikes! What can you do to offset this image of gross incompetence?

If you have a grade point average (GPA) above 3.5, or have worked as a tutor, emphasize that fact on your resume and at the top of job interviews. You are trying to create the "halo" effect; that is, if one big first-impression factor is perceived as being good, an assumption is made that other factors must be good as well.

If your GPA is poor or marginal, omit it from your resume but bring it up midway in a job interview. Instead, show that you had to work to pay for your school and living expenses. And explain that you devoted much time to "real life" experiences, such as leadership in campus organizations for jobs working with people. Ideally, you also can show that your grades in your major are excellent, and that your GPA rose as you learned better study habits.

Tips for recent graduates

REMEMBER

Times and resumes have changed since your older pals graduated. As I explain in Chapter 1, start by writing a multiple-page core resume that includes familiar requirements for your career field. If popular requirements include A, B, C, and D, be sure your core resume reflects your qualifications in A, B, C, and D. This source document is your wellspring for cranking out shorter and targeted marketing communications.

Customize your spinoff resumes for replying to specific job ads. And, if logical, customize your spinoff resumes for posting in resume databases; if you're a marketing graduate, for example, you might choose to match different requirements for a resume database for the chemical industry than a resume database for the healthcare industry. You can handle the matching of requirements with your qualifications in your opening skills summary (Chapter 6) and throughout your resume.

Keep the following resume boosters in mind, as well.

Beef up your sales pitch

Thicken your work experience by including all unpaid positions — internships, special projects, and volunteer jobs. List them in chronological order in your Work Experience section. Statements like these are powerful agents on your resume:

> *Sales: Sold $1,200 worth of tickets to college arts festival*
>
> *Counseling: Advised 16 freshman students as peer counselor*
>
> *Public Policy Coordination: Coordinator for student petition drive to save California Cougar from sports hunting, gaining 2,000 signatures in 35 days*

Highlight the work experience most relevant to your intended future. If you have at least one year of full-time professional experience, place education after experience — unless your education is changing your career path.

Clarify your aim

Make your objective clear if you use an objective statement. Don't use a lofty statement of the absurd, like this one:

> *I'm seeking a challenging position that will allow me to actualize my talents in saving the world, with good potential for professional growth and pay commensurate with my ability.*

Instead, cut to the chase, like this:

> *Research position in urban planning field in Chicago area.*

You can add a summary, too, as I show you in Chapter 6.

Ditch unhelpful information

Don't enclose your resume in a report cover or bulky package or attach school transcripts or letters of recommendation, unless they're requested.

Include an activity only if it reveals skills, competencies, accomplishments, results, or other qualifications to support your intended job. Omit high school data unless it adds a unique fact to the total impression that you're creating.

What about the laundry list of your college courses — do they earn their keep on your resume? No, unless the course work is unusual or you have little to say without them.

Data-mine your college experience

Need a job? Get experience! Need experience? Get a job! This predicament has frustrated new graduates since the continents broke apart.

Having nothing but education to work with makes for a difficult resume scenario. Only dedicated job research and customizing each resume gives you a chance of producing a persuasive product. Perhaps you overlooked something; even child-sitting or pet-sitting offers experience in accepting responsibility and demonstrates reliability.

Consider the following factors in identifying the experience and skills you garnered in college and matching the information with the job you hope to land:

- **Work:** Internships, summer jobs, part-time jobs, campus jobs, entrepreneurial jobs, temporary work, and volunteer work
- **Sports:** Proven ability to achieve goals in a team environment

> ✔ **Awards and honors**
> ✔ **Research papers and projects**
> ✔ **Campus leadership**
> ✔ **Grade Point Average (GPA):** If it's 3.0 or above; otherwise, omit it (some advisers set the GPA floor at 3.5).
> ✔ **Technical skills and software facility**

Concerning student jobs, one technique to make the most of your experience is to separate your jobs into fragments and explain them. For example, don't say that your job title was "office help" or "office clerk" and stop there. Divide the job into such functions as telephone reception, telephone sales, contract negotiations, purchasing, inventory, staff training, computer application training, Web design, public speaking, and written communications. Describe each one in terms of your accomplishments and their outcomes.

If an exhaustive search of your hobbies, campus activities, or community service turns up absolutely nothing worth putting on your resume, your education must carry the entire weight of candidacy for employment. Milk it dry, as the example in Figure 9-1 suggests.

Gaffes common to new graduates

New graduates are more likely than experienced job seekers to make the following mistakes.

Falling short of image standards

If you present a paper resume flawed with little printing errors, or an online resume blemished with unwrapped lines of type that seem to run on for miles, you flunk.

Omitting heavy-hitter points

You distinguish yourself by creating an opening summary that calls to mind an image of your unique selling points. Use categories described in "Data-mine your college experience" stated earlier in this section. For example: *As team captain, used strong influencing skills and tremendous personal energy. Got marketplace experience through multiple Internships and 6 student jobs, including tutoring. GPA 3.8 despite heavy course load.* Keep your summary brief — three to four achievements is plenty.

New Graduate — Little Experience

Deanna R. McNealy
(111) 213-1415

1234 University Drive,#56B
Irvine, California 78910

Seek retail management trainee position. Offer more than three years' intensive study of public communication. Completed Bachelor's degree, developing strong research, language, interpersonal, computer, and disciplinary skills. Proven interactive skills with groups and individuals. Energetic, adaptive, fast learner.

BACKGROUND & EDUCATION

- **Bachelor of Arts, University of California at Irvine (UCI), May, 20##, Literature & Social Studies**

Self-Directed Studies [date] - Present
Focusing on mainstream culture and trends, study merchandising and population demographics of individuals between the ages of 18 and 49. Browse media and advertising extensively, developing an in-depth understanding of material consumption in U.S. culture.

University Studies
[dates]   Literary Philosophy, Graduate, UCI, Irvine, California
Accumulated skills in prioritizing, self-management and discipline, accomplishing over 90 pages of commentary on the subject of philosophical thought.

[dates]   Social Text and Context, UCI, Irvine, California
Developed in-depth understanding of public consensus and modern value systems.Concentration: the relationship between ideals and historical and economic patterns.

[dates]   Critical Thinking, UCI, Irvine, California
60 hours of self-directed research and lecture attendance, studying essential elements of critical thought. Developed skills in argumentative dialogue, logic, analysis, and approaching perception from an educated and diverse persepctive. Focus: anatomy of critical thought.

[dates]   Public Communication, UCI, Irvine, California
Intensive study of the psychological and social techniques of speech and communication. Developed comprehensive understanding of debate, physical language, formal and informal delivery, subliminal communication, and advertising. Focus: written and visual advertising techniques.

Other Experience [date] - Present, UCI, Irvine, California
15th and 16th Century Rhetoric, French Poetry, Literature in Music, Women, Words & Wisdom, FilmTheory, Shakespeare, British Fiction, U.S. Fiction, World Literature.

SKILLS
Computer: All word processing applications on Macintosh and PC, Internet savvy.
Interpersonal: Experienced in working with groups and individuals using teamwork and collaboration, setting goals, delegating and communicating effectively.

Figure 9-1: The resume of a graduate with little experience but marketable skills.

Overcompensating with gimmicky language

Don't tart up your resume to compensate for a lack of qualifications. Avoid using exotically original language, such as "eyelinered genius," a term used by a business graduate applying for an entry-level marketing position in the cosmetics industry. The term may be colorful, but charm communicates better in the interview.

Making employers guess

Employers hate it when they're asked to decipher your intent. Merely presenting your declared major and transcript excerpts is not enough to kick off a productive job search. Add either an objective to your resume and/or a skills summary directed at a specific career field.

Leveling the experience field

Your resume is no place to give every job equal billing. Many rookie resumes are little more than rote listings of previous jobs — subpoena server, TV satellite dish sales representative, waiter, landscape helper, and computer coach, for example. Separate your jobs into an A list and a B list. The A list contains the jobs that relate to what you want to do next, even if you have to stretch them to make a connection. Briefly mention jobs on the B list in a section called *Other Experience* or *Other Jobs*.

Stopping with bare bones

Some rookies look at a sheet of paper and then at their embarrassing, bedraggled collection of jobs in their paid-experience stew. Desperate to get *anything* written, they settle for name, rank, and serial number (employer, job title, and dates of employment).

The solution is to pull in *all* experience, including volunteer and part-time gigs. Sit, think, think some more, and add all your relevant competencies and skills pointing in the direction in which you hope to thumb a ride. One strategy is to sign up for a postgraduate internship. Speak with your college's career counselors or internship counselors about this possibility.

Still stymied? Look online for sample resume ideas; try www.collegegrad.com.

Hiding hot information

Data entombed is data forgotten. Employers remember best the information you give first in a resume, not the data folded into the middle. Decide what your selling points are and pack that punch upfront. Ask three friends to read your resume and immediately tell you what they remember about it.

Highlighting the immaterial

Featuring the wrong skills and knowledge acquired on each job is an error that many first-time resume writers make. Suppose you want to be a multimedia producer and one of your work experience citations is your three years of effort for campus student theatrical productions. You painted scenery, sold tickets, and designed sets. It's the experience in designing sets that helps qualify you for multimedia producer, not painting scenery or selling tickets. Cloak yourself in the skills that help employers imagine you playing a role in their company.

Ignoring employers' needs

Even the smartest new graduates, who may have survived research challenges as rigorous as uncovering the body language of ancient French cave dwellers, make this mistake. They forget to find out what employers want from new hires. Your college career center can sprinkle your search path with gems of wisdom in reading employers' wish lists.

Writing boastfully

Appearing too arrogant about your talents can cause employers to question your ability to learn as a junior team member. Even when you're just trying to compensate for your inexperience, avoid terminology that comes across as contrived or blatantly self-important. If you're not sure, ask older friends to describe the kind of person they think your resume represents.

Grabbing Good Jobs as a Baby Boomer

If you're on the shady side of 50 (maybe even 40 in today's world), it's pointless to debate whether or not age discrimination lives. It does. Society continues to wink at age bias. My readers daily attest to that fact. In this section, I don't discuss legal remedies or self-employment. Instead, I show you how to do all within your power to beat off pesky bias and display your excellent qualifications on your resume.

First, a primer on the pluses and minuses of being a boomer job seeker.

Quick take: Boomer strengths

You have at least five main selling points and a slew of minor ones:

✔ You have more knowledge and greater wisdom than you did when you were half your age. Your judgment is a valuable commodity. You could easily save an employer substantial "mistake dollars" because you've seen most situations play out in some form over the course of your learning lifetime. You have the common sense that comes with experiencing life. You won't rush into hasty or rash decisions.

✔ You're dependable. You won't take off for frivolous reasons. Employers can rely on you showing up and doing the job as expected. You're more grateful for a good job than younger workers. You show your appreciation with a strong work ethic. Your work history shows that your word is your bond.

✔ You're motivated to be flexible and adaptable. You may value working less than a full-time schedule. You can adapt to the changing needs of a business.

✔ You may be able to work for less money than your competition. Your kids are grown and your expenses are down.

✔ You see the big picture in dealing with people. You've had years to discover what makes them tick. You know from firsthand experience the quality of customer service consumers expect and appreciate.

Other positive characteristics you have acquired as time kept on going by include the following: You've acquired a taste for team playing because you've seen how all hands can work collectively for the good of a business. Unlike mountain-climbing younger employees, you won't skip out for a flashy opportunity when you've got a bird in hand — you're happy to be working and you've seen enough of the dot-com bubbles to last a lifetime.

Quick take: Boomer soft spots

The notion that older people have had their day and should make room for the next generation is deeply ingrained, say researchers. The stereotype is that you can't teach an old dog new tricks and that all mature workers are alike in their abilities to learn, perform, energize, remember, and deal with change in a new kind of world.

Here is a selection of prevalent myths about workers of a certain age, followed by the realities you should try to reflect in your resume:

✔ **"Older workers can't or won't learn new skills."** A smart, well-executed resume proves this bit of conventional wisdom wrong, as it certainly is: The over-50 crowd is the fastest growing group of Internet users. Use technical terms on your resume if appropriate. Mention new skills recently acquired. Studies show only negligible loss of cognitive function of people under 70.

✔ **"Training older workers is a lost investment because they won't be around for long."** The life of a new technology for which workers are trained often won't last as long as the work life of an employee over 50. Find ways to tell employers that you

- Are committed to doing quality work

- Can get along with co-workers and younger bosses

- Have strong skills in reading, writing, and arithmetic

- Are someone who can be counted on in a crisis

- Are willing to be flexible about doing different tasks

✔ **"Benefit and accident costs are higher for older workers."** According to a study by the AARP organization, older workers take fewer sick days per year than do other age groups because they have fewer acute illness and sporadic sick days. Although it's true that individual older workers' health, disability, and life insurance costs do rise slowly with age, they are offset by lower costs because of fewer dependents.

Overall, fringe benefit costs stay the same as a percentage of salary for all age groups. Older workers take fewer risks in accident-prone situations and statistically have lower accident rates than other age groups. Handling this on a resume is tricky but you could say, if true: "Robust health; no dependents other than spouse."

Tips for baby boomers

Perhaps you've heard the baby boomer generation's battle cry: 70 is the new 50? Okay, then 60 is the new 40! And 50 is the new 30! Take the attitude to heart in your resume. In addition to what it says, a clean, young-looking resume design is a shield against age bias.

To forestall age discrimination, tailor your resume to make yourself look like a well-qualified candidate — not a well-preserved one — by using the following tips.

Match your target job description

Find or write job descriptions of your target occupations. If you like your current field and are leaving involuntarily because it's disappearing from under your feet, start with job descriptions in closely related jobs. Compare requirements of related jobs with your transferable skills profile. If you don't like your current field, forget I mentioned it.

To identify occupations closely related to your current field, check a library copy of the *Occupational Outlook Handbook* published by the U.S. Department of Labor. Or, read it online at www.bls.gov/oco.

Knowing what you have to offer gets you up off your knees, out of the past, and into the future; it enables you to write a resume that readers will respect, by saying, "This is what I can do for you that will add to your productivity, efficiency, or effectiveness. Not to mention a little bump on the bottom line."

Shorten your resume

The general guideline is "Go back no more than 15 years." But if that doesn't work for the job you seek, one answer is to create a functional resume where you emphasize your relevant skills in detail toward the top of the resume and downplay overly impressive titles that might intimidate younger employers. For example, *Senior Vice President, Sales* becomes *Sales Executive.*

Focus your resume

For emphasis, I'll repeat that: Focus your resume (see Chapter 6). Concentrate on highlighting your two most recent or most relevant jobs. Don't attempt to give equal attention to each of your past jobs. If your job experience has been diverse, your resume may look like a job-hopping tale of unrelated job after unrelated job.

Show that you're a tower of strength

Give examples of how you solved problems, recovered expenses, and learned to compensate for weaknesses in your working environment. Emphasize how quickly such adjustments occurred. Gray heads who've survived a few fallen skies are valuable assets in difficult times.

Demonstrate political correctness

This is especially important for positions that have contact with the public. Show that you're familiar with contemporary values by using politically correct terms wherever appropriate. Examples include *diversity, cross-cultural, mainstream, multiethnic,* and *people with disabilities* (never *handicapped*), and *women* (not *girls* or *gals*).

Distribute your resume online

Doing so helps dispel any ideas that you're over the hill. See Part I for more on digital resumes.

Murder ancient education dates

Of course, the absence of dates sends a signal: This is a geezer who read a resume book. But at least it shows that you have sufficient faculties left to read the book and play the game.

Trim your resume to fighting weight

For very experienced professionals, sorting out the most powerful resume points can be difficult. It's like being a gifted child — so many choices, and you're good at all of them! You know what they say, though: The longer the cruise, the older the passengers.

Use appropriate headings

If you're using freelance, hobby, or volunteer experience, use the heading *Work Experience* and list it first, unless you have changed your focus through education. Then, begin with the heading *Education.* To refine this heading, substitute target-job-related education, such as *Accounting Education* or *Healthcare Education.* Your employment history follows.

What do you do with all the experience that was great in your old job but means zero where you want to go? Lump it together at the end of your resume under *Other Experience* or *Earlier Experience.* Shrink it to positions, titles, employers, and/or degrees and educational institutions. If extraneous experience is older than five years, squash it entirely.

Taking a lower-level job

When you're willing to step down from your previous level of work, the first thing to know is don't try to do it with a resume. Do it by a personal first contact where you get a chance to color your positioning in the best hue, and to defuse intuitive rejection. Tell your story before recruiters and, employers can say they don't want to hear it.

Positioning your status counts. You aren't a manager lowering yourself by looking for a much less responsible job. You're a career changer exploring new fields:

> *In the past decade, I've put in very long hours and exceeded expectations in jobs in the same industry. I realized I'm a doer who needs new mountains to climb. I have too much to give to the business world to ride on autopilot the rest of my life. I want to check out other ways I can make a contribution in a different career field, hopefully at your company.*

Show skills as they apply to new position

Making a career change? As you list your skills, competencies, education, and experience, lead with the information relevant to the new position and then list the other data. You have to quickly convince the employer that you have the ability to handle the position.

Assume an engineer wants to move into sales. The resume should mention things like "client liaison," "preparing presentations for meetings," and "strong communications skills."

You may begin by writing: "Used a strong technical background and excellent communications skills in a sales role." Then continue to speak of your ability to provide good technical advice in a business relationship.

Writing that you "enjoy learning" is a coin with two sides; the employer may see you as flexible in your desire to further your education, or, conversely, make a negative judgment that you don't have the skills right now to hit the ground running.

Go directly to the hiring manager and explain your reasoned willingness to accept lower compensation:

> *I have a great work attitude and excellent judgment. Show me a new task, and I get it right away. I understand, of course, that the trade-off in moving into your industry is less pay and responsibility.*

When you've opened the door, hand over your resume. Write a hybrid resume (detailed in Chapter 5) with heavy emphasis on the functional part. You need breathing room to shape your resume in a way that spotlights your transferable skills as they pertain to the job you seek, such as talent for working with numbers, reliability, and good attendance record, as well as fast-learning ability.

When you're a major seeking a minor position, emphasize that, sometimes, good people need new chapters in their lives.

Gaffes common to boomers

When you have a long job history, you're more likely to need updates on the following issues.

Choosing the wrong focus

Choosing the wrong focus is a problem shared with new graduates who fail to elaborate on those jobs that best address the hoped-for next job. Like the real estate adage that the operating principle is location, location, location, the operating principle for the better jobs is target, target, target.

Presenting short-term work on your resume

Baby boomers may find that they're doing work for a specific company but are being paid through a temporary staffing firm or other intermediary and be unsure about how to report the information on their resumes. You don't have to list the middleman firm. Note only the companies for which the work was performed. Here's a brief template:

Company A, Company B, Company C   [date] to present

For **Company A,** Name of Department/Division

As **job title,** performed:

✔ achievement

✔ achievement

✔ achievement

For **Company B,** Name of Department/Division

As **job title,** implemented:

✔ achievement

✔ achievement

✔ achievement

For **Company C,** Name of Department/Division

As **job title,** credited with:

✔ achievement

✔ achievement

✔ achievement

P.S. If your job titles are extreme — insignificant or overly exalted — don't bold them.

Using old resume standards

Many baby boomers, still working on last decade's calendar, have an outdated concept of what a resume should be. An office neighbor recently expressed surprise when I told him to leave out his personal information, which once was standard fare on resumes.

"Oh, I thought personal information was supposed to humanize you," the seasoned ace said. Busy employers and job computers don't care that you're a par golfer or play tennis; this kind of personal bonding information comes out at the interview.

Lacking a summary

Because of the extensiveness of your experience, your resume may be unwieldy without a summary. Suppose you're fed up living as a city slicker and want to move to a small town where agribusiness is dominant. Your objective may take only one line — "Wish to work as internal auditor in the farm equipment industry." Follow that statement with a one- or two-paragraph summary of why you're qualified. Think of a summary as a salesperson's hook. It describes some of your special skills, your familiarity with the target industry, and your top achievements.

Revealing age negatively

Don't blurt out your age. Start with ageless — you can always move to senior. Do not put old education first on your resume (unless you're a professional educator). Avoid listing jobs with dates older than 10 or 15 years. If you must include dusty jobs, de-emphasize the dates or omit them. You can summarize old jobs under a heading of "Prior to 20XX" and avoid being too specific. Alternatively, you can include all jobs under functional headings. Try not to describe older jobs in detail.

Appearing low-tech

Seasoned aces who do not have computers still type resumes; others with computers have old-fashioned dot matrix printers. Their resumes are often stopped at the door. Today's readers like crisp, attractive layouts that only a computer and laser printer can create. Trade a dinner or two for resume services from a friend, use a computer free at a library, rent a computer by the hour at a copy center, or pay a professional to do your resume.

Not supplementing a high school education

If your highest education attainment is high school, don't forget to mention any continuing education, including seminars and workshops related to your work — if it applies to what you want to do next.

Winning Interviews as a New Civilian

If you're trading in military life for your first civilian gig, be sure to sign up for the invaluable Transition Assistance Program (TAP), the three-day class that helps active-duty personnel write resumes and prepare for interviews. Experts say that a lot of young military retirees overlook TAP. As executive search consultant Mike Dodd commented to *Newsweek* magazine: "[They're thinking] 'I'm a gun fighter. I'm going to go out into the world and do great things. I don't care about resumes.'" Dead wrong.

Unless you're partial to the school of hard knocks and reality bites, pay attention to this section. In it, I show you how best to present your military experience as you look for a civilian job.

Quick take: Transitioning military strengths

You've got a chest full of selling points. Here are six super marks of merit:

- ✔ You have exceptionally good training. Military schools are recognized to be superior institutions, and you've shown that you are trainable.

- ✔ You have substantial real-life experience. You may have things like high-tech skills and leadership skills that you acquired at an early age and that are not typically available to the civilian workforce. Maybe you managed a troop and even advanced to a position responsible for policymaking and strategic planning.

- ✔ You know how to be a team player and show up on time. You perform well under pressure. You know how to accomplish assignments in a structured organization.

- ✔ You may have experience with a direct fit to the civilian job market: operations management, supply chain procurement, human resource management, systems administration, or financial planning.

- ✔ You have a strong work ethic to get it right the first time.

- ✔ You're flexible and able to quickly adapt to changing situations.

Quick take: Transitioning military soft spots

Communication is the biggest reason recruiters or hiring managers overlook well-qualified military candidates, say career coaches who specialize in transitioning from military to civilian jobs. They just don't get what your resume says when you speak military-ese, not civilian-ese.

The military-talk habit is hard to shake. A news report describes an incident involving a former soldier named Perkins who was transitioning to civilian life after a 20-year hitch. Applying to a staffing company, Perkins spelled out his last name in military alphabetic code: Papa-Eco-Romeo-Kilo-India-November-Sierra.

The problems resulting from noncommunication when you use military-ese (also called *milspeak*) on your resume are discussed in more detail later in the section "Get the message about milspeak."

When finished writing your resume, put it through the civilian translation wringer by asking friends and neighbors who know not a whit about things military to read it and see whether they understand what you're talking about.

Admittedly, some employers do hold a stigmatized stereotype of military service members as being rough, tough, rigid, and hard-headed types whose idea of leadership is command and control. A resume won't do much to alter that perception, but if it's well done will help get you inside an interview room where your pleasing personality may be able to reverse false, preconceived notions.

Tips for new civilians

Many employers do appreciate vets as employees and will give you preference above a comparable nonvet competitor. The federal government awards five to ten extra points beyond a passing score to veterans — good news if you're applying for a government position.

Government contractors hire a lot of former military members. That's why it's especially important when preparing your resume to factor in the new federal requirements in online recruiting processes designed to promote equal employment procedures. Federal contractors must play by the rules set by the Office of Federal Contract Compliance (OFCCP).

These rules favor customizing your resume for the position you're targeting. Specialty job boards, such as www.militarystars.com, now publicize the fact that their online candidate databases meet the standards of the federal compliance mandates announced in 2006 by the Office of Federal Contract Compliance Programs. The new rules are a little tricky to understand, so turn to Chapter 1 for particulars on how the new OFCCP mandates affect you.

Here are other resume pointers to boost your cause.

Advertise what you're selling

Avoid building your resume around your military rank or title. Instead, emphasize the qualifications you bring to the employer.

Consider your best format

A hybrid resume (Chapter 5) is a good choice, say many career coaches who work with transitioning military, because it features competencies and skills in professional categories, rather than chronological history by rank or job title. But this doesn't mean a reverse chronological resume format can't be used to your advantage.

If you're working with a third-party recruiter, do as the recruiter — who is carrying your immediate future in his or her hands — advises.

Zero in on job fairs

Job fairs are one of the most potent employment avenues for service members and veterans to meet employers, network and even be interviewed on the spot. The classified pages of your Sunday newspaper may carry big ads announcing fairs; some are aimed at attracting transitioning military, especially individuals who have current top-secret clearances.

Check out the Web sites in the "Visit key Web sites" section in this chapter to track military transition fairs.

Protect your identity from theft

Your Social Security number is the key to the vault for identity thieves. Unfortunately, the military has been slow to give up its open and widespread use of Social Security numbers for even routine transactions at commissaries and base libraries. And then there's the matter of the 2006 theft from the Veteran's Administration of records on almost everyone who has served in the military since 1975.

Unless you're applying for a federal job, which does require your Social Security number, keep it off your resume, cover letter, or application form. If you suspect your data has been compromised, ward off identity theft by monitoring your credit reports and putting a fraud alert or a freeze on your credit accounts. The California Office of Privacy Protection's Web site (www. privacy.ca.gov) offers detailed information about the mechanics of combating identity theft.

Be a resource collector

You deserve entire books dedicated to your special needs when transitioning from military to civilian life, and luckily, good ones are available. Here are my five picks:

- *Military Resumes and Cover Letters,* by Carl S. Savino and Ronald L. Krannich, Ph.D. (Impact Publications, 2004)

- *Expert Resumes for Military–to-Civilian Transitions,* by Wendy S. Enelow and Louise M. Kursmark (JIST Publishing, 2006)

- *Military to Federal Career Guide,* by Kathryn Kraemer Troutman (The Resume-Place (resume-place.com), 2006)

- *Job Search: Marketing Your Military Experience,* by David G. Henderson (Stackpole Books, 2004)

- *Military Transition to Civilian Success,* by Mary T. Hay, et al. (Impact Publications, 2006)

Hey Uncle Sam — how about a job?

If you've ever thought about looking into a federal job, time's wasting. Uncle Sam's 1.7 million civilian workforce averages 20,000 vacancies every day. Benefits are handsome: great health insurance, decent retirement plans, and flexible leave. Annual pay raises — often 3 to 4 percent — are automatic. You may not even have to relocate. Although Washington holds the mother lode of federal jobs, they exist as well in locales across America and even overseas.

The number-one best way to spot a federal job that may interest you is to land online at the official USA Web site: `usajobs.gov`. You can even search by salary. For instance, on a recent day there were 11 jobs in Chicago in a pay range of $35,000 to $45,000. A few examples:

Financial accounts technician, Veteran's Administration

Supervisory Contact Representative, State Department

Adjudication officer, Homeland Security, Citizenship & Immigration Services

Federal resumes are different

1. Federal resumes tend to be longer and require information not typically found on a private-sector resume, including: Social Security number; citizenship; veteran's information; employers' names and contact data; supervisors' names and phones; ending pay for jobs; and hours worked per week.

2. Federal language is more bureaucratic than private-sector documents. Here's how a private-industry example is translated into government-speak:

Private industry: Prepare all levels of correspondence, reports, and other documents. Make consumer-smart travel arrangements for senior managers.

Government: Prepare a wide variety of recurring and nonrecurring correspondence, reports, and other documents. Make travel arrangements, such as scheduling transportation, making reservations, and preparing travel orders and vouchers, based on general travel intentions, known preferences of traveler, and in accordance with appropriate travel regulations.

Read the federal vacancy announcements (recruitment advertisements) carefully to get it right, and pay special attention to the qualifications and KSA (knowledge-skills-abilities) requirements.

Find a specialist

For federal job employment help, my recommendation is Kathryn Troutman. Widely regarded as the go-to guru for job seekers hoping to outmarket and outcommunicate the competition for federal hiring, Troutman has helped tens of thousands of people get hired. Her resume-writing services are described on Troutman's Web site (`resume-place.com`), as are her stellar books, two examples of which are

✔ *Federal Resume Guidebook, Fourth Edition* (The Resume-Place, 2006)

✔ *Student's Federal Career Guide* (The Resume-Place, 2004)

Visit key Web sites

Dozens of Web sites offer help for transitioning military personnel. Start with the following resources, which may link to other Web sites you'll want to know about:

- TAOnline (www.taoline.com)
- VetJobs.com (www.vetjobs.com)
- The Landmark Destiny Group (www.destinygroup.com)
- Corporate Gray (www.corporategray.com)
- Military Officers Association of America (www.moaa.org/tops)
- Non Commissioned Officers Association (www.ncoausa.org)
- Intelligence Careers (www.intelligencecareers.com)
- MilitaryStars.com (www.militarystars.com)

Get the message about milspeak

Bill Gaul, himself an Army veteran, is president and CEO of The Landmark Destiny Group (www.destinygroup.com), a job board with a lot of benefits for transitioning military members. A long-time expert on the military transitioning job market, Gaul answers questions about demilitarizing your resume.

Q: Can you give an example of what you call *milspeak?*

A: An Army colonel's resume we were recently sent read: "As commanding officer of a 500-person organization, I was responsible for the health, morale, and welfare of all personnel." Health, morale and welfare? Just think of the incredible range of skills and experience completely overlooked in that milspeak phrase. Far-reaching accomplishments and important responsibilities are whitewashed into boilerplate terms that mean nothing to a civilian hiring manager.

For example, digging into "health, morale, and welfare," we found "policy development, human resource management, budget planning and administration, process improvement, operations management, and staff development."

Q: What's the deal with job titles?

A: Many military job titles are ambiguous. Some are misleading. For example, a Navy fire control technician does not put out fires but operates and maintains electronic weapons targeting systems.

Translate your job title without misleading the employer:

- Mess cook (food service specialist)
- Fire control technician (electronic weapons systems technician)
- Motor pool specialist (automotive maintenance technician)
- Provost marshal (law enforcement officer)
- Quartermaster (supply clerk)

Q: What about when your specific work experience doesn't closely relate to the job you're applying for?

A: You can list your organizational position instead of your job title. An E-5 Marine Corps embassy guard applying for a management position in the security industry listed his job title as "facility supervisor." He then added the details of his experience within the body of his resume. This drew readers further into his resume because it represented more of a fit than someone who kept people in proper lines applying for visas.

Q: Aren't most military members in combat-related jobs?

A: Yes, and that can be a problem, trying to relate the job you've had to the job you want, unless you're applying for law enforcement positions. But for the straight combat MOS (military occupational specialty) — infantry, tank gunner, reconnaissance Marine, and the like — there are several options to choose from:

List your relative position in an organization — "unit supervisor" instead of "platoon sergeant" as your title.

Your work in collateral duties may be the key. A platoon sergeant seeking a position in staff development and training, based on duty as a training NCO (noncommissioned officer), could list training supervisor as her title. The dates listed must accurately reflect the time you spent in the specific collateral duties, of course. As you know, it is often the case that you will have more than one collateral duty while performing a key role for an organization.

Q: How should you list your level of authority?

A: Omit references to rank or grade like "NCO, "petty officer," and "sergeant." Unless an employer has military experience, these terms won't communicate your relative position within an organization. Instead, list civilianized equivalents appropriate to your level of authority:

- Safety Warrant Officer OSHA (coordinator)
- Training NCO (training supervisor)
- Barracks sergeant (property manager)

Q: What about education and training?

A: Many courses and schools leave recruiters wondering exactly what you trained for because the course titles can be esoteric and arcane. The rule is this: List your training in a way that will provide immediately apparent support for your job objective.

If the name of a school or course doesn't communicate exactly what was taught there, modify it because you are trying to inform, not mystify. You are trying to demilitarize the language to help resume reviewers understand the nature of your military training.

These examples illustrate:

- SNAP II Maintenance School (Honeywell Computer Server Maintenance School)
- NALCOMIS Training (Automated Maintenance and Material Control System Training)
- Mess Management School (Food Service Management School)
- NCO Leadership Training (Leadership and Management Training)

Q: Is that all there is to civilianizing a military background?

A: Not quite. To help resume reviewers understand the depth of your training, list the number of classroom hours you studied. To determine the number of hours, multiply the number of course days by 8, or the number of weeks by 40. If you completed the course within the last 10 years, list the competition date. If the course is older, leave off the date. Here are two examples:

- Leadership and Management Training, 3/07 (160 hours)
- Leadership and Management Training (160 hours)

Changing Course with an OnTarget Resume

You're on the way to finding your new place in the world. Whether your new place turns out to be a stopover or a long-term occupational address, smooth your passage with effective traveling papers — that is, a core resume from which you spin off targeted resumes.

Resumes going up to the top floor

Whether you're seeking an executive position as a move up from middle management or are already in the executive league looking for greener pastures, distinguish between the two categories as you prepare your resume. That's the word from noted executive coach Dilip Saraf (7keys.org).

Job seekers who are breaking out of middle management levels should focus a resume on technical successes — leading teams and working across functional boundaries, Saraf advises. He explains that job seekers already in the executive space should focus on the four functions of managing: leading, planning, organizing, and setting up controls.

If you have an eye on the top levels of the workforce — preferably at C-level (as in chief executive officer or chief financial officer), this book is useful to learn state-of-the-art resume moves. But you do need additional coaching to prepare high-end executive resumes, a specialized job market.

Arguably, the number-one authority on upscale resumes is John Lucht, author of the classic *Rites of Passage at $100,000 to $1 Million+*, published by Viceroy. Lucht's *Executive Job-Changing Workbook* is a gold-standard guide to top-floor resumes. There's more: Lucht's RiteSite.com is an excellent subscription Web site for executives. Another upscale book getting rave reviews is *Executive's Pocket Guide to ROI Resumes and Job Search,* by Louise M. Kursmark and Jan Melnik (JIST Publishing, 2006).

Keep polishing your work until your traveling papers are excellent. As famed economist and author John Kenneth Galbraith said about the need to keep writing until you get it right: ". . . there are days when the result is so bad that no fewer than five revisions are required. In contrast, when I'm greatly inspired, only four revisions are needed."

Reflect on the stakes for your efforts to move along. By writing your transitional OnTarget resume, you're more than the author of your traveling papers — you're the author of your life.

Chapter 10

Successful Solutions to Resume Problems

. . . .

In This Chapter

▶ Squashing the overqualified objections

▶ Standing tall as a reentering woman

▶ Dealing with disability issues

▶ Patching over employment gaps and demotions

▶ Coping with too many layoffs

▶ Counting out too many jobs

▶ Explaining a substance-abuse history

▶ Handling a bad credit/background check

▶ Relaunching after a prison stay

. . . .

Chances are that not everything in your career history is a plus. Minuses — either fact or perception — like your age (be it a little or a big number) and experience (whether too much or not enough) need special care to keep them from setting off alarm bells. It's always better to anticipate factors in your background that could screen you out of the running and do what you can to minimize them.

Nobody's perfect. But rarely are we jammed up against problems so severe that they can not be solved in some way. Careful resume management is a good start.

Here are some ideas on how to turn lemons into lemonade.

Too Much Experience

Not only is inappropriate experience — too much or too little — often the real reason that you're turned down, but it's also too frequently a cover story for rejections that are really based on any factor from bias to bad breath.

Too many qualifications or ageism?

A reader writes that his qualifications for a training position are superior but too ample. He explains:

> *Preoccupation with age seems to be the pattern. I'm rarely called for an interview; when I call after sending a resume in response to an ad or a networking contact, I'm told I'm too experienced for the position — that I seem to be overqualified. How can I keep my resume from looking like lavender and old lace?*

Ageism often is the subtext in the *overqualified* objection. Deal with it by limiting your work history to the most recent positions you've held that target the job opening. To avoid seeming too old or too highly paid, limit your related experience to about 15 years for a managerial job and to about 10 years for a technical job.

What about all your other experience? Leave it in your memory bank. Or if you believe that the older work history adds to your value as a candidate, you can describe it under a heading of *Other Experience* and briefly present it without dates. Figure 10-1 is an example of a resume that shows recent experience only.

The recent-experience-only treatment doesn't work every time, but give it a try — it shows that you're not stuck in a time warp, and it's a better tactic than advertising your age as one that qualifies you for carbon dating.

If the employer is notorious for hiring only young draft horses, rethink your direction. Try to submit your resume to employers who can take advantage of your expertise, such as a new or expanding company operating in unfamiliar territory.

What if the overqualified objection is just that and not a veil for age discrimination? The employer legitimately may be concerned that when something better comes along, you'll set a sprint record for shortest time on the job.

Recent Experience Only

Work Experience.

FEIN AND SONS – Operates continuously in Long Beach, Calif. **Sole Proprietor, Broker.**
Real estate brokerage, development, asset management, and consulting. In-house brokerage
company, specializing in eight- and nine-figure acquisitions, shopping centers, and
commercial space, obtaining entitlements and economic analysis. Personal volume: over
$100 million.

SONNHAARD INC. – Solana Beach, Calif. [dates]. **Marketing Manager.**
Real estate development corporation. Primary project: Le Chateau Village, a French-theme
100-lot residential development in Del Mar. Sourced architect, designers, and contractors.
Limited liability company built 60 upscale custom homes by architect Jacques Donnaeu of
Toulouse. Supervised 10 sales representatives. Sales gross exceeded $40 million, selling 58
homes ahead of project schedule by six months.

WEST COAST ASSOCIATION – Los Angeles, Calif. [dates]. **Executive Vice President**.
International trade association with 190 firms holding annual fairs, from 25 states and all of
Canada, including two theme amusement parks, 15 affiliated breed organizations and 300
service members who provide goods and services to members. Annual convention attended
by over 2,000 executives. Acted as legislative advocate for California district and county
fairs, nine of which have horse racing and pari-mutuel wagering. Increased membership by
200%, administering seven-figure budget, with staff of five professionals.

Other Experience.

• BBH & Co., d.b.a. ENVIRONMENT AFFILIATED, **Executive Vice President.**
Administered six-figure budget and supervised 27 managers. Directed recruitment and
marketing activities.

• CSU Long Beach, **Development Director.** Managed 40-million-dollar project to expand
campus grounds 30%. Maintained lowest campus construction budget in state, including
contracting and materials.

• TRADE ALTERNATIVE, **Commercial Properties Manager.** Marketed, leased, and
acquired $900,000 in commercial property. Catered to such upscale clientele as high-end
law firms.

Figure 10-1: Focusing on recent experiences is an effort to avoid the problem of being seen as too old.

On the other hand, another version of rejection based on too many qualifications or ageism occurs when a candidate who qualifies for AARP membership wants to kick back a bit and work at less demanding, lower-paying work. The employer questions the applicant's true intent — why would an older engineer want a technician's job? — and consequently doesn't bother to interview a candidate she suspects of seeking any port in a storm.

When you really prefer to take life easier physically or to have more time to yourself, spell it out in your resume's objective. Writing this kind of statement is tricky. You risk coming across as worn-out goods, ready to relax and listen to babbling brooks while you collect a paycheck. When you explain your desire to back off an overly stressful workload, balance your words with a counterstatement reflecting your energy and commitment:

> *Energetic and work-focused but no longer enjoy frenzied managerial responsibility; seek a challenging nonmanagerial position.*

Too much experience in one job

A reader writes:

> *I've stayed in my current and only job too long. When my company cut thousands of workers, we received outplacement classes. I was told that job overstayers are perceived as lacking ambition, uninterested in learning new things, and too narrowly focused. What can I do about this?*

Here are several strategies for meeting this issue head-on.

Divide your job into modules

Show that you successfully moved up and up, meeting new challenges and accepting ever more responsibility. Divide your job into realistic segments, which you label as Level 1, Level 2, Level 3, and so on. Describe each level as a separate position, just as you would if the levels had been different positions within the same company or with different employers. If your job titles changed as you moved up, your writing task is a lot easier.

Deal honestly with job titles

If your job title never changed, should you just make up job titles? *No.* The only truthful way to inaugurate fictional job titles is to parenthetically introduce them as "equivalent to . . . ." Suppose that you're an accountant and have been in the same job for 25 years. Your segments might be titled like this:

   ✔ Level 3 (equivalent to supervising accountant)

   ✔ Level 2 (equivalent to senior accountant)

   ✔ Level 1 (equivalent to accountant)

To mitigate the lack of being knighted with increasingly senior job titles, fill your resume with references to your continuous salary increases and bonuses and the range of job skills you mastered.

Tackle deadly perceptions head-on

Diminish any perception that you became fat and lazy while staying in the same job too long by specifically describing clockless workdays: "Worked past 5 p.m. at least once a week throughout employment."

Derail the perception that you don't want to learn new things by being specific in describing learning adventures: "Attended six semesters of word-processing technologies; currently enrolled in adult education program to master latest software."

Discount the perception that you're narrowly focused by explaining that although your employment address didn't change, professionally speaking, you're widely traveled in outside seminars, professional associations, and reading.

Highlight the issue

In a departure from the normal practice of omitting from your resumes reasons for leaving a job, consider indicating why you're making a change after all this time.

Neutralize the issue burning in every employer's mind: "Why now? Why after all these years are you on the market? Kicked out? Burned out?" If the question isn't asked, that doesn't mean it isn't hanging out in the recruiter's mind. Even though you may be seen as a moss-backed antique, reveal yourself as interested in current developments by adding this kind of phrase in your objective:

> *Focusing on companies and organizations with contemporary viewpoints*

In an even more pioneering move to solve the same problem, create a whole new section at the tail of your resume headed "Bright Future," with a statement along the lines of this one:

> *Layoffs springing from a new management structure give me the welcomed opportunity to accept new challenges and freshen my work life.*

Don't let too little experience kick you to the curb

When a job posting calls for a specific number of years of experience — say, three years' experience and you come up short with only two years' experience — but you know you can do the job, the basic technique is to work with what you've got. Dissect your two years' experience, and then add a statement in parentheses that says: (skills acquired equivalent to three years' experience). The expansion technique won't work every time, but it's worth the gamble.

Too Long Gone: For Women Only

The reentering woman still has it tough. Usually, Mom's the one who puts her career on hold to meet family responsibilities. When she tries to reenter the job market, by choice or economic necessity, she feels as though she's been living on another planet. A reader writes:

> *Employers don't want to hire women if they've been mothers and out of the market for more than a year or two. Hey, ya know, for the last ten years, I've worked my tail off! Don't they understand that? Doesn't intelligence, willingness to work hard, creativity, attention to detail, drive, efficiency, grace under pressure, initiative, leadership, persistence, resourcefulness, responsibility, teamwork, and a sense of humor mean anything these days?*

Every characteristic that this reader mentions is still a hot ticket in the job market, but the burden is on Mom to interpret these virtues as marketable skills:

- Grace under pressure, for example, translates to *crisis manager,* a valuable person when the electricity fails in a computer-driven office.

- Resourcefulness translates to *office manager,* who is able to ward off crank calls from credit collection agencies.

- A sense of humor translates to *data communications manager,* who joshes a sleepy technical whiz into reporting for work at 2 a.m. for emergency repair of a busted satellite hovering over Europe.

You can't, of course, claim those job titles on your resume, but you can make equivalency statements: Like a crisis manager, I've had front-lines experience handling such problems as electrical failures, including computer crashes.

If you're a returning woman, use the tips in the following sections to develop a great resume that connects what you can do with what an employer wants done. Figure 10-2 gives you an example of how it might come together.

Reentry

JOY R. NGUYEN

12 Watt Road, Palmira, Florida 34567   (321) 654-9876

SUMMARY OF EXPERIENCE

More than five years' experience in event-planning, fundraising, administration and publicity. More than nine years' experience in administration for retail and manufacturing firms. B.A. in Business. Florida Teaching Certificate.

NONPROFIT/VOLUNTEER SERVICE

[dates]   **Palmira Optimists' Association, Palmira, Florida Membership Committee Chair**

Planning, organizing programs, exhibits and events to recruit association members. Coordinated annual new member events.

[dates]   **Okeefenokee County Y.M.C.A., Okeefenokee, Florida Member, Board of Directors and Executive Committee**

Spearheaded first Y.M.C.A. organization in county. Designed programs, procedures, and policies, monitoring trustees in the construction of $3 million facility. Led $2.5 million fundraising campaign.

> • **Fundraising Chair**, [dates] Raised funds for entire construction project, establishing hundreds of donors and supervising project. Sourced contractors and directed fundraising activities, using strong interpersonal and networking skills.

HOME MANAGEMENT EXPERIENCE

• **Scheduling:** Assisted business executive and two children in the scheduling of travel and 160,000 miles of transportation. Arranged ticketing, negotiated finances of $12,000 in travel expenses.
• **Conflict Resolution:** Arbitrated personal, business issues. Effective interpersonal skills.
• **Relocation:** Launched inter state relocation of entire family, coordinating moving services, trucks, and packing schedules.
• **Budget & Purchasing:** Managed family finances, including budgeting, medical, dental, insurance packages, two home purchases, three auto purchases, expenses, and taxes. Developed finance and math skills.

ADDITIONAL PROFESSIONAL EXPERIENCE

[dates]   **Sunrise Books, Cabana, Florida**
                 Assistant Manager, Sales Representative

Managed daily operations of coffee house and bookstore, directing staff of 35. Supervised entire floor of merchandise and stock. Purchased all sideline goods.

• Spearheaded store's first sales campaign, resulting in tripled sales.
• Designed system for inventory analysis, streamlining purchasing. and display control.
• Redirected staff duties for more effective work hours.
• Promoted from sales to supervisor in 38 days; three months later to asst. mgr.

EDUCATION

• **Bachelor of Science in Business,** [year], University of Miami, Miami, G.P.A.: 3.75
• **Florida Teaching Certificate,** Business and English, 2001, Florida State, Palmira

Figure 10-2: A sample resume showcasing the skills of a family caregiver reentering the work place.

Sift through your past

Identify transferable skills that you gained in volunteer, civic, hobby, and domestic work. Scout for adult and continuing education experiences, both on campus and in nontraditional settings.

Reexamine the informative Web sites you've used, the educational television programs that you've watched, and the news magazines that you've monitored. Go to the library and read business magazines and trade journals, or online if the ones you want are available without subscription.

Use professional terms

In recounting civic and volunteer work, avoid the weak verbs: *worked with* or *did this or that.* Instead say *collaborated with* or *implemented.* The use of professional words can help de-emphasize informal training or work experience. Chapter 7 lists words to jog your memory.

Professionalizing your domestic experience is a tightrope walk: Ignoring it leaves you looking like a missing person, yet you can't be pretentious or naive. *Housewife* dates you; *family caretaker* sounds more modern and better describes your role. Refer to *home management* to minimize gaps in time spent as a homemaker.

Fill the home management period with transferable skills relevant to the targeted position. Examples range from time management (developing the ability to do more with less time) to budgeting experience (developing a sophisticated understanding of priority allocation of financial resources). Other examples include using the telephone in drumming up support for a favorite charity (developing confidence and a businesslike telephone technique) and leadership positions in the PTA (developing a sense of authority and the ability to guide others).

Know the score

Gender bias lives, and, of course, you should omit all information that the employer isn't entitled to, including your age, marital status, physical condition, number and ages of children, and husband's name. Even though the law is on your side, in today's interview-rationed job market, why drag in facts on your resume that could stir up bias? Your resume's job is to open interview doors.

When you've been out of the job market for some years, you have to work harder and smarter to show that you're a hot hire. To help in your quest, seek out seminars and services offered to reentering women.

Selected home-based skills

Don't overlook skills that you may have acquired inside the home. Here are a few examples of occupations in which they can be used. This illustration assumes that you lack formal credentials for professional-level work. If you do have the credentials, upgrade the examples to the appropriate job level.

✔ **Juggling schedules:** Paraprofessional assistant to business executives or physicians, small service business operator, dispatching staff of technicians

✔ **Peer counseling:** Human resources department employee benefits assistant, substance abuse program manager

✔ **Arranging social events:** Party shop manager, nonprofit organization fundraiser, art gallery employee

✔ **Conflict resolution:** Administrative assistant, customer service representative, school secretary

✔ **Problem-solving:** Any job

✔ **Decorating:** Interior decorator, interior fabric shop salesperson

✔ **Nursing:** Medical or dental office assistant

✔ **Solid purchasing judgment:** Purchasing agent, merchandiser

✔ **Planning trips, relocations:** Travel agent, corporate employee relocation coordinator

✔ **Communicating:** Any job

✔ **Shaping budgets:** Office manager, department head, accounting clerk

✔ **Maximizing interior spaces:** Commercial-office real estate agent, business furniture store operator

Job Seekers with Disabilities

Millions of job seekers are protected by the *Americans with Disabilities Act* (ADA), which makes it illegal for an employer to refuse to hire (or to discriminate against) a person simply because that person has one or more disabilities.

ADA protection covers a wide spectrum of disabilities, including acquired immunodeficiency syndrome (AIDS) and human immunodeficiency virus (HIV), alcoholism, cancer, cerebral palsy, diabetes, emotional illness, epilepsy, hearing and speech disorders, heart disorders, learning disabilities (such as dyslexia), mental retardation, muscular dystrophy, and visual impairments. The Act does not cover conditions that impose short-term limitations, such as pregnancy or broken bones.

Generally, the ADA forbids employers that have more than 15 employees from doing the following:

✔ Discriminating on the basis of any physical or mental disability

✔ Asking job applicants questions about their past or current medical conditions

✔ Requiring applicants to take pre-employment medical exams

The ADA requires that an employer make reasonable accommodations for qualified individuals who have disabilities, unless doing so would cause the employer "undue hardship." The undue hardship provision is still open to interpretation by the courts.

If you have a disability that you believe is covered by the ADA, familiarize yourself with the law's specifics. The U.S. Department of Justice's ADA home page can be found at ada.gov. For even more information, call your member of Congress, visit your library, or obtain free comprehensive ADA guides and supporting materials from the splendid Web site maintained by the Job Accommodation Network (janweb.icdi.wvu.edu).

Deciding whether to disclose a disability

Do not disclose your disability on your resume. Remember, your objective is to get an interview. Save disclosure until a better time, if at all. Here are a couple of guidelines for deciding when and whether to disclose a disability:

✔ If your disability is visible, the best time to disclose it is after the interview has been set and you telephone to confirm the arrangements. Pass the message in an offhanded manner: "Because I use a wheelchair for mobility, can you suggest which entrance to your building would be the most convenient?" Alternatively, you may want to reserve disclosure for the interview.

✔ If your disability is not visible, such as mental illness or epilepsy, you need not disclose it unless you'll need special accommodations. Even then, you can hold the disclosure until the negotiating stage once you've received a potential job offer.

No matter what you decide to do, be confident, unapologetic, unimpaired, and attitude-positive.

Explaining gaps in work history

What can you do about gaps in your work history caused by disability? In years past, you may have been able to obscure the issue. No longer. New computer databases make it easy for suspicious employers to research your medical history. And with health insurance costs so high, they may do exactly that.

If your illness-related job history has so many gaps that it looks like a hockey player's teeth, I've never heard a better suggestion than writing "Illness and Recovery" next to the dates. It's honest, and the "recovery" part says, "I'm back and ready to work!"

If you have too many episodes of "missing teeth," your work history will look less shaky in a functional format, discussed in Chapter 5. Online resume discussion groups, which you can find through the Job Accommodation Network (`janweb.icdi.wvu.edu`), can serve as further sources of guidance on this difficult issue.

Asking for special equipment

If you need adaptive equipment, such as a special kind of telephone, I wouldn't mention it — even if the equipment is inexpensive or you're willing to buy it yourself. Instead, stick with the "time-release capsule" method of sharing information: Dribble out those revelations that may stifle interest in hiring you only when necessary. Never lose sight of your objective: to get an interview.

When Demotion Strikes

Kevin Allen (not his real name) was the district manager of five stores in a chain when he was demoted to manager of a single store. The higher-ups were sending him a message — they hoped he'd quit so that they could avoid awarding a severance package of benefits. Kevin ignored the message, retained a lawyer, kept his job, and started a job hunt after hours.

He finessed his resume by listing all the positions he had held in the chain, leaving out dates of when each started and stopped:

> **Demoting Store Chain, Big City**
>
> District Manager, 5 stores
>
> Store Manager, Windy City
>
> Store Assistant Manager, Sunny City
>
> Store Clerk, Sunny City

Throwing all of Kevin's titles into one big pot seemed a clever idea, but it didn't work for him. After a year of searching, Kevin got interviews, yes, but at every single face-to-face meeting, he was nailed with the same question: "Why were you demoted?" The interviewers' attitudes seemed accusatory, as if they'd been misled. Kevin failed to answer the question satisfactorily and didn't receive a single offer during a year's search. How did all the potential employers find out the truth?

Among obvious explanations: (A) Kevin worked in a "village" industry where people know each other and gossip. (B) Employers ordered credit checks on him; credit checks show employment details. (C) Employers authorized background checks.

No one knows what really happened, but in hindsight, Kevin may have done better had he accepted the message that the chain wanted him out, negotiated a favorable severance package that included good references, and quit immediately while his true title was that of district manager.

After two humiliating years of demotion status, Kevin took action by "crossing the Rubicon," an ancient Roman phrase that universities have adapted. It refers to those who seek a new beginning by returning to college for a law or business degree. Kevin enrolled in law school. (A happy ending: Twelve years later, Kevin is a happily employed attorney.)

In cases like Kevin's, a strategy that's forthright but doesn't flash your demotion in neon lights may work better than trying to cover up the demotion. Combine only two titles together, followed quickly by your accomplishments and strengths, as shown in Figure 10-3.

[dates] Demoting Company Name
Assistant Manager, Manager

As assistant manager, support the manager and carefully monitor detailed transactions with vendors, insuring maintenance of products and inventory; use skills in invoicing, billing, ordering, and purchasing. As manager, supervise all aspects of purchasing, display, and merchandise sales. Trained team of more than 30 employees in two-week period. Trained three assistant managers in essential functions of customers, employees, and finance. Increased sales revenues 25 percent in first six months.

Figure 10-3: Sample of combining a demotion with a higher position.

No matter how well you handle your resume entry, the reference of the demoting employer may ultimately end your chances of landing a new job that you want. In trying to mend fences, you may appeal to the demoting employer's fairness or go for guilt. Point out how hard you worked and how loyal you've been. Find reasons why your performance record was flawed. Ask for the commitment of a favorable reference and a downplaying of the demotion. If fairness or guilt appeals are denied, see an employment lawyer about sending the demoting employer, on law-firm letterhead, a warning against libel or slander.

The basic way to handle demotions throughout the job-hunting process is akin to how you handle being fired: by accentuating the positive contributions and results for which you are responsible. But being demoted is trickier to handle than being fired. Being fired no longer automatically suggests personal failure — but being demoted does.

Gaps in Your Record

Periods of unemployment leave black holes in your work history. Should you (A) fill them with positive expressions such as *family obligations,* (B) fill them with less positive but true words such as *unemployed,* or (C) show the gap without comment?

Choosing B, *unemployed,* is dreary. Forget that! Choosing C, *leave-it-blank-and-say-nothing,* often works — you just hope that it isn't noticed. My choice, however, is A: Tell the truth about what you were doing but sugarcoat it in a dignified, positive way. A few examples: *independent study, foreign travel, career renewal through study and assessment.*

An info-blizzard of tips has been published on how to repair resume holes. Unless you were building an underground tunnel to smuggle drugs, the principles are simple:

- Present the time gap as a positive event.

- Detail why it made you a better worker — not a better *person,* but a better worker with more favorable characteristics, polished skills, and mature understanding, all of which you're dying to contribute to your new employer.

How can these principles be applied? Take the case of a student who dropped out of college to play in a band and do odd jobs for four years before coming back to finish his biology degree and look for a job. The student knows that employers may perceive him as uncommitted. In the resume, he should treat the band years like any other job: Describe the skills that were polished as a band leader. Identify instances of problem-solving, teamwork, leadership, and budgeting.

You do the real problem-solving in the cover letter that accompanies such a resume. You might say something like this:

> *After completing two years of undergraduate study, it was necessary for me to work to continue my education. Using my talents as a musician, I organized a band and after four years was able to continue my education. I matured and learned much about the real world and confirmed that an education is extremely important in fulfilling my career goals.*

The consultant/entrepreneur gap

Professional and managerial job seekers are routinely advised to explain black holes by saying that they were consultants or that they owned small businesses. Not everyone can be a consultant, and there's substantial risk in the small-business explanation.

If it should happen to be true that you were a consultant, name your clients and give a glimmer of the contributions you made to each. If you really had a small business, remember: Employers worry that you'll be too independent to do things their way or that you'll stay just long enough to learn their business and go into competition against them.

Strategic antidotes: Search for a business owner who is within eyeshot of retirement and wouldn't mind your continuing the business and paying him or her a monthly pension.

Resume antidotes: Describe yourself as "manager," not "CEO" or "president," and if you have time, rename your business something other than your own name: "River's End Associates, Inc.," not "Theresa K. Bronz, Inc."

The chief mistake people make is assuming that a positive explanation won't sell. Instead, they fudge dates from legitimate jobs to cover the black holes. You may get away with it in the beginning. But ultimately, you'll be asked to sign a formal application — a legal document. When a company wishes to chop staff without paying severance benefits, the first thing that happens is an intense investigation of the company's database of application forms. People who lied on their applications can be sent out into the mean streets with nothing but their current paychecks on their backs.

Lying isn't worth the risk — it's a mistake.

Another method of papering-over glaring gaps is to include all your work under "Work History" and cite unpaid and volunteer work as well as paid jobs.

Suppose that you've been unemployed for the past year. That's a new black hole. Some advisers suggest the old dodge of allowing the recruiter to misperceive the open-ended date of employment for your last job: "2008–" as though you meant "2008@ndPresent." The open-ender solution often works — until you run into a reader who thinks that it's way too calculating.

Black holes are less obvious in a functional format, which I discuss in Chapter 5. In this final analysis, if you can't find a positive explanation for a black hole, say nothing.

If you possess a not-so-pristine past, stick with small employers who probably won't check every date on your resume.

Too Many Layoffs That Aren't Your Fault

Hard to believe, but good workers sometimes experience one layoff after another. One of my readers wrote that he'd experienced four no-fault severances within seven years.

When you've been to the chopping block a few too many times, explain the circumstances after each listing of the company name:

> Carol Interiors (company closed doors) . . . Salamander Furnishings (multirounds of downsizings) . . . Brandon Fine Furniture (company relocated out of town) . . . Kelly Fixture Co. (plant sold and moved overseas).

Offering brief explanations takes the blame from your shoulders — but I suppose that a cynic could think that you're a jinx.

Explaining Mergers and Acquisitions

A reader writes:

> *Upon graduating from college, I went to work for Company A. Several years later, Company A was acquired by Company B. More years passed, and Company B was acquired by Company C. Eventually, Company C merged with Company D, and as a result, after ten years with the four companies, I was laid off.*
>
> *My question is how best to handle this work history on my resume? I worked for four different corporate entities, with four different names, without ever changing jobs. Do I list all four on my resume? Or just the last one?*

Always try to show an upward track record — that you acquired new knowledge and skills, and just didn't just do the same thing over and over each year. And, you don't want the reader to assume that you worked for only one company that laid you off after a decade.

Taking these two factors into consideration, can you show correlation between your job titles and responsibilities with the changes in ownership? If yes, identify all four owners:

> Job title, Company D (formerly Company C), years
>
> Job title, Company C (formerly Company B), years
>
> Job title, Company B (formerly Company A), years
>
> Job title, Company A, years

If you can't show an upward track record that correlates with changes in ownership, just use the current owner name with a short explanation:

Job title, Company D, years
(Through a series of mergers and acquisitions, the entities for which I have worked since college graduation were known as Company A, Company B, and Company C.)

The reason for naming every entity is perception. Background and credit checks will turn up those company names, and if your resume doesn't mention them, it sends up a red flag for your potential employer!

Here a Job, There a Job, Everywhere a Job, Job

I once interviewed a man who had held 185 jobs over the course of his 20-year career, encompassing everything from dishwasher to circus clown and from truck driver to nursing aide. He wrote to me, not requesting resume advice, but to complain that a potential employer had the nerve to call him a *job hopper!*

Talk about an antiquated term: In the 21st century, the notion of job hopping is as far out of a reality circle as the concepts of job security, company loyalty, and a guaranteed company pension. The Great American Dumping Machine will continue to sack people who sometimes have to take virtually any job they can to survive.

Adding insult to injury, some employers cling to a double standard — hiring and firing employees like commodities, then looking with disfavor on applicants who have had a glut of jobs by circumstance, not by choice.

Overcoming a job-hopping image

Even when it wasn't at your initiative, holding five or more jobs in ten years can brand you as a job hopper. The fact that you're out of work now underscores that impression. Even employers who are guilty of round after round of employee dismissals instinctively flinch at candidates they perceive to be hopping around.

 Take pains to reverse that disapproval. When you draft your resume, post a list of negative perceptions on your desk; when you're finished writing, compare your resume with the list. Offer information that changes negative perceptions of you as a job hopper. The following list identifies perceptions employers often have of a job hopper and ways to counter them.

BEWARE

Omit interview-killer data

The best way to handle some land mines on your resume is to ignore them. Generally, revealing negative information on a resume is a mistake. Save troublemaking information for the all-important job interview, where you have a fighting chance to explain your side of things.

Stay away from these topics when constructing a resume:

- Firings, demotions, forced resignations, and early termination of contracts

- Personal differences with co-workers or supervisors

- Bankruptcy, tax evasion, or credit problems

- Criminal convictions or lawsuits

- Homelessness

- Illnesses from which you have now recovered

- Disabilities that do not prevent you from performing the essential functions of the job, with or without some form of accommodation

Should you ever give reasons for leaving a job? Almost never. In most instances, resume silence in the face of interview-killing facts is still the strategy of choice. But the time has come to rethink at least one special issue: losing a job.

Now that jobs are shed like so many autumn leaves, losing a job is no longer viewed as a case of personal failure. It may be to your advantage to state on your resume why you left your last position, assuming that it was not because of poor work performance on your part. If you were downsized out, the recruiter may appreciate your straightforward statement, "Job eliminated in downsizing."

A related circumstance is when it may appear that you were fired (job tanked quickly, for instance) but you really were not fired, or the employer agreed to say you were laid off, it is acceptable to add "Layoff" after the date of employment — *3/2008 to 5/23/2009 (Layoff).*

But remember, if you elect to say why you lost one job, for consistency, you have to say why you left all your jobs — such as for greater opportunity or advancement.

Perception	Counter
Is disloyal and self-focused	Perfect attendance, volunteer office gift collector
Will split in a blink for a better offer and take company secrets along	Competition of projects
Doesn't know what he/she wants and is never satisfied	Diverse background that promoted impressive results

After checking for damage control, go back and review your resume for accomplishments that enhance your image, such as the following:

- ✔ **A fast learner:** Give examples of how your skills aren't company-specific and you rapidly adjust to new environments.

- ✔ **A high achiever:** Show favored skills much courted by headhunters, and at end of each job mention, put "Recruited for advanced position."

- ✔ **A quick adapter:** Mention examples of agreeable flexibility in adjusting to new ideas, technology, and position requirements.

- ✔ **A relationship builder:** List praise from co-workers for commitment to team success.

If your current joblessness comes after a background that a quick-change artist would admire, use your resume to prepare the way to acceptance. Emphasize project completion and career progression, using years not months. If you still have trouble landing interviews, use positive statements in your cover letter to tackle your history.

Cleaning out your job closet

Large numbers of people have to write resumes that explain holding too many jobs in too short a time. The harsh realities of business may force you to detour from a single career path to alternative tracks where you can acquire new skills and experiences, even if they're not skills and experiences of choice. If so, you need serious creative (but truthful) writing to keep your resume focused on the work history that is relevant for the next job sought.

Use these workarounds when you find that you have too many jobs in your history:

- ✔ Start by referring to your *diversified* or *skills-building* background.

- ✔ Use a functional or hybrid resume format (see Chapter 5) and present *only your experience relevant to the job you seek.*

- ✔ Alternatively, you can list jobs relating to the position you now seek first under "Relevant Work Experience" and cluster the nonrelevant jobs under "Other Good Work Experience."

- ✔ Express your work history in years, not months and years.

When Substance Abuse Is the Problem

Substance abuse is a disability under the Americans with Disabilities Act. If you're recovered from the addiction, you're entitled to all the Act's protections. If you're still abusing a substance, such as alcohol or illegal narcotics, you're not covered by the Act. Don't disclose previous substance abuse on your resume.

Cover gaps in your work history with the *Illness and Recovery* statement (see the "Job Seekers with Disabilities" section earlier in this chapter) or simply don't address the issue at all.

Be careful when deciding which information you put on a job application — remember that it's a legal form and that lies can come back to haunt you (see the "Gaps in Your Record" section earlier in this chapter).

If you were ever arrested for smoking pot or being intoxicated — even once in your life — the fact may surface to damage your employment chances. Asking about arrest records is illegal, but a few private database companies don't let that stop them — they compile electronic databases of such arrest information and sell them to any employer who will buy.

Avoid mentioning booze or drugs, be careful about application forms, and be honest at interviews — *if* you have recovered or *if* the experience was a brief fling or two.

If you're still held prisoner by a chronic, destructive, or debilitating overuse of a chemical substance that interferes with your life or employment, no resume tweaks will benefit you. Get help for your addiction.

A Bad Credit Rap

Job seekers who won't be handling money are surprised that employers may routinely check credit records. Credit histories — called *consumer reports* — hold much more than payment history. A consumer report contains data from names of previous employers and residential stability to divorces and estimated prior earnings.

Employers are wary of hiring people awash in debt because they fear that stress will impact job performance or that you have inadequate management skills or even that you may have sticky fingers with the company's funds.

Consumer reports have serious implications for students who graduate with sky-high education loans and credit card balances, especially if they or their families have missed payments. Divorced individuals may have interview-killing credit problems caused by the split-up and never know why their resumes aren't delivering interviews.

Among consumer protections against unfair credit treatment is the require-ment that employers must get your permission in a stand-alone document to check your credit (Fair Credit Reporting Act) — no blending the request into fine print in the employment application.

After an employer receives a report on you — but before any adverse action is taken, such as rejecting your application for a job — the employer must give you a free copy of the report with related legal documents. Receiving a copy of the documents gives you a chance to correct mistakes and clean up your credit record if you can.

Background checks are even more invasive than credit reports. They include records for driving infractions, court and incarceration histories, workers' compensation, medical histories, drug testing, and more. For details, visit The Privacy Rights Clearinghouse (`privacyrights.org` — search on Background Checks).

Ex-Offenders Job Hunting

Each year nearly 650,000 individuals leave state and local prisons for the free world. Another 11 million individuals yearly circulate in and out of American jails and detention centers at the city and county levels. If you're one of these people, this book can help you — especially when it comes to meeting the new need to customize your resume to a job or to the career field (described in Chapter 1) — but you need specialized help of the type that I describe at the end of this section.

Know that negative information is dangerous

Always remember that the purpose of your resume is to get a job interview. Your resume is not the place to confess your sins, accentuate your weaknesses, or lie about yourself. Make sure your resume is future-oriented and employer-centered. Use your resume to clearly communicate to employers what it is that you can do for them. Issues concerning your criminal record are best dealt with during the job interview.

Avoid the chronological format

The reverse chronological format (Chapter 5) is not your friend. This format, with its ordering of employers and dates, tends to point up the two major weaknesses of ex-offenders — limited work experience and major employment time gaps. Instead, choose a functional or hybrid combination format (Chapter 5) that emphasizes your qualifications as they relate to the job you seek — skills, competencies. and personal qualities.

Present your prison experience in nonprison terms

If you acquired education, training, and work experience in prison, be careful how you list that experience on your resume. Instead of saying that you worked at "Kentucky State Prison," say you worked for the "State of Kentucky." Both statements are truthful, but the first statement immediately raises a red flag that can prematurely screen you out before you get an interview.

Get help with your resume and job search

Unless you have strong analytical and writing skills, reach out for help from a local nonprofit group that functions to assist ex-offenders in writing resumes and finding jobs.

You also can hire a professional resume writer; find one at any of these three organizations: parw.com, prwra.com, or nrwaweb.com. To check out other re-entry resources in all 50 states, jump online to this gateway site: hire network.org/resource.html. Still other resume and job search information related to ex-offenders is offered on exoffenderreentry.com.

To find the depth of advice you need for your specialized situation, I highly recommend the following books published by Impact Publications (impact publications.com):

- ✔ *Best Resumes and Letters for Ex-Offenders,* by Wendy Enelow and Ron Krannich
- ✔ *The Ex-Offenders' Job Hunting Guide,* by Ron and Caryl Krannich
- ✔ *The Ex-Offender's Quick Job Hunting Guide,* by Ron and Caryl Krannich

Look for Ways to Scoot Past Resume Blocks

As you find out in this chapter, it's not always possible to move directly from start to finish of a successful job search with a single resume strategy. I suggest some solutions to difficult resume situations but may not have addressed your specific concern. If not, use the illustrations here to inspire a creative solution to your difficulty that doesn't rely on telling lies.

Need encouragement? Michael Jordan, widely considered to be the greatest player in the history of basketball, has a few words to say about the very kinds of obstacles you may face in creating a great resume on your way to a job interview:

> *Obstacles don't have to stop you. If you run into a wall, don't turn around and give up. Figure out how to climb it, go through it, or work around it.*

Part III

Bringing It All Together: Sample OnTarget Resumes

The 5th Wave   By Rich Tennant

"Your resume won me over. Not many people can list looting and pillaging as a transferable skill."

In this part . . .

Nearly 50 sample resumes show you what an OnTarget resume looks like. In this part, I show you how to use the strategies I tell you about throughout the book to create your most effective resumes.

Chapter 11

A Sampling of OnTarget Resumes by Industry and Career Field

No skeletons in your work history? No problems? If you're as perfect as they come, this is your kind of chapter. The sample resumes here reflect the job market by type of expertise and work skills being recruited or offered.

A box atop each sample resume contains a mission statement — that is, what the job seeker aims to accomplish, which usually is a better job. The mission statement also includes the requirements for a specific position — or a summary of the typically requested requirements for an occupation or career field. You may be surprised that the requirements have numbers. And that the numbers are cross-matched to qualifications in the resume. Does this mean you are supposed to put numbers on your resumes as these samples show? The answer is: No! No! A thousand times no!

The cross-matched numbers between a job's requirements and the candidate's qualifications shown here are for just for illustration, *not for your actual resumes.*

These samples are intended to laser your attention to requirement-and-qualification matching, the single most important factor in causing your candidacy to get noticed in an online swarm of resumes.

Sales. <u>Sales Representative</u>. Reverse chronological. College grad seeks Manufacturer's Representative position in home theater/electronics equipment industry. Requirements: Bachelor's Degree,[1] 3-5 years in consultative sales,[2] relationship development skills,[3] product knowledge,[4] and experience in sales management.[5]

CHARLES A. TRENTON

3256 Mountain Way • Detroit, MI 48201
Cell: (555) 999-9999 • Email: catrenton@gmail.com

OBJECTIVE: SALES CONSULTANT – HOME THEATER/ELECTRONICS

SYSTEM EXPERTISE

Audio Formats[4]– Dolby Digital, Dolby Pro Logic II, and DTS; encoding surround sound.

Media Formats[4]– Introduce home theater systems with integrated video and audio sources such as HD (720p, 1080i, 1080p) and Standard (480p) video, DVD-Jukebox (Fireball) systems, Hard-Drive based (Kaleidoscope) systems and AV distribution including Cable, Satellite, WiFi, Bluetooth and Cat5e (Control-4, Elan).

Speaker Recommendations[4]– Satellite, center channel and subwoofers to achieve optimum sound. Advise on room placement to achieve maximum sound experience.

Sound Engineering License – Omega Studio, Detroit, Mich. [date]

SALES EXPERIENCE

Supreme Home Theater and Audio, Detroit, Mich.

SENIOR AUDIO VIDEO CONSULTANT – SYSTEM DESIGNER [dates][2]

- Identify and analyze customer's home theater project interests and budget, understanding and anticipating needs and wants and recommending appropriate products and systems.[3] Discover unrealized music, home theater, and projection interests to grow sale.
- Build customer relationships based on trust;[3] personally manage sale and installation coordination.
- Develop innovative approaches to sales, such as demonstration CDs, to feature audio and visual equipment, resulting in increased enthusiasm and commitment to total quality system.
- Prepare and present sales proposals to decision makers and negotiate purchase agreement.

SYSTEM DESIGNER [dates]

- Member, architect/interior design team, planning total installation of new and renovated homes.
- Conducted site inspections, including planning wiring, special construction and cabinetry.
- Designed whole-house audio and video networking solutions and home automation, including lighting, security, CCTV and HVAC control.
- Developed relationships with architects, general contractors, builders and interior designers.

SALES MANAGER, AUDIO VIDEO CONSULTANT – SYSTEM DESIGNER [dates]

- Drove strategic business initiatives and managed daily operations.[5] Set standards and trained staff on customer assessments, product knowledge and introduction, sales techniques, relationship development and demo presentations.
- Motivated and mentored sales team on current technology and advanced applications.

Sales Accomplishments: Beat quota by 5-25% annually, increasing gross sales totals by $100,000+ per year for year-on-year growth. Top seller for [year] and [year]; Number 2 for [year].

Piano Town, Chicago, Ill. [dates]
SALES CONSULTANT – RETAIL SALES. Achieved 105-135% of sales quota in keyboard department.

EDUCATION: B.A.,[1] **Psychology,** Wayne State University, Detroit, Mich., [date]

Healthcare. Medical Technologist. Reverse chronological. Medical Technologist I seeks level II position. Requirements: Bachelor's degree in Medical Technology, Biology, or Clinical Laboratory Sciences,[1] 2-4 years' experience in clinical laboratory setting,[2] and excellent computer, verbal and written communication skills.[3]

CELESTE PEREZ

9084 Robinson Road • San Francisco, CA 94107
Cellular: 777-222-5757 • Email: celesteperez@yahoo.com

PROFILE: Dedicated **Medical Technologist** with over 3 years' experience.[2] Skilled in clinical laboratory methodology and activities, including performing complex analyses using sophisticated instruments and good judgement. Strong computer proficiencies, with excellent communication skills.[3] Customer service focused, with polished interpersonal skills. Organized and detail-oriented; reliable and able to take the initiative. Energetic and hardworking; able to work well under pressure.

~ **B.S.,**[1] Medical Technology, San Francisco State University, San Francisco, Calif. [date] ~

Completed six-week rotation, performing all aspects of analytical testing within clinical laboratory sections, including Blood Bank, Hematology, Microbiology, and Chemistry.

PROFESSIONAL EXPERIENCE

Medical Technologist I
LabCenter, San Francisco, Calif.   [dates]

- Specimen Testing: Perform complex qualitative and quantitative immunochemistry analyses and testing; prepare detailed reports summarizing findings. Anticipate and plan work to complete assigned tasks in allotted time. Ensure compliance with company policies, as well as federal, state, and local regulations. (Also possess 2 years' experience conducting virology assays.)

- Quality Control/Troubleshooting: Perform and document all instrument checks and quality control tests. Conduct daily preventative maintenance and troubleshooting; recognize, analyze, and take corrective action to resolve instrument and clinical testing problems. Contact manufacturers' technical service departments to troubleshoot and correct equipment problems, as needed. Assist co-workers in resolving similar problems.

- Administration: Perform clerical functions associated with designated laboratory area. Review reports for clerical accuracy and clinical indications, help maintain files, and accurately input results into computer database. Track inventory and reagent use; request supplies from supervisor on weekly basis.

- Training: Attend and participate in regular department staff meetings and volunteer for cross-training. Train other laboratory personnel and students within designated area.

Accomplishments:

- Consistently receive highest rating on quarterly and annual reviews. Contributed to achievement of annual laboratory goals and objectives; awarded bonus.

- Volunteered to attend week-long new equipment training; upon return, trained select group of employees on new procedures and machinery.

- Routinely volunteer to work hard-to-cover shifts.

Project Management. Construction Project Manager. Reverse chronological. Seeks position with commercial building firm. Requirements: 5-7 years' construction experience,[1] B.S. degree in Construction Sciences or Engineering,[2] stable employment background [3] and proficiency in estimating and project management software.[4]

CASEY DAVIS

5050 Bellevue Circle
Orlando, FL 32801

(888) 444-5656
e-mail: davis_c@earthlink.net

CONSTRUCTION PROJECT MANAGER

• Project Scheduling	• Historic Building Renovation
• Value Engineering	• Planning and Budgeting
• Regulatory Compliance	• Contract Negotiation

OBJECTIVE: Project Manager – Commercial

SUMMARY OF QUALIFICATIONS

Over 7 years of success in managing multi-million dollar building construction and renovation projects from inception through occupancy.[1] Recent experience includes restorations and renovations of historic and public buildings, as well as new construction. Skilled in managing multiple projects simultaneously. Adept at working with engineers, architects, subcontractors, and field superintendents to coordinate activities and solve problems. Skilled in developing spreadsheet cost estimates, budgets, and project schedules using Master Builder, Primavera P3, MS Project, and MS Excel.[4] Supervisory experience includes functional supervision of subcontractors, field superintendents, and diverse workforce. Stable, upward job record.[3]

WORK EXPERIENCE

Construction Project Manager

Bauer Craig Becker Edwards, Inc., Tallahassee, Fl.   [dates]

Manage multi-million dollar building construction and renovation projects from inception through occupancy. Direct projects and ensure on-schedule completion within or below budget to meet contractual obligations.

- Define scope of work and review and interpret design specifications, and plans. Organize, plan, and conduct meetings with engineers, architects, and owners using tact and diplomacy.
- Forecast project costs and budget. Establish man-hour production rates, and crew requirements. Perform quantity take-off and material pricing.
- Solicit/review subcontractor proposals and ongoing project change orders with company executives and execute contractual agreements.
- Prepare job schedule for each phase of construction, order, and schedule material deliveries.
- Inspect workmanship for adherence to design specifications and quality standards. Ensure compliance with federal and state health and safety laws and regulations (OSHA), recognition/mitigation of HAZMAT, and company safety policies.
- Perform monthly project billing and final project closeout.

Recent Accomplishments:
- Tallahassee Community College Nursing School, $15M, 24-month project
- Leon County Public Parking Garage #5, $5M, 6-month project
- Florida State House of Delegates, $10M, 12-month project
- Florida State Central Services Facility, $12M, 18-month project

Facilities Construction Contract Compliance Inspector
Larmore County Government, Growth and Environmental Management, Tallahassee, Fl.   [dates]

With minimal direct supervision, monitored various facility contracts and vendors to ensure delivery of services and completion of tasks. Worked on a team to complete construction projects effectively.
- Evaluated scope and duration of work requests to produce legal agreements/permits. Reviewed blueprints to answer technical questions and produce takeoffs.
- Identified, researched, and resolved complex problems, and recommended and implemented solutions. Answered questions regarding bids, proposals, and contracts.
- Communicated effectively with the public, County Attorney, Structural Engineers, and other professional staff. Conducted pre-bid conferences; reviewed certificates of insurance and performance bonds. Inspected sites for completion of work and authorized release of bond documents.

Housing Inspector
Larmore County Government, Growth and Environmental Management, Tallahassee, Fl.   [dates]

Inspected privately-owned single and multi-family properties for HUD compliance.
- Determined fair market values. Estimated property damages in preparation for claims.
- Used effective interpersonal communications to defuse tense landlord/tenant situations.

Tradesworker II
Larmore County Government, Growth and Environmental Management, Tallahassee, Fl.   [dates]

Coordinated and instructed trades helpers on how and why of specific assignments.
- Estimated labor, equipment, and materials needed to accomplish structural renovations/repairs.
- Constructed, altered, and repaired structures where accuracy, space, and fit were essential, and structural soundness and appearance were meaningful.
- Read, interpreted, and applied complex building plans, specifications, blueprints, sketches, and building codes.

EDUCATION

B.S.,[2] Construction Engineering Technology, Florida A & M University, Tallahassee, Fl.   [date]

PROFESSIONAL TRAINING

Scaffold Training Institute, Scaffold User certification   [date]
Construction Specification Institute; Documents Technology certificate   [date]
American Management Association; Facilities Management certificate   [date]

Nursing. Nurse R.N. Reverse chronological. Healthcare professional seeks advancement. Requirements: current appropriate R.N. licensure,[1] graduate of accredited School of Nursing,[2] minimum of one-year medical-surgical nursing and hemodialysis experience,[3] ability to assist in lifting patients and equipment,[4] and ability to provide coverage at area facilities during times of short staffing.[5]

SOPHIE McCALL, R.N. [1]

50010 Broad Boulevard • St. Paul, MN 55101
Residence: 333-777-3434 • Cell: 333-444-1010 • Email: nursesophie@hotmail.com

PROFILE: Dedicated **Nurse R.N.** [1] with over 11 years' medical experience providing superior clinical care to broad-based patient populations. Skilled leader and team-member, able to maintain positive attitude and productive work environment.[5] Strong interpersonal, administrative and patient/family education skills. Demonstrated ability to establish trust, emote genuine patient caring, and manage crisis situations. Highly organized and able to efficiently prioritize multiple tasks. Able to lift 60 lbs. [4]

PROFESSIONAL EXPERIENCE

Charge Nurse/Clinical Nurse

Med-Surg/Renal Unit,[3] Medical Care North America, St. Paul, Minn.   [dates]

- Provide specialized care for renal patients on 32-bed unit on human dialysis floor. Rotate as charge nurse, overseeing staff members (LPNs, NAs, Nurse Extenders, and Unit Secretaries) and participating in team/unit meetings.
- Conduct patient assessments, and develop, implement, and evaluate individualized care plans. Provide appropriate care and achieve patient outcomes by combining patient involvement and education into total care plan. Adjust treatment plan as needed.
- Perform technical aspects of hemodialysis,[3] assessing and documenting response to therapy. Administer medications, monitor patient progress, develop discharge plans, provide health and nutrition education, and maintain charts and documentation.
- Key team member of unit study project to assess quality of patient care. Analyzed 12 months of patient records to review care, treatment plan, and outcome. Drafted revised policies to improve care and ensure best practices.

Staff Nurse/Charge Nurse

Medical Specialty Unit, Oakdale Rehabilitation Center, Oakdale, Minn.   [dates]

- On 28-bed subacute care unit, rotated as charge nurse. Scheduled and supervised staff.
- Provided primary nursing care and educated patients and family. Assessed patients; developed and implemented treatment plans. Performed variety of procedures and treatments including paritometrial dialysis, ventilator care, central lines and IV therapy.
- Administered medications and monitored patient response. Maintained charts and worked with other healthcare professionals to provide total quality care.

Charge Nurse

Valley Creek Convalescent Center, Woodbury, Minn.   [dates]

- Oversaw all phases of night shift clinical care on 46-bed specialized care unit. Scheduled and supervised LPNs and Nursing Assistants.

EDUCATION

B.S.,[2] Nursing, College of St. Catherine, School of Nursing, St. Paul, Minn.   [dates]

Accounting. Civilian Pay Technician. Reverse chronological. Candidate seeks more challenging accounting work. Requirements: 5+ years of accounting experience,[1] 1-2 years of business school or accounting training,[2] proficiency in Excel, Word, Outlook and PowerPoint,[3] strong analytical skills and attention to detail,[4] and verbal and written communication skills.[5]

SHANNON BRODY

61 South Bend Road • Dayton, OH 45420-1472
(777) 683-5614 • shannonb@brody.net

OBJECTIVE: Staff Accountant

SKILLS SUMMARY: Customer-focused accounting professional with over 10 years of experience maintaining employee payroll accounts and managing billing and accounts receivables.[1] Effective troubleshooter and researcher with exceptional verbal and written communication skills.[5] Detail-oriented with strong analytical skills [4] and ability to produce quality work under strict deadlines. Associate of Science, Accounting[2] The Ohio University, Athens, Ohio, [date].

COMPUTER SKILLS: SAP Business One, Exact Finances, and several other accounting and reporting systems. MS Word, Excel, Outlook, PowerPoint;[3] Remedy Problem Management Software.

PROFESSIONAL EXPERIENCE

Defense Finance Accounting Agency (DFAS), Dayton, Ohio   [dates]

Civilian Pay Technician   [dates]
- Managed payroll accounts under Defense Civilian Pay System for 200 employees; verified employee timesheet information was correctly entered on-time for bi-weekly payroll. Assured pay stubs and yearly tax information. Updated records and tax information.
- Determined validity of timekeeping debts and prepared letters to notify employees of indebtedness and mandatory involuntary deduction based on debt regulations. Complied and evaluated reports for data accuracy and made necessary adjustments.
- Responded to questions and provided payroll information to state taxing authorities, attorneys, family courts, employees and human resources staff. Assigned to call center for two years; effectively responded to numerous inbound customer service requests.

Accounting Technician   [dates]
- Received, sorted, processed and coded accounting documents, including invoices and checks. Prepared vouchers, invoices, checks, account statements, and reports for accounts receivable and payable. Produced batch control worksheets, processed voucher copies according to appropriation, and maintained monthly reports. Prepared financial statements, journal entries, month-end close, and collection vouchers.
- Matched hard copy accounting documents to automated system transmittals; identified and corrected erroneous transactions. Researched and reconciled incomplete accounting data and requested additional supporting documentation when needed; filed completed cases.
- Monitored budget activity, utilizing Merged Accountability Funds Reporting (MAFR) system and Excel spreadsheets to input and track billing information.

Supply Chain. <u>Production/Logistics Manager</u>. Reverse chronological. Seeking Supply Chain Manager Position. Requirements: 7-10 years' experience in Supply Chain Management: Distribution, Logistics, Transportation.[1] Previous experience in multi-site industrial or consumer products manufacturing,[2] solid track record of cost reduction and productivity improvement,[3] project management experience,[4] excellent leadership and communication and negotiating skills.[5] Degree required, MBA and/or Six Sigma Black Belt preferred.[6]

PAUL A. BUTLER

408 Grendel Road • Nashville, TN 37013
Residence: 111-777-1010 • Email: <u>pabutler@verizon.net</u>

SUPPLY CHAIN MANAGER

Distribution ~ Production Planning ~ Logistics Manager

PROFILE: Over 9 years' supervisory and managerial experience in **operations, warehouse, supply chain management** and **distribution** environments.[1] Proven track record of managing and improving operations and logistics for multi-million dollar entities, applying strong analytical skills and innovative and successful problem resolution expertise. Experienced in contract management and negotiations [5] and building vendor relationships. Outstanding budget management skills. Results-oriented leader with excellent communication and motivational skills.[5] Able to develop staff and build productive teams. Certified PMP;[4] Six Sigma Black Belt.[6] **B.S.,**[6] Business Administration, University of Tennessee, [date].

PRODUCTION & DISTRIBUTION EXPERIENCE

VITAMIN PRODUCTS, INC.   [dates]

Manage and coordinate complete production and delivery cycle for medical foods company,[2] *producing up to 10,000 cases of liquid and 500,000 units dry per cycle.*

Manager, Production & Logistics   Brentwood, Tenn. [dates]

- Production Planning: Track and analyze raw materials and finished goods inventory at third-party production facility and at local distribution warehouse. Coordinate production cycles. Assess vendors' proposals best value. Procure raw components from vendors.
- Vendor/Production Oversight: Assure vendors meet Good Manufacturing Practices. Conduct post-production review of product to ensure quality, as well as analyze production losses and causes. Assure labeling and packing integrity.
- Transportation/Logistics Management: Coordinate delivery of product to customers, distributors and local warehouse.

Key Accomplishments:
- Created significant cost reduction: reduced overall production costs by 8.5%, transportation costs by 4%, and packaging costs by 4.5%.[3]

PAUL A. BUTLER, page 2   111-777-1010

BIG BOX ELECTRONICS, INC.   [dates]

Held a series of increasingly responsible positions at the nation's largest electronics retailer. [2]

General Manager   Mt. Juliet, Tenn. [dates]

- Managed 280,000 sq. ft. warehouse with full $18M P & L annual responsibility.
- Supervised 30+ employees. Trained management staff in procedures and policy implementation.
- Controlled costs by continually analyzing and streamlining operations procedures.
- Directed transportation contracts for replenishment carriers and home delivery service.
- Developed and maintained close working relationships with retail partners.

Key Accomplishments:
- Successfully managed $26M inventory by instituting audit processes.
- Consistently surpassed inventory budget expectations; facility-wide bonuses awarded.
- Increased productivity by 18% by instituting performance metrics to monitor activity. [3]
- Developed customer service standards with peer manager to create regional standards, improving customer services, resulting in increased customer loyalty.

General Manager   Deptford, N.J. [dates]

- Opened new market, third-party distribution facility; responsible for $10M annual P & L.
- Managed third-party logistics operations contract, including warehousing, store replenishment and home delivery; controlled contract costs.

Key Accomplishments:
- Developed and implemented audit processes to ensure accurate management of company's $17M inventory by third-party warehouse company.
- Consistently came in below budget on inventory; awarded bonuses.

Warehouse Supervisor   Madison, Tenn. [dates]

- Oversaw and directed daily warehouse operations, including preparation of shipments to 32 retail stores and 375 home delivery customers, with $26M inventory.
- Supervised warehouse staff of 20, in an 180,000 sq. ft. facility.

Key Accomplishment:
- Developed and instituted consistent procedures and policies to improve processes.

TENNESSEE COURIER SERVICE   Nashville, Tenn. [dates]

Distribution Coordinator
- Directed 30 carriers and routing of 300 packages and consignments for priority morning delivery. Trained couriers and drivers; participated in review and discipline process.

COMPUTER PROFICIENCIES: MS Word, Excel, Outlook, PowerPoint, Access, SAP

Banking. Bank Manager. Reverse Chronological. Career progression to bank manager; now seeks position as VP in larger bank or regional manager. Requirements: 5-7 years branch management experience,[1] extensive knowledge of operations and lending,[2] customer service managment,[3] staff development and training,[4] and business marketing and development.[5]

CLAUDIA RAMOS

1405 Bishop Dr. • Highland Park, IL 21702
Residence: 777-202-2323 • Cellular: 222-555-8989

BANK FINANCIAL/OPERATIONS MANAGER

Over 15 years' banking experience. Demonstrated competence in branch management,[1] staff recruitment and training, community relations, and business development.[4] Promoted 3 times in 4 years. Strong customer service and communications skills,[3] with keen ability to build relationships with diverse clients. Noted excellence in financial operations[2] and administration. Creative and resourceful in community relationships and marketing.[5] Grew new business portfolio 300% in 3 years. Professional and motivated, with strengths in problem resolution, team building, and research and analysis. Bilingual: English and Spanish. Over 300 hours of banking and management classes and 2 years' undergraduate studies. PC proficient.

PROFESSIONAL EXPERIENCE

PROVIDENT BANK, Highland Park, Ill.   [dates]
Branch Manager [dates]; [1]
Customer Relations Manager [dates]; **Head Teller** [dates]

- *As Branch Manager,* direct operational, service, and administrative activities of branch. Lead staff of 20 in providing customer service and financial care.[3] Manage:
  - HR tasks, including hiring, coaching, training, and performance management.[4] Compliance with all policies and procedures; fraud control; loss prevention.
  - Procurement, service contract administration, and technology issues; action plans to improve controls, mitigate losses, and ensure superior client experience.
  - Overall branch performance and financial reports/analyses; sub-ledger, general ledger, and cash reconciliation.

- *As Customer Relations Manager,* opened new accounts, sold numerous bank services, resolved customer issues. Trained and supervised Customer Service Representatives.

- *As Head Teller,* interviewed, trained, and supervised daily functions of tellers. Ordered and received cash.

Recognition:
- Outstanding Performance Award, [date]; Employee of the Month Award, [date]; Outstanding Performance, [date]; Certificate of Excellence, [date]; Outstanding Performance Award,[date].

WACHOVIA BANK, Highwood, Ill.   [dates]
Financial Services Representative

- Opened retail and commercial accounts, including savings, checking, IRA, CDs, and Keoghs. Exceeded new account goals by 36%. Improved customer service satisfaction by 16%.

Office Work. Administrative Assistant. Hybrid. College graduate seeks Executive Assistant position in chemical industry. Requirements: Bachelor's Degree,[1] 3-5 years in responsible administrative role for chemical manufacturer,[2] strong computer skills,[3] excellent written and verbal communication skills.[4]

ERIN KINGSTON

1510 Franklin Drive
Phone: 443.555.8989   Baltimore, MD 21237   emkingston@aol.com

ADMINISTRATIVE/OPERATIONS ASSISTANT

Highly-motivated, personable Administrative Professional with over 3 years' experience in chemical industry.[2] Recognized for enhancing productivity through exemplary operational, client service, and sales support. Efficient with exceptional time management, problem-solving, and analytical skills. Very strong oral communication[4] and interpersonal skills. Flexible and adaptable to changing priorities.

CORE STRENGTHS
- **Administrative Operations:** Special event, meeting, and travel logistics; correspondence, file, records, and database management; project administration and executive-level support.
- **Sales Support:** Client service, accounts management, problem trouble-shooting and resolution; contract administration, order review, and shipping management; sales tracking and reporting.
- **Communications:** Polished telephone skills. Experienced business writer, proofreader, and editor.[4]
- **Financial/Budget Administration:** Budget oversight, invoice verification, and expense tracking; purchasing, supply, and inventory management.
- **Computer Expertise:** Skilled in creating reports, spreadsheets, presentations, and graphs. Proficient in MS Windows, Word, Excel, PowerPoint, and Outlook.[3]

PROFESSIONAL EXPERIENCE

ADMINISTRATIVE ASSISTANT, BioProducts, Inc. - Columbia, Maryland   [dates]

Provide high level of administrative, sales operations, and client service support for leading manufacturer and supplier of biopesticides and chemical pesticides. Directly support VP of Sales and Marketing and 19 regional sales managers and field development researchers. After 2 months, promoted to permanent position.
- **Administrative Support:** Effectively orchestrate a full range of strategic administrative functions, including correspondence and publications management; database and file management; travel, special events, and meeting planning; and general purchasing/budget oversight. Create scientific/technical PowerPoint presentations, spreadsheets, graphs, and reports for managers.
- **Sales, Operations & Customer Service:** Direct liaison between customers and sales. Field 20+ calls per day for product and order information. Input domestic sales orders into database, updating contracts, pricing information, and customer account data. Schedule and track shipments; troubleshoot problems. Conduct operations and management process analyses.

Accomplishments:
- Independently developed new sales report/pivot table, now company's primary tracking tool.
- Developed and implemented a linked paper-and computer-based filing system, incorporating an Excel spreadsheet, to provide fast and easy access to new product and regulatory information.

ADDITIONAL WORK EXPERIENCE

Target, Ellicott City, Maryland **-** Backroom Stocker/Flow/Replenishment.   [dates]
Kohl's, Ellicott City, Maryland **-** Overnight Sales Floor Stocker.   [dates]

EDUCATION & TRAINING

B.A.,[1] History, University of Maryland Baltimore County, Baltimore, Maryland.   [date]

Information Technology. Information Technology Help Desk Analyst. Hybrid. Recent MBA graduate with sales and IT experience seeks Technical Sales Analyst position. Requirements: Bachelor's Degree,[1] 1-2 years IT experience and/or training,[2] excellent customer service skills, knowledge of Microsoft Access, Word, mail merge, Excel, Internet and graphic design,[3] and excellent oral and written communication skills.[4]

WILLIAM J. FRANKLIN, JR.

billjfranklin@comcast.net

300 Frederick Road, Apt. 2C
Catonsville, MD 21228

Home: (888) 888-1212
Cell: (888) 777-3434

OBJECTIVE: Technical Sales Analyst, Solimar Systems, Inc.

QUALIFICATIONS SUMMARY

Accomplished technical marketing and sales value for employer with over two years' progressively responsible experience in sales, customer support, and end-user training for telecommunications technologies and services.[2] Strong technical background with proven success building and managing customer relationships with major corporate and government clients. Keen problem solving, analytical, and negotiation skills. Excellent presentation and oral/written communications skills.[4] BS Marketing degree.[1]

Business, marketing, sales, & technology expertise:

➢ Business Development, Client Relationship Management, & Needs Assessment
➢ Competitive Product Positioning, Technical Support & Troubleshooting, Technology Training
➢ Strategic Alliances, Government & Corporate Partnerships
➢ Strategic Sales & Marketing Planning/Research, Presentations, & New Product Launch
➢ Managing Vendor/Supplier Relationships
➢ Statistical Analyses, Graphical Presentation of Data, & Competitive Benchmarking
➢ Wireless Voice and Data Communications, including Pagers, PDAs, and BlackBerry Products
➢ PC hardware, Software & Peripheral devices, including all Microsoft applications

PROFESSIONAL EXPERIENCE

Help Desk IT Analyst
NET SOLUTIONS, INC. International Unit, Washington, D.C.   [dates]

Provide first tier end-user technical support via telephone to over 8,000 staff. Assist and resolve complex technical issues and questions on Lotus Notes; MS Office XP; remote access; BlackBerry devices; and other internal software applications. Conduct remote diagnostics to troubleshoot and resolve desktop application issues.

Accomplishment:
➢ Currently facilitating seamless migration of windows 2000 Enterprise Desktop (ED3) to XP (ED4) and Lotus Notes R5 to Notes ND6 with virtually no interruption to workflow.

SPRINT COMMUNICATIONS, Vienna, Va.   [dates]

Fast-track promotion through positions of increasing challenge and responsibility, based on consistently strong performance in sales support, account management and technical support of multi-million dollar wireless technology contracts with Fortune 1000 companies and federal government agencies, including the Department of Defense, the CIA, and the Federal Energy Regulatory Commission.

William J. Franklin, Jr. ~ Cell: (888) 777-3434

National Account Sales Consultant [dates]

Established and fostered relationships with government and corporate clients to promote integrated wireless data and messaging services, including pagers, PDAs, and BlackBerry products. Directly supported four Account Executives.

➤ Expanded and strengthened sales and marketing efforts through new product and training presentations. Contributed to new product development of key accounts.
➤ Challenged to identify, evaluate, and capture opportunities for upgrade or expansion of contracts.
➤ Provided technical support and problem resolution and led end-user training.
  Accomplishments:
    ➤ Consistently achieved or surpassed team quota at 100% each month for 3 years.
    ➤ Coordinated and managed up to 30 strategic accounts simultaneously and provided direct customer support to 40-50 individual customers.
    ➤ Monitored, researched, and summarized market trends and competitor data and developed integrated product analyses for accounts executives that drove sales growth.

Team Customer Account Executive [dates]

Integral member of four-person account service team that developed and orchestrated multi-media presentations and on-site technical training sessions for clients nationwide. Fostered open communications with customers to gather vital feedback on products, pinpoint problems, and end-user issues. Resolved diverse range of technical, service, and billing problems.

  Accomplishments:
    ➤ Contributed sales support to government channel to reach over 137% of plan for [years].
    ➤ Improved customer satisfaction and retention by responding promptly to user and billing issues, staying alert to potential problem areas, and developing creative solutions.

Regional Implementation Specialist [dates]

Integral member of a seven-person team that supported pre-sales and closing presentations for federal and corporate accounts.

  Accomplishments:
    ➤ Successfully implemented over 60 accounts, improved customer satisfaction by 50%.
    ➤ Closed 20 new government and corporate accounts.

ADDITIONAL WORK EXPERIENCE

Credit Manager, MBNA, Baltimore, Md. [dates]
  Managed up to 500 customer loan and real estate accounts. Generated new business leads, cross-sold financial services, and refinanced loans through cold-calling, telemarketing, and field sales.

EDUCATION

Bachelor's Degree, Marketing,[1] Temple University, Philadelphia, Pa. [date]

COMPUTER SKILLS [3]

Proficient in popular applications, including Microsoft Windows, Excel, Word, Access, PowerPoint, Outlook, and Works; Lotus Notes; WordPerfect; Adobe Acrobat, Illustrator; Internet applications. Expertise with specialized data management, mail merge and analytical software.

Retailing. <u>Retail sales worker</u>. Reverse chronological. Retail worker seeks assistant manager position. Requirements: 1-2 years of retail experience,[1] positive sales attitude and proven sales leadership,[2] strong verbal and written communication skills,[3] strong customer service skills,[4] and basic computer skills.[5]

CYNTHIA MARIE ROMANI

765 Glassboro Ave., Apt. 2E   Cell: 555-444-0909
Alexandria, VA 22301   Email: cmromani@gmail.com

OBJECTIVE: Assistant Manager, Retail Beauty Company

PROFILE: Motivated **retail sales professional** with three years[1] of outstanding customer service experience.[4] Demonstrated sales leader,[2] with ability to consistently surpass goals and build client base. Positive attitude,[2] able to go above and beyond for customer satisfaction. Skilled in problem resolution, time and asset management and team leadership. Strong administrative and visual merchandising skills, with keen attention to detail. Excellent verbal and written communication skills.[3] Prior management experience in food service.

RETAIL EXPERIENCE

Key Holder, Sales Representative
Perfect Skin Co., Arlington, Va.   [dates][1]

> <u>Customer Service:</u>[4] Build customer base through friendly, attentive service. Educate customers in skin care and make-up products and techniques. Perform facials and color makeovers. Drive revenue by communicating and demonstrating benefits of products and special offers to new and returning customers. Maintain customer files and follow up on sales to create brand loyalty and increase customer retention. Answer questions and resolve customer complaints and problems.

> <u>Merchandising/Loss Prevention:</u> Plan and organize displays to correspond with current promotions and best-selling products. Maintain store appearance and stock shelves; identify and respond to security risks and thefts.

> <u>Sales Administration:</u> As Key Holder, open/close store; prepare daily deposits and sales reports. Process customer payments, balance cash drawers and maintain sales records. Interact with other stores as needed. Motivate staff to meet goals.[2]

Key Accomplishments:
> Promoted three times in 18 months, from part time to full time, then to Key Holder.
> Exceeded personal daily, weekly and monthly sales goals. Ranked top seller for [year].

OTHER EXPERIENCE

Administrative Assistant, National Fleet Leasing, Co., Fairfax, Va.   [dates]

Teacher, KinderCare Learning Center, Kingstowne, Va.   [dates]
> *Key Accomplishment:* Employee of the Quarter [date]

EDUCATION: Howard University, Washington, D.C., General Education   [dates]

COMPUTER SKILLS: MS Word, Excel, Outlook, PowerPoint; Internet; proprietary databases; hardware, software and peripheral troubleshooting.[5]

Food Service. <u>Server</u>. Functional. Experienced restaurant worker seeks higher-paying job. Requirements: 2 years of experience in reputable dining establishment,[1] ability to communicate using a positive and clear speaking voice, listen to and understand requests, and respond appropriately,[2] ability to perform essential physical job functions,[3] ability to work under pressure,[4] and be a team player.[5]

RENEE MARGARET JONES

4808 Juneberry Way, Apt. 102 • Mesa, AZ 21236
Cellular: 999-777-3434 • Email: rmjones@gmail.com

RESTAURANT SERVER

PROFILE: Over 5 years of customer service experience in restaurant and retail settings. Highly motivated, able to multi-task and prioritize workload under pressure, as well as increase pace as workload demands.[4] Excellent interpersonal skills, with ability to build rapport and develop regular clientele. Team player,[5] noted for volunteering to work additional shifts, in other departments. Keen attention to detail.

KEY SKILLS

- **Customer Service/Sales:** Skilled in essential physical job functions[3] — anticipating needs and empathizing with diverse customers. Speak clearly, quickly identify and resolve problems, listen and respond to requests, and follow up to assure complete satisfaction.[2] Outstanding upselling ability, without over-selling.

- **Server:** Accurately and quickly take and place all food orders. Answer all questions about cooking methods, menu items, specials and prices. Prepare and/or deliver food, beverage, and dessert orders. Check food for appearance, temperature and portion size, and deliver food orders in a timely fashion. *Recognized as top server. Routinely manage 6-table station on busy Friday and Saturday night shifts.*[3] *Consistently achieve sales goals.*

- **Team Lead/Trainer:** Experienced in leading teams, delegating work, enforcing policies, and ensuring assigned tasks are completed. Motivate co-workers.

- **Accounting/Inventory:** Accountable for cash and credit transactions. Also, skilled in receiving deliveries and verifying 400-piece orders; noted discrepancies, damages, and missing items.

- **Computer Proficiencies:** Various POS software programs, including QuickBooks POS Pro and Keystroke POS System.

PROFESSIONAL EMPLOYMENT

Server [1]   [dates]
Olive Garden, Mesa, Az.
Server [1]   [dates]
Ruby Tuesday, Phoenix, Az.
Student Marshall   [dates]
Arizona State University, Tempe, Az.
- *Received Outstanding Service Award, [date]*

EDUCATION

Undergraduate Coursework, Health Science Policy; Arizona State University, Tempe, Az.,
93 credits.   [dates]

Healthcare. Office manager. Hybrid. Recent healthcare management graduate with medical office experience seeking Medical Office Business Manager position. Requirements: 5 years' experience as medical practice administrator,[1] 3 years' supervisory experience,[2] experience with marketing and referral development,[3] experience in billing and accounts receivable[4] and demonstrated accomplishments and career growth in the healthcare field.[5]

MARY L. TREY

845 Nature Way * Anaheim, CA 92807
111-998-5555 * maryltrey@yahoo.com

CAREER FOCUS

Healthcare Management
Administration • Operations & Processes • HR • Generalist • Sales • Education Coordinator

PROFILE & SKILLS VALUED BY YOUR COMPANY

- Five years' direct experience in Healthcare Administrative Management.[1] Professional working knowledge of procedures applicable to hospital and physician settings. Completed healthcare internship while earning Bachelor of Science degree in Healthcare Management.

- Multi-task/detail oriented: provide functional guidance on multifaceted projects. Prioritize and distribute workloads, carefully balancing skill sets. Manage calendars and schedules, meeting fast-paced deadlines. Oversee staff.

- Accomplished professional with refined interpersonal and communications skills. Ensure smooth flow of communications between management, patients/clients, and team members, speaking frequently with patients and medical or insurance professionals. Maintain strict confidentiality of sensitive information following HIPAA regulations.

• Resilient & Energetic	• Relationship Builder	• MS Word, Excel, PowerPoint
• Leader	• Medical Terminology	• Information Management
• Manager	• Medical Insurance	• Medical Billing/Coding
• Diplomatic & Tactful	• Risk Management	• Medical Legal Requirements

EXPERIENCE

Office Manager, Plumbing Inc., Irvine, Calif.   [dates]
- Manage administrative and financial tasks for company of 15. Complete AP/AR, weekly payroll, banking, and invoices. Construct quarterly business taxes.[4]
- Conduct research and compile information to generate bids (for construction contracts).
- Provide excellent customer service and answer multi-line telephone system.
Key Accomplishments:
- Analyzed and streamlined business processes, reducing paper records and input time. Reduced labor expenditures by 10%.[5]
- Researched providers and reviewed bids for equipment lease and service; secured better price/product for copier and telecommunications. Achieved cost savings of $12,000 per year.[5]

Medical Office Coordinator, Doctors & Associates, Brea, Calif.   [dates]
- Hired as Medical Office Coordinator and within eights months, was informed center would close. Shifted into high gear to oversee difficult task of managing operating medical clinic, while

Mary L. Trey, Page 2

simultaneously closing the clinic. Successfully met closure deadline with all patient files copied and sent to selected doctors.

- Worked closely with patients to find new doctors, ensuring they had proper medications during transition period.
- Copied charts for new medical practitioners, sent closure notices to all patients, and mailed medical records to each patient or made arrangements for storage.
- Operated Medical Information Management software (patient registration, charge entries, and appointment scheduling). Scheduled appointments, checked patients in and out of clinic, prepared encounter forms, prepared daily log sheet, posted charges daily, entered and updated insurance information, entered ICD and CPT codes, and made daily bank deposits.

Medical Secretary, Klebanow Family Care; **Maintenance Supervisor,** Property Management
Company: Kelly Personnel Services, Yorba Linda, Calif. [dates]
- Scheduled appointments, checked patients in and out of clinic, prepared encounter forms, prepared daily log sheet, posted charges daily, entered and updated insurance information, entered ICD and CPT codes, and made daily bank deposits.
- Greeted patients with professionalism and courtesy to set appointments or resolve complaints/conflicts.
- Managed administrative requirements as temp employee in various offices.

Office Manager, Intensive Care Ambulance Service, Fullerton, Calif. [dates]
- Managed office requirements including bookkeeping and AP/AR, payroll for 10 employees, and marketing. Balanced four separate bank accounts. Produced financial/statistical reports and worked closely with the CPA. Directed two assistants.[2]
- Supervised and dispatched eight EMTs and paramedics.
- Scheduled appointments with nursing homes and hospitals for patient transport.
- Wrote correspondence and marketing materials to gain new business with nursing homes, dialysis clinics, and hospitals.[3]
- Worked with vendor companies to purchase ambulance supplies including stretchers, wheel chairs, IV bags, bandages, uniforms, and medications issued during transport of patients.

EDUCATION

Bachelor of Science Degree, Health Care Management [5]
California State University, Fullerton, Calif. [dates]

Relevant Health Care Management Courses:

• Health Policy	• Public Speaking	• Risk Management/Health Care
• Anatomy & Physiology	• HR & Labor Relations	• Legal Aspects of Health Care
• Management Problems	• Facilities Fiscal Aspects	• Health Care Services Analysis
• U.S. Health Care System	• Marketing	• Equipment & Materials Mgmt.

Healthcare Administrative Internship: [dates]

Shadowed **Healthcare Administrator** (an RN) of assisted living facility with 50 residents. Cross-trained in all departments: **HR and Office Manager's offices** (staff scheduling and administration; interviewed job candidates), **Admissions** (interviewed hospital applicants and processed applications for admission), **Health Inspection** (shadowed health inspector), and **Marketing** (visited local hospitals and medical offices).

Business. Business Analyst. Reverse Chronological. Technical Writer seeks Business Analyst position. Requirements: college degree,[1] minimum five years of relevant work experience,[2] experience/understanding of business process reengineering and business modeling concepts,[3] awareness of the business and information technology functions,[4] and strong analytical and technical writing skills.[5]

MICHELLE ANN GERSHON

346 Shipwright Way, #716 • St. Louis, MO 19807
Cell: 555-333-6767 • Email: m-a-gershon@hotmail.com

BUSINESS ANALYST

Over 10 years' experience in managing and integrating information technology (IT) applications[2] for financial service and healthcare providers. Expertise: business and end-user requirements, project management, communicating business needs to IT staff, and quality assurance (QA) testing. Strong technical written communications skills, including ability to convey complex IT and industry-specific information clearly.[5] Deadline-driven. Pay attention to detail. Excel in team and individual work settings.

RELEVANT PROFESSIONAL EXPERIENCE

Technical Writer
Medical Billing Co., Chesterfield, Mo.   [dates]

Technical writing for non-profit medical billing and collection company, serving 50 major hospitals in the Midwest. Hired to author Health Insurance Portability and Accountability Act (HIPAA) compliance and IT information security policies.

- Policy Development: Wrote corporate and IT security policies to satisfy HIPAA regulations. Created corporate standard for policy and procedure documentation. Wrote and edited IT software documentation, policies, and procedures.[4]
- Project Management: Facilitated company's conversion from paper to automated data tracking and recordkeeping. Led project team to develop online Documentation Center. Researched commercial off-the-shelf and open-source software.
- Disaster Recovery: Worked with contractor to develop and implement disaster recovery plan and established business continuity plan. Managed disaster recovery testing; taught system to users.

Key Accomplishment
Successfully passed 2 external audits with no items of concern. (Company had previously been cited/fined for lack of information security policies with regard to HIPAA regulations.)

Project Coordinator (Contract position)
First Credit Co.,Clayton, Mo.   [dates]

Hired to coordinate several high-profile IT projects for this global financial services provider. Reported directly to a VP of the Consumer Internet Group. Supported project management staff (5 project managers with up to 30 people per team) to complete 15 IT projects, including Disney custom Internet site, Disney Rewards Card, Disney reporting, and Verified by Visa.

- Project Coordination: Developed and maintained project documentation including Project Plans, Action Items/Issues Logs, Critical Tasks lists, and Meeting Minutes.
- Resource Management/Liaison: Balanced changing priorities and business expectations to meet strict deadlines. Served as point of contact and liaison for all project staff.

Key Accomplishment
Significant contributor to Disney Rewards Card project—completed on time and under budget.

Business Analyst
College Finance Co., St. Louis, Mo.   [dates]
Performed business process analyses for this national postsecondary education loan services company.

- Business/Process Analysis: Reviewed and analyzed business modeling operations; flowcharted all company processes and functionality.[3] Developed and recommended business process improvements, identifying end-user and business requirements. Designed and prepared reports.

Key Accomplishment
Critical contributor to implementation of Phone Pay system, a PC application which automated loan payment process, saving over 100 manhours per month. Worked extensively with developers and QA testing; trained end-users.

Business Analyst/Technical Writer
Applied Card Systems, St. Louis, Mo.   [dates]
Initially hired as Technical Writer; promoted to Business Analyst for this growing financial services company.

- Project Management: Managed projects according to System Development Lifecycle, ranging from application processing and collection system enhancements to new products, using MS Project. Identified end-user requirements and developed business requirements documents.
- Software Implementation: Developed documentation (user and technical manuals) for software applications and procedural documentation for all IT units.

Key Accomplishment
Provided liaison for IT-related projects with multiple business units serving 1,000 internal users.

EDUCATION, TRAINING, & CERTIFICATIONS
B.A.,[1] English, University of Missouri, Columbia, Mo.   [date]
Webmaster Certificate, Penn State University   [date]
Spherion eSQM Training Course (Internet Software Quality Management Methodology) [date]

COMPUTER PROFICIENCIES
MS Office: Word, Excel, PowerPoint, Access; SharePoint, Visio, MS FrontPage, MS Project; Adobe Acrobat, FrameMaker, Photoshop; TYPO3; HTML; Javascript; Test Director 6.0; Winrunner 6.02

Chapter 12

A Sampling of OnTarget Resumes by Experience Level and Age

⬤ ⬤

*H*ave reason to think that you have too much experience — or not enough — to rack up the job offers you want? Or that you're too young — or too old? Or that even when you're barely out of your mid-40s (a kid, really), you're stuck in low gear? The sample resumes in this chapter show techniques aimed at downplaying negative perceptions about your experience or your age.

A box atop each sample resume contains a mission statement — that is, what the job seeker aims to accomplish, which usually is a better job. The mission statement also includes the requirements for a specific position — or a summary of the typically requested requirements for an occupation or career field. You may be surprised that the requirements have numbers. And that the numbers are cross-matched to qualifications in the resume. Does this mean you are supposed to put numbers on your resumes as these samples show? The answer is: No! No! A thousand times no!

The cross-matched numbers between a job's requirements and the candidate's qualifications shown here are just for illustration, *not for your actual resumes.*

These samples are intended to laser your attention to requirement-and-qualification matching, the single most important factor in causing your candidacy to get noticed in an online swarm of resumes.

New Graduate. <u>Business Administration degree.</u> Hybrid. Candidate seeks Junior Financial Analyst position. Requirements: BS Business or Finance,[1] 1-3 years' relevant experience,[2] strong Excel skills,[3] independent work style,[4] highly motivated,[5] strong problem-solving skills,[6] excellent communication skills[7] and team player.[8]

JOSHUA GANSL

1450 Mount Sinai Lane, Apt. 102   Tel: 555.111.1712
Charleston, SC 29401   joshgansl@yahoo.com

OBJECTIVE: Junior Financial Analyst

SKILLS & QUALIFICATIONS

- Strong financial, quantitative/qualitative analytical, and problem-solving skills.[6]
- International and domestic summer work experience. Gained essential knowledge evaluating properties, structuring financing, conducting pro-forma cash flow analysis, and executing leases for residential and commercial real estate sales and acquisitions.
- Poised, self-confident. Proven public speaking, interpersonal and multicultural communications skills.[7]
- Highly motivated with strong work ethic.[5] Well-developed team player abilities.[8] Able to prioritize tasks, work independently,[4] and meet deadlines.
- Competitive and ambitious. Welcome new challenges.
- Computer Skills: Advanced proficiencies in Microsoft Windows, Word, Excel,[3] and PowerPoint.

EDUCATION

B.S.,[1] Business Administration, Clemson University, Clemson, S.C., GPA 4.0   [date]

- **Relevant Courses:** Corporate Finance, Accounting, Financial Statement Analysis, Micro/Macro Economics, Business Statistics, and Management Information Systems
- **Team Project:** In-depth business case analysis of sporting goods industry. Conducted top-down financial statement analysis to determine predictors of future stock prices.

WORK EXPERIENCE

Tillman Securities, PLC, London, England [2]   [dates]

Worked directly with CFO on commercial real estate acquisitions and financing. Reviewed properties and conducted future cash flow analysis. Prepared and presented regulatory and financial documentation to financial institutions.
- Involved in executing purchase of over $100 million in commercial real estate properties.
- Part of team that refinanced several multimillion dollar real estate properties.

JOSHUA GANSL

Page 2

Seaside Realty Partners, Inc., Los Angeles, Calif.   [dates]

Summer [year]: Participated in successful acquisition of 18 commercial properties leased to U.S. Drugstore Corporation in upstate New York. Created Excel spreadsheets, performed due diligence, analyzed and prepared leasing agreements, conducted pro-forma cash flow analysis, and conducted on-site inspections with acquisition team.

- Presented summary financial data to outside investors and the company's executives to be used for acquisition decision-making.

Summer [year]: Shadowed Vice Chairman. Gained valuable experience evaluating real estate properties, and predicting future cash flow and property income. Developed passion and talent for identifying, structuring, and executing sound commercial real estate investments.

Gansl and Greenberg, LLP, Los Angeles, Calif.   [dates]

- Delivered administrative and operational support for high-volume law firm. Ensured all documents were accurately filed. Provided customer service and supported legal staff.

Camp International, Jerusalem, Israel   [dates]

Camp counselor at an international summer camp for 200 campers from all over the Americas and Europe; including England, France, and Belgium.
- Led broad range of team activities and supervised tours throughout Israel.
- Promoted open communications and camaraderie among all campers. Reinforced importance of respecting cultural differences.
- Developed talent for fostering communication despite language barriers.

SPECIAL INTERESTS & ACTIVITIES

Community Service
- Chai Lifeline Volunteer, an organization that supports cancer patients and their families. Maintained ongoing relationships with seriously ill youngsters. Participated in "Big Brother" program for two years.

Team Sports
- Captain of college basketball team, 2 years.

International Travel
- Extensive travel to over 10 European countries, as well as trips to the Middle East. Enjoy experiencing and learning about other cultures, history, and customs.

Foreign Languages
- Write and speak Hebrew.
- Conversational Yiddish — an international dialect of German.

Reading
- Avid reader. Especially enjoy financial publications.

Mid-Career Trades. HVAC expert. Functional. Experienced heating/cooling specialist seeks HVAC Manager, Technical Training & Service position. Requirements: Min. 15 years of experience in theory and practice of HVAC – installation, service, repairs, heat pumps, air conditioners, gas/oil furnaces, boilers, and standard controls,[1] strong communication and leadership skills,[2] must be performance-driven, motivated,[3] and computer savvy. [4]

GREG BOREK

903 Longmeadow Lane • Raleigh, NC 27602
Cell: 999-333-2323 • Email: greg_borek@comcast.net

HVAC/Refrigeration Systems Expert

OBJECTIVE: HVAC Manager, Technical Training and Service

AREAS OF EXPERTISE

- **HVAC/R Expert**, with over 20 years' experience. Highly skilled in every phase of heating and air conditioning, chillers, heat pumps, furnaces, and boilers for residential, commercial, plumbing and refrigeration lines: **design, installation, troubleshooting, service, and repair**.[1] Experienced with Metasys and Johnson 350 controller. Proficient in Control systems design and installation–Analog and DDC.

- Experienced **project manager and team leader,**[2] with jobs averaging $500,000, up to 500 tons. Adept at estimating job schedules, choosing quality, cost-effective materials and designing and installing control systems, as well as supervising apprentices, journeymen and subcontractors on the job.

- Mentor, coach, and train junior staff. Develop and implement work standards and provide guidance on technical processes, safety, and operations.

- Performance-driven and motivated;[3] consistently complete job ahead of schedule and under budget. Regularly receive written and verbal recognition and bonuses.

- Strong customer service, interpersonal and communications skills.[2]

- Skilled at any and all **electrical** or **electronic diagnosis** and **repair**.

- Knowledgeable A/C systems **programmer**; PC proficient and familiar with HVACPRO software.[4]

CERTIFICATIONS

North Carolina Licensed Journeyman, #6666; EPA Certified, Universal & Automotive, #999999999

SAMPLE PROJECTS

Designed and installed controls systems for:
WNCN 17 NBC • Fool Lion food stores
Borders book stores • Wake Forest University

Installed & set up Metasys system for:
Durham Regional Hospital • CVS drugstores
State government building, Raleigh

WORK HISTORY

Johnson Controls, *Controls Technician*	[dates]
Aire Right Mechanical, *Commercial A/C*	[dates]
Servicemark Mechanical Services, *Residential A/C and Refrigeration; Appliance Repair*	[dates]

EDUCATION/SPECIALIZED TRAINING

Metasys ASC engineering, Johnson Controls, [date]
DDC control, M & M Controls, [date]
Trane Microcontrol Voyager, Trane, [date]
Pneumatic Controls I & II, [date]
Honeywell: Fireye, M & M Controls, [date]

Carrier Parker System, Carrier, [date]
Wake Tech. Comm. College, 36 credits [dates]
Diploma, Roosevelt High, Raleigh, SC [date]

Young Adult. Intern. Reverse Chronological. Recent MPA graduate seeks Program Officer/Researcher position with nonprofit or public policy organization. Requirements: Bachelor's degree (preferably Master's),[1] strong research, writing, and legislative skills,[2] experience working on policy and advocacy campaigns,[3] solid Microsoft Office skills,[4] and strong attention to detail and ability to multi-task.[5]

ROCHELLE HENDERSON

1908 Clarkson Ave., Apt. 900
Brooklyn, NY 11203
Cell: 888-444-9090
E-mail: r_henderson@ny-u.edu

EXPERIENCE

[dates] **UNITED NATIONS DEVELOPMENT PROGRAMME** New York, N.Y.
Programme Assistant Intern, Equator Initiative [dates]
Mid-term Evaluation Intern, United Nations Capital Development Fund [dates]
- Researched and wrote [2] reports and position papers on capacity building in local communities.
- Authored and edited [2] articles for *Between the Lines* newsletter.
- Evaluated and analyzed documents to extract recommendations for improving design and cost effectiveness of microfinance donor training workshops.

[dates] **NEW YORK UNIVERSITY SCHOOL OF MEDICINE** New York, N.Y.
Research Associate, [2] Center for Immigrant Health
- Conducted highly detailed [5] research in English and Spanish on quality of medical services for immigrant populations for advocacy campaign,[3]
- Designed and implemented quality assurance mechanisms to improve accuracy of study's data.[5]
- Supervised and trained staff of 9 research interns.

[dates] **PEACE CORPS** Tarija, Bolivia
Gender and Development Representative [dates]
Natural Resources Management Extensionist [dates]
- Directed all logistical components, drafted budget, and raised funds for 4-day national gender and development conference for 35 high school students and 5 community representatives.
- Selected to use participatory modules to train 28 volunteers for gender mainstream projects.
- Managed locally focused natural resources projects for over 80 indigenous women.
- Planned, prioritized, and managed multiple tasks and assignments in fast-paced environment.[5]

[dates] **WORLD WILDLIFE FUND** Washington, D.C.
Government Relations Intern [2]
- Wrote and edited documents on environmental legislation and international development concerns to educate staff on policy issues. Represented lobbyist at World Bank and Capitol Hill meetings.

[dates] **THE WHITE HOUSE** Washington, D.C.
President's Council on Sustainable Development Intern [2]
- Prepared overviews of environmentally sustainable strategies presented to international delegations.
- Edited *Towards a Sustainable America* report presented to President William Clinton.

EDUCATION
Master of Public Administration,[1] New York University, New York, N.Y., [date]
   Specialization: International Public and Nonprofit Management and Policy
Bachelor of Arts,[1] Environmental Science and Policy, Hood College, Frederick, Md., [date]
   Concentration: Environmental Policy; Minors: Sociology and International Economics

COMPUTERS
Microsoft Office [4] (Word, Excel, Outlook, PowerPoint, Access, Visio) and SPSS

LANGUAGES
Fluent in Spanish. Intermediate proficiency in Portuguese and Quechua.

Mid-Career Professional. Teacher. Reverse chronological. Experienced drama teacher seeks community college drama director position or chair of drama department. Requirements: 5-10 years' teaching theater in educational setting,[1] master's degree in theater arts.[2]

TERESA LYNN MORROW

33 Enjay Ave. • Catonsville, MD 99999
Residence: 444-555-1234 • Cellular: 444-555-5678
Email: dramacate@aol.com

Talented **Drama Instructor** with 10 years[1] plus of hands-on theatre and teaching experience. Outstanding ability to build programs and interest, both at school and community levels, as well as to develop rapport, relationships, and resources. Innovative and creative, willing to try new ideas; strongly committed to fostering the next generation of playwrights, actors, and production staff. Master's degree in theater arts (this year).[2]

TEACHING EXPERIENCE

Drama Teacher/Director of Drama   [dates]
Lincoln High School, Columbia, Md.

Revitalized struggling drama department of this former tech-magnet Howard County high school. (Program went through 10 teachers in year prior to hire.) Built interest in drama program as well as offerings and opportunities. Currently teach 5 drama classes and direct Drama Club.

✓ Productions: Direct 3 large stage productions and 2 smaller classroom productions per year. Coordinate student technicians, directors, production staff, and actors. As appropriate, select plays, direct casting, coordinate auditorium calendar and events, and supervise design and construction of scenery and costumes. Manage production budget and direct marketing of productions. Continually challenged to present quality, award-winning productions on small budget.

Provide advice, support, and direction to students, encouraging high level of student involvement.

Productions include *Get Bill Shakespeare Off the Stage, George M!, A Night with Edgar, Starmites, Sugar, The Princess Bride, The Wizard of Oz, Finian's Rainbow, After Juliet, Seven Brides for Seven Brothers, Anything Goes,* and *The Importance of Being Earnest.*

✓ Teaching: Prepare and present materials on drama and communications for culturally diverse student base. Classes include: Introduction to Drama, Advanced Drama, Stagecraft, Musical Theatre, and Speech Communications. Incorporate variety of teaching strategies, including Essential Elements of Instruction, cooperative learning, and portfolio writing.

✓ Curriculum Development: Designed "Theater as Resource" Instructional Projects for middle school English classes, to introduce/integrate theatre and increase interest in drama prior to entering high school. Participate on Curriculum Development team; as a contributor, drafted guidelines, goals, and recommendations, as well as outlines and lesson plans.

✓ Community Festivals/Field & Class Trips: Coordinate student participation/attendance of variety of theatre presentations and workshops, locally, nationally, and internationally, including the Shakespeare Festival, the Folger Theatre Festival, Howard County Drama Festival, Magic Music Days (Epcot Center), and the Stratford Theatre Festival (Canada).

T. L. MORROW	Page 2	Cellular: 444-555-5678

Achievements:

✓ Received 9 statewide awards for "best in" categories (Long Reach High School students).

✓ Organized trip to prestigious Stratford Theatre Festival in Canada, Summer [date]. Orchestrated invitations for 20 students and 4 adults—partially government-supported program is usually only open to Canadian students/teachers. Festival included workshops, backstage tours, and plays.

✓ Created Stagecraft class, teaching students to plan and create sets.

Substitute Teacher [dates]
North Hill High School, Hampstead, Md.

Taught Mythology and 11th grade English. Voted Teacher of the Month for [date]. Also, recruited as substitute Theatre Director for [date]. Supervised/performed selection, casting, costuming, set design and construction; produced *Anne of Green Gables*.

VOLUNTEER & OTHER EXPERIENCE

Coordinator, Howard County (Maryland) Drama Festival [dates]

Organized and coordinated one-day festival with 250 student attendees and support/teaching staff of 20. Scheduled seminars, entertainment, and workshops, including room planning and lunch. Served as co-coordinator for [date] festival.

Instructor, The Teaching Shakespeare School (Stratford, Canada) [dates]

Specially invited to participate in program open to Canadian teachers. Additionally, paired with Stratford actor to team-teach *The Tempest* and *As You Like It* to 20 Long Reach students. Served as Teachers' Festival Liaison (3 years) for Stratford Festival teacher's conference, [date].

Graduate Assistant, New York University Study Abroad Program [dates]

Made daily preparations for on and off-campus classes at Trinity College (Dublin, Ireland). Coordinated receptions for students, visiting dignitaries, and professors; provided administrative support to Program Director.

Producer/Technical Director, The Howard County (Maryland) Players [dates]

Coordinated musical theatre performances for program that pairs high school students and adults.

EDUCATION

Master's Degree, in progress, Educational Theatre, Community Concentration, New York University, New York, N.Y., 24 credits; expected completion: GPA: 3.75 [dates]

Bachelor of Arts, English and Theatre, York College of Pennsylvania, York, Penn., [dates] received Helen Gotwald Drama Award

Secondary Certification, English Theatre, York College of Penn., York, Penn., [dates]

Continuing Education, The Academy at the Stratford Festival, Stratford, Canada. [dates] Classes completed: Shakespeare: Text and Performance, Voice and Movement, Set Building and Scene Painting, and Design in the Theatre

Young Professional. Graphic Artist/Visual Information Specialist. Reverse chronological. Graphic Artist seeks corporate communications graphics position. Requirements: Bachelor's degree,[1] 3 years' experience in graphics design and photography,[2] experience in production management and utilizing video, 35MM and audio equipment,[3] knowledge of advertising and marketing communications,[4] excellent communications skills,[5] and willing to travel 50% of the time.[6]

SCOTT E. PASQUALE

340 Decatur Lane
Baton Rouge, LA 70801

Cell: 111.444.4444   E-mail: spasquale@gmail.com

GRAPHIC ARTIST/VISUAL INFORMATION SPECIALIST

Skilled graphic artist, photographer, and video producer with three years' professional experience.[2] Creative and resourceful in coordinating and producing training videos, photography for print and Web and graphic design. Proficient in production management, as well as use of video, graphics software, 35 MM, digital and audio equipment and systems [3] to produce advertising and marketing materials, Web content, and training programs. [4] Strong communications skills;[5] able to travel. [6]

Professional Experience	**Computer and Information Specialist**	[dates]

Training Professionals, Inc.; Baton Rouge, La.
- Maintain Web site utilizing HTML, scanning and forms management
- Develop graphics, photographic images, and content for print and electronic media
- Maintain customer service, evaluate customer feedback, and determine appropriate action
- Produce videos and edit into training films
- Photograph training sessions for Web site production

Commercial Photography Intern and Independent Contractor   [dates]
Online Real Estate Listing Service; New Orleans, La.
Judith Salmona, Freelance Photographer; Kenner, La.
- Accomplish portrait, real estate, and documentary photographic assignments
- Produce professional quality custom color prints and graphic images
- Scan negatives and slides; manipulate and correct images
- Maintain and service printing and graphics equipment
- Organize and catalog negatives and proof sheets

Technical Supervisor: *Performance Anxiety* **Installation**   [dates]
Smith College; Northampton, Mass.
- Produced interactive video exhibition combining real-time computer image processing with variety of short videos
- Used Image software and Infusion Systems' I-Cube X hardware

Education   B.A.,[1] Visual and Performing Arts, Louisiana State University, Baton Rouge, La.   [date]
Relevant Coursework: Introduction to Computers, Programming in C, HTML, Dreamweaver, Illustrator, Quark, Macromedia Flash, B&W Photography, Color Photography, Advanced Photography, Electronic Image Processing, Final Cut Pro, Alternative Processes, Visual Concepts, Ideas in the Arts, Introduction to Recording Techniques, History of Photography, Contemporary Art in Process, History of Film, American Life in Films

Skills   ***Computer:*** Macintosh and PC – Word, Excel, PowerPoint, Photoshop, Illustrator, Acrobat, QuarkXpress, Flash, digital imaging, scanning, Corel Draw, non-linear video production and editing, C Programming, HTML Web page development, database management

Photography: digital video production, 35mm photography, B&W and color processing, printing and toning, studio portraiture, and dry mounting

Baby Boomer. Director of Marketing and Communications. Reverse chronological. Marketing expert seeks Director of Marketing position for international nonprofit. Requirements: Bachelor's degree (Master's preferred)[1] and a minimum of 10 years' experience in marketing, brand management, and corporate communications,[2] experience conducting market research and utilizing market research to guide planning and decision making,[3] knowledge of the not-for-profit fundraising environment,[4] excellent communications, presentation and negotiation skills,[5] and willing to travel 20% of the time.[6]

CONSTANCE M. CONNOLLY

222 Strawberryfields Rd.
Sioux Falls, SD 99999

Home: 555.444.5656   E-mail: c_connolly@hotmail.com

Director of Marketing

Creative, dynamic Marketing professional with 14+ years of experience.[2] Demonstrated success developing and implementing strategic and tactical global marketing plans to improve product positioning, brand management, corporate communications, and competitive market share.[2] Results-oriented team leader with proven expertise managing marketing programs from concept through project completion. MBA in Marketing. Key strengths include:

- ✓ Superior communications, presentation, negotiation, and management skills[5]
- ✓ Experience formulating and implementing comprehensive multi-media campaigns.
- ✓ Expertise developing global and product-specific marketing plans, strategies, and budgets for nonprofit and for-profit organizations[4]
- ✓ Strong analytical capabilities. Extensive market research expertise, including demographic and market trend analyses; competitive assessments; and consumer segmentation and needs studies to guide planning and decision making.[3]
- ✓ E-Commerce & Web creation, development, and management experience.
- ✓ Proficiency in new product development, launch, and evaluation.
- ✓ Published writer and accomplished presenter, able to travel for meetings, trainings, and conferences.[6]
- ✓ American Marketing Association, American Society for Association Executives.

PROFESSIONAL EXPERIENCE

Director, Marketing and Communications
MUSCULAR DYSTROPHY ASSOCIATION, Sioux Falls, S.D.   [dates]

Develop and implement marketing and communications strategies to support major, organization-wide refocusing of MDA's operations, role and relevancy, community impact and image. Reached funding goal. Charged with conceptualizing and designing central messaging strategies to reposition MDA as leading health and human service organization.

- ✓ Aggressively promote notable accomplishments, and develop communications tools to improve internal branding, public relations, and sales.

- ✓ Develop and execute annual marketing program integrating television, radio, direct mail, print, electronic media, and special events.

- ✓ Conduct in-depth market research to evaluate public/customer perception and satisfaction, guide organizational investments in set-vices and impact areas, and support special projects to drive improvements.

Key Contributions & Achievements

- ✓ Developed technical blueprint that provided foundation for software development for new Volunteer Matching Program that will facilitate marketing and matching of volunteer opportunities.

- ✓ Conceived and spearheaded development of first Speakers Bureau to improve visibility of key constituencies (volunteers, health and human service representatives) in community. Speakers Bureau set for launch in [date].

Director of Marketing, Research, and Product Development
SCHOLARLY ASSOCIATION, INC., Washington, D.C.   [dates]

Supported global marketing needs of four distinct product lines: special interest groups, membership, conferences, and publications. Worked directly with Executive Director, internal management team, Board of Directors, and 62 committees to translate collective vision into strategic marketing plan.

- ✓ Built key consumer relationships, designed and implemented solutions-based sales strategies, and positioned company as market leader in scholarly publishing market.

- ✓ Developed and managed integrated, multimedia marketing program. Implemented new product development, launch, and evaluation. Developed strategies for increased product sales, brand awareness, and communications.

Key Contributions & Achievements

- ✓ Co-developed and implemented pricing model that created financially-sound basis to increase professional journal subscription revenues by $1 million on sustained basis.

- ✓ Conceptualized innovative direct mail marketing program that boosted new consumer base by 40% in one year.

- ✓ Spearheaded organization's first-ever global consumer satisfaction and performance improvement study, enabling management to formulate decisions based on consumers' expressed needs and desires.

- ✓ Strategic player in company's entrance into arenas of e-commerce and Web communications. Co-initiated effort to restructure Web site to increase navigability, aesthetics, brand, and commerce opportunities.

- ✓ Reevaluated vendor network and negotiated more competitive terms, resulting in savings of over 30%.

- ✓ Named 'Marketer of the Year' by Council of Educational Organizations   [date]

CONSTANCE M. CONNOLLY   Page 3

Director of Marketing and Public Relations
ARCHDIOCESE OF SIOUX FALLS, Division of Catholic Schools, Sioux Falls, S.D.   [Dates]

Launched one of the first programs in nation to market Catholic schools to counter 20-year trend of declining enrollment. Collaborated with Superintendent and Marketing Advisory Committee to generate marketing vision. Conceptualized message and developed strategies for multimedia advertising. Primary liaison with advertising agency and media. Managed advertising designs, scripts, and placement of spots. Maintained press relations and briefed educational reporters. Hired as Marketing and P.R. Assistant: promoted after 3 years.

Key Contributions & Achievments

✓ Launched successful multi-media campaign that increased Catholic school enrollments by 13% and generated construction of three new schools. By [date], there were more applicants than placements for county schools.

✓ Co-negotiated exclusivity contract with local TV station and advertising agency to produce commercials for Archdiocese on pro-bono basis, reducing campaign costs by 50%.

✓ Wrote, presented, and received grant to fund position and program for three-year period.

✓ Authored demographic study to guide Archdiocesan leadership in new school construction.

✓ Designed training program that incorporated facets of the marketing position: marketing, public relations, and development work. Trained school boards and committees at 101 schools to maximize local impact.

EDUCATION

Master of Business Administration, [1] [date], University of South Dakota, Vermillion, S.D.
Bachelor of Business Administration/Marketing Major, [date], Dakota Wesleyan University, Mitchell, S.D.

PUBLICATIONS & PRESENTATIONS

"Strategic Planning for State and Local Associations" – Guest speaker at National Association of Home Builders, Destin, Ha., [date]

"Application of Market Research to New Product Design: Case Studies" – Guest speaker at Council of Engineering and Scientific Society Executives, Houston, Texas, [dates]

Connolly, C. [date], **"Using Market Research to Make Strategic Decisions"** Association Management

Connolly, C. [date], **"Applying Marketing Success Principles to International Organizations,"** New Organizations World.

Connolly, C. [date], **"Nonprofits When Effectivly Marketed Can Save Lives,"** Nonprofits Review.

Young Professional. <u>Sales and Marketing Manager</u>. Hybrid. Seeks Marketing Coordinator position in larger company in advertising field. Requirements: 3-5 years of marketing experience – printing industry experience a plus,[1] degree in business, marketing, advertising or related discipline,[2] highly motivated,[3] detail and goal-oriented,[4] and high proficiency with MS Word, Excel, PowerPoint – Quark and Photoshop a plus.[5]

YOEL MORECK
1111 Sage Lane • Las Vegas, NV 99999
Cell: 555-333-3939 • Residence: 702-999-8989
Email: yoel_morick@gmail.com

MARKETING COORDINATOR with 5 years of marketing experience.[1]

- Sales, marketing, and advertising in printing/publishing,[1] real estate, and landscaping.
- Highly motivated,[3] with demonstrated ability to develop and maintain new sales territories and accounts, create new revenue streams, and increase profits.
- Strong ability to develop customer rapport and build loyal relationships.
- Excellent attention to detail and ability to meet and surpass sales goals.[4]

SALES & MARKETING EXPERIENCE

Sales and Marketing Manager/Field Supervisor
Local Lawn Services, Las Vegas, Nev.   [dates]

Recruited to spearhead sales and marketing efforts for this growing landscaping company.

<u>Marketing:</u> Develop marketing and advertising programs and materials, including direct mail and internet. Conduct market and customer research and develop new revenue streams to build business. Advise on market penetration and business development strategies.

<u>Sales:</u> Manage customer relationships from initial contact through consultation/estimate and service delivery. Develop sales leads, estimate projects, and write service contracts. Determine customer needs and recommend best options. Resolve customer problems and follow up to ensure customer satisfaction and loyalty.

<u>Management:</u> Analyze business operations and processes and identify improvements. Review profit and loss statements; recommend ways to reduce costs and maximize profits. Develop and implement policies. Direct laborers onsite; track time and attendance.

Key Accomplishments:

- Achieved year-on-year growth, increasing revenue by 31% in first year to $550,000; and an additional 18% the following year, for total revenue of $650,000. Established 70+ new accounts.
- Authored 14-page Employee Handbook; developed formal standards and policies for labor staff.
- Created new business line, hardscaping. Also created Web site for retail mulch sales.

Account Executive
Star Publishing, Las Vegas, Nev.   [dates]

Sold advertising to local and national clients for primarily business-to-business publications, including area chamber of commerce directories. Total circulation was approximately 100,000.

Maintained established accounts and developed new leads and clients. Consulted directly with clients' executive staffs to secure ad sales. Kept track of and met multiple, concurrent publication deadlines. Worked with creative design staff to develop advertising concepts and content. Managed full sales-cycle, ensuring client satisfaction.

Key Accomplishments:

- Consistently met/exceeded sales goals; sold $100,000 of advertising in 6 months.
- Established territory for newly won contract — Susquehanna Chamber of Commerce Quality of Life Guide, a full-color directory. Landed 35 new accounts, worth $35,000.

President
Your Lawn and Garden, LLC, Henderson, Nev.   [dates]

Founder/operator of landscaping business. Oversaw all aspects of company start-up and operation, including sales and marketing, business development, accounting, and management.

Researched market and identified specific demographics of targeted client base. Developed marketing strategy; created and distributed advertising materials. Managed customer relationships; met with potential clients, negotiated contract, and closed sale. Directed staff of 1-3, coordinating projects and ensuring completion.

Sales Manager
Sailor's Restaurant and Seaside Guide, San Francisco, Calif.   [dates]

Sold advertising for 2 regional editions of full-color, glossy boating magazine, circulation of 110,000.

Created sales territory for new regional edition of this yearly publication, distributed at local marinas. Generated leads through direct contact and cold calls. Clients included hotels, restaurants, yacht brokers, and retail shops. Negotiated contracts, established payment schedules, and designed ads. Managed billing and publication distribution. Once established, maintained and expanded client base.

OTHER WORK EXPERIENCE

Flight Attendant
Delta Airlines, Las Vegas, Nev.   [dates]

Provided customer service, resolved passenger and employee problems, and responded to emergency situations. As Chief Purser, supervised crews of 2-10; provided liaison with captain. Received numerous commendations and customer appreciation letters.

Editor: [dates]

Created and published 20-page bimonthly staff newsletter. Selected and compiled content and artwork; edited, formatted, designed, proofread, and laid out publication.

EDUCATION

B.S.,[2] **Marketing,** in progress, University of Nevada, Las Vegas, Nev.; 96 credits. Expected graduation: [date]

A.A.,[2] **Business,** City College of San Francisco, San Francisco, Calif.,   [date]

COMPUTER SKILLS:[5] MS Word, Excel, Outlook, Publisher, PowerPoint; Photoshop; ACT! database

Baby Boomer. Publisher turned Author. Hybrid. Retired from a successful publishing career and self-published his own book. Author Publisher seeks speaking engagements via radio, TV, and conferences about life experiences and career successes. Requirements: strong, professional speaking skills and appearance,[1] a message to give,[2] energetic,[3] people-person [4] and drive to share experiences.[5]

FRANK S. JUDAKIS

555 Warren Pl. • Providence, RI 99999

Phone 666-777-4040 • Fax 401-777-2020 • E-mail: fjudakis@comcast.net

MOTIVATIONAL SPEAKER

Seasoned, popular speaker,[1] energetic,[3] inspirational, witty, and direct. Passion to share life experiences and expertise[5] and enrich lives of others. Enjoy reaching out to diverse groups[4] to communicate message.[2] Topics include publishing, journalism publicity, marketing, entrepreneurship, and contemporary business professionalism.

HIGHLIGHTS OF EXPERIENCE

BEST-SELLING AUTHOR, *To Love Mercy,* published by MidAtlantic Highlands, Huntington, W.V. A non-fiction book of memoirs and close-to-true-life fiction by residents of Mid-Atlantic States. Completed two successful book tours, interviews on more than 20 radio shows, and second printing in just three months. Featured in the Chicago Sunday Sun-Times.

PUBLISHER/CONSULTANT, COMMUNICATIONS GROUP, Chevy Chase, Md.
Provide publishing, marketing, editorial and strategic consulting to publishers and other clients. Published over 60,000 FEDERAL PERSONNEL GUIDES until [date]; readership averaged 70,000 per print and on-line guide. Previously published nationally influential newsletters including Health Policy Week, Managed Care Report, Prospective Payment Guide, Law Firm Profit Report and others.

PARTNER, AMERICAN COMMUNICATIONS GROUP, Bethesda, Md.
One of three partners in firm that published six newsletters and one database service serving gasoline marketers, credit unions, small banks, day care providers and business mailers.

ASSISTANT EDITOR, THE WASHINGTON POST, Washington, D.C.
Edited Watergate copy for L.A. Times/Washington Post News Service client newspapers.

REPORTER AND EDITOR, THE ASSOCIATED PRESS, Chicago, Ill.
Covered numerous famous disorders, riots, and demonstrattions.

OTHER ACCOMPLISHMENTS/EXPERIENCE

Gold (first prize), best newsletter promotion, by The Newsletter Clearinghouse, [date]

Adjunct Professor, American University School of Communications, Washington D.C., [dates]
Adjunct Professor, George Washington University, Washington D.C., [dates]
Chair, Small Publishers Working Group, Newsletter Publishers Association, [year]

Young Professional. Associate Editor. Reverse chronological. Journalist seeks features/projects designer position. Requirements: 3 years of weekly newsroom design experience,[1] solid news judgment,[2] communication skills,[3] attention to detail,[4] and knowledge of InDesign.[5]

JANCIE ULREY
360 Cinnamon Way, Apt. 304 • Jamaica Plains, MA 02130
Cell: 617-777-6767 • Email: jan_ulrey@gmail.com

JOURNALIST/LAYOUT & DESIGN SPECIALIST

OBJECTIVE: Features/Projects Designer

PROFILE: Nearly six years' experience in weekly newspaper settings, serving as writer, editor and page designer.[1] Passionate about newsgathering and creating eye-catching, reader-friendly content. Solid news judgment and design skills,[2] coupled with imagination and creativity, able to produce aesthetically pleasing pages. Organized, detail-oriented [4] and deadline-driven. Strong time management and communications skills;[3] excel in team and individual work settings. Proficient in AP Style. **Computer Skills:** Word, Outlook, Excel, PowerPoint, Access; Quark Express; InDesign;[5] Photoshop; HTML

~ **A.A.S.,** Communications, Bunker Hill Community College, Boston, Mass., [date] ~

RELEVANT EXPERIENCE

Associate Editor   [dates]
Bay Windows   Boston, Mass.

Design, layout and write for weekly newspaper, averaging 64-136 pages, with circulation of 16,000.

- Design/Layout: Plan and execute advertising and editorial page design, including front and back pages, news and features sections, headlines, column titles, and cutlines. Review weekly ad sales and determine page count and color slots. Formulate layout design and presentation using InDesign, including style and size of type, photographs, and graphics. Take layout direction from editor and work with advertising and design staff to correct problems. Use Photoshop to make color corrections on photos and crop and rotate images; track photo archives.

- Writing/Editing: Research, develop and write news and feature stories. Contribute to editorial planning, develop story ideas and arrange and conduct interviews. Review copy and correct errors in content, grammar and punctuation, following appropriate formatting and AP style guidelines. Write/rewrite cutlines and headlines. Correct final copy and prepare files for Web upload.

Key Accomplishments:
- Successfully completed layout/production on largest paper (136 pages) in publication's history for 30th anniversary issue.
- Supported new editor, staff writer and editorial assistant during major staff transition.
- Wrote over 40 feature and news stories while handling design/production responsibilities.

Staff Writer   [dates]
The Sunday Voice   Cambridge, Mass.

Key player on four-person staff of this small weekly community newspaper.

- Writing/Content Selection: Contributed to and/or managed news coverage, determining emphasis, length, and format. Wrote hard/soft news, including school news and obituaries. Gathered information through research, interviews, experience, and attendance of events.

- Production/Administration: Planned and executed layout of school news section and obituaries, as well as determined page count and scanned photos. Edited and proofread editorial content. Assumed managing editor's duties as needed, leading news meetings, assigning stories, and gathering news content. Also, screened phone calls and purchased supplies.

Mid-Career Professional. <u>Vice President</u>. Reverse chronological. Banking executive seeks regional finance manager position. Requirements: Bachelor's degree in finance or accounting, MBA or CPA preferred,[1] 5-7 years experience in accounting, finance, and auditing,[2] proficient in SAS, SQL, Access, Excel, and PowerPoint,[3] results oriented,[4] and strong written and verbal communication skills.[5]

DAVID M. SHERLE

9080 Hopscotch Circle • Denver, CO 80012
Residence: 555-777-9090 • Office: 303-333-4545
Email: sherle_dm@comcast.net

FINANCIAL SERVICES EXECUTIVE

Special Assets/Credit Administration/Risk Management

Over 7 years' broad banking experience, including accounting, finance, and auditing.[2] Technical expertise in special assets, loan workout, and credit administration. In-depth knowledge of foreclosure and multiple bankruptcy procedures. Excellent ability to communicate and build consensus with diverse groups having dissimilar interests. Results oriented,[4] with strong negotiation, organization, and written/verbal communication skills.[5] Proficient in MS Word, Excel, Outlook, PowerPoint, Access; SQL; SAS.[3]

Leadership & Organizational Expertise

- Business & Market Development
- Strategic Planning & Development
- Team Building & Performance Improvement
- Inter- & Intra-Banking Relationships

Financial Expertise

- Corporate & Individual Credit Analysis
- Cost Benefit Analysis
- Asset Recovery
- Risk Management

PROFESSIONAL EXPERIENCE

Vice President
Community Bank, N.A., Denver. Colo.   [dates]

- Senior Workout Officer/Credit Administration Division. Monitor due diligence and integrity of distressed commercial loan, commercial real estate, and charged-off loan portfolios in excess of $15M.
- Loan Workout. Reduce non-performing assets via restructure, renegotiation, or vacate strategy. Meet with client to discuss loan status and ascertain best options to improve and/or recover loan and related expenses. Conduct cost-benefit analysis, consider credit/cash flow constraints and bankruptcy/legal remediation prior to formulation of Action Plan.
- Implement Action Plan. Work with bank's legal counsel from default initiation through account reconciliation and/or exit.
- Establish bid-in guidelines, coordinate, and finalize public auctions of real estate.
- Manage Other Real Estate Owned.
- Standing Member, Problem Loan Committee.

- Perform Quality Review, examining select loans for regulatory and internal policy compliance. Prepare reports for senior management.

Key Accomplishments:
- Reduced delinquencies from 8.85% to 2.05% of aggregate loans outstanding ($150M), net charge-off recovery of $1.95M or 36% of assigned footing ($5.48M).
- Liquidation of all Other Real Estate Owned properties.

Assistant Vice President, Special Assets Department
Southern Trust Co., Denver, Colo.   [dates]

- Managing Officer of Commercial Loan/Mortgage Workout Department. Generated monthly Action Plans for assets classified/criticized by Office of the Comptroller of the Currency.
- Underwriting Officer of SBA loan portfolio and agency leasing program.

Key Accomplishments:
- Garnered "Favorable" department rating for [dates] O.C.C. examinations.
- Reduced delinquency from 8.78% to 1.05% of aggregate loan/mortgage base ($97.5M).
- Downsized Other Real Estate Owned by 95% ($2.98M).

Assistant Vice President, Special Assets Department
Bank of the West, Tacoma, Wash.   [dates]

- Vice President of a bank subsidiary, specifically created for the sale of Other Real Estate Owned commercial properties and industrial machinery/equipment; aggregate portfolio tiered at $17.5M, with collections approximating $3.5M.
- Workout Officer for Credit/Support Services Division. Collected or restructured non-performing outstandings under commercial loan, real estate and equipment leasing portfolios. Maximized monetary recovery through credit/collateral risk analysis and distressed-asset liquidation under auction and direct sale. Managed loan portfolio in excess of $18M.
- Special Assets Officer.

Vice President, Commercial/Consumer Loan Department   [dates]
Ado State Bank, Alamosa, Colo.

- Senior Credit Officer, overseeing dual-loan portfolio in excess of $42.5M. Supervised two managers and five support staff. Implemented operational procedures and regulatory controls as required by Federal statutes.

Early Professional Career
Business Development Officer, Central Bank   [dates]
Loan Review Officer, Corporate Loan Group, Mercantile Bank   [dates]
Regional Loan Officer, Community Banking Division, Union Trust Company of Colorado [dates]

EDUCATION
MBA,[1] University of Colorado at Denver, Denver, Colo. 3.80 GPA   [date]
BA, Accounting, Adams State College, Alamosa, Colo., 3.75 GPA   [date]

DONNA LUNA

4214 Kensington Rd. • Dallas, TX 99999
Residence: 111-869-4716 • Email: DLuna@hotmail.com

PROFILE: Recent BS Biology plus 8 years' experience in veterinary and medical fields. Skilled in latest technology. Work cheerfully on team or independently. PC proficient. Dependable, conscientious veterinary paraprofessional ready for senior level veterinary hospital staff position.

LABORATORY SKILLS

✓ Dexterous use of laboratory equipment and instrumentation, including isolating environmental samples, performing assays, and identifying samples. Prepare, analyze, and test laboratory specimens. Stain slides to microscopic test for specific disease pathogens and unknowns.

✓ Assist with veterinary surgical and autopsy procedures. Perform micro animal surgeries and anesthetizations.

✓ Collect blood, and other samples from animals. Perform red/white blood cell counts.

✓ Keep comprehensive lab notes and researched, prepared, and presented detailed reports and papers. Lead and organized group project work.

WORK EXPERIENCE

Veterinary Technician   [dates]
Westview Animal Hospital, Dallas, Tx.

Veterinary Support:[1] Assist veterinarians to diagnose and treat variety of animal diseases and conditions including surgeries. Take and test blood, urine, and fecal samples, testing for disease, viruses, and parasites. Skilled with instrumentation, including radiograph and ultrasound.[3] Use Avimark, MS Word, & QuickBooks software.[4]

Reception: Receive and direct calls and visitors, answering customer inquiries and resolving problems. Assure customer satisfaction, exercising empathy and tact. Take and relay detailed messages regarding animal patients. Collect and process payments. Set appointments and send reminder notices. Update and maintain electronic and paper filing systems. Direct and provide guidance to Animal Care Assistants.

Receptionist   [dates]
Dr. Roger Lax, Plano, Tx.
Administration: Receptionist for busy private practice. Answered phones and received patients. Created and updated medical files. Gained competence with medical terminology.

EDUCATION

Bachelor of Science,[2] Biology; Towson University, Towson, Md.   [dates]

Relevant Coursework: Biostatistics, Biology: Ecology, Evolution, & Behavior, Botany, Chemistry, Comparative Animal Physiology, Dangerous Diseases, Fish Biology, Genetics, Medical Microbiology, Organic Chemistry, Physics, Zoology.

Mid-Career Professional. Project Manager. Reverse chronological. PM seeks Managerial HRIS (Human Resource Information Systems) position. Requirements: Bachelor's degree in computer science, management information systems, or equivalent, MS/MBA a plus,[1] five+ years increasing responsibility in HR Technology and/or HR discipline leading medium to large scale projects,[2] three+ years experience in project management,[3] knowledge of current HRIS technology,[4] good analytical, interpersonal, leadership and managerial skills,[5] and strong oral and written communication skills.[6]

JANICE E. DEMER

11111 Constant Road
Anaheim, CA 22222

Day/night: 999-555-5555
Email: Janiceedemer@aol.com

MANAGER
HUMAN RESOURCE INFORMATION SYSTEMS

- Project Management
- Implementation Consultant
- Quality Customer Service
- Corporate Start-ups
- Procedural Development
- Corporate & Government Contracts

- Skilled Negotiator
- Strategic Planner
- Sales Process/Full Life Cycle
- Market/Competitor Research
- Product Solutions
- Payroll

Over 5 years' solid career history in HRIS operations including start-ups, reviewing and determining software solutions for payroll and HR issues, training, and large scale project management.[2] Keen eye for analyzing problems and determining viable solutions. Demonstrated experience in effectively managing implementation cycles. Expertly control high-level client problem resolution. Develop and establish 'customer service first' environments, attaining significant levels of customer retention. Proven ability to build and lead teams, establish rapport and manage personnel.[5] Excellent written, presentation, and negotiation skills.[6]

TECHNICAL PROFICIENCY [4]

Web Based Recruiting Tools	HRIS	LANs/WANs	Visio	Word
Internet & Research	Web-based HR/PR	Pivotal	Networks	Excel
Database Management	Tools	MS Project	Access	Outlook
Client Server Technology	SQL Reporting			PowerPoint

PROFESSIONAL EXPERIENCE

Treemont Employer Services, Irvine, Calif.   [dates]
Treemont is a payroll and HR solutions outsourcing company.

Project Manager [3]   [dates]
- Implement and manage responsibilities of multiple, integrated projects. Ensure consistent success of service initiatives across customer segments and business units.
- Collaborate with senior and functional managers to plan business and technology initiatives and budgets. Use formal and informal networks to accomplish objectives.
- Manage cost, schedules and performance of large, highly complex projects. Fully accountable for complex/diverse projects with high degree of business risk.

Janice Demer, Page 2

Key Projects:
- Managed multi-product Web-based implementation worth $250K. Successfully moved a 4,000 employee global client from Windows-based PR/HR software to a Web-based HR/Payroll package. Supervised project team of 17, completing project on time and under budget.
- Carefully managed sensitive outstanding balance issue with hostile client. Directed team of five to troubleshoot complex issues, retain the account, and collect balance in full, equaling $400K.

System Consultant   [dates]
- Generated leads and secured new HRIS clients. Created and delivered proposals and demonstrations to key management personnel (user, technical user, buyer and decision-makers), meeting customer specific requirements. Maintained $8.2 million quota annually. Proposed product solutions and applications working with IT directors for system requirements and functionality. Wrote RFPs.
- Effectively tailored responses and proposals using strategic models to best position firm in marketplace. Managed large and complex client accounts, averaging 500 to 5,000 personnel.
- Reviewed current technology trends. As product expert, educated field staff on cutting edge advances in payroll & HR, recruiting, employee self-service and benefit outsourcing.

Account Executive   [dates]
- Selected at regional level for special project team studying customer retention to proactively manage and develop profitable, long-term customers.
- Met with clients to ensure complete customer satisfaction. Reviewed and recommended solutions to HRIS problems and suggested specific software. Managed conflict resolution.
- Developed account strategies to establish trends and identify opportunities to capitalize on retaining and growing customer base. Coordinated customer training. Negotiated long-term agreements.

Consultant/Implementations   [dates]
- Analyzed customers' payroll needs and provided recommendations for streamlining payroll processes. Negotiated contracts up to $5M.
- Trained customers on Source 500 software. Provided quality on-going customer support, ensuring successful implementation of payroll, human resources, and tax filing accounts.

Mountain High Health Services, Villa Park, Calif.

                                                                               [dates]
Mountain High held a government contract for the military insurance program—housing multiple large databases with hundreds of thousands of files and records.

Operations Supervisor
- Developed and implemented start-up plans/operations/audits to employ and operate call center with 700 employees. Implemented new database software and controlled large databases.
- Hired and trained 60 direct-report employees, set-up department, and staffed call center with 500 additional personnel. Determined all staffing requirements, providing timely hiring and training.

EDUCATION

   M.A.,[1] Information Access and Management, University of California, Irvine, GPA: 4.0   [date]
   B.A., Human Resources Management, California State University Fullerton, GPA: 3.85   [date]
   Project Management Institute, Irvine, Calif., Member

Chapter 13

A Sampling of OnTarget Resumes for Special Circumstances

· ·

*J*ust because you're changing careers or stepping out of your military uniform, or explaining resume gaps, or running away from home back into the workforce, or are ready to belt the next person who calls you "overqualified," don't think you're necessarily at a disadvantage. You can create a riveting resume. The samples in this chapter give you some ideas about how to do just that by deftly handling your special circumstances.

A box atop each sample resume contains a mission statement — that is, what the job seeker aims to accomplish, which usually is a better job. The mission statement also includes the requirements for a specific position — or a summary of the typically requested requirements for an occupation or career field. You may be surprised that the requirements have numbers. And that the numbers are cross-matched to qualifications in the resume. Does this mean you are supposed to put numbers on your resumes as these samples show? The answer is: No! No! A thousand times no!

The cross-matched numbers between a job's requirements and the candidate's qualifications shown here are just for illustration, *not for your actual resumes.*

These samples are intended to laser your attention to requirement-and-qualification matching, the single most important factor in causing your candidacy to get noticed in an online swarm of resumes.

Career Change. Flight Attendant. Reverse chronological. Experienced flight attendant seeks new career in sales/account management outside travel field. Requirements: Bachelor's degree,[1] 5+ years' Customer Service Support or Sales Experience,[2] proficiency in Word, Excel, and Outlook,[3] excellent communication, organization, time management, and presentation skills,[4] and willingness to be part of a high-performing team![5]

Pamela Wright

111 Baldwin Station Rd., Apt. #304
Seattle, WA 99999

Day/Evening: (777) 333-2525   p_wright@yahoo.com

OBJECTIVE: Customer Service Account Manager

QUALIFICATIONS SUMMARY:

Results-driven Customer Service professional with over 5 years of customer service support experience.[2] Self-confidence, integrity, and commitment to customer service excellence. Creative, pragmatic and proactive problem-solver. Organized and attentive to detail, with demonstrated time management skills. Strong research, mediation, and negotiation skills gained from work place experience. Dynamic oral, writing, interpersonal, and presentation skills.[4] Energetic team member.[5] PC proficient.

PROFESSIONAL EXPERIENCE

Lead Flight Attendant   [dates]
Northwest Airlines, Inc., Seattle, Wash.

Supervise Staff, Customer Liaison:
- Answer customer inquiries and resolve problems, working with diverse clientele. Anticipate and assess needs; assist passengers with baggage and boarding. Build customer rapport; use diplomacy and tact to avoid confrontational situations and defuse hostile customers.
- Oversee work performance of up to four flight attendants during flights. Consult with cockpit and cabin crew for trip briefings. Use communication log to update staff and management.

Plan and organize in-flight services flow and ensure safety and comfort of passengers. Collect payment for retail products. Account for meals, beverages, and other supplies.

Leadership of Flight Attendants.
- Elected to lead 525 flight attendants. Coordinated six employee support committees.
- Developed and managed database systems to track and distribute information.
- Developed leadership training and budget requirements.

Maintain knowledge of government regulations.
- Interpret and communicate complex regulations, policies, and procedures in language the public can understand.
- Continually analyze work processes and recommend ways to improve operations and services.

Notable Achievements:
- Awarded three Certificates of Excellence for providing exceptional service to customers.
- Developed new procedure to improve flexibility for handling emergencies.

EDUCATION/COMPUTER SKILLS

Bachelor of Arts, [1] **Communication**   [date]
The George Washington University, School of Media and Public Affairs, Washington, D.C.

Windows; Word, Outlook, PowerPoint, Excel.[3]

Returning Homemaker. <u>Nurse</u>. Functional. Homemaker seeks R.N. position. Requirements: Current Registered Nurse license,[1] graduate of approved School of Nursing,[2] current physical assessment skills,[3] comprehensive knowledge of nursing principles,[4] current CPR certification,[5] strong attention to detail,[6] and patient/family interaction skills.[7]

Pearl Izumi, R.N.

666 Bisbury Road • Dallas, TX 99999
Cell: 222-888-4040 • Email: pearlizumi@hotmail.com

SUMMARY: Licensed Registered Nurse[1] with comprehensive knowledge of nursing principles.[4] Three years of field/classroom experience. Dependable and highly organized, with excellent attention to detail [6] and follow through. Personable, able to develop positive rapport and empathize with patient and family.[7] Strong communication skills—speaking, listening, and writing. Experienced in managing crisis situations and resolving problems. Enjoy working as a team member or individually. Experienced instructor.

KEY SKILLS/QUALIFICATIONS

➢ Direct patient care; patient charting and client care documentation; robust physical condition [3]
➢ Assessing patient condition, planning appropriate treatment and administering patient care and discharge plans
➢ Educating patients and family for home care [7]
➢ Maintaining sterile fields and applying dressings; catheter, IV, and suctioning training; cleaning instruments and surgical equipment
➢ CPR certified, valid through [date] [5]

EARLIER EXPERIENCE

Trainer   [dates: more than a decade ago]
Best Solutions Group, Irving, Texas
➢ Developed training program and presented software curriculum for healthcare companies.
➢ Analyzed client needs and created appropriate training materials. Wrote curriculum and materials for companies in four states. Designed/presented "The Trainer's Trainer" program for Canadian counterparts.

EDUCATION

A.A.,[2] Nursing, El Centro College, Dallas, Texas; GPA 4.0   [date]
Clinical: Parkland Memorial Hospital, Irving Coppell Surgical Hospital, Dallas Southwest Medical Center, Renaissance Hospital

General coursework, Boston College, Boston, Mass., 60 credits   [dates: more than a decade ago]

> **Military to Civilian.** <u>Operations Manager</u>. Hybrid. Army officer seeks to transition into Supply Chain Management for Government Contractors. Requirements: 10+ years supply chain management experience,[1] 10+ years supervisory experience,[2] degree in Logistics, Industrial Engineering, or related discipline,[3] strong relationship-building skills,[4] and excellent communication and presentation skills; high integrity.[5]

JERRY W. THOMAS

CR 475 Box 12 * APO AE 09000
011-49 (0) 555-5555555 (c) * jerryw.thomas@yahoo.com

CAREER FOCUS
SUPPLY CHAIN MANAGEMENT

TRANSPORTATION • OPERATIONS • INSTRUCTOR • FORCE PROTECTION

PROFESSIONAL AND PERSONAL VALUE OFFERED

- Current Secret Clearance
- Twenty years' professional experience as an Operations Manager with specific expertise in large-scale transportation and supply management operations.[1]
- Superior technical and interpersonal communications, building strong relationships and alliances.[4] Excellent written, verbal and presentation skills.[5] Thoroughly enjoy challenges and creative problem resolution. Maintain high integrity.[5]
- Draft and implement policies and procedures. Manage logistical and administrative requirements for hundreds of personnel supporting thousands of customers in multiple countries—knowledge of treaties and regulations governing arms control and property book control.
- Quickly assess operations and initiate improvements in staffing, organization and procedures. Manage multiple, simultaneous and complex projects and programs.
- Assemble, motivate, train, and inspire talented working teams/staffs. Consistently produce quality.

PROFESSIONAL EMPLOYMENT AND SELECTED EXAMPLES OF QUALIFICATIONS IN ACTION

MANAGER, RANGE CONTROL & SAFETY [dates]
U.S. Army, Deployed to Kosovo

- Manage administration, resource planning, safety coordination, and operations for a range serving complex 30 separate organizations in Europe. Create schedules and communicate with customers for scheduling requirements. Write reports and submit documentation.
- Serve as a consultant and advisor to Director on safety, operations, and specific issues.
- Formulate safety guidelines and policies and provide operational guidance. Assure that customers adhere to safety policies and procedures.
- Acted as consultant to area managers to prepare quotes, negotiate contracts, monitor shipments, and coordinate deliveries within Europe and Eastern Asia.

JERRY. W. THOMAS   011-49 (0) 555-5555555 (c)

OPERATIONS MANAGER   [dates]
ACCOUNT MANAGER   [dates]
Brown and Root Contractor, Germany

- Supervised warehouse operations including receiving merchandise and delivery. Supervised 38 personnel[2] including five administrative staff, seven subcontractors, 23 warehouse personnel, and three contract security personnel responsible for warehousing and storage of $33M perishable and non-perishable products. Supervised, evaluated work performance, and rated employees.
- Coordinated incoming shipments with shipping contractors (military and civilian), managed the workload, monitored manpower requirements, processed special orders and critical deliveries.
- Managed customer service, ensuring customer satisfaction. Developed an SOP to track shipments.
- Supply Center Program – Europe Account Manager: Managed new and existing requisition and supply accounts. Supervised and coordinated resources with local vendors for purchases up to $15M.

U.S. Army (Senior Noncommissioned Officer)   [dates]
SENIOR ADMINISTRATOR   [dates]
First Infantry Division, Germany

- Managed and supervised logistical operation procedures. Oversight direction for administration and coordination of training support, safety control, and supply requirements during deployment and contingency training in a split-country operation.
- Directed logistical operations for 42 sub-divisional units including field deployments, division gunneries, and maneuver densities. Managed $900K worth of equipment.
- Assisted the Food Service Supervisor in interpreting and implementing Army's Food Service program and provided multifunctional logistical support for operations in garrison and field. Supervised staff of 89, provided class I support to 1,200 soldiers, accounted for $7M in equipment, and managed annual budget of $90,000.
- Selected to provide logistical training support and foreign military training in Hungary. Coordinated logistical requirements for 4,200 personnel and trained individual delegations on logistical support from setting up a command to managing a supply channel.

OPERATIONS SUPERVISOR, Korea   [dates]

- Coordinated and directed maneuvers, supply operations, inventories, hand-receipts, special procurements and other logistical requirements for 20 sub-divisional organizations including inspections and evaluations.
- Implemented emergency, disaster, and combat feeding plans (computed supply usage factors). Developed SOPs for safety, security, and fire prevention programs.

Education, Training & Awards

B.S.,[3] Business/Integrated Supply Chain & Operations Management,   [dates]
University of Phoenix, Phoenix, Az

International Merchant, Purchase Authorization Card training, [date] • Requisition and Local Procurement Management Training, [date] • Senior Advisor and Management Course, [date] (3 weeks) • Automated Management Information System, [date] • Advanced Leadership and Management Course, 6 weeks, [date]

Overqualified. Manager. Reverse chronological. Equal Employment Program Administrator seeks lighter responsibility as EEO consultant or investigator.(Candidate has a master's degree but doesn't mention it because the job ad doesn't call for an advanced degree. She would mention the fact in an interview. And the candidate would include her master's if the job ad stipulated a preference for an advanced or professional degree.) Requirements: Minimum of three years' Human Resources, EEO Claims, Employment Law and/or related experience,[1] Bachelor's degree in Business Administration, Human Resources or related field.[2] Solid investigative and writing skills,[3] organizational, time-management, and interpersonal skills.[4]

PAMELA THIERRY

123 East Lake St. Apt. 111   Home: 111-333-0505
Kansas City, MO 12345   E-mail: pam_thierry@aol.com   Cell: 111-444-0909

OBJECTIVE

EEO Consultant. Energetic and dedicated, though no longer enjoy frantic managerial pace. Seeking challenging non-managerial position.

PROFESSIONAL SUMMARY

- Exceptional conflict resolution, investigation and mediation skills [3]
- Proven ability to organize work, prioritize tasks and produce high quality work products in a timely manner [4]
- Expert knowledge of EEO laws and procedures.
- Demonstrated interpersonal,[4] written and oral communications skills [3]
- Results oriented and effective team leader
- Dedicated, with strong work ethic
- Word, Excel, Outlook, Access, PowerPoint, Internet research skills

PROFESSIONAL EXPERIENCE

CENTERS FOR MEDICARE & MEDICAID SERVICES   [dates] [1]
Kansas City, Mo.

Supervisory Equal Employment Opportunity Specialist
- Team Leader for the Office of Equal Opportunity and Civil Rights' EEO complaints processing team. Consult with customers to acquire information, collect and analyze evidence, and prepare investigative reports. Negotiate conciliations and interact with complainants, agency staff, and legal staff.
- Direct and monitor Alternative Dispute Resolution (ADR) Program for EEO complaints.
- Direct and monitor EEO Contract Investigations Program.
- Prepare and deliver presentations and training for agency EEO counselors, Federal ADR professionals, and agency managers and employees.

PAMELA THIERRY Cell: 111-444-0909

Key Accomplishment:
- Brought agency into 100% compliance with all EEO regulatory time frames. Reconciled EEO complaint inventory. Eliminated backlog of complaints. Improved quality of written work products. Established office as a model for complaint processing.

U.S. EQUAL EMPLOYMENT OPPORTUNITY COMMISSION   [dates]
St. Louis, Mo.

Held a series of increasingly responsible positions in **Equal Employment Opportunity** and **Alternative Dispute Resolution**.
Alternative Dispute Resolution Coordinator (Acting), [dates]; Mediator/Facilitator, [dates]; Intake Supervisor, [dates]; Investigator/ADR Coordinator, [dates]; Systemic Investigator, [dates]; Investigator, [dates]

- Managed and evaluated EEOC, St. Louis District Field Office's mediation program.
- Used variety of ADR processes to resolve employment discrimination complaints involving private companies and state, local, and Federal agencies.
- Investigated class allegations of employment discrimination.
- Investigated individual charges of discrimination involving private companies and state and local government agencies.
- Managed and responded to Congressional inquiries, White House correspondence, interagency referrals, and public inquiries.

Key Accomplishments
- Effectively managed inventory of 100 cases, while consistently receiving positive feedback from clients regarding timeliness, responsiveness, and outcome of mediation sessions. Expanded Field Office use of ADR.
- Recognized for high level of success in resolving complex cases.
- Contributor to development of nationwide Mediation Training Program for staff and contract mediators.
- High percentage of investigations resulting in findings of discrimination and conciliation agreements.

ADDITIONAL PROFESSIONAL EXPERIENCE

U.S. Department of Justice, Community Relations Service; Internship
U.S. Office of Personnel Management; Investigator
National Institute on Aging, Gerontology Research Center; Library and Research Assistant

EDUCATION

Bachelor's Degree,[2] Business Administration, Truman State University, Kirksville, Mo.

PROFESSIONAL AFFILIATIONS

Co-Chair, Federal Executive Board, Alternative Dispute Resolution Council
Volunteer Mediator, Federal Executive Board, Mediation Services Program
Volunteer Mediator, Department of Justice, Office of Civil Rights, Disability Rights Section

Grouping Temp Jobs. Legal Assistant. Reverse chronological. Legal Assistant seeks Paralegal position, based on recent certification and 7 years' experience in legal field. Requirements: Paralegal certificate,[1] at least 5 years' experience in legal setting,[2] experience in preparing contracts and agreements,[3] excellent communications skills,[4] advanced computer skills,[5] minimum typing speed 75 wpm,[6] project management skills,[7] professional demeanor.[8]

BRINDA BASU

333 Bladensburg Avenue • Dallas, TX 12345
Residence: (444) 777-1212 • Cell: (444) 999-1919
Email: brinda_basu@gmail.com

OBJECTIVE: Paralegal

Over 7 years' experience as legal assistant and legal secretary,[2] with additional administrative experience. Expertise in legal research, drafting pleadings and motions, scheduling depositions and coordinating hearings, case file management and analysis, record keeping and data tracking, client interviewing and recommending actions. Law experience includes Personal Injury, Medical Malpractice, Family Law, Estate Planning, Workers' Comp and Corporate Law.

Core competencies include efficiency, organization, working well under pressure and deadlines and attention to detail. Professional demeanor,[8] with excellent interpersonal and communications skills.[4] Typing speed: 75 wpm.[6]

COMPUTER PROFICIENCIES [5]

Expert in MS Office: Word, Excel, Outlook, Access; WordPerfect; Quicken; Internet; familiar with Lexis-Nexis and various legal billing and litigation management software

EMPLOYMENT HISTORY

Paralegal Intern [dates]
Public Defender's Office, Dallas, Texas

• Reported directly to and provided support for Public Defender in busy city district. Researched cases and transcribed tapes. Summarized police reports and compiled trial notebook. Maintained and updated legal case files. Wrote speedy trial motion.

Legal Assistant
Harlow Staffing Services, Dallas, Texas [dates]

Assigned to Dallas/Fort Worth law firms, including: James & Marks; Dean M. Holly; Linda K. Ryan; Gonzalez & Gonzalez; Dixie and Moor

- Office Management: Coordinated office functions for small law firms, including client file management, billing and accounts payable and receivable. Supervised administrative and word processing staff.

- Research/Writing: Conducted thorough research of federal and state statutes, using Internet and law libraries. Identified and summarized relevant points in primary and secondary authorities of law. Applied court opinions, statutes and court rules in writing recommendations for course of action on complex personal injury and property damage claims. Prepared contracts, agreements and other legal documents.[3]

- Litigation Support/Case Management: Served as project manager for casework and litigation support.[7] Summarized depositions, medical records, employment records and other relevant documents. Organized documents for trial. Drafted various pleadings and documents for medical malpractice, personal injury and family law actions. Coordinated expedited hearings and met all filing deadlines. Scheduled and assisted with depositions.

- Personal Injury, Tort Law/Medical Knowledge: Experienced in tort law, case analysis procedures, discovery and client/witness interviewing. Knowledge of medical terminology.

Legal Assistant
The Ramirez Law Firm, Dallas, Texas   [dates]

- Executive assistant to Senior Partner and associate. Wrote and followed up on longshoremen and workers' compensation claims. Interviewed claimants for relevant information and summarized cases. Scheduled depositions and ensured all parties received notices. Provided liaison with opposing counsel to determine and/or confirm course of action. Contacted insurance companies to follow up on claims and communications.

Legal Secretary
Law Offices of Danes and Smith, Dallas, Texas   [dates]

- Assisted in timely and complex preparation of cases from discovery to trial phase. Prepared case files, including case summaries, supporting forms and documentation. Processed wide range of business contracts. Researched cases, decisions, laws and statutes.
- Managed scheduling functions. Received and reviewed all incoming correspondence. Prepared outgoing correspondence, including client, court and opposing counsel communications. Screened and directed calls and visitors.

EDUCATION/TRAINING

Paralegal Certificate,[1] Southeastern Career Institute, Dallas, Texas, GPA: 4.0/4.0   [date]

Mediation & Conflict Resolution Certificate, Texas Women's University   [date]

A.A. Degree, Liberal Arts, Camden County College, Camden, N.J.   [date]

Military Spouse. <u>Military Family Member</u>. Reverse chronological. Instructor and Training Coordinator seeks Trainer position. Requirements: Bachelor's degree,[1] minimum of 5 years of experience in adult education, curriculum design and development,[2] experience coordinating and administering training programs,[3] knowledge of curriculum evaluations including qualitative and quantitative analysis,[4] excellent communications and program marketing skills,[5] and willing to travel.[6]

MELODY ANN RICHARDS

456 Pine St. • Falls Church, VA 99999
Evening Phone: 666-333-4444 • Day Phone: 666-333-3333
Email: <u>melody.richards@comcast.net</u>

TRAINER
Training and Curriculum Specialist, Instructor, Coordinator

- ✓ Experienced instructor with 5+ years' experience in training and curriculum design [2]
- ✓ Public speaking, teaching professional adults clearly, comfortably and memorably [5]
- ✓ Excellent content developer utilizing interactive exercises and multi-media images in PowerPoint presentations
- ✓ Skilled in curriculum design and lesson planning
- ✓ Critical analysis, including qualitative and quantitative review of course evaluations for continuous improvement [4]
- ✓ Excellent listening and consulting skills meeting management and personal training objectives; willing to travel [6]

PROFESSIONAL EXPERIENCE

Employment Readiness Assistant   [dates]
Army Community Service, Ft. Myer Military Community, Va.

<u>Career Instruction.</u> Instruct military personnel and family members in job search strategies, interview skills and resume writing techniques.

<u>Employment Counseling.</u> Train military community in employment strategies both individually and in classroom settings. Coordinate appointments and group trainings.[3] Assist clients with job search, resume writing and interviewing skills. Market qualified applicants to local employers in private industry, county, state and federal government.

<u>Job Fair and Special Event Coordination.</u> Organize and facilitate job fairs, career expos and luncheons. As team member, manage events for up to 200 family members seeking employment.

Accomplishments:
- ✓ Successfully developed relationships with more than 20 local small and mid-sized businesses for consideration of spouse employment.[5]
- ✓ Established cooperation with federal agency human resources recruiters to establish placement opportunities with Federal Career Internship programs.
- ✓ Developed successful interactive curriculum, which has resulted in excellent class attendance and evaluations.

MELODY ANN RICHARDS, page 2   666-333-4444

Senior Core Instructor   [dates]
Universal Movement, Virginia Beach, Va.

    <u>Program Design.</u> Developed syllabus and implemented marketing strategies for numerous yoga classes and workshops. Coordinated program offerings and class schedules.[3] As Core Instructor, managed program oversight, assessment and evaluation.

    <u>Coaching and Instruction.</u> Regularly met with students to review required hours and complete grid for registry application.

    Accomplishment:
    ✓ Co-designed initial teacher training program in accordance with industry guidelines.

Program Developer/Instructor   [dates]
Adult Learning Center, Virginia Beach, Va.

    <u>Course Development and Marketing.</u>[5] Expanded yoga program from one class to eight classes per week in addition to monthly weekend workshops.

    <u>Curriculum Design and Evaluation.</u> Wrote class descriptions and syllabus. Developed marketing materials, class evaluations, and lending library for students.

    Accomplishment:
    ✓ Increased classroom enrollment by 110% over one year.

EDUCATION

    B.S.,[1] Business Administration, University of Nebraska, Lincoln, Neb.   [date]

AFFILIATIONS AND LICENSES

    Career Masters Institute   [dates]
    Association of Job Search Trainers   [dates]
    Licensed Yoga Instructor   [dates]
    Licensed Yoga "Train the Trainer" Instructor and Curriculum Design   [date]

TRAINING COURSES

    Training and Presentation Coaching, Worldwide Media, New York City   [dates]
    Training in PowerPoint Design and Program Marketing, 16 classroom hours   [date]
    Extensive Yoga Training and Development, US and International courses   [date]

COMPUTER SKILLS

    Microsoft Office: Word, Excel, Outlook, PowerPoint, Access; Adobe Photoshop (basic skills).

Too Many Layoffs. <u>Information Technology</u>. Hybrid. Information technology network expert seeks Network Analyst position. (Through no fault of his own, candidate has been laid-off three times in about four years. To prevent employer's assuming he was terminated for cause or is a job hopper, candidate makes exception to the resume rule of giving no reasons for leaving a job.) Requirements: Bachelor's degree in Computer Science or equivalent training and several years of related full-time experience,[1] experience operating and configuring security and networking on enterprise systems,[2] excellent customer service skills,[3] knowledge of networks routing and switching equipment, authentication systems, network diagnosis tools,[4] and experience with Windows and Unix.[5]

JASON P. KING

222 Birmingham Ave.   Pittsburgh, PA 99999
Cell: 555-444-1010   Email: jpking@gmail.com   Home: 555-555-9090

Network analyst and security administrator more than three years of LAN administrative experience.[1] Recognized for expert troubleshooting, using network analyzers and test equipment to quickly solve network hardware problems. Able to research past problem resolutions and develop new solutions. Adept in planning, coordinating, and controlling automated systems.

AREAS OF EXPERTISE

- <u>Local Area Networks:</u> Experienced in installation/configuration of new software modules, user training, diagnostic and problem resolution, testing and providing operational support and maintaining/monitoring automated systems.

- <u>System Design:</u> Adept at analyzing, designing and implementing computer software to manage central systems.

- <u>Customer Service & Communications:</u> Good at understanding and resolving client problems.[3] Outstanding documentation, written and verbal communication skills. Comfortable in high-pressure, 24/7 on-call environment. Team member and mentor.

IT KNOWLEDGE AND SKILLS

Software: [4,5] Novell NetWare 3.1/4.0, Win95/98/XP/Vista, IIS, Linux (RedHat), Checkpoint Firewall1/VPN1, Visio, Cisco PIX, Unix Citrix

Hardware: [4] PC maintenance/installation, servers, desktops and laptops, Cisco Routers/Catalyst Switches, Cabletron Ethernet/Fast Ethernet, Ascend/Lucent ISDN

Networking: Peer-to-Peer, Client/Server, TCP/IP, DHCP, WINS, DNS, Routing, Network Cabling, FDDI, Gateways, Firewalls, Ethernet, VPN

CERTIFICATIONS [1]

MCSE, MCP+Internet,   [date]
MCP: NT Workstation, Server, Enterprise, TCP/IP, IIS3.0,   [date]
A+ certified,   [date]

JASON P. KING   Cell: 555-444-1010   Email: jpking@gmail.com

PROFESSIONAL EXPERIENCE

Network Administrator   [dates]
Allegheny Computer Systems, Inc., Pittsburgh, Penn.
(Company being sold.)

- Administer, direct and integrate networks in multiple platforms.
- Develop, assess, maintain and configure LAN/WAN network hardware, software telecommunications and systems solutions.**2** Troubleshoot network security, servers, LAN/WAN hardware, software and integration. Perform vulnerability assessment testing.
- Manage corporate network and servers. Configure routers, switches, servers and firewalls.

Key Accomplishment:
Managed selection, installation, configuration and testing of monitoring software, ensuring 99.99% uptime. Spent half of allotted $50,000 budget.

Firewall Administrator/Contractor   [dates]
GBH Consulting, Ingram, Penn.
(Company closed.)

- Built firewall security policy from the ground up; created security policy for customers based on need and services provided. Monitored and maintained customer firewalls, building and troubleshooting VPNs and secure dial-in connections
- Troubleshot customer issues.
- Technical point-of-contact for sales staff; trained personnel in networking and firewall security.

Cisco Engineer/Contractor   [dates]
TechSys Solutions, Mt. Oliver, Penn.
(Company lost major contract, resulting in significant staff layoffs.)

- Monitored and maintained 135+ diverse and complex Web hosting client network environments. (24/7, 99.99% uptime.)
- Reviewed router and switch configuration, checked for anomalies, anticipated/averted problems.
- Monitored and managed multiple data lines through six global data centers.

Systems Integration Manager   [dates]
Three Rivers Computers, Pittsburgh, Penn.

- Managed, trained and supervised production staff of 11 technicians.
- Configured, integrated and serviced PCs; installed and configured software applications for workstations, servers and laptops. Troubleshot hardware and software.

EDUCATION

BS Degree, Computer Science*, College of Allegheny County   [date to present]

*48 of 62 required credits completed

Page 2

Employment Gap. Program Manager. Hybrid. Former project officer seeks to return to professional project work after 5-year unemployment gap and recent teaching experience. Focused on employment with government contractors. (Education showing updated skills positioned before outdated 10-year old technical relevant experience. Unemployment gap explanation buried at end of resume.) Requirements: significant senior experience as Project Manager,[1] demonstrated success in coordinating with government contracting personnel,[2] negotiating and managing expectations with senior government executives,[3] managing task order operations on time and on budget,[4] hiring and managing staff,[5] and program administration.[6]

JACKSON FELS

111 W. Cherry Avenue • Atlanta, GA 30302 • 777-999-1212 • Email: jacksonfels@aol.com

Summery of Qualifications

Integrity-driven, versatile **Project Manager** 17 years of increasingly responsible experience in the government sector; 6 years of project management experience.[1] Cross-functional expertise supporting core business functions, including Technical Research, Contract Development/Procurements, Customer Relations, Project Planning/Coordination, Budget Analysis, and Technology Utilization. Strong analytical, organizational, and administrative skills. Positive, adaptable, and motivated.

Areas of Expertise

- **Organization:** Logical and highly-organized. Excel in prioritizing and completing tasks and meeting budget goals and deadlines without compromising quality or productivity.[4] Extensive project management, budget management, scheduling, and procurement experience.

- **Expert Technical Skills:** Ability to define systems requirements, coordinate hardware/software purchases, and adapt commercial-off-the-shelf software (COTS). Programming background.

- **Oral/Written Communications:** Experience interfacing with people of diverse backgrounds, including coordinating tasks with government and contracting personnel.[2] Skilled in writing and editing.

- **Client/Customer Service:** Excellent negotiation and customer interface skills. Direct liaison to senior management,[3] external clients, vendors, and consultants.

Selected Education & Certifications

Master of Education, University of Georgia, Athens, Ga.,	[date]
A+ and Network+ Certifications	[date]
B.S., Computer Science, Georgia Institute of Technology, Atlanta, Ga., Honors graduate	[date]
B.A., Organizational Communications/Journalism, Minor: Government,	[date]

Relevant Professional Experience

Technical Intelligence Project Officer [dates]
Defense Intelligence Agency (DIA)
Directed information technology program[6] to upgrade information security and improve intelligence data management and dissemination. Developed requirements, budgets, and schedules. Coordinated all project phases from development through implementation. Liaison to internal and external clients, vendors, contract officers, consultants, military and national intelligence organizations.

- **Contracts/Logistics:** Oversaw procurements of large computer systems. Wrote Request for Proposals and Statements of Work. Defined and documented technical requirements. Reviewed funding.
- **Personnel/EEO Support:** Resolved personnel matters. Held successful conflict resolution meetings with military and civilian staff. Selected by supervisor to serve on Personnel Hiring Panels. Oversaw interview and hiring of professional and administrative personnel.[5] Trained and managed staff of 10.
- Researched and analyzed Counter Intelligence Research Branch operations to determine computer systems requirements to support intelligence data collection, analysis, retrieval, and dissemination.
- Interviewed senior intelligence staff to gather source data. Planned and executed in-depth study of DIA intelligence work stations. Managed deadlines and briefed branch chiefs on project progress, status, and timelines.

Selected Accomplishments:
- Successfully executed all team projects on schedule and within budget.
- Planned and implemented organizational studies to evaluate workflow, system requirements, and collection needs. Summarized and presented detailed analyses to DoD officials.
- Successfully planned and accomplished the total hardware and software automation of the Human Intelligence and Counter Intelligence Offices.

Computer Systems Project Officer   [dates]
Computer Programmer [dates]
Department of Defense (DoD), U.S. Army

Computer Systems Project Officer [dates]: Oversaw the contractual, logistical and financial processes for large-scale office automation projects. Planned and executed analysis of the INSCOM center's operations. Provided technical advice and support to cross-functional teams. Independently planned and conducted in-depth research and analysis of ADP system design, interrelationships, operating mode, software, and equipment configuration. Promoted from Computer Programmer.

Other Experience & Additional Information

Substitute Teacher   [date to Present]
Atlanta City Public Schools, Atlanta, Ga.

Roving substitute for Title 10 schools in Atlanta, Ga. Teach reading, implement lesson plans, and manage classrooms for first to fifth grade students with learning and physical disabilities and behavioral problems.

Full-Time Student   [dates]

While still caring for now school-aged child, completed Master's degree in Education. Also, volunteered as reading instructor and coach.

Caretaker   [dates]

Resigned full-time position to adopt and care for toddler and care for dying elder relative, allowing spouse to retain full-time position. Also, resolved stress-related illness.

Military to Civilian. <u>Sourcing Manager</u>. Hybrid. Newly retired Army Contracting Officer seeks senior private-sector job with federal government contractor (Note: Unlike most private-sector businesses, military terminology/jargon is understood and valued by civilian government contractors). Requirements: minimum 10 years' procurement,[1] college degree (advanced degree preferred),[2] ability to coordinate overall material management effort,[3] strong leadership and decision-making skills,[4] and excellent computer skills.[5]

MICHAEL HSIEH

6565 S. Northway Dr.   Residence: 999-444-9090
Jackson, MS 92000   Email: michael_hsieh@army.mil

MATERIAL MANAGEMENT SENIOR MANAGER

Sourcing Manager with over 12 years' experience managing full contract life cycle for multi-million dollar procurements in military/federal area.[1] Combine in-depth knowledge of federal acquisition regulations and performance-based acquisition solutions with Six Sigma project management expertise. Expert on logistics and supply chain management, acquisition planning, material management, pre/post-award contract documentation, and contractor compliance monitoring.[3] Innovative problem solver with keen business acumen, demonstrated skill in making sound decisions, motivating leadership skills,[4] and demonstrated win-win philosophy. Excellent computer skills.[5] Clearance: DOD Secret.

CERTIFICATIONS

DAWIA Level II Certification (Contracting) [date]
Contracting Officer Warrant: $5 million

EXPERTISE

- **Acquisitions:** Manage full procurement life cycle, from acquisitions planning through solicitation, selection, award, and contract management.

- **Logistics:** Plan, coordinate, and evaluate logistical actions in support of agency mission.

- **Program Analysis:** Conduct program and cost analysis in the preparation of Business Case alternatives to achieve short- and long-term strategic goals.

- **Consulting:** Provide expert planning, analysis, and advice on program alternatives, strategies, and costs.

ACCOMPLISHMENT HIGHLIGHTS

- Awarded over 170 contracts valued in excess $160M during six-month deployment. Major awards include a $25M bus transportation requirement and $78M agreement between the United States and the Hashemite Kingdom of Jordan to train Armed Forces.

- Completed site survey and $32M contract awards to complete a major building in 18 days.

- As Contractor Administrator with Contingency Contracting Administration team overseas, realized $1.5M in cost savings for construction of camp to house refugees.

PROFESSIONAL EXPERIENCE

United States Army   [dates]

Emergency Essential Contingency Contracting Officer   [dates]

As a warranted ($5M) Contracting Officer for the Project and Contracting Office (PCO), directed full contract life cycle for wide range of complex acquisitions with high visibility in Iraqi Reconstruction Effort. Acquisitions have supported construction projects throughout the country, primarily focused on renovation of critical police stations and commodities for Armed Forces. Administered and awarded Delivery Orders against $20M requirements contract for clothing and textile commodities in support of the nation's uniformed services. Developed Solicitation Plan for $200M vehicle maintenance contract. Applied Six Sigma principles to develop continuity files and contracting templates to streamline acquisition process.

Supply Chain Management Analyst, Fleet Industrial Supply Center   [dates]

Provided program management support for Supply Chain processes in Southeast Asia. Identified inefficiencies and redundancies achieving annual cost savings of over $830K [date]. Orchestrated bottom up review of Personal Property program. Reconciliation of 3,356 line items and $11M worth of Minor Property resulted in "Outstanding" rating.

Chief Logistics and Contracting Officer   [dates]

Managed all logistical support for 250-solider detachment deployed to Camp Zama, Japan. Supervised 25 officer and enlisted soldiers managing wide range of services including budget, contracting, payroll, retail sales, mail, and hazardous materials. Reduced base-wide inventory costs by 10% ($150K) by application of automated inventory control systems. Prepared $900K budget request for an Unfunded Requirement resulting in 100% funding for critical programs.

Deputy Logistics Director, Regional Contracting Center   [dates]

Managed Logistics Support Center operations, including oversight for all contract administration, warehousing, stock, transportation, mail, fuel supply management, and support for troops operating in Southeast Asia and Australia. Developed a Business Case resulting in approval of $1.1M for Web-enabled Enterprise Resource Management solution, projected to save $1.5B.

Contingency Contract Specialist, Defense Contract Management Agency   [dates]

Managed all DCMA post-award functions including evaluating contractor performance, interpreting contract laws and provisions, negotiating contract modifications, determining price and cost analysis, and ensuring timely delivery. Coordinated with United Nations Health Care Relief, Halliburton, and U.S. Navy and Air Force LOGCAP program managers to execute multi-million Cost-Plus Award Fee contracts. Realized $1.5M in cost savings by reducing procurement lead times.

EDUCATION

Master of Business Administration,[2] University of Baltimore, Baltimore, Md. [date]

Bachelor of Science,[2] General Science/Math, Jackson State University, Jackson, Miss., [date]

Too Many Jobs. <u>Administrative Security Specialist in federal agency</u>. Functional. Seeking Administrative Security Manager position in civilian government contracting firm. (Because candidate risks being perceived as job hopper, she uses two techniques: Group jobs by theme, and make exception to rule of not giving reasons for leaving jobs.) Requirements: Experience with facility, personnel, information, operations, personnel and physical security,[1] 3 years security experience,[2] strong interpersonal, speaking and writing skills,[3] must pass background investigation.[4]

MOLLY DANNER

5400 Via Romaza, Colorado Springs, CO 80927

Cell 555-555-9999   molly.danner@comcast.com   Home: 555-555-8812

OBJECTIVE: Administrative Security Manager

PROFILE: Security specialist with three years of security experience;[2] former contract administrator and budget analyst. Expertise includes gathering information and preparing security reports, conducting security training, and establishing and enforcing security procedures. Strong interpersonal, speaking and writing skills.[3] Fast learner, adaptable. Hold SCI Security Clearance.[4]

SECURITY SKILLS ON JOB

- Ensure compliance with departmental security policies, procedures and instructions to safeguard classified information, facilities, equipment and human resources.
- Advise senior staff on security awareness, classification, travel, courier and communications policies.Develop and update Security Operating Procedures and Training Manuals/Materials.
- Implement security violation detection, prevention and reporting programs.
- Areas of security expertise: information, physical, personnel, operations and facility.[1]

SECURITY/LAW ENFORCEMENT EXPERIENCE

SPACE & MISSILE DEFENSE COMMAND, COLORADO SPRINGS, COLO.   [dates]
Administrative Security Manager

Referred by OP communications (training vendor) as best person for this security-sensitive position.
Operate and administer computer equipment and Directorate of Combat Development's (DCD) Sensitive Compartmented Information (SCI) Program and collateral facilities. Administer SCI program and ensure that SCI data is properly accounted for, controlled, transported, sorted, packaged, safeguarded and destroyed. Ensure continuous systems integrity and secure communications within SCI facility.

- Conduct inspections, investigations, inquiries and assistance visits and provide reports. Make recommendations for corrective actions. Develop security plans and procedures to safeguard classified information.
- Establish and maintain emergency action plans (EAP) and Standard Operating Procedures (SOPs).
- Oversee physical security program for operations in two facilities. Ensure compliance with national and agency security directives and policies. Monitor Fixed Facility Checklist and access controls.
- Manage SCIF intrusion detection system, including, CCTV system, alarms and central panel operations. Establish alarm response procedures, perform live testing and document findings.
- Responsible for personnel security program. Prepare Visit Requests for over 65 staff members and officers for field trips and temporary duty assignments. Ensure staff has appropriate level of access.

OP COMMUNICATIONS, COLORADO SPRINGS, COLO. [dates]
Manager and Registrar

Coordinated Security Operations Officer Qualification Course Training for 350 students. Performed administrative duties for instructors and administrators.

CITY OF COLORADO SPRINGS, COLORADO SPRINGS, COLO. [dates]
Metropolitan Police Officer

Resigned to care for critically ill family member, who passed away after two months.
Completed 8-month police study program and 3-month advanced field training courses.

- Certified in 9mm handgun, shotgun, police equipment, cameras, automated police information retrieval systems, crime scene evidence collecting equipment and use of chemical aerosol irritants.

CONTRACTING & ADMINISTRATIVE EXPERIENCE

ALLEN CONSTRUCTION, INC., COLORADO SPRINGS, COLO. [dates]
Contractor Administrator

Recruited to more challenging position.
Provided support to project managers on Federal contracts, ranging in value from $300,000 to $8M.

STATE OF WYOMING, CHEYENNE, WYO. [dates]
Contract Administrator and Budget Analyst

This was a 9-month contract position
Performed accounting and contract review for $50M Wyoming State Prison Construction Project. Important liaison to senior attorney general, with direct interface on arising construction issues and discrepancies. Supervised one employee located in another location and served as purchasing agent.

- Prepared legal notices and correspondence for each phase of construction contracts, including review, closeout and final retainage release. Composed correspondence and reports.
- Compiled construction progress and financial reports, including accounts receivable and payable.

EDUCATION, TRAINING, CERTIFICATIONS & COMPUTER SKILLS

Undergraduate Coursework, Business Administration, Wyman College, Cody, Wyo., 42 credits, [dates]

Professional Training & Certifications

- Joint Personnel Adjudication System Training for Security Professionals, in progress
- Certified Information System Security Officer (ISSO), [date]

Proficient in Microsoft Word, Outlook, Publisher, Excel, Access, PowerPoint, Quattro Pro, QuickBooks, Dac Easy Payroll & Accounting, Internet. Familiar with AutoCAD 12.

Chapter 14

A Sampling of Extreme Resume Makeovers

* *

*E*ach of five before-and-after sets of resumes in this chapter makes a specific point: bare-bones quick notes don't make the sale; attention wanders with too much (unusable) information; persuasive information grabs attention; credibility grows when focus meets accomplishments; and white space encourages readability.

A box atop each resume in this chapter contains a mission statement — that is, what the job seeker aims to accomplish, which usually is a better job. The mission statement also includes the requirements for a specific position — or a summary of the typically requested requirements for an occupation or career field. You may be surprised that the requirements have numbers. And that the numbers are cross-matched to the qualifications in the resume. Does this mean you are supposed to put numbers on your resumes as these samples show? No! No! A thousand times no!

The cross-matched numbers between a job's requirements and the candidate's qualifications shown here are just for illustration, *not for your actual resumes.*

The samples are intended to laser your attention to requirement-and-qualification matching, the single most important factor in causing your candidacy to get noticed in an online swarm of resumes.

BEFORE

DAVID YOUNG

Walter Reed Army Medical Center   *Permanent Address:* P.O. Box 3901
Malogne House Omaha, NE 68105-3901   Omaha, NE 99999
6900 Georgia Ave., N.W.
Washington, D.C. 20307
Cell: 402-777-3030   Email: davidyoung@yahoo.com

I received a purple heart and I will be a 10 point vet pref.

EMPLOYMENT

[dates]   INTERN, VETERAN'S AFFAIRS
             Congressman Gene Taylor, 4th Congressional District of MS

             I assisted his staff in office work during Hurricane Katrina and had my own project which I worked on. There was a soldier's home in Gulfport that had to be evacuated. Over 300 vets had to be brought up here to the D.C. soldier's home. My job was to make sure they were being taken care of. I got them in touch with their families and friends and made sure everyone was accounted for. I worked with different organizations to set up clothes drives and phone card drives.

[dates]   MILITARY POLICE OFFICER
             Nebraska Army National Guard

             I received police officer training, both garrison and combat MP. As soon as I graduated, our brigade was deployed to Iraq as combat MP's. While deployed, I completed all the MP duties: convoy escorts, personal security, mounted patrol, holding and transporting prisoners, searches, etc.

[dates]   EQUIPMENT OPERATOR AND SUPERVISOR
             Pepper Turbines, Inc.

             I operated heavy machinery, vehicles, and forklifts.

EDUCATION

             Approx. 60 college credit hours in the fields of criminal justice and social work

             High School Diploma

AFTER

Military to Federal. Active Duty Reserves. Reverse chronological. Wounded veteran seeks Program Support Clerk job at VA Hospital, GS-5 position, $37,000. Federal resumes must include SSN, prior hours and earnings, citizenship, military service & federal job announcement number.Requirements: knowledge of VA policies, procedures, objectives and regulations pertaining to patient care,[1] ability to tactfully and courteously deal with a variety of people from diverse backgrounds and with varied levels of understanding,[2] working knowledge of PC software packages,[3] ability to work independently and under pressure,[4] and ability to organize, plan and prioritize work. [5]

DAVID YOUNG

Cell: 402-777-3030   Email: davidyoung@yahoo.com

Current Address: *Permanent Address:*
Walter Reed Army Medical Center   P.O. Box 3901
Malogne House   Omaha, NE 99999-3901
6900 Georgia Ave., N.W.
Washington, D.C. 20307

Social Security Number: 123-45-6789   Citizenship: United States of America
Military Service: Nebraska National Guard [dates]   Veteran's Preference: 10 points

OBJECTIVE: Program Support Clerk, GS-0303-5, Announcement Number: ATL-06-06-031TA

JOB SKILLS

- Experience communicating with soldiers and veterans from various backgrounds, both in active duty and hospitalized for serious injuries sustained in Operation Enduring Freedom. Able to build rapport and use tact, courtesy and professionalism in interpersonal relations.[2]
- Knowledgeable of physical therapy and medical terminologies.
- Skilled in office administration procedures, including answering calls, preparing correspondence and documents and filing. Type 40 wpm.
- Able to work under pressure effectively, both independently and in team settings.[4]

PROFESSIONAL EXPERIENCE

Intern, Veteran's Services   [dates]
Congressman Gene Taylor, 4th Congressional District of Mississippi
Rayburn House Office Building, Washington, DC
Salary: n/a; 15 hours/week
Supervisor: Rep. Gene Taylor, 202-444-9090. May be contacted.

- Administrative Assistant: Performed administrative duties such as word processing, managing files and records, designing forms, and other office procedures. Prepared correspondence and producing reports on veteran's benefits activities and research.
- Constituent Services: Provided customer and personal services to veterans concerning benefits and programs. Answered written and phone inquiries, providing information on policies, procedures, objectives and regulations pertaining to patient care and services.[1]
- Veterans' Benefits Research: Researched TRICARE health insurance issues for national guardsmen and reservists while not on active duty. Advocated for veterans' benefits and provided

- 1 -

DAVID YOUNG   Cell: 402-777-3030
Announcement Number: ATL-06-06-031TA   SSN: 123-45-6789

information to Department of Veterans Affairs representatives. Wrote summaries of veterans' problems and situations concerning processes and treatment services.

Key Accomplishment:

- Hurricane Katrina/Veterans Home Coordinator: Coordinated relocation of 300+ veterans from Armed Forces Retirement Home in Gulfport, Miss. to U.S. Solders' and Airmen's Home located in Washington D.C. during aftermath of Hurricane Katrina. Established phone card and clothing drives to ensure that each veteran had sufficient clothing. ***Awarded Humanitarian Service Medal and Nebraska Emergency Service Medal.***

Military Police Officer   [dates]
Nebraska Army National Guard
155th Separate Armored Brigade
2222 Hwy 51 South, Lincoln, NE 99999
Salary: $21,500/year; 40 hours/week
Supervisor: Capt. James Sutter, 402-444-9090. May be contacted.

- Security: Performed law enforcement duties for U.S. forces and commands, preserving military control and providing perimeter, escort and physical security. Investigated, processed and prepared incident reports. Debriefed and interviewed witnesses and sources for pertinent information concerning investigations and incidents; wrote reports and summaries.
- Operational Support: Provided ordnance and logistical support to operational forces. Coordinated compound and work projects.

Equipment Operator and Supervisor   [dates]
Pepper Turbines, Inc.
5555 Wilkens Boulevard, Omaha, NE 99999
Salary: $25,500/year; 40 hours/week
Supervisor: Mike Jones, 402-555-3434. May be contacted.

- Supervisor: Managed equipment operators in safety and operations for this government contractor manufacturing firm. Organized, prioritized and planned workload; assigned tasks.[5]
- Equipment Operator: Operated vehicles, forklifts and heavy machinery.

EDUCATION

Undergraduate Coursework, Criminal Justice and Social Work, Metropolitan Community College, Omaha, NE 99999, 56 credits   [dates]

Diploma, Pine Grove High School, Omaha, NE 99999,   [date]

AWARDS

Army Commendation Medal, Iraq Campaign Medal, Global War on Terrorism, Expeditionary Medal, Purple Heart, Humanitarian Service Medal, Mississippi Emergency Service Medal, National Defense Service Medal, Army Service Ribbon, Armed Forces Reserve Medal

COMPUTER SKILLS [3]

MS Office: Word, Outlook, Excel, PowerPoint, Access; Internet

BEFORE

Sales to Administration. Salesperson who wants to return to administration writes a generic resume with a cliché objective that focuses on what she wants, not what she brings to the employer. Nor does she strategically position her administrative experience but begins with sales, although she no longer wants to work in sales. The makeover resume that follows addresses both of these problems.

LEAH C. JENKINS
CELL(212)768-4545•LEAH_JENKINS@YAHOO.COM
999 AMESBURY PLACE•NEW YORK, NY 11111

OBJECTIVE

To obtain a challenging full-time position in a dynamic atmosphere where my hard work and customer service capabilities can be efficiently utilized. Should be career oriented and allow for an opportunity for growth within the company.

EXPERIENCE

[dates]   Ikea   Long Island, NY
Sales Worker
- Assist customers with purchases, such as planning wardrobe systems and bathrooms. Recommend options and answer customer and co-worker inquiries. Place customer orders using automated system; search database for item availability.

[dates]   Medix School   Towson, MD
Admiissions Receptionist
- Supported Director and Director of Admissions. Typed letters, scheduled meetings, and maintained student files. Managed receptionist duties.

[dates]   Outback Steakhouse   Baltimore, MD
Restaurant Administrator
- Coordinated all special and charity events, such as first Baltimore Marathon, Charity Golf Classic, etc.
- Employee of the year for [date], employee of the month [dates].
- Implemented training system for all servers, bartenders, hosts, and bussers.
- Handled all payroll, accounts payables/receivables, employee issues, corporate reports (monthly P&L, daily sales reports, etc.) and all money handling responsibilities.

[dates]   Hycalog Drilling Co.   Houston, TX
Office Manager
- Created annual operating plan using PowerPoint.
- Established and maintained new office for regional manager.
- Reviewed engineer's expense reports, handled all travel arrangements, administered petty cash box, and acted as English/Spanish translator.

[dates]   Law Offices of Leonard Bunch, P.C.   Houston, TX
Receptionist/Secretary
- Prepared legal documents such as last wills and testaments, trusts, corporation & association papers, IRS forms and claims.
- Greeted clients, answered 5-line phone system, and scheduled all appointments for attorneys. Completed general filing and office duties.

EDUCATION

[dates]   Cooper Union School of Art   New York, NY
Pursuing Continuing Studies Certificate in Photography.
[dates]   Lamar State University   Beaumont, TX
45 credits toward B.A. in Business Administration and Spanish.
[dates]   Juan Agustin Maza University   Mendoza, Argentina
90 credit hours toward B.S. in Industrial Engineering.

SKILLS

Bilingual Spanish/English; Computer proficient; Extensive experience in customer service; International work experience; High attention to detail and ability to multitask

AFTER

LEAH C. JENKINS

999 Amesbury Place • New York, NY 11111
Cell (212) 768-4545 • leah_jenkins@yahoo.com

EXPERTISE: Administrative Management

Motivated and accomplished office manager and administrative professional with over 5 years' experience.[1] Attentive to detail, able to take initiative, prioritize multiple tasks and manage workload. Resourceful with can-do attitude;[5] team player. Bilingual: Spanish/English (fluent).[4]

SKILL SUMMARY

- **Administration:** Managing office workflow, purchasing, developing policies and procedures to improve operations, maintaining filing and database systems, meeting/event planning,

- **Accounting:** Managing and monitoring financial transactions, accounts, invoices and payroll.

- **Communications:** Preparing business documents, letters and memos, serving as receptionist, POC and first contact.

- **Expert Computer Skills:**[3] MS Word, Excel, PowerPoint, Outlook; Internet; Photoshop; CAD; Peachtree; Quicken; proprietary databases and software programs

ADMINISTRATIVE EXPERIENCE

Admissions Receptionist
Medix School, Towson, Md.   [dates]

- <u>Reception:</u> Served as first contact for callers and visitors; determined nature of contact and directed/forwarded to correct department. Provided information, answered inquiries, took messages and scheduled appointments.

- <u>Administration:</u> Provided direct support to Director and Director of Admissions. Scheduled and coordinated meetings, arranging for refreshments, reserving meeting space, inviting attendees and preparing materials. Coordinated service for and procured new/upgraded equipment, technology, service plans and office supplies. Developed and implemented administrative policies and procedures, maintained student records and files and managed incoming and outgoing correspondence. Prepared and typed letters, minutes, memos and other documentation. Assured correct use of grammar, punctuation, language, format and spelling.

- <u>Admissions Support:</u> Tracked and managed student information via database. Scheduled appointments with Admissions Counselor. Served as proctor for student testing; prepared and sent admissions letters to applicants and students.

Key Accomplishments:
- Discovered accounting error, saving $4,700 in purchasing overcharges.
- Created new form letter templates and developed database system to manage mailings.
- Upgraded postage and phone systems, securing more cost-effective service and better equipment.

Office Manager
Hycalog Drilling Co., Mendoza, Argentina   [dates]

- <u>Office Management:</u> Tapped to establish new regional office. Coordinated initial furnishing and set up; managed continual administrative operations. Supported regional manager and engineering staff. Served as Point of Contact, resolving customer and staff issues. Managed all correspondence, travel arrangements and purchasing. Prepared letters and reports, including P&L and annual operating plan for senior management. Maintained files. English/Spanish translator.

- <u>Accounting:</u> Managed all A/R and A/P. Reviewed, processed, coded and paid invoices and expense reports. Sent invoices and collection letters, audited accounts and managed petty cash.

Receptionist/Secretary
Law Offices of Leonard Bunch, P.C., Houston, Texas [dates]

- Managed office workflow and reception. Greeted, screened and directed visitors and callers. Scheduled appointments and managed attorney calendars. Sorted and forwarded incoming mail; prepared outgoing correspondence. Typed, formatted and prepared letters, memos and legal documents. Maintained and updated filing system.

OTHER WORK EXPERIENCE

Sales Worker
Ikea, Long Island, N.Y. [date to Present]

- <u>Sales/Customer Service:</u> Assist customers with room planning and purchases. Ascertain needs, recommend options and answer customer and worker inquiries. Place customer orders using automated system; search database for item availability.

- <u>Administrative/Inventory:</u> Take daily inventory and input requisitions into database. Maintain communications with coworkers, including written updates on tasks, projects and goals. Write weekly product updates for staff. Conduct yearly and need-based inventories.

- <u>Design/Merchandising:</u> Plan and design space and furniture layout and systems, using automated programs and paper sketches. Design customer and internal room settings.

Key Accomplishments:

- Received excellent performance evaluations: "Exceeds job expectations." [dates]
- Received 5 Ambassador Awards, for excellent customer service.

Restaurant Administrator
Outback Steakhouse, Baltimore, Md. [dates]

- <u>Accounting:</u> Managed payroll, A/R, A/P and cash deposits. Tracked and submitted payroll for staff of 75; reviewed payroll report, identified errors and made corrections. Received and tracked invoices, entered and coded accounting data and paid vendors. Prepared daily, monthly and yearly corporate reports, including P&L. Maintained and stored files and records.

- <u>Administrative:</u> Scheduled part-time administrative staff; trained employees and replacement. Purchased office supplies and coordinated equipment maintenance. Coordinated all special and charity events. Contacted corporate and business donors, scheduled time and location, prepared invitations and gift bags for participants and coordinated events with kitchen and waitstaff.

Key Accomplishments:

- Promoted twice in less than 2 years. Hired as server, promoted to bartender and then to RA.
- Employee of the Year, [date]; Employee of the Month, [date].
- Implemented new training system for all new servers, bartenders, hosts, and bussers.

EDUCATION

Undergraduate Studies,[2] Business Administration/Spanish, Lamar State University, Beaumont, Texas, 45 credits completed, [dates]

BEFORE

> **Data to Education.** Data analyst transitioning to Instructional/Curriculum Design based on new education. Resume with laundry list of skills and duties is overwhelming and hard to follow. Also, lists only last two jobs – about 3 years' experience; she's been working for about 10 years. Small font makes it hard to read.

Evelyn Baker

55 Keswick Ct.
Honolulu, HI 99999   **ebaker@gmail.com**

Home Phone: (808) 444-1212
Cell Phone: (808) 333-6060

Objective: To obtain a position as a Curriculum Design Specialist in an organization that would allow me to develop my skills, while contributing to organizational goals.

Professional Profile: An ambitious, organized individual experienced at working in a fast paced environment demanding strong, organizational, technical and interpersonal skills. Prioritize tasks and meet deadlines.

Technical Skills

- **Languages:** C/C++, Visual Basic 2005, Java, HTML
- **Operating Systems:** UNIX, DOS, Windows 95 – 2003, XP
- **Applications:** Microsoft Office (Excel, Access, Word, PowerPoint, Outlook), PeopleSoft, GroupWise
- **Database:** Oracle8i Database Administrator Track Training for SQL and PL/SQL, Enterprise DBA Part 1A: Architecture and Administration, Enterprise DBA Part1B: Backup and Recovery, Enterprise DBA Part 2: Performance and Tuning, Enterprise DBA Part3: Network Administration
- **Instructional Design and Development:** Apply theories, philosophies, and current research driving learning, teaching, and Instructional Design. Create basic Internet-based instructional content, and basic multimedia-based instructional content. Manipulate current database technologies, desktop publishing technologies, spreadsheet technologies, and digital graphic editing technologies.
- **Information Technology Infrastructure:** Hands-on experience of Information systems architectures including software systems, hardware, operating systems, databases, object-oriented technology, networking, and enterprise-wide systems.
- **Internet and Network Security:** Footprinting, scanning, and enumeration tools, testing Windows security (95-2000), testing UNIX/Linux security, testing network devices and firewalls, scanning for remote control and testing backdoors and Trojans, testing Internet users.
- **Technical Writing:** Develop and edit technical communication such as user manuals, installation instructions, Marketing Collateral: Grant Proposals. Researches, analyzes, and edit system information and perform technical writing. Interpret and simplify information technology concepts for defined audiences.
- **MIS Capstone Project:** Developed an Information System for an organization. Made modifications in design techniques and strategies to accommodate several different contingencies.

Professional Experience

The Queen's Medical Center, Honolulu, HI   [dates]
Adult Intensive Care Unit – APACHE 11 Data Analyst/Coordinator

- Collate data of all admissions into the Adult ICU on a daily basis using the APACHE 11 System.
- Collate data of all admissions into the Adult ICU and prepare quarterly reports with that data.
- Prepares Summary Sheets for each ICU patient noting all appropriate statistics.
- Coordinate the daily activities of the Adult ICU.
- Performs data management and data analysis for research.
- Gathers data requirements, design reports, analyze the results and implement and test Reports.
- Maintains data collected for research purposes (including acquisition, editing and reporting); providing statistical consulting primarily in collaborative studies involving the Adult Intensive Care Unit.
- Follow up with various ancillary departments to obtain statistics necessary to be presented in the quarterly report.

Home Phone: (808) 444-1212	Evelyn Baker ebaker@gmail.com	Cell Phone: (808) 333-6060

- Design and implement new Reports and modify existing Reports.
- Maintain user security within the Reporting application and make changes/updates as necessary.
- Support and maintain Reporting and Data Analysis Tools.
- Work with business users to understand business requirements and develop appropriate solutions.
- Direct day-to-day office operations, providing fundamental support to Director, Assistant Director and three Intensivists in the Adult Intensive Care Unit.
- Manage accounts payable, receivable, and billing charges.
- Oversee administrative budget. Prepare expense reports and credit card/bank reconciliations.
- Train Medical Residents in use of office computer resources.

Volunteer Experience
Bridgestone Classic, Honolulu, HI [dates]
PGA Tournament Intern
- Assist Event Coordinator and work in conjunction with the tournament site Operations staff on certain aspects of the event.
- Conference planning.
- Serves as point of contact with clients and committees.
- Provides onsite supervision for conferences and meetings.
- Prepares contracts for corporate review and signature.
- Compile, sort, code and enter clients' invoices into computer.
- Account reconciliation experience.
- Maintain communication with clients' regarding payments.
- Responds to clients inquires regarding conference billings and procedures.
- Management of event database (volunteers, sales, VIPs, club members).
- In conjunction with Bridgestone, create and maintain Tournament Web site.
- Post event; generate letters from Tournament Director to all contestants and sponsors thanking them for participating in the tournament.
- Distribute and process volunteer applications.
- Coordinate with tournament, Bridgestone, and P.E.J. Productions regarding volunteers.
- Coordinate registration packets/credentials, yardage books and uniforms.

Education
- **Master of Science: Instructional Technology,** Instructional Design and Development
  Certificate in Information Security and Assurance
  Hawaii Pacific University, Honolulu, HI; [date]
- **Bachelor of Science: Management Information Systems**
  University of Hawaii at Manoa, [date]
- **Oracle 8i Database Administrator Training**
  University of Maryland Baltimore County, [date]
- **Associate of Applied Science: Computer Information Systems**
  Leeward Community College, Pearl City, Hawaii, [date]

Professional Affiliations
- Member of Beta Alpha Pi (Accounting and Information Systems Organization), Hawaii Pacific University
- Member - Computer Club, Leeward Community College

Honors
- Honors List, Meritorious Scholar

References and salary requirements available upon request.

AFTER

Data to Education. <u>Career Change</u>. Reverse chronological. Data analyst with new degree in instructional technology seeks position in instructional systems design and development. Requirements: Master's degree in instructional systems design or closely related field,[1] experience in multimedia authoring of instructional systems,[2] demonstrated ability to work in teams,[3] project management experience,[4] and experience with Web development technologies.[5]

EVELYN BAKER

55 Keswick Ct. • Honolulu, HI 99999
Residence: 808-444-1212 • Cellular: 808-333-6060
Email: ebaker@gmail.com

PROFILE: Over 7 years of experience in administration, instruction and information technology. Broad range of skill sets in Instructional Design, IT and office management. Organized, with demonstrated ability to manage workload and meet deadlines. Strong written and oral communications skills.

KEY COMPETENCIES

- **Instructional/Curriculum Design and Development:** Maintain knowledge of theories, philosophies and current research driving learning, teaching and Instructional Design. Create Internet-based and multimedia-based instructional content.[2] Use and apply database, desktop publishing, spreadsheet and digital graphic editing technologies.

- **Information Technology Expertise:** Hands-on experience in Information Systems architectures including software, hardware, operating systems, databases, object-oriented technology, networking and enterprise-wide systems. Special project management:[4] Developed MIS Capstone Information System for organization. Conducted needs assessment, developed, implemented and tested system. Made modifications in design techniques and strategies to accommodate contingencies.

- **Technical Writing:** Experience in developing and editing technical communications such as user manuals, installation instructions and grant proposals. Able to research, analyze and edit system information, as well as interpret and simplify IT concepts for defined audiences.

EDUCATION

M.S.,[1] Instructional Technology, Instructional Design and Development, Hawaii Pacific University, Honolulu, Hawaii; Certificate in Information Security and Assurance   [date]
 Relevant Coursework: Applied Psychology of Learning, Research and Information Technology, Computer Based Instruction, Information Technology and Infrastructure

B.S., Management Information Systems, University of Hawaii at Manoa, GPA: 3.75   [date]

PROFESSIONAL EXPERIENCE

Data Analyst/Coordinator
Adult Intensive Care Unit (ICU), The Queen's Medical Center, Honolulu, Hawaii   [dates]

- **Data Management:** Collect, enter, update and manage Adult ICU data, ensuring data accuracy and integrity. Track for management analysis, resource allocation, financial management. Prepare statistical reports with interpretive summary narratives. Work with other departments to obtain or verify data. Maintain user security.
- **Office Administration:** Manage daily office operations, providing support to director, assistant director and 3 intensivists in Adult ICU. Administer budget, managing all accounts payable and receivable functions. Train new and current staff on processes and technology systems.

Intern

Bridgestone Classic, (PGA Tournament), Honolulu, Hawaii   [dates]

- **Event Management Support:** Assisted Event Coordinator and as team member,[3] worked with tournament site operations staff. Provided onsite supervision for conferences and meetings. Prepared contracts and performed accounts receivable activities and reconciliation; sorted, coded and entered invoices.

- **Data Management/Communications:** Served as point of contact for clients and committees. Updated and maintained event database. Created and maintained tournament website. Drafted and sent thank you letters to contestants and sponsors.

Teacher

Manoa Elementary School, Honolulu, Hawaii   [dates]

- **Computer Instruction/Curriculum Development:** Taught computer fundamentals to students in grades K-5th. Prepared daily lesson plans. Collaborated with other teachers on technology integration curriculum.

Lab Assistant

Leeward Community College, Peal City, Hawaii   [dates]

- **Computer Specialist:** Provided user support for 6,000 college students in computer lab. Managed 72 multimedia workstations.

COMPUTER COMPETENCIES

Languages: C/C++, Visual Basic 2005, Java
Operating Systems: Windows 95-2003, XP
Applications: MS Office (Excel, Access, Word, PowerPoint, Outlook), PeopleSoft, UNIX, DOS, GroupWise, HTML, Dreamweaver, CSS, XML, PhP, Macromedia Flash, Macromedia Captivate [5]
Databases: Oracle8i Database Administrator Track Training for SQL and PL/SQL, Enterprise DBA Part 1A: Architecture and Administration, Enterprise DBA Part1B: Backup and Recovery, Enterprise DBA Part 2: Performance and Tuning, Enterprise DBA Part3: Network Administration

PROFESSIONAL AFFILIATIONS

Beta Alpha Pi (Accounting/Information Systems Organization)   [dates]
Hawaii Pacific University, Honolulu, HI

Computer Club, Leeward Community College, Pearl City, HI   [dates]

BEFORE

> **Culinary Career.** Sous Chef seeking Chef position. Lacks focus, direction, organization, visual appeal.

MATTHEW BELASKI
1930 Wye Woods Rd.
Hartford, CT 06105
Residence: 860-999-1212
Email: matthew_b@comcast.net

EDUCATION
[dates]   Computer Programming Degree, Anne Arundel Community College, in progress
[dates]   A.A., Degree, Restaurant Cooking Skills, Baltimore International College
[dates]   B.S., Business Administration, Shepherd University

EMPLOYMENT
[dates] Sous Chef, Government House
- Logistical kitchen planner for food and beverage events for the Governor of Connecticut.
- Plan, purchase and execute specific menus. Coordinate meeting and convention service requests. Inventory, inspect and rotate fresh, frozen and grocery stocks.
- Coordinate and communicate relevant information with the Governor's office, State Police and other state agencies.
- Provide and deliver personal needs of the first family.
- Protect privacy of the first family, as well as, proprietary information pertaining to Government House. Provide information to the media as needed.
- Direct usage of Department of Corrections trustees.
- Develop, implement and insure sanitation programs.
- Maintain and reconcile departmental petty cash funds.
- Successful implementation of private sector ideas and technologies to a public sector environment.

[dates] Banquet Chef, Hartford Marriott
- Designed and executed high-end food operations for exclusive catered events.
- Led production team by communication of specific customer directed protocols regarding national and international clients.
- Implemented quality assurance and cost control measures.
- Made purchasing, cost and quality recommendations to upper management.
- Was recognized by management for innovative ideas that improved operational effectiveness.

[dates] Food and Beverage Director; Executive Chef, Aramark
Food and Beverage Director: Executive Dining Room at Sprint Network Services.
- Supervised staff of 8 employees, both front and back of the house.
- Designed and directed production of breakfast and lunch menus for service 5 days a week.
- Increased new catering sales, while maintaining repeat customer clients.
- Developed and led employee training sessions for customer service, food production and sanitation.
- Updated computer technology to modernize purchasing and just in time inventory systems.
- Developed marketing and advertising campaigns to grow business. Installed thorough accounting and customer service tracking systems.
- Introduced and maintained hazardous area critical control points program to promote safe food handling.
- My duties also included management of all vending operations.

AFTER

Culinary Career. Sous Chef. Reverse Chronological. Sous Chef seeks Chef position. This customized resume addresses requirements with matching qualifications, and directs reader's eyes to "sell don't tell" achievements. Requirements: bachelor's degree or related culinary degree,[1] 8+ years of industry and culinary management experience,[2] ability to manage staff in a diverse environment with focus on client and customer services,[3] experience controlling food and labor cost,[4] menu development,[5] and skill in development of culinary team.[6]

MATTHEW BELASKI
1930 Wye Woods Rd. • Hartford, CT 06105
Residence: 860-999-1212 • Work: 860-444-3535 • Email: matthew_b@comcast.net

CHEF

Over 10 years of kitchen management experience[2] in state government and corporate settings. Demonstrated expertise in project management, team building, budget management and improving operations. Able to assess needs, processes and performance and recommend and implement improvements. Strong skills in customer service, as well as interpersonal, written and verbal communications. Excellent ability to establish priorities, multi-task and meet strict deadlines. Proven proficiency in developing innovative solutions to problems and achieving results. PC competent.

PROFESSIONAL EMPLOYMENT

Government House, State of Connecticut   [dates]
SOUS CHEF, HARTFORD, CT

- Operations Management: Direct daily operations of full-service kitchen, planning, coordinating and preparing formal and informal meals and events for up to 3,000 people, both planned in advance and last minute, with range of guests from international dignitaries to constituents. Continually analyze operations and recommend and implement range of process improvement initiatives. Develop, implement, apply and interpret policies, regulations and directives.

- Project Management: Conduct needs assessment surveys and determine needs based on event specifications and labor demands. Plan event menus with consideration to protocol, preferences, caliber of event, attendees and lead time.[5] Create project timeline; assign tasks and monitor progress. Manage multiple task lists to complete projects with adjacent deadlines. Resolve problems and issues, including crisis situations. Conduct post-event assessments.

- Supply Management: Take inventory and plan orders to regulate flow of product and ensure stock levels meet event and daily needs. Research best products and vendors to comply with state purchasing regulations. Rotate stock, monitor usage and storage to ensure efficiency, sanitation and security and reduce waste. Negotiate, administer and oversee vendor and service contracts.

- Budgeting/Funds Management: Develop pricing and cost accounting procedures. Analyze and forecast product and labor costs estimates. Resolve budget issues and develop food and labor cost-cutting solutions to ensure budget adherence.[4] Brief management and recommend cost control improvements and budget adjustments.

- Personnel Management:[6] Direct diverse kitchen and wait staff,[3] promoting teamwork and communication. Provide continual training and coaching to improve employee performance, job knowledge and career advancement; serve as point of contact for benefit information. Write position descriptions and assist in hiring process. Resolve employee issues and provide employee input and feedback to management.

MATTHEW BELASKI   Residence: 860-999-1212

- **Logistics Management:** Integrate logistics of event planning, including manpower and personnel, supply, training, storage and facilities. Research and plan manpower, equipment and fiscal resources.

- **Customer Service:** [3] Serve as personal and administrative assistant to First Family. Anticipate and respond to needs, maintaining flexible and service-oriented attitude. Purchase personal and business related goods. Protect privacy and security of First Family at all times.

- **Communications/Information Management:** Build rapport with internal staff and external departments to improve operations and flow of information. Develop and utilize spreadsheets, databases and documents to improve operational readiness, manage projects and research information. Maintain records on events, including menus, demographics and after-action reports.

Key Accomplishments:
- Plan, coordinate and execute breakfast, lunch, dinner for First Family and other events, including seated dinners and open houses for up to 4,000, with usually 3-5 events per week, up to 2 per day.
- Instituted process changes to alter staff mind-set from reactive to proactive. Created plan to work one meal ahead, enabling accommodation of last minute requests and events.
- Received letter of appreciation from the White House for organizing luncheon attended by President with less than 24-hour notice.
- Implemented industrial production system, automated systems and information management for production, scheduling and cost control.
- Actively built team mindset and morale, achieving improved attendance and performance. Stressed employees' role in organizational success and interdepartmental cooperation.

Downtown Marriot   [dates]
BANQUET CHEF, HARTFORD, CT

- Designed and executed high-end food operations for exclusive catered events. Led production team, communicating customer-directed protocols for national and international clients. Implemented quality assurance and cost control measures. Recognized by management for innovative ideas that improved operational effectiveness.

Aramark   [dates]
FOOD AND BEVERAGE DIRECTOR; CHEF, HARTFORD, CT

- Food and Beverage Director, Executive Dining Room: Sprint Network Services. Designed and directed production of breakfast and lunch menus for service 5 days a week, for 100 employees. Supervised staff of 8. Increased new catering sales and established new client services. Developed and led employee customer service, food production and sanitation training sessions. Updated computer technology to modernize purchasing and just in time inventory systems. Implemented hazardous area critical control points program to promote safe food handling.

- Chef, *Hartford Pride*: Oversaw menu design, coordination and execution for lunch, dinner and catered events on 450-passenger vessel. Led galley team of 20 employees and 2 supervisors. Employed commercial and banquet-style food production methods to achieve time and product management. Directed purchasing, inventory control and training involved with menu execution. Achieved increased efficiencies in purchasing, inventory and scheduling using computer technology. Developed, trained and employees in sanitation and food safety.

EDUCATION

    B.S.,[1] Business Administration, Shepherd University, Shepherdstown, W.V.   [date]

    A.A.,[1] Restaurant Cooking Skills, Baltimore International College, Baltimore, Md.   [date]

BEFORE

Law Enforcement/Security. Protection Professional. Reverse chronological. Overcrowded, challenging to read. Mid-career government security professional seeks senior position with large corporate firm or government contractor. Requirements: related MA/MS/MBA plus 15 years experience,[1] knowledge of security program planning, funding, and information management systems,[2] ability to coordinate and evaluate staff and programs,[3] adjust plans and schedules to meet requirements,[4] and must be eligible for Secret Security Clearance.[5]

MARION J. JACOBI, CPP
P.O. Box 1111 • San Diego, CA 99999
email: m_jacobi@juno.com

Day: (111) 444-6565   Evening: (111) 333-1212

Senior Executive • Law Enforcement & Security Operations

Results-driven **Certified Protection Professional (CPP)** with more than 20 years of progressively responsible national security and federal investigative experience,[1] in the public sector preceded by a career in municipal law enforcement and emergency medical services. A hands-on senior executive with extensive experience planning and managing investigative operations and personnel in a 24/7 environment. Exceptional qualifications in strategic planning, program development and management, budget development and administration, team building, staff development, and human resources management. Advanced knowledge of public administration law, police operations, and national security issues. Strong public speaker. Top Secret Security Clearance.[5] PC proficient.

Areas of Expertise:

- Criminal/Administrative Investigations
- Internal Affairs Investigations
- Physical Security / Antiterrorism Programs
- Investigative Case Management
- Personnel Security/ Background Investigations
- Training & Performance Measurement
- Non-traditional & Traditional Investigations

- Strategic / Budget Planning & Execution
- Law Enforcement Operations & EMS Leadership
- Program Administration / Project Management
- Organizational Management
- Risk, Fraud Management / Regulatory Compliance
- Human Resources Management, Union/Salaried
- Tactical Field Operations / Electronic Surveillance

PROFESSIONAL EXPERIENCE

DEPARTMENT OF HOMELAND SECURITY (DHS)   [dates]
U.S. Immigration and Customs Enforcement (ICE) / Immigration & Naturalization Service (INS)
-- Promoted through increasingly responsible national security supervisory and law enforcement positions.

Section Chief / Supervisory Special Agent, San Diego, Calif. (dates)

Selected to lead DHS/ICE's Law Enforcement Support Center (LESC), a national, non-traditional operations center supporting local, state, and federal law enforcement investigations 24/7, 365 days/year. LESC uses government and commercial criminal history databases to provide current immigration and identity information.

Lead five key departments: Investigations Branch, Computer Services Division, Operations, Program Analysis Unit, and the Administrative Section. Oversee 250+ union and salaried employees.[3] Concurrently serve as Facility Security Manager and NCIC Criminal Justice Information Services Officer. Scope of responsibility:

- Managing development and implementation of internal and external operations protocols affecting investigations, communications, and administration; long and short-range budget planning and execution.[2]
- Provide liaison to FBI, National Crime Information Center (NCIC), Advisory Policy Board, National Law Enforcement Telecommunications System (NLETS) Board of Directors and other investigative agencies. Provide operational, procedural, and compliance oversight.
- Senior advisor to multi-agency state and federal executive working groups on national and international enforcement and security initiatives involving critical infrastructure industries, employment, law enforcement communication, and information sharing.

Current Leadership Projects & National Security Initiatives:

- Consultant for the new Federal Air Marshal NCIC program. Advised on and contributed to creation of policy recommendations for new handheld wireless device initiative.

- Leading and managing Task Force for $200,000 project to transfer the national U.S. Customs and Border Protection (CBP) tip-line (1-800-BE-ALERT) to ICE, merge the two systems, create a new internal telephone system, and new national policies and procedures affecting information processing.
- Consultant to Transportation Security Administration for developing background check procedures.

Major Accomplishments:

- Orchestrated reorganization of NCIC national program, resulting in its centralization at LESC. Totally redesigned policies, procedures, and institutional practices, agency-wide.[4]
- Directed start-up of LESC to provide enhanced investigative support to federal, state, and local security agencies investigating criminal foreign nationals (in the post 9/11 environment). Developed and implemented highly effective new search and response protocols that improved response time and records accuracy.
- Established DHS toll free tip-line (1-866-DHS-2ICE) for public use to facilitate reporting of suspicious activities affecting national security and public safety.
- Streamlined methods for investigative records management, established strategic partnerships with FBI management and staff. Effectively led major organizational changes and staff growth of 280 employees.
- Authored and implemented Emergency Occupant/Site Disaster Recovery Plan and contract security guard post orders, driving improvements in facility security.

Organized Crime Drug Enforcement Task Force Coordinator, INS (dates)
Senior Special Agent, Atlanta, Ga.

Directed the West Central Organized Crime Drug Enforcement Task Force (OCDETF), a region encompassing 12 states and four INS District Offices. Decision-making responsibility for all immigration task force matters, including the role of the regional task force, investigative case planning and management, and INS resource allocations. Advisor to INS district and regional components investigating criminal activities. Federal task force team leader. Evaluated personnel performance, mediated interagency disputes, and led regulatory training.

- One of only two national coordinators selected to define, implement, and manage an international human trafficking investigation. Served as INS liaison to the Criminal Division in the Department of Justice.
- Frequently selected for long-term assignments at the Central Region Investigations Branch in Dallas. Formulated national guidelines on undercover operations and consensual monitoring.

Senior Special Agent, INS, Detroit, Mich. (dates)

- **Violent Gang Task Force (VGTF) Program**: Developed and orchestrated complex narcotics distribution investigations employing standard investigative techniques, undercover operations, and electronic surveillance. Led two long-term investigations as an undercover operative.
- Successfully dismantled active human trafficking/identity document vending organizations. Made calm, sound judgments based on experience and initiated appropriate enforcement actions.

Journeyman Border Patrol Agent, San Diego, Calif. (dates)
Captain / Paramedic Operations Supervisor, Louisville, Ky. (dates)
Police Officer, City of Plantation Police Department, Plantation, Ky. (dates)

EDUCATION, LAW ENFORCEMENT CERTIFICATIONS, & TRAINING

M.A., Security Management,[1] Webster University Graduate School, St. Louis, Mo.

B.S., Liberal Studies, University of the State of New York, Albany, N.Y.

Certified Protection Professional (CPP), [date], American Society for Industrial Security (ASIS)

Certified Police Officer, Kentucky Department of Criminal Justice, Police Academy, Richmond, Ky.

MEMBERSHIP ORGANIZATIONS

American Society for Industrial Security (ASIS) / Federal Law Enforcement Officers Association (FLEOA)

AFTER

Law Enforcement/Security. <u>Protection Professional</u>. Reverse chronological. White space makes reading easier. The previous and identical 2-page resume presented here as a 3-page resume. Mid-career government security professional seeks senior position with large corporate firm or government contractor. Requirements: related MA/MS/MBA plus 15 years' experience,[1] knowledge of security program planning, funding, and information management systems,[2] ability to coordinate and evaluate staff and programs,[3] adjust plans and schedules to meet requirements,[4] and must be eligible for Secret Security Clearance.[5]

MARION J. JACOBI, CPP

P.O. Box 1111 • San Diego, CA 99999
email: **m_jacobi@juno.com**

Day: (111) 444-6565   Evening: (111) 333-1212

Senior Executive • Law Enforcement & Security Operations

Results-driven **Certified Protection Professional (CPP)** with more than 15 years of progressively responsible national security and federal investigative experience,[1] preceded by a career in municipal law enforcement and emergency medical services. A hands-on executive with extensive experience planning and managing investigative operations and personnel in a 24/7 environment. Exceptional qualifications in strategic planning, program development and management, budget development and administration, team building, staff development, and human resources management. Advanced knowledge of public administration law, police operations, and national security issues. Strong public speaker. Top Secret Security Clearance.[5] PC proficient.

Areas of Expertise:

- Criminal/Administrative Investigations
- Internal Affairs Investigations
- Physical Security/Antiterrorism Programs
- Investigative Case Management
- Personnel Security/Background Investigations
- Training & Performance Measurement
- Non-traditional & Traditional Investigations

- Strategic/Budget Planning & Execution
- Law Enforcement Operations & EMS Leadership
- Program Administration/Project Management
- Organizational Management
- Risk, Fraud Management/Regulatory Compliance
- Human Resources Management, Union/Salaried
- Tactical Field Operations/Electronic Surveillance

PROFESSIONAL EXPERIENCE

DEPARTMENT OF HOMELAND SECURITY (DHS)

U.S. Immigration and Customs Enforcement (ICE)/Immigration & Naturalization Service (INS)   [dates]
Section Chief/Supervisory Special Agent, San Diego, Calif.   [dates]

Selected to lead DHS/ICE's Law Enforcement Support Center (LESC), a national, non-traditional operations center supporting local, state, and federal law enforcement investigations 24/7, 365 days/year. LESC uses government and commercial criminal history databases to provide current immigration and identity information.

Lead five key departments: Investigations Branch, Computer Services Division, Operations, Program Analysis Unit, and the Administrative Section. Oversee 250+ union and salaried employees.[3] Concurrently serve as Facility Security Manager and NCIC Criminal Justice Information Services Officer. Scope of responsibility:

- Managing development and implementation of internal and external operation protocols affecting investigations, communications, and administration; long- and short-range budget planning and execution.[2]

- Liaison to FBI, National Crime Information Center, Advisory Policy Board; National Law Enforcement Telecommunications System Board of Directors.

Current Leadership Projects & National Security Initiatives:

- Consultant, Federal Air Marshal NCIC program. Advisor: new handheld wireless device initiative.

- Leading and managing Task Force for $200,000 project to transfer the national U.S. Customs and Border Protection (CBP) tip-line (1-800-BE-ALERT) to ICE, merge the two systems, create a new internal telephone system, and new national policies and procedures affecting information processing.

- Consultant to Transportation Security Administration for developing background check procedures.

Major Accomplishments:

- Orchestrated reorganization of NCIC national program, resulting in its centralization at LESC. Totally redesigned policies, procedures, and institutional practices, agency-wide.[4]

- Directed start-up of LESC to provide enhanced investigative support to federal, state, and local security agencies investigating criminal foreign nationals (in the post 9/11 environment). Developed and implemented highly effective new search and response protocols that improved response time and records accuracy.

- Established DHS toll free tip-line (1-866-DHS-2ICE) for public use to facilitate reporting of suspicious activities affecting national security and public safety.

- Streamlined methods for investigative records management, established strategic partnerships with FBI management and staff. Effectively led major organizational changes and staff growth of 280 employees.

- Authored and implemented Emergency Occupant/Site Disaster Recovery Plan and contract security guard post orders, driving improvements in facility security.

Organized Crime Drug Enforcement Task Force Coordinator, INS   [dates]

Senior Special Agent, Atlanta, Ga.

Directed the West Central Organized Crime Drug Enforcement Task Force (OCDETF), a region encompassing 12 states and four INS District Offices. Decision-making responsibility for all immigration task force matters.

- One of only two national coordinators selected to define, implement, and manage an international human trafficking investigation. INS liaison to Department of Justice.

- Frequently selected for long-term assignments at the Central Region Investigations Branch in Dallas. Formulated national guidelines on undercover operations and consensual monitoring.

Senior Special Agent, INS, Detroit, Mich.   [dates]
- **Violent Gang Task Force (VGTF) Program**: Developed and orchestrated complex narcotics distribution investigations employing standard investigative techniques, undercover operations, and electronic surveillance. Led two long-term investigations as an undercover operative.

- Successfully dismantled active human trafficking/identity document vending organizations. Made sound judgments based on experience; initiated appropriate enforcement actions.

Journeyman Border Patrol Agent, San Diego, Calif.   [dates]

Captain/Paramedic Operations Supervisor, Louisville, Ky.   [dates]

Police Officer, City of Plantation Police Department, Plantation, Ky.   [dates]

EDUCATION, LAW ENFORCEMENT CERTIFICATIONS, & TRAINING

M.A., Security Management,[1] Webster University Graduate School, St. Louis, Mo.   [date]

Certified Protection Professional (CPP), American Society for Industrial Security (ASIS)   [date]

Certified Police Officer, Kentucky Department of Criminal Justice, Police Academy, Richmond, Ky.   [date]

MEMBERSHIP ORGANIZATIONS

American Society for Industrial Security, Federal Law Enforcement Officers Association

Part IV

You've Sent Your Wow. What to Do Now

The 5th Wave By Rich Tennant

"I checked the references for Ms. Snow White. While one seemed quite happy, the others were just bashful, grumpy, or out and out dopey."

In this part . . .

You've sent off your OnTarget resumes; is it time to sit back and wait for the calls to start pouring in? Hardly. Following up is an important part of getting the interview, and in this part, I show you how to keep your information safe, how to prepare your references to highlight your assets, and how to be politely insistent about getting your resumes read.

Chapter 15

References Safeguard Your Resume

In This Chapter

▶ Acknowledging the power of a lackluster reference

▶ Managing references to back up claims on your resume

▶ The care and feeding of your reference folder

▶ Overcoming toxic references that kill your resume efforts

A nd just like that, the job offer goes missing. The one you thought was in the bag. Chances are, if the job itself wasn't cancelled or a background check didn't knock you out of the offer, you can blame your references for shooting you down.

Although verifiable statistics are elusive, I've come across several startling small-scale reference-checking surveys. The surveys assert that 50 to 64 percent of all recommenders rate their subjects as mediocre to poor! Upon reflection, I think the assessment could well be true. That's because the management of references is the last frontier to be recognized as an activity vital to promising career development.

The Harm Caused by a So-So Reference

A reference doesn't have to be a broadside to sink your ship. A few of the many subtle ways to wreck your chances include such seemingly innocuous comments from reference givers as these:

> ✔ *Oh, is she still working in this field?*

> ✔ *He gave my name as a reference?*

> ✔ *I can't go into detail but she's not eligible for rehire.*

> ✔ (Long pause, followed by a disgusted tone of voice) *Oh yes; I do remember him.*

Sometimes reference givers use the avoidance dodge — they simply don't return calls asking about your performance. (Employers aren't legally required to provide references.)

A little foresight on your part can help ensure that your references aren't wrecking your job search.

References are power hitters in the hiring process because they provide validation of your claims to be a superior performer and candidate.

We tend to view good references as entitlements, merely assuming they'll be there when we need them if we've done good work. Sorry, but that's yester-year's thinking. Today's thinking is more like "Trust, but verify."

Managing your references — or, reference management — is a key factor in managing your career. As a job search tool, reference management seems to have soared to a new height during the past five years or so. There are several reasons: the globalization of employment, a churning job market, and increasingly risk-adverse employers who want to be assured again and again that they're making the right choices.

References aren't resumes, but they are the subject of a chapter in this book because as guardians that backstop resumes, references have become deal breakers if not handled correctly. And after all the hard work on your OnTarget resume, you don't want that to happen, right?

Seven Things You Should Do about References

Now is a good time to rethink references and to consider how they hurt your chances when they're negative, or modest, or even positive but not concretely connected to your aspirations. These pointers show you how to make sure others sing your praises.

Ban references from your resume

Create a second document filled with the names, correct telephone numbers, and addresses of references. Supply this sheet only when a potential employer requests it. Don't burn out your references by allowing too many casual callers access to their names and contact information. Employers typically don't spend the time and money to check references until after you're interviewed and are on the short list of potential hires.

Sending reference letters with a resume to recruiters is not a good move, advises Jim Lemke, this book's technical reviewer. Recruiters are likely to assume the letters are either bogus or written by close friends. Including a reference letter with your initial submittal may make you seem desperate (and that's not good).

Expect employers to check references

In times gone by, employers didn't always bother to check references. The majority check now. Small employers still may not, but midsized and large companies, afraid of making a hiring mistake, are taking aim on your past.

Rules vary slightly in different states, but employers can legally investigate not only references but an applicant's credit history, record of criminal convictions (not arrests), moving violations and accidents, performance at previous jobs, and workers' compensation claims. Your state labor agency may post the rules for your state on its Web site. If not, call the agency or consult with a reference librarian.

When it's no secret that you're going to leave your current job, ask your company's human resource specialist what the exact company policy is for providing references. You may find it's essentially job title and employment verification dates, and perhaps salary confirmation and whether you're eligible for rehire.

You may discover that your company is outsourcing reference information to private companies that charge a fee to prospective employers for your reference information. If that's your company's policy, try to get your work history in writing before you leave your job, which will save a prospective employer money, time, and irritation.

Choose references with thought

List references who have direct knowledge of your job performance. If necessary, go beyond your immediate supervisor and include past or present co-workers, subordinates, customers, suppliers, members of trade associations, or anyone else who can praise your work. Don't use relatives or friends for personal references; they have no direct knowledge of your performance on the job. (Exception: some job seekers, such as ex-offenders, may require personal references.)

What's a good way to line up references? Skip this technique if you are doing a secret search, but if it's out in the open you can ask your boss whether he or she will give you a good reference. Ask for particulars regarding how your boss sees your accomplishments, competencies, skills, strengths, and weaknesses. If your boss squirms and mumbles, you're probably a sitting duck for a less-than-glowing recommendation.

Checking out co-workers, you can say: "Terry Ann, I am beginning a job search. Do you feel you know me well enough to provide a reference commenting on my skills in budget management?" If Terry Ann declines, it's a blessing in disguise to find out before giving her name as a recommender.

With the exception of your immediate boss, never — *never* — list a reference until you have gained that person's permission to do so.

Make a dry run: Have a brave buddy call your references to make certain that no sly naysayers are hiding behind friendly faces.

Help references help you

Providing recommenders with your resume is standard operating procedure. Go further: Write a short script of likely questions with a summary of persuasion points under each question.

In addition to general good words about your industriousness, creativity, and leadership, focus on the industry. If you're applying at a financial institution, suggest that your references dwell on trustworthiness, conservatism, and good judgment. If you're applying at a high-tech company that has proprietary software and inventions, ask your references to stress your ethics and loyalty.

Send a brief e-mail to recommenders identifying the qualifications you highlighted when you customized your resume for a given position (see Chapter 1). Say "I hope you can work that qualification in if you have an opening."

Although you don't want to wear out your welcome and become a pest, try to keep in touch with your references. Let them know how you're doing. Take them to coffee or lunch occasionally.

Cover your bases with a reference folder

A letter of recommendation isn't particularly effective, but it is better than nothing in cases where a company disappears, your boss dies, or the reference is difficult to reach. Begin now to collect praise in a reference folder, also called a reference dossier. Routinely arrange for a reference letter when you leave a job, as well as copies of your evaluation reports, and place them in the folder.

Writing the recommendation

What do you say in a recommendation letter? The reference giver verifies an individual's experience, affirms competence, and adds credibility. A strong reference letter typically does some combination of the following:

- Introduces the recommender, explaining the recommender's basis of knowledge for the reference

- Confirms dates and job title(s)

- Identifies competencies, skills, and other qualifications that make the individual an ideal candidate for a potential employer

- Describes performance and attitude

- Highlights one or more exceptional qualities with an example

Here's an excerpt of an example highlighting an exceptional quality I received in a letter from a Toronto, Canada, reader:

Jane was able to develop her assertiveness skills under my supervision. When she first came into the department as a payroll clerk, she was not as assertive as was necessary in dealing with the other departments when they were late submitting time cards and payroll information. After taking an assertiveness course and developing great self-confidence, Jane was able to develop her conflict resolution skills and she was promoted twice in the accounting department before leaving the company to take a manager's position elsewhere. I highly recommend her for her willingness to work on areas in which she needed improvement.

The above example — plainspoken and warmly sincere — praises a quality of interest to all employers: willing worker takes steps to improve job performance.

You can't assume recommenders will come up with the points and words you need, so you may have to draft the letters and statements yourself. Try to have each reference cover a different qualification with some overlap for emphasis. Tactfully offer to draft the letter to save your recommender time.

What else goes in your reference folder? Acclaimed Boston resume writer Louise Kursmark recommends a page or two of endorsements — the quoted actual words of several reference givers.

"Each testimonial consists of about eight lines within quotation marks," Kursmark says, "topped by a headline lauding an achievement — 'Trusted Manager Driving Results through Better Consumer Communication.' Each statement is signed with the name, title, and company of the recommender."

Use the endorsement sheets as follow-ups to your resume to gain an interview, or to leave behind as reminders at interviews.

A script to neutralize a damaging reference

Katie worked 18 months at a small company, where she received consistently good write-ups from the owner, but was fired by Jenny, a supervisor who was jealous of Katie's positive relationship with the company owner. Katie's friend made some calls and verified that Jenny was lying to prospective employers and telling them that Katie didn't do her job and wasn't a good employee. What should Katie do to improve her reference from Jenny?

Tony Beshara's inspired answer

Enter Tony Beshara, a top-flight placement and recruiting professional in Dallas, who gave Katie this terrific advice:

Katie should call Jenny, speaking in a very calm, nonthreatening tone, saying that she understands a bad reference is being given and that the reference is closing doors to employment. Katie nicely, but firmly, tells Jenny that this has to stop.

If Jenny is unresponsive or won't come to the phone or return a voicemail — which is very likely — Katie should write a letter to Jenny with the same message and send a copy of it to the owner of the company. Katie doesn't have to threaten litigation in the letter because any business manager with common sense will read between the lines that Katie's next step is to sue.

Katie's goal is not a total reversal of the negative evaluation but to obtain a neutral (but not mediocre) reference from the ex-employer.

Additionally, Katie should call the owner and explain the situation, saying that she doesn't want to cause any problems but wants to be able to go to work. She should ask the owner to be the one to provide future references since he has first-hand knowledge of her work and she's only asking that he tell the truth. Katie should remind the owner that she had been at the company for a year and a half, had a good track record, good reviews, and until the particular run-in with Jenny, everything had been smooth. If she can't get the owner on the phone, Katie should write him a letter saying the same thing. The last thing the owner of a small company wants is a lawsuit over an employment reference.

When all efforts fail

If every effort Katie makes fails, and she is dead certain of an upcoming bad reference, Beshara suggests she say to interviewers: "I do have excellent references with every previous employer. My last supervisor's personality was very difficult. I believe she will not give me a glowing reference. Others in the company will testify to my diligence and work ethic. I will provide those names and numbers. So if you check references with my previous employer, please check *all* of the people I was associated with there."

As a last resort, Beshara recommends that Katie offer to work on a temporary basis for 90 days to prove herself, a willingness that along with collateral good references, communicates a brand of commitment that's hard to resist.

Stamp out bad references

If you were axed or pressed to resign, or if you told your boss what you thought of him and quit, move immediately to damage-control alertness. Even if you were cool enough to obtain a letter of reference before you left, you absolutely must try to neutralize the reference.

Appeal to a sense of fair play or guilt. Sometimes, just saying that you're sorry and you hope that the employer won't keep you from earning a living will be enough. Sometimes it won't.

When you've tried and failed to overcome a bad reference, you have three options:

- ✔ Drown the poor reference in large numbers of favorable references.

- ✔ Find a lawyer who, for $200 or so, will write a letter threatening legal action for libel or slander to the person who is giving you a bad rap. This approach is surprisingly effective.

- ✔ Continue your job hunt, concentrating on small firms that may not check references or that may be more inclined to take a chance on someone.

Thank everyone

When your job search is finished, remember your manners: Thank the people who were willing to help you. Not only is it common courtesy but you never know when you'll need them again.

Finding References without Shedding Your Cloak of Secrecy

You know that it's smart to snare a new job before hanging it up at your current position. But the Catch-22 is that you can't give as references your boss or other managers at your current company or your secrecy jig's up.

You have two options for getting references while keeping your job search under wraps:

- ✔ Use the names of former supervisors at other companies, preferably people you have kept in touch with and tipped off in advance about your search as well as reliable contacts from professional organizations.

   Don't give the names of co-workers or current suppliers or vendors: You can't be sure they won't inadvertently let slip that you're on the market, or even purposely curry favor with your management by whispering in the boss's ear.

> ✔ Emphasize to prospective employers that your job search is confidential. When an offer looks eminent, say that upon receiving a signed offer letter, you will be pleased to have the prospective employer check with your current management and that if you don't stack up as expected, you understand the job offer is null and void.

Allow Enough Time for Skillful Reference Management

In this time-starved world, busy people may take longer than you expect to come to your aid in perfecting a quality reference tool. When the timeline between your request for a reference and the giver's follow-through seems stretched beyond endurance, it helps to remember that you give the tardy reference a higher priority than does the recommender. A much higher priority.

Allow yourself plenty of lead time to drum up reference deliveries from people who like you and would like to cheer you onward and upward, but, well, it's a busy life.

Chapter 16

Twisting in the Wind? Follow Up!

- -

In This Chapter

▶ Following up after sending your resume

▶ Handling voicemail like a pro

▶ Punching through screens to talk to the boss

▶ Adapting sales techniques that really work

▶ Applying the Follow-Up Matrix to best use your time

- -

You submitted your resume describing how you qualify for a targeted position. It's a work of art, a wow! Or so you thought. Four weeks have passed and the silence is deafening. Except for an automated response of receipt, you've heard nothing. Doesn't anyone care? You do. The problem is, you care more than the employer does.

I know that because I haven't heard from a single employer complaining about a lack of resumes. But the most-asked question I receive these days is this one:

> *My online resumes have gone missing; what can I do about it?*

The quick answer, assuming you didn't set up your resume's journey with networking or employee referrals in advance (see Chapter 3), is to learn the ropes of resume postsubmission and to follow up in ways you never had to think about before.

Job-hunting dynamics have dramatically changed over the past half-dozen years or so. Driven by the pull of market forces, and the push of government rules, and made possible by advancing technology (as I explain in Chapter 1), employers are having a hard time dealing with the zillions of resumes floating around the Internet.

The old advice of a decade ago, including my own, is outdated. Forget about amateurish messages that so politely ask someone who doesn't know you to call you back. Those were Clark Kent days. For job seekers, this is the Superman age.

This is the time to leap tall buildings doing battle for the job interviews you want. This is the time to learn hard-hitting new tactics to turn the tide in your favor. This is the time to get very serious about using resume follow-up as a critical job search tool.

But, you ask, in an age where time is rationed, isn't solid follow-up a time-eating monster? Well, yes, it can be. Bird-dogging all of your resumes *is* time consuming. That's why, later in this chapter, I present a new time-saving tool that you can use to selectively choose which resumes to chase and which to relegate to second- and third-string opportunities.

Are you tough? Disciplined? Ready to charge ahead? If so, this chapter is for you. In it, I suggest advanced tactics to reach out and snag interviews while your competition stands slack-jawed at the side of the road watching you make connections.

Why Follow-Up Efforts Are Essential Today

When employers and recruiters don't see the benefits of spending time talking with you, they become masters of the game of "catch me if you can." Even if you do manage to talk your way through assistants and get managers on the phone, they may be evasive, even brusque. Despite the risks of rude receptions, learning the art of following up for something you want can be one of the smartest things you ever do for the following reasons:

- **Lightning strikes.** Sometimes a hiring manager, who has been meaning to fill a position but has been too busy putting out fires, responds favorably to the candidate who happens to call on a day when the manager has time to exhale. It's a bit of the luck of the draw.

- **Persistence produces.** Some employers wait to judge which candidates have the most followthrough by how well they follow up. This "test" applies not only to sales but to other endeavors where a prized competence is the ability to "stay on top of things."

- **Control empowers.** By learning and adapting the successful strategies crack sales professionals use to set an appointment, you dramatically reduce the amount of frustration, letdown, and low self-esteem you could be feeling because you're taking charge and doing everything you can do.

The vast majority of employers — as many as eight of ten who use applicant tracking systems (see Chapter 6) — send out an automatic response to your application. The response says you'll be contacted if you match a job opening.

The automatic response rate of independent recruiters is unclear, but if you're a potential candidate for a job opening they're trying to fill, a recruiter will call you fairly quickly; if not, you may get an autoresponse or no response.

If you get a canned response, you won't look like a quiz-show winner if you call to ask a transparent question, "Did you receive my resume?" Duh. Instead, say some version of the following script:

1. When an autoresponse message tells you that your resume has been received, call the person to whom you sent it (usually a human resources specialist) and ask what happened to it:

   Was my resume a match for an open position? Was my resume passed onto a hiring manager? Can you tell me which manager?

2. If you find out the name of the hiring manager, try to contact that manager, because that's who will quarterback the decision to hire you or not hire you. (See Chapter 2 for more about how to reach the hiring manager.) If you were referred by someone, such as an employee in another department, use the following type of question:

   My name is Kelly Novak and I'm calling you because Henry Johannsen in engineering, who recommended that I send you my resume, says that you intend to hire a top-of-the-line planner as soon as possible. I've been able to design plans that were quickly approved by the California Coastal Commission. Would you like to talk with me before I leave on a scheduled vacation?

And if you don't have a name to throw around, try a question like this one:

   I've had strong interest from another employer, which prompts me to ask whether you had planned to contact me within the week? Your company has a good reputation and I'd like to meet with you before making other commitments. Does this week work for you?

Questions to Ask Yourself Before Following Up

When you're uncertain about how to make employers and recruiters hear what you're saying and offer you an interview, plan your follow-up campaign in advance. These questions and answers can help you fill in the blanks.

Should I phone or e-mail my follow-up?

Resume blasting rarely gets interviews. E-mail pitches rarely get interviews. Most search experts agree with Jeffrey E. Christian, CEO of Christian & Timers, a prominent executive search firm headquartered in Cleveland. Christian explains that you shouldn't spend time hiding behind technology like e-mail and instead do three things: Call, call, and call. "The old-fashioned personal call is the new way to go these days," Christian advises.

You may argue with that judgment, noting that you lose your nerve and don't come across as accomplished and confident and so you should stick with e-mail. You think some "shy" people just can't sell themselves on the phone even if they can sell other things.

You may be right. Telemarketing yourself is tough stuff. So is getting yourself recognized on the Internet. You probably need help from others in overcoming telephonophobia.

You might gather several jobless friends and practice on each other. Or go way out and take a temp job as a telemarketer to become somewhat desensitized to rejection after rejection. You may never become really comfortable pitching yourself, but at least you won't faint or fold when you're told to "get off this phone and never call me again!"

The consensus of specialists in job search and sales is that human voices are more persuasive than e-mail messages. E-mail can, however, pave the way for your phone call. You might address a hiring manager and say:

> My proven background in supply chain management looks like a good fit for your advertised requirements and my qualifications for the assistant manager position. I'm unsure whether you're at the interview phase yet but I would be delighted to answer any preliminary questions you may have. I'll call you tomorrow at 9:30 a.m.

What if the ad says "no phone calls"?

Call and call again. You'll get your share of hang-ups and rude responses ("Can't you read, you cluck?"), but you'll also get some positive responses. When you're told to bug off, be ready with an immediate hook that grabs attention:

> I understand you don't want to be swamped with unqualified candidates, but that's not me. My team cut inventory losses by 30 percent in nine months. I was a key team member and I'm ready to make similar savings happen for you. My accomplishments and future value to your company are much too good to pass up. Can we talk sometime this week?

Your challenge is to prepare a memorable, brief statement — a sound bite — designed to melt a hiring manager's frosty no-calls defense shield. Promise good things but avoid specifics until you're interviewed.

If you're stonewalled by a gatekeeper — administrative assistant or HR specialist — with a no-calls defense shield, you can modify your response to push for an interview or a good time to call back. More likely, you're going to have to skirt the gatekeeper by calling before and after the workday hours when screeners aren't so likely to be answering the phone.

What is the most powerful opening statement I can make?

The most powerful message to launch your call is to immediately mention the name of someone who referred you, someone who the hiring manager cares about. This may be a company executive, company employee, client, fellow professional, family member, lodge brother, and so on.

Jim Lemke, this book's technical reviewer, says that the second most powerful statement is to start out by mentioning that you're currently working for or recently left the employment of a major competitor.

What are other compelling opening statements?

Your accomplishments and results in past jobs or endeavors are what give your pitch a critical edge. Here are several examples:

> *In my current position, I led a team to develop new sales strategies which this year boosted each store's sales by $90,000 per month.*

> *I was vice president of the campus economics club – second in leadership for 45 members. Our competitive project, which I chaired, was rated tops in a national competition.*

> *When my employer's offshored customer service experiment failed, the department was recalled to Florida. I put in place a new process to handle complaints that boosted customer satisfaction by 45 percent.*

After making your accomplishment opening statement, follow with a request to meet face to face: "If you're interested in knowing more about that, can we schedule a time when I could come in for a short talk?"

How much information can I find out from a central phone operator?

If the company you're calling employs a central phone operator or reception-ist, you may get lucky and find out the very information you need from that individual to follow up on your resume.

One road block: Companies sometimes slam on an information freeze that forbids releasing the names of their employees. The companies train people who answer phones to conform to the no-loose-lips policy. (Read the next question for some ideas on how to counter an information freeze.)

In many offices, the central phone operator is a welcoming individual who's probably treated like a robot and will buy into an approach that recognizes her or his inner human being. Be friendly, and then say something like this:

> *I'm sure the incoming calls keep you hopping, so please put me on hold when you find it necessary. Please tell me, who is the manager for the new product marketing department? Oh thank you. I appreciate your help. And could you also tell me who the manager reports to? Thanks a billion.*

If you're bonding with the central phone operator — you may be the only real conversation the operator has in a long day of fielding call after call — go for broke. Ask for the manager's secretary's name, best time to call, how to pro-nounce the manager's name and does the manager work early, late, or week-ends. Aim to uncover your target's direct telephone number — or his extension number, from which you can figure out the direct line.

Now you can use the old top-down approach: Call the manager's boss, who will probably refer you to the manager. But now when you call the manager you say you've been referred by his boss, which will get you more respect.

What are some tips to get past screeners, a.k.a. gatekeepers?

Start with a charm offensive on every gatekeeper you encounter. Leave con-frontational behavior to amateurs. Think of gatekeepers as human toggle switches that either pass you on to your target or off to oblivion.

Try the following phone techniques that have been worked out by legions of successful salespeople and recruiters since the telephone was invented:

> ✔ **Name identification:** When you don't know who the hiring decision-maker is, start easy by just asking a receptionist: "I'm trying to locate your company's sales manager for Western Ohio. Who is that, please?"

What's behind the no-loose-lips policies?

Reasons central phone operators are trained not to give out employee names range from concerns about employee privacy to concerns about employees wasting time on nonproductive phone calls. The most colorful reason is aimed at preventing competitors from raiding a company's best talent.

Here's the inside story: Some recruiters have made an art form of spinning fictional tall tales. The tales are deceptions fed to receptionists to pry out names of skilled employees whom the recruiters wish to pirate for their own clients. The fiction is called "pretexting" or "rusing." The pretexts can be wild and barely believable but are delivered with seeming sincerity. For example, a recruiter calls a receptionist and begins the ruse:

> One of your nuclear engineers left me a message that he said was urgent but my daughter wrote it down in invisible ink and I could read only part of it — Bob or Bill Something — before the dog lapped it up — big vet bill — and I wonder whether you can think who it might be? Who in your nuclear engineering department could have called me?

Recruiters who've gone "rusing" in the past tell me it works more often than you might think.

If the decision-maker's name is protected like a national security asset and you know the easily found extension for the sales department (ext. 123), call related extensions (121, 122, 124, and 125) and say to anyone who answers, "Oh gee, I was trying to call the sales manager." An employee untrained in the use of no-loose-lips scripts may tell you what you seek.

✔ **Readiness alert:** Be prepared with your elevator speech (30-second summary of who you are and your selling points for the target jobs) in case the sales manager answers one of your calls.

Breaking through digital walls is easier when you realize that gatekeeping scripts don't vary much; almost all require your name, company, and purpose of call before the gatekeeper decides what to do with you.

✔ **Ideal screen buster:** The best tip is sailing in on the wings of a mutual acquaintance: "This is John Jason. Tim Pitman, a fellow professional of your boss, thinks your boss and I should talk." If coattail wings aren't available, throw a curve ball into the gatekeeper's script and take charge of the conversation. Do it by interrupting her script. Sound confident. Use first names.

You: *Good morning. To whom am I speaking?*

Gatekeeper: *This is Lois.*

You: *Lois, good morning. This is John Jason calling for David.*

Effect: You interrupted the script! The gatekeeper may assume you work in the company or are an approved vendor and pass you on.

When you suspect a first-name-only approach is too cheeky for the situation, modify: "Can I speak to David (small pause), David Wintergate?" If the gatekeeper asks you to repeat who is calling, use the same formula: "John (small pause), John Jason." The implication is that you know each other.

But what if the gatekeeper is super diligent and wants chapter-and-verse detail on your call's purpose? Try this:

> *Lois, I appreciate why you're asking that question. You see, my call involves confidentiality concerning my mastery of a business process in which David has expressed a current interest. I believe that needs to start with David and we can move forward from there. Please connect me. Thank you. (Say "thank you" often.)*

✔ **New good buddy:** By being friendly, sincere, warm, and humorous, and asking for help, you may convert the gatekeeper to an ally.

When asked for your company connection; say:

> *I'm calling as an individual today.*

When asked why you're calling, skip phony reasons like "It's a personal matter." That wheeze falls on deaf ears. Instead, research pays:

> *I understand that your boss has a mandate to cut costs. I've had serious experience with cost trimming, saving 10 percent and more. I think he'd get value in speaking with me for a few minutes. I need your help in arranging to speak to David.*

The "I'm here to help" approach allows the gatekeeper to present you as a solution to the hiring manager's problem, not as a pesky job hunter.

Similar to the patter you use with a central phone operator or receptionist, encourage your newfound mentor/coach to name the best and worst times to call, how to pronounce the boss's name if it's unusual, and for the boss's e-mail address. You're building rapport.

Send the gatekeeper a note of appreciation, or perhaps an e-card from a commercial online greeting card service.

What can I do if I keep getting booted to voicemail?

When you can't break through voicemail, leave a short message showing upbeat interest, not desperation — and a time when you will call back.

> *My name is Maureen Farmer, and I'm calling you because I've successfully outgrown my job, and you have a reputation for running a progressive department. I think you have my resume. If you like what you see, can we talk? I'll call you tomorrow morning at 11:30 to set a convenient time.*

Pronounce your name clearly and say your telephone number at a moderate pace. Give the hiring manager a chance to write it down without replaying the message. Otherwise, the manager hears a "garbledrushofwords" and decides "Idon'thavetimeforthis, and moves on.

How often should you call? Some very smart experts suggest calling every five to ten days until you're threatened with arrest if you call again. But busy employers insist that — unless you're in sales or another field requiring a demonstration of persistence — after you're certain your resume was received, call one to two weeks later, and then no more than once every three to four weeks.

Although you don't want to become a pest, the volume of resumes in the New Era job market is turned up beyond rock-concert level. If your decision is between not being a pest or being ignored, tilt toward more follow-up.

Following up by phone is your most effective tool, but you can, from time to time, substitute contacts by sending notes or e-mail with additional facts about your qualifications, ideas to solve a problem you know the company is facing, a news clipping of mutual interest, or just an expression of our continuing interest in working for the company and the manager.

Is your telephone number blocked from caller ID? Two dozen hang-ups make you look decidedly uncool.

Why shouldn't I leave a message asking the target to call me back?

Because "They're not going to do it," says sales expert George R. Walther, author of *Heat Up Your Cold Calls* (Kaplan Publishing, 2005). Speaking from the sales trenches, Walther explains that when you wash out on your first voicemail call, it's a big mistake to leave your name and number and ask employers to call you back. Instead leave a very brief message indicating that you will call again at a specific time. You may have to make a dozen calls before connecting, each time again giving a time frame for your next call. The trick, Walther observes, is to

- Set a specific time and keep your word, which makes you look like a reliable person.

- Use phrases that prevent the target from feeling "guilty" for missing your call after call. ("Please don't feel bad about missing my call. Afternoons may be better for you . . .")

Find a hook for each time you call back. Here are examples from executive search firm guru Jeffrey Christian, who says it's a good idea to make each message cite a different accomplishment:

✔ Monday: Sorry I missed you; I'll try again Wednesday afternoon. I'm hoping to meet and go into detail about my sales channel strategy, which could work very well for you.

✔ Wednesday: Too bad we missed connecting today. I'll get back to you tomorrow to explain how I worked the lost-customer database and reclaimed 38 percent of them as paying customers. Until tomorrow, then . . .

✔ Thursday: You undoubtedly have your plate full, which is why you need to meet with me — I'm persistent and I follow through. I'll get back with you next week. I want to help.

How can I keep track of all my calls, e-mails, and contacts as I follow up?

You can fall back on the usual suspects: notebooks, card files, Excel, or another computer spreadsheet program.

Alternatively, you can use a new Web-based program called JibberJobber (`www.jibberjobber.com`), which at this writing is free. JibberJobber allows you to enter information about your job search and not have to worry about how to set up or design the organizational system. You have to play around with it a little to get started, but you need not be technically minded.

When is it time to throw in the towel and move on?

Suppose you do reach the hiring manager but just can't close the interview invitation. Salvage something of your time and effort. Ask the "Who should I call?" question. Does the manager, whom we'll name Buz Shore, know anyone at another good company who might gain by talking with you? You begin that call with a referral: "Buz Shore over at Top Ship suggested we might meet for a discussion of mutual benefit."

Or suppose you never reach the hiring manager despite your dedicated effort. When is it time to say I've done all I can do and I'll explore other opportunities?

I asked Tony Beshara that question. Beshara is the author of *The Job Search Solution* (AMACOM Books, 2006). A dynamo, Beshara runs Babich and Associates, one of America's most successful job placement firms, and has years of experience in working follow-up campaigns.

Answering the question about when it's time to give up and pursue other opportunities, Beshara shared his rule of thumb: "I move on after about 15 calls spread out over two months."

Monitoring Your Follow-up Efforts

When you've sent out a boatload of resumes and are hardly, if ever, contacted for a job interview, you know it's time to power up your follow-up.

Now the big question becomes how much time you should spend on each follow-up mission. You could make a trip to Mars faster than you could chase after all your resume submissions. You may even be thinking that the old 80/20 rule, which says only 20 percent of your job search activities produce 80 percent of results, applies to resume follow-up.

Frankly, I don't know whether the 80/20 rule has any merit here. But I am sure you should be selective about the efforts you make for each resume submission. Here's an idea.

Figure 16-1 shows a Resume Follow-Up Matrix. It's a tool you can use to make objective and comparative judgments about which resume submissions offer you the biggest returns for your time investments.

The Matrix, which was created by James M. Lemke, this book's technical reviewer, and John S. Gill, my technical associate, allows a simple, easy comparison of jobs for which you've thrown your hat in the ring. It spotlights the most promising jobs for you personally that you should pursue quickly, and tags the less promising jobs that can wait until you have time on your hands.

Using the Follow-Up Matrix

The Follow-Up Matrix is divided into six main factors. The factors are divided into five value levels ranging from 0 to 4 (see the Values Key). The values are based on the presumed quality of the position for which the resume was submitted.

You won't have all the information for each category. You may have to make some educated guesses. But if you follow the New Era strategy of customizing your resume to each position, you'll have more than normal research at your fingertips.

The values inserted in each category of the Matrix are subjective. If you disagree with the examples, substitute your preferences to reflect your views about what's hot and what's not about any new position.

Lemke-Gill
RESUME FOLLOW-UP MATRIX

	Job 1	Job 2	Job 3	Job 4	Job 5
Your fit					
Company/Industry					
Salary/Benefits					
Training					
Location					
Personal Factors					

Total					

Figure 16-1: The Resume Follow-Up Matrix.

Additionally, you can change the point values in any category to suit yourself. If, for example, avoiding commuter stress is overwhelmingly important to you and you're willing to accept less in every other factor (like pay and training) for a job that's ten minutes from your residence, add 5 to 10 points to the neighborhood job.

Factors on the Follow-Up Matrix

The following are some considerations that you may want to keep in mind when mulling over your options.

> ✔ **Fit:** How well do your qualifications align with the position's stated requirements? For example, if there are six requirements, how many can you match with qualifications?

- **Company/Industry:** Does the employer's focus reflect your own interests and culture? Is the company stable, an industry leader?

- **Salary/Benefits:** Does the compensation package, if revealed, fit within your desired range? When you can't find out, award average points. Visit www.salary.com to get an idea of what the position should pay. Does the company pay college tuition?

- **Training:** Working with a progressive company that has the latest technology and generous training opportunities helps keep your skills up to date and marketable.

- **Location:** In your area, the time, stress, and expense of commuting are factors. If you must move to another section of the country, consider relocation (relo) costs and who pays them, as well as the availability of housing and transportation, and the quality of schools, recreational facilities, and lifestyle.

- **Personal Factors:** Figure out what counts most with you and switch the values to conform to those things. Working mothers might choose to keep "Telecommuting and Life/Work Fit" as the top value. Baby boomers might value "flexible hours or part-time work." It's your call.

If you sent a resume for a job that you give 4 points in each of the six categories, that's 24 points and you should run, not walk, to follow up on that winner. By contrast, if you sent a resume for a position that you give only 1 point in each of the six categories, depending on what else is on your plate at the time, you may want to exert a minimum of effort to follow up on that loser.

The Values Key

Fill in each job's six factors using this key (which you should feel free to change if the values differ from your own).

Fit

0 = Not qualified at all, but I'm desperate

1 = I think I could do the job, but my resume says no

2 = I'm qualified but so are many others

3 = I'm very qualified so I should get noticed

4 = I'm extremely qualified and can make an immediate impact

Company/Industry

0 = No future/too many layoffs

1 = Steady/limited growth opportunities

2 = Solid performer

3 = Industry leader

4 = Bleeding edge leader

Salary/Benefits

0 = Unemployment better option

1 = Beats unemployment

2 = Average

3 = Great

4 = Outstanding

Training

0 = Going nowhere job

1 = Little training/old technology

2 = Some training/current technology

3 = Good training/new technology

4 = Great training/new technology

Location

0 = Ghastly commute/unpaid relo to swamp land

1 = Each way 1 hour

2 = Each way 30-45 minutes

3 = Less than 30 minutes each way/mass transit

4 = Home office, or paid relo to paradise

Personal Factors

0 = Wrong culture

1 = Plenty of women/men

2 = Fancy office

3 = Telecommuting

4 = Work/life balance

Checking out a sample Matrix

Figure 16-2 illustrates how the Resume Follow-Up Matrix helps you allocate your follow-up time. Go after Job 2 and Job 3 immediately. Follow up on Job 5 and Job 1 when convenient. Don't waste your time on Job 4.

	Job 1	Job 2	Job 3	Job 4	Job 5
Your fit	0	4	1	1	. 2
Company/Industry	3	4	3	0	2
Salary/Benefits	0	4	4	3	3
Training	2	4	3	0	1
Location	2	4	2	0	1
Personal Factors	1	4	1	0	1
Total	8	24	14	4	10

Figure 16-2: Example of how you might use the Resume Follow-Up Matrix.

Fast-Tracking Your Successful Follow-Up

Although following up does take an investment of your time, it need not suck all the oxygen from your life's free hours. The Resume Follow-Up Matrix encourages smart time management while reminding you that good things no longer come to he or she who waits.

Often the wait is longer than you expect. Many people think the hiring cycle is about 30 to 45 days, when the actual figure is closer to 90 to 120 days, say veteran job placement experts.

Any number of things delay decisive employment action: The first choice candidate backs out, employers change their priorities while dealing with a crisis, management freezes budgets, hiring managers go on vacation, or rumors surface of an impending merger, to name a few.

Job seekers who diligently follow up resume submissions sometimes discover that on their fifth or sixth call to a target company, seven or eight weeks later, that the company's interviewing process has risen from the dead and given new emphasis. There you are, metaphorically speaking: on the right street corner at the right time when the right bus comes along — and you get on the bus.

Chapter 17

Almost Got the Interview Date? Read This First

In This Chapter

▶ Setting or rescheduling a mutually agreeable interview date

▶ Assuring same-room interviews

▶ Showing enthusiasm without losing money

▶ Handling a rush of employer interest

▶ Paying for travel interviews

So you've sent out your resumes and been tapped for an interview. Now it's merely a matter of the where and when. At this point, nothing can monkey-wrench your meeting. Or can it? The inconvenient answer is "yes."

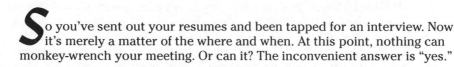

Countless factors that are beyond your control — such as a sudden budget crunch that kills the position — can derail your home-stretch run for promising interviews.

Fortunately, most of the accidents waiting to happen are small things you can control. Unfortunately, even small missteps can have a big bad impact. To make sure you don't snatch defeat from the jaws of victory, here are five illustrations of developments where little things mean a lot to your future.

When Your Job Conflicts with an Interview Date

You're employed, with a hectic job, which is one reason you want to make a getaway. A recruiter contacts you with an interesting interview request to meet with a hiring manager. The problem is the manager wants to meet with you during a busy work day.

If you have no vacation or other leave time available and you've replaced every tooth in your mouth, your best option is to frame your proposal for a night or weekend meeting in terms of your honorable work ethic:

> *I am excited about meeting with Harry Lucas but, in good conscience, I can't cheat my current company and take a work day off to do so right now. My management is counting on me to complete a company-wide inventory all next week. When I sent you my resume as a candidate for your open technical service position, I knew that I am probably a close match for the job. Your position requires A, B, and C. And, as you noted on my resume, I have a dozen highly productive years' experience in A, B, and C. Can we possibly set up an early evening meeting, say Tuesday or Wednesday?*

Should an emergency arise at your present job requiring you to change an interview time, use the same approach — you're a conscientious employee and never let your team down. Just remember, rescheduling an interview once is risky; twice is fatal.

Face-to-Face Beats Ear-to-Ear

Telephone interviews are screening interviews to find out whether you're worth the investment of time that a regular interview requires. You aren't going to be hired for a good job until you get in the same room with a person who has the authority to hire you. That's why even in a formal telephone interview with a screener you should keep pushing for a face-to-face interview.

One way to earn a face-to-face interview is to hold back on a few key questions to give the decision-maker a reason to see you. Decide in advance which likely important questions you'll use to leverage a meeting with a hiring authority, who typically is the manager to whom you would report. You might say something like this in response to a question:

> *With my skills in management, it's one that I feel I can't adequately answer over the telephone. Can we set up a meeting so that I can better explain how my qualifications dovetail with your stated requirements? I'm free on Tuesday morning. Is that a good time for you?*

Whenever possible, avoid answering employment questions on a mobile phone; they have a propensity for audio mishaps. ("Can you hear me now?") Say you'll call right back on a landline.

Going Overboard on Ardor Can Cost You Money

Accepting an interview invitation is cause for celebration. But when you're making the interview arrangements, be friendly and agreeable, warm and pleasant, but show a little restraint. Exhibiting thrilled, puppy-dog excitement and face-licking gratitude can plant the idea that you're desperate and willing to accept below-market-rate pay, as well as raise doubts about why you're desperate for new employment. Set up the interview appointment as though you're looking forward to it but not because you "need" the job.

Zeal and youthful enthusiasm work well for young graduates but not so well for job seekers over the age of 25. It's a negotiation issue.

When the Interview Is Out of Town

If a company contacts you and requires an out-of-town interview, the company should pick up the tab.

If you made the contact, the issue is murkier. A cool way to find out who will pay travel costs for you to travel for a company-site interview is to finesse the question. Here are two examples:

> *Should I contact your company's travel department or do you use an outside travel agent?*
>
> *Will your company be making the travel arrangements for me?*

If you're on your own for travel costs, your decision may be difficult. It helps if the interviewing location is in a pleasant spot and you can combine your trip with a little vacation (ask your tax adviser if the travel is deductible).

If you're a starving college senior or a new graduate, you can get away with pleading poverty, saying you'd love to come see them in a city far away but that you spent your last dime getting the quality education that qualifies you as a candidate for employment by the target company.

Schools and nonprofit organizations may have a policy requiring all candidates to pay their own interview travel expense. Don't reject the interview invitation outright; accept it. You can always cancel later.

Take stock of your situation and determine whether you can make the trip work: Do you have a friend or family member who will welcome you as a guest? Can you get a cheap flight? Can you double (or triple) up and interview with other prospective employers in the area?

Making the Most of Your Moment

You seem to be the candidate of the hour: Four companies are requesting your presence for an interview — all in the same week! What a happy dilemma, you say.

And it is, particularly because you can put yourself in the best position possible — and get a little interviewing practice — if you utilize the following strategy:

1. **Review the Resume Follow-Up Matrix in Chapter 16.**
2. **Rank the four companies from one to four, with one being your top pick.**
3. **Interview with numbers three and four first, and one and two last.**

Not only will you be in interviewing mode by the time you talk with your top picks, but companies number three and four may make you an offer that you can use to leverage a quicker decision by your top choice.

Prioritize and set up your interviews quickly. If you don't move fast enough to schedule an interview, an employer who's impatient to fill the position may make a choice before seeing you. It's unlikely, but possible.

Little Things Do Mean a Lot

When the interview you want is within grabbing distance, you'll have other issues to address and choices to make — some of which may seem insignificant. Try not to ignore the small stuff. It can come back to bite you.

Part V
The Part of Tens

The 5th Wave — By Rich Tennant

"I sent my resume to 9 PR firms. If any of them call back, tell them I'm magically cleaning my clothes at a breakthrough laundromat where the who's-who of Oak Street meet and greet."

In this part . . .

Quick tips and checklists for perfecting your resumes make up this part. I show you how to back up your claims, find an effective resume writer when you want to call in a pro, how to sidestep common mistakes, and give your resumes a last once-over to make sure they're OnTarget.

Chapter 18

Ten (×3) Ways to Prove Your Claims

· ·

In This Chapter

▶ Ten number statements to prove your accomplishments

▶ Ten percentage statements to document your claims

▶ Ten dollar-amount statements to back your results

· ·

So you have excellent communications skills, or you meet people well, or you can make a computer work magic. At least, that's what you assert. How can I (an employer) believe you?

I'm more likely to believe your claims of skills and accomplishments when you back them up with specifics.

A good start on backing up your statements is *measuring* them with numbers, percentages, and dollar amounts.

Compare the following statements in Column A with the statements in Column B. Which is the strongest, most attention-grabbing, most convincing?

Column A	Column B
Easy Ways to Be More Popular	50 Easy Ways to Be More Popular
Towels on Sale	Towels 40% Off
Designed internal company insurance plan to replace outside plan at great savings.	Designed $30 million self-insured health plan, saving estimated $5 million per year over previous external plan.

I think you'll agree that the Column B statements win hands down! The take-home message is *measure, measure, measure.* Look at the following statements in the three categories of numbers, percentages, and dollar amounts. Fill in the blanks as a reminder to measure your accomplishments and results.

Say It with Numbers

1. __ (#) years of extensive experience in _____ and _____.

2. Won ____ (#) awards for _____.

3. Trained/Supervised ____ (#) full-time and ____ (#) part-time employees.

4. Recommended by _____ (a number of notable people) as a _____ (something good that they said about you) for excellent _____ (an accomplishment or skill).

5. Supervised a staff of ____ (#).

6. Recruited ____ (#) staff members in _____ (period of time), increasing overall production.

7. Sold ____ (# of products) in _____ (period of time), ranking ____ (1st, 2nd, 3rd) in sales in a company of ____ (#) employees.

8. Exceeded goals in __ (#) years/months/days, establishing my employer as ____ (1st, 2nd, 3rd, or whatever number) in industry.

9. Missed only ____ (#) days of work out of ____ (#) total.

10. Assisted ____ (#) (executives, supervisors, technical directors, others).

Say It with Percentages

1. Excellent_____(your top proficiency) skills, which resulted in ____ (%) increase/decrease in _____ (sales, revenues, profits, clients, expenses, costs, charges).

2. Recognized as a leader in company, using strong skills to effect a/an ____ (%) increase in team/co-worker production.

3. Streamlined _____ (industry procedure), decreasing hours
   spent on task by ____ (%).

4. Used extensive _____ (several skills) to increase customer/
   member base by ____ (%).

5. Financed __ (%) of tuition/education/own business.

6. Graduated within the top ____ (%) of class.

7. Responsible for an estimated __ (%) of employer's success in
   _____ (functional area/market).

8. Resolved customer relations issues, increasing customer satisfaction
   by ____ (%).

9. Eliminated _____ (an industry problem), increasing productivity by ____ (%).

10. Upgraded _____ (an industry tool), resulting in ____ (%)
    increase in effectiveness.

Say It with Dollar Amounts

1. Supervised entire _____ (a department) staff, decreasing
   middle-management costs by ____ ($).

2. Purchased computer upgrade for office, saving the company ____ ($) in
   paid hours.

3. Eliminated the need for _____ (one or several positions in
   company), decreasing payroll by __ ($).

4. Averaged ____ ($) in sales per month.

5. Collected ____ ($) in memberships and donations.

6. Supervised the opening/construction of new location, completing task
   at ____ ($) under projected budget.

7. Designed entire _____ program, which earned ____ ($) in
   company revenues.

8. Implemented new _____ system, saving _____ ($) daily/weekly/ monthly/annually.

9. Reduced cost of _____ (substantial service) by developing and implementing a new _____ system at the bargain price of _____ ($).

10. Restructured _____ (organization/system/product) to result in a savings of _____ ($).

Chapter 19

Ten Ways to Improve Your Resume

In This Chapter

▶ Eliminating anything that doesn't support the job you're targeting

▶ Not pussyfooting around about what you're applying for

▶ Finding success in the 5 percent rule

Think your resume could sparkle with a few tweaks? Here are ten easy fixes to power up to OnTarget status.

Match Your Resume to the Job

To dart past job software filters, a resume must closely meet the requirements in the job description. If you know what company recruiters are looking for, make sure you put it in the top quarter of your resume. If instead you're posting your resume in databanks, research the career field for typical requirements and include those that apply to you.

Use Bulleted Style for Easy Reading

Using one- or two-liners opens up your resume with white space, making it more appealing to read. Professional advertising copywriters know that big blocks of text suffocate readers. Let your words breathe!

Discover Art of Lost Articles

Although using articles — "a," "an," and "the" — in your resume isn't *wrong*, try deleting them for a crisper and snappier end result. Recruiters and employers expect to read resumes in compact phrases, not fully developed sentences.

The first person "I" is another word that your resume doesn't need. Look at the following examples:

With Articles	**Without Articles**
I report to the plant manager of the largest manufacturer of silicone-based waxes and polishes.	Report to plant manager of largest manufacturer of silicone-based waxes and polishes.
I worked as the only administrative person on a large construction site.	Worked as only administrative person on large construction site.

Sell, Don't Tell

Forget sticking to the old naming-your-previous-responsibilities routine. Merely listing "Responsible for XYZ" doesn't assure the recruiter that you met your responsibility or that the result of your efforts was worth the money someone paid you.

By contrast, read over your resume and make sure you have answered that pesky "So what?" question, which is lying in ambush for each bit of information you mention. Try to imagine what's running through a recruiter's mind when you relate that you were responsible for XYZ: *So what? Who cares? What's in it for me?* Anticipate those questions and answer them before a recruiter has a chance to toss your resume. (Chapter 5 discusses this advice in more detail.)

Show Off Your Assets

Recruiters are wild about snaring the cream of the crop. If you're in the top 5 percent of any significant group (graduation, sales, attendance record, performance ratings) make sure that fact appears prominently on your resume.

Make Sure Your Words Play Well Together

Old wisdom: Use a lot of action verbs to perk up reading interest in resumes (see Chapter 7). *Later wisdom:* Cash in some of the action verbs for nouns, the keywords that ward off anonymity in sleeping resume databases. *New wisdom:* Use both nouns and verbs.

Just don't mix noun and verb phrases in the same resume section. The following example explains.

> ***Highlights:***
>
> - Founded start-up, achieving positive cash flow and real profits in the first year. [verb]
> - President of point-of-sale products. [noun]
> - Proven ability for representation of high technology products. [noun]
> - Consistently achieved highest profit in 45-year-old company history. [verb]

Change the noun statements to be consistent with the verb statements:

- Served as president of point-of-sale products.
- Proved ability to represent high-technology products.

Writing instructors call this agreeable notion *parallel construction.*

Reach Out with Strength

Highlight the qualifications and past job activities that speak to the kind of job you want and the skills you want to use. If, for instance, you want to transition from military training to civilian training, remain riveted to your training skills without diluting your message by mentioning your ability to use several simple computer programs.

Don't muddle your resume's message with minor skills or skills you no longer wish to use; stay on message.

Trash a Wimpy Objective

Imagine an actor striding onto a stage, stopping, and then standing there like a log addressing the audience: "I came to find out what you can do for me."

Not exactly a curtain raiser — any more than beginning your resume with simply awful objective statements like: "Seeking a chance for advancement," or "where my skills will be utilized."

Retire trite messages like this one: "To obtain a responsible job with "challenging and rewarding duties." Does someone out there really want an irresponsible position? One that's dull and unrewarding?

Be an editor! Draw a line through wussy wording that leaves everyone wondering whether you're a washout. Your statement can be simple, yet effective: "Management position in finance where more than ten years' experience will strengthen the bottom line."

Check the Horse's Mouth

Pick up the phone and call the HR department where you want to work and are about to submit your resume. Ask: "Before I send you my resume online, I want to get the facts. Do you accept MS Word attachments, store them as formatted documents, and route them to line managers as images?"

If the answer is *yes,* wrap fish in that ugly ASCII plain text resume and throw it away, reveling in the fact that you'll get to send the attractive version of your resume. If the answer is *no,* well, good try in this era of transition. After all, ugly is still better than unreadable.

Erase the "Leave-Outs"

Eliminate clutter by removing useless information that doesn't support reasons you're a qualified candidate. Here's a short list of the worst offenders:

- ✔ "References available on request." Listing the actual references on your resume is even worse.

- ✔ Your Social Security number or driver's license number.

- ✔ The date your resume was prepared.

- ✔ Your company's telephone number.

- ✔ Your high school or grammar school if you're a college graduate.

- ✔ Dates you spent involved in college extracurricular activities.

- ✔ Dates you were involved with professional or civic organizations unless using them to fill in gaps or add heft to your claims.

- ✔ Names of (human) past employers; put these on your reference sheet with contact information.

Chapter 20

Ten Tips on Choosing Professional Resume Help

In This Chapter

▶ Selecting a professional resume writer

▶ Checking out the goods

▶ Shopping for price quotes

*T*o use a professional resume writer or not? That is the question.

"No!" answers one recruiter, "I don't recommend professional services. Write your own. Interviewers have certain expectations from the resume. When a professional writer creates an overblown image that you can't live up to, the interview crashes because the interviewer feels she's been fooled. That wastes everyone's time, including yours."

"Yes!" Another career counselor disagrees: "Seldom would I recommend that job seekers write their own resumes, regardless of their intelligence or writing ability. They lack objectivity. They often spin their wheels focusing on the wrong things, either over- or underreacting to their experiences."

These two opinions differ because effectively packaging yourself on paper is not a naturally acquired ability but a skill you purposely set out to learn.

I come down on the side of the second counselor's opinion — use a pro to write your resume, if you wish. You should, however, organize your own material to present to the professional writer just as you organize your taxes to hand over to an accountant. The reason is simple: Organizing your information primes your mind for job interviews.

In an age of personalization — personal financial advisers, personal trainers, personal tax preparers, personal career coaches — why not a personal resume pro? Prime candidates for resume services are first-time resume writers, people with a checkerboard history, and people who haven't thought about resumes in years. Follow these tips to choose a personal resume pro wisely.

Choose a Resume Writing Service, Not a Clerical Service

Many *clerical services* do a nice job of word processing your resume for a fair price of $100 or more. A clerical service is a useful option if that's all you need.

But most people need much more, and clerical services are in a different business from *professional resume writing services.* Clerical services sell such clerical processes as keyboarding and printing. Resume firms sell specialized knowledge in fluently articulating what you want to do and the evidence that proves you can do it.

A resume pro knows a great deal about the business of marketing you to employers, has the latest trends and buzzwords on tap, and coaches you through potholes in your history.

Ask Around for a Great Resume Pro

After you've decided to use a resume professional, your next step is finding a winner. The best way to do so is to get a referral, either from a satisfied customer or from someone in the business — a local career center consultant, recruiter, employment agency consultant, or outplacement consultant.

If you're being laid off, inquire within your corporate human resource department. These people often know who's doing the best work.

The fact that a resume firm has been in business for a long time and has done thousands of resumes is no guarantee of competence — but it's a sign that some customers must like what they do and have spread the word. The acceptance of major credit cards is another indicator of stability.

Request a Free Initial Consultation

Request a free, brief, get-acquainted meeting in person or on the phone. Speak not to the boss or a sales representative, but to the writer. The same firm can have good and poor writers. Ask the writer what general strategy she'll use to deal with your specific problems. If you don't hear a responsible answer, keep looking.

A responsible answer does not imply discussion of the specifics of how your resume will be handled. Much like people shop retail stores to look at the merchandise and then order from a discount catalog, people shop professional resume services to pick writers' brains and then write their own resumes. Resume pros caught on to this move and developed laryngitis. Moreover, it is irresponsible for a resume pro to go into detail about how your resume will be handled until she knows more about you. You want to know the general approach — the kinds of strategies discussed in this book.

Watch Out for Overuse of Forms

Most resume pros ask you to fill out a lengthy, detailed form — much like the one new patients fill out in a doctor's office. The form is a good start, but it's far from enough. Eliminate the firms that don't offer dialogue with the writer. The resume pro should interview you to discover your unique experience and strengths. You and the resume pro are colleagues, sharing a task.

The problem with form dependency is you may merely get back your own language prettied up in a glitzy format. That's not what you want a resume pro to do for you.

Look for a Fair Price

Prices vary by locale, but expect to pay between $150 and $1,000 for most resumes. Executive resumes may range from $500 to $1,600.

If you're using a two-page resume, you can probably pay for a core resume and customize only the first page for each different job, while retaining the second page across your search. You may have to pay extra for a few customizations of your core resume to see how it's done.

Never pay by the page — longer isn't better. Find out the rate for branching out from a core resume to create a targeted resume specifically for an individual employer or occupation. Other questions to ask include:

- Can I get a volume discount for several resumes targeted in different directions?
- What's the charge for minor alterations?
- What's the charge for an update two years later?
- What's the cost for extra copies?

Don't be persuaded by an offer of, say, 100 copies for a discount price. Even if it seems like a bargain, you may want to make changes long before your inventory is gone. Beware also of a resume professional who gives lifetime free updating — it's unrealistic to expect quality work when the professional isn't being paid.

Check Out Samples

Ask the resume pro to show you samples of his resumes. Look not only at content but at production values. Choose a resume pro who has invested in state-of-the-art technology: a good computer and a laser printer. You judge the quality of the content, layout, word processing, paper, and printing.

Take Aim

For maximum impact, target each resume you send out to a specific employer or career field. Look for a resume pro who understands this concept. You need a resume that has "you" written all over it — *your* theme, *your* focus, and *your* measurable achievements — all matched to a career field you want. Skip over those who sell the same cookie-cutter resume over and over.

Avoid resume pros who offer assembly-line presentations, virtually indistinguishable from thousands of others created by the service. Ignore resume pros who plug your information into a fill-in-the-blanks standard form, garnished with prefab statements. Double ignore those who try to cover the sameness of their work by printing out resumes on 11 x 17-inch parchment paper and folding them into a pretentious brief. Employers use these resumes for kindling.

Also, be careful of the pro who caters to you instead of to your target audience. A heavyweight resume pro warned me that some resume services cater to their customers, not their customers' customers — with fancy brochures, excessive color, and whimsical paper.

Consider a Certified Resume Writer

Resume writers who belong to resume-certifying organizations are likely to stay up to date in resume effectiveness; some earn continuing education units (CEUs). Here are the "big three" certifying organizations:

- ✔ The **Professional Association of Resume Writers & Career Counselors** (www.parw.com) is a for-profit organization. It was the first in the resume-writing industry to certify professionals who meet the required criteria of experience and examination. Those who become certified are allowed to use the title Certified Professional Resume Writer (CPRW) after their names.

- ✔ **Career Directors International** (www.careerdirectors.com) is a for-profit organization. While the newest of the "big three" resume-certifying organizations, it's well regarded in the industry. Career Directors International offers four levels of resume certification: Certified Advanced Resume Writer (CARW), Certified Expert Resume Writer (CERW), Certified Master Resume Writer (CMRW), and certified Federal Resume Writer (CFRW).

- ✔ The **National Resume Writers' Association** (www.nrwa.com) is a not-for-profit organization. It started as a spin-off of PARW but is now totally independent. Those who become certified through this group are allowed to use the title Nationally Certified Resume Writer (NCRW) after their names. Visit the organization's Web site to locate members who are well qualified to write your resume.

Visit the Web sites of the above organizations to locate members who are well qualified to write your resume — no matter where you live. You can reside thousands of miles away from the resume writer and still get a great product.

Remember That Design Counts

Review pointers in Chapter 9 to recall how a professional resume is supposed to look. You'd be amazed at how "borax" and junky the products are that I get as spam from resume mills. Your resume must look professional.

Know That a Poor Resume Is No Bargain

Appreciate the hidden costs of a poor resume: A hack job can cost you good job interviews. When the finished product is in your hands, you should be able to say:

- ✔ This is an OnTarget resume — it looks great and makes me look great!
- ✔ This resume doesn't leave out qualifications that are targeted to the jobs I'm after.
- ✔ I like reading my resume; it won't put the recruiter to sleep.

Chapter 21

Ten Pet Peeves of Recruiters

In This Chapter

▶ Reading recruiters' inside talk

▶ Recognizing irksome resume flaws

▶ Knowing when to overrule recruiters

Check out what recruiters write when they think no "civilians" (job seekers) are reading. Both third-party (independent) recruiters and inside corporate recruiters share their thoughts freely on various Internet forums.

Here are ten categories of transgressions that various e-recruiters cite as making them grumpy. Some categories contain comments from different recruiters. I report them anonymously to protect their privacy. My comments conclude each category.

Resume-Free Pitches

I bristle at applicants who e-mail me a general question, "Do you have any technical positions open in Kansas City?" instead of a resume.

Spare yourself a nonanswer for a nonresume. Attach a resume to your question.

Major Mismatches

I find it extremely annoying when people send resumes without reading our job posting. If we advertise for a pizza chef, a bike mechanic is just as likely to self-nominate himself for the job, leaving us to figure it out. We don't have time for goose chasing.

Our management positions require a background in a certain industry plus experience. We get responses from people with one year of experience and no management background. We get resumes that claim their experience is ideal or that they read the position and found it to fit their skills exactly, when in reality they have none of the experience detailed in the job posting.

We advertised for a telecommunications consultant with call center experience and received a resume of someone with experience in movie production and no experience in anything we look for. I am sure applicants would have a more positive outcome if they applied for positions that are relevant to their experience, although I doubt this will ever change.

Some job seekers, particularly in technical fields, operate on the lottery theory and scatter resumes everywhere. A number of job seekers adhere to the old-school 80 percent strategy (if you fit 80 percent of the job's requirements, give it a go) or believe that if you can manage one thing, you can manage anything.

Others seek ways to apply viable transferable skills to new environments and, failing to make a strong enough case, are rejected because some recruiters are too inexperienced, overworked, or insular to recognize the legitimacy of transitioning skills.

Still other job seekers just don't get it and waste everyone's time in applying for jobs for which they're dramatically unqualified.

Solution: The targeted resume. (See Chapter 1.)

E-Stalking

One applicant e-mailed his resume and a few days later sent another, saying he was waiting for a response. I replied that we would contact him if we are interested. A few days later, and once a week for a few months, he sent e-mails that said only, "Still waiting." Creepy.

I would like to tell job seekers to send only one resume. If someone is "open" to all appropriate positions, just say so!

Checking back periodically works best if you send new information of interest to the recruiter. You may send a relevant news article with a brief "In case you missed this" note, adding that you continue to look forward to the right timing for an interview.

Censor before sending your complaint

This is the true story of what can happen when you give into feelings of stress, frustration, irritation, and anger and call it like you see it. The following is an actual e-mail letter to a major defense contractor that employs tens of thousands of people:

To Whom It May Concern:

In response to the job openings posted at your Web site, I have applied for numerous jobs (probably over 100 different positions) by sending my resume to you along with e-mails during the last 4 to 5 weeks. I am extremely disappointed by the way my online job applications have been handled by [company name withheld].

The recruiter who handled the complaint replies:

"This person was interviewed at a job fair and told that if he qualified for any positions, we would notify him. He then submitted 111 actual resumes for more than 40 different career positions. I have never met anyone who could qualify for that many positions. This individual doesn't get it. We now have removed him from all job searches in our company."

Talk about target resume overkill!

Saying that you're available for any appropriate position carries the risk that you'll be seen as too much of a generalist and expert at nothing, or desperate. If you do it, define the field — "appropriate in the accounting field" or "appropriate in the retail financial field," for example.

The technical reviewer for this book, HR expert Jim Lemke, says that stuffing the recruitment box with your resumes may become moot:

"Most applicant tracking systems that companies are using now require job seekers to create a login ID before permitting job seekers to attach a resume. After the job seeker logs into the company career site, he or she can easily modify a current resume, save multiple versions, and apply to multiple positions with the click of the mouse.

"The job seeker may still be required to answer specific questions before a resume can be submitted for a specific job. If the questions are answered correctly (according to the company's standards), the recruiter or hiring manager is notified by e-mail that a new qualified resume is available for review. If the applicant doesn't pass the litmus test for qualification, the applicant's resume stays in the company's database and is searched on for future openings.

"It doesn't stop the persistent applicant from sending additional resumes or e-mail or making phone calls. The trick is not to become a pest."

Caps and Taps and Typos

My sore spot is receiving e-mails with no use of capitalization whatsoever, or with some words mysteriously capitalized and those that should be capitalized (proper names, beginning of a sentence) in lowercase.

For heaven's sake, use spell check. A neat resume will always be my preference over one that is not.

Every single book or article on resume writing I've ever seen recommends impeccable work. It would be a crying shame to put together a well-researched resume only to have it discarded because of misspellings and typos throughout the text.

Too Much Information

I give bad marks to people who think that sending their resume multiple times will increase their chance of getting a call for an interview. It won't.

I dislike it when the applicant puts several addresses in the "to" e-mail box and mass mails the resume. This unprofessional shortcut looks like no care is taken in applying to each individual position.

Another practice to avoid is postal mailing a hard copy of your e-mailed resume. Carry hard copies to an interview, but don't mail or fax an additional copy because doing so is unnecessary. As for e-mailing your resume, not only is it disrespectful to mass mail your resume addressed to multiple names, but it's no one's business but your own where you're applying for work.

Moreover, as the sea change of target resumes sweeps across the job market, the old-school "blast" style mailings (one-size-fits-all) stand little chance of delivering you into an interview room.

Date Grate

What annoys me is when job seekers send resumes and don't specify start and end dates for jobs. As if this won't be at the top of my list to ask in an interview and a reference check — if they get to the interview process at all.

Two old dodges don't fly with me: (1) Trying to hide a resume gap by listing employment dates at the end of the summaries rather than in the left-hand margin and (2) substituting the number of years at a company for the real dates.

Reporters are taught to put the most important facts at the lead of a story. Using the same theory of first things first, list your experience in this order: title of position, name and locale of employer, and dates of employment. Dates of employment don't have to be placed in the left margin. The right margin is perfectly acceptable and even preferred by some resume experts.

Guess Who

It's a pain when I get incomplete resumes and cover letters without contact information. We have offices in several countries and a hotmail.com address doesn't suffice.

A pet peeve of mine is receiving resumes without the current employer listed — "confidential" resumes. I can understand this treatment for Web job site postings but when sending a resume to a specific employer, the current employer should be identified.

As for the first comment, you can add to the "hotmail.com" (or other free mailbox established for a job search) a post office box and a dedicated telephone answering machine. That combination will protect your privacy but make it easy for a recruiter to contact you.

As for the second comment, you can use a generic description of your current position and skills, noting that you'll reveal the current employer's name in a job interview. I urge caution in fully revealing your identity and personal workplace information on the Internet.

File Style

I can't imagine why, but some people have to be told to submit a resume as a normal attachment in a common program (Word, WordPerfect, Notepad, and so forth). I have received two-page Word documents as zip files! I have the software to handle zips, but many people do not.

Zip files are for documents the size of Connecticut, not resumes or CVs. No one wants to bother unzipping.

Useless and Uninformative

I grow peevish when forced to read through fluff that does not relate to a workforce position. It doesn't matter to anyone in my office that you were the local beauty queen. It doesn't matter to anyone in my office that when you are 35, out of college, and have held several jobs that you attended a prestigious prep school as a teenager. It doesn't matter to anyone in my office that your wife is the vice president of a well-known company.

Another thing that bugs me is the use of fancy graphics and poems on resumes.

Stick to information related to your ability to do the job for which you are applying.

Probable Prevarication

I hate wasting my time on resumes from people who claim to have attended a school they never saw the inside of and to have worked for a company that they didn't.

Lying about a point of fact easily proved or disproved is riskier than ever in today's era of fact-checking background investigations.

Recruiters and employers are getting wise to lies and are turning fib finding into a big business. The Society for Human Resource Management, a membership organization, says the number of third-party screeners has exploded in the past ten years into a $2 billion industry because 96 percent of businesses now conduct some sort of background check on job applicants. Some companies even conduct checks upon promotion.

Despite the glib assurances from some that you must inflate your resume or be put at a disadvantage because "everybody's doing it," tall tales court trouble, as a number of high-placed executives have discovered on their way out the door.

Employers often assume that those who cheat on resumes and job applications also cheat in school and in life.

Chapter 22

Your Ten-Point Resume Checklist

In This Chapter

▶ Making sure your resume matches up with specific job qualifications

▶ Using a fire hose on tacky resume errors

▶ Standing back for a fresh look at the impression you're making

▶ Trusting your resume skills but verifying overall results

*B*efore going public with your resume, give it a final walk-through. Check the box in front of each item only when your resume meets OnTarget standards. Give yourself 10 points for each checkmark. If you don't get a score of 100, go back to your keyboard and try again.

Tit for Tat

❑ **You remember the new drive to customize resumes by matching your qualifications (skills, education) with the specific positions of a job, or by matching your qualifications with the expected qualifications in a career field.**

If you write a two-page resume, you remember to customize the first page, even if you do not customize the second page. (Chapter 1 discusses the customizing requirement and why it's now important.)

Format and Style

❑ **You select the best format for your situation.**

For example, *reverse chronological* when staying in the same field, or *functional* when changing fields. (Chapter 5 covers resume formats.)

Focus and Image

❏ **You say what you want to do and why you should be interviewed to do it.**

You let your resume "rest" for a day or so, and then look at it with fresh eyes. You consider its overall impression. What kind of "brand" do you project? Your resume has a theme. You present yourself as focused — not merely desperate to accept just any job.

Achievements and Skills

❏ **You relate your skills to the skills needed for the job.**

You cite at least one achievement for each skill. You measure by using numbers, percentages, or dollar amounts for each achievement. You measure any statement you can. You highlight results, not just responsibilities.

Language and Expressions

❏ **You make the most of your word choices.**

You use adequate keywords (nouns) to make your resume searchable. You use action verbs to put vitality in your resume. You eliminate words that don't directly support your bid for the job you want, as well as such meaningless words and phrases as "References available." You use industry jargon where appropriate, but you translate acronyms, technical jargon, or military lingo into easy-to-understand English. (Chapter 7 reviews word usage.)

Content and Omissions

❏ **Your content supports your objective.**

You begin with either a skills summery or a job objective. Next, you state your experience. You begin with your education only if you're a new graduate with virtually no experience, or if your target job is related to education and training. You don't list personal information that isn't related to the job you seek, such as marital status, number of children, or height. (For a refresher on content, see Chapter 6)

Length and Common Sense

❏ **You use a length that makes sense for the amount of information you're presenting.**

You limit your resume to one or two pages if you're lightly experienced, or two or three pages if you're substantially experienced. These page counts are only guidelines; your resume can be longer if necessary to put your qualifications in the best light. Additionally, your resume can exceed three pages if it's a professional resume or a CV (curriculum vitae). *Remember:* Don't jam pack a jumble of text on one page; doing so makes your resume too difficult to read.

Appearance: Online Attached and Paper Resumes

❏ **Your resume is a real looker.**

Your e-resume in a fully formatted Word document (or equivalent) looks much like a fully formatted paper resume. You use an open layout with white space, minimum one-inch margins, headings in bold typeface or capital letters, bullets, and other low-key graphic elements that make your resume look professional (see Chapter 8). Your paper resume is printed on white or eggshell paper, both for a business impression and because it may be scanned into a database.

Sticky Points and Sugarcoating

❏ **You thoughtfully handle all problem areas, such as grouping irrelevant jobs, long-ago, part-time, and temporary jobs.**

You account for all the gaps in the time frame of your resume. You scour your resume for possible hidden negatives and eliminate them as described in Chapter 10.

Proofreading and More Proofreading

❏ **Your resume contains no typos, no grammar disasters — no errors of any kind**

You not only use your computer's spell-checker, but you also double-check (and triple-check) it. You ask others to carefully read it. Typos are hot buttons to many employers — two goofs and you're gone.

Tap the Power of OnTarget Resumes

Most jobseekers don't understand the phenomenon of how the second gust of innovative winds, called *Web 2.0,* is changing the way the Internet is connecting people with jobs.

That's why — after reading this book— you're ahead of your competition in understanding the variety of changes, including

- ✔ Employers' demands for dead-on matches of job requirements and your qualifications.
- ✔ Social networking and employee referral systems you can use.
- ✔ Blogs that carry targeted job ads for your interests and skill sets.
- ✔ RSS (Real Simple Syndication) feeds that sprint job openings to you immediately as they're posted.
- ✔ Vertical job search engines that attempt to collect for you every job opening in the universe.

Get a leg up by starting now at the beginning of a New Era in job search. Plunge into writing your OnTarget core resume sooner rather than later. You can't meet today's job market challenges relying on resume strategies from the past century.

All best wishes for you,
Joyce Lain Kennedy, *Resumes For Dummies,* 5th Edition
San Diego, California

Index

• Symbols and Numerics •

37Signals Web site, 52

• A •

abbreviations, 98, 137
The About.com Guide to Job Searching: Tools and Tactics to Help You Get the Job You Want (Doyle), 32
academic curriculum vitae resume format
  creating, 94
  defined, 80, 91
  example, 92–93
  executive summary, 91
  length, 91
  strengths, 91
  weaknesses, 91
  who should use it, 91
  who shouldn't use it, 91
accommodations employers must make for people with disabilities, 184
accomplishment resume format, 98
accounting example resume, 205
achievements
  checklist, 332, 335
  proving, 311–314
  rankings, 316
  responsibilities versus achievements, 139
  what to include, 112, 121
acquisitions, 189–190
activities, 117–118
ADA (Americans with Disabilities Act)
  conditions covered, 183
  substance abuse, 192–193
  undue hardship provision, 184
adaptive equipment requests, 185
addresses
  current address, 105
  e-mail address, 105
  mailing address, 104–105

permanent address, 105
Web page address, 105
administration
  keywords, 132–133
  sales to administration example resume, 263–265
  wow words, 124
ads
  classified print ads in newspapers, 39–41
  corporate Web sites, 41–43
  job boards, 36–39
  mirroring language of, 14
age discrimination
  forestalling in resume presentation, 160–162
  myths about older workers, 159–160
  overqualified objection, 162–163, 177–178
aggregators, 30
Agilent, 42
AIRS Job Board and Recruiting Technology Directory, 38
alignment of ASCII resume, 64
A-list candidates, 26
all-purpose resumes, 9–10
also, avoiding the word, 139
American Institutes for Research, 152
Americans with Disabilities Act (ADA)
  conditions covered, 183
  substance abuse, 192–193
  undue hardship provision, 184
analysis skills
  case studies, 71
  wow words, 128–129
AOL Instant Messenger, 56
appearance of resume
  breaking up text, 143–144
  digital version, 141, 333, 336
  fonts, 145
  footer, 146
  groupings, 143
  header, 146
  importance of, 323

appearance of resume *(continued)*
  layout, 146–150
  paper selection, 142
  paper version, 141, 333, 336
  placement of information, 146
  printing, 142
  readability, 150
  style consistency, 143
  theme papers, 142
  typefaces, 145
  white space, 145
  word processing, 142
  word wrap, 64
applicant management system, 103–105
applicant tracking system (ATS), 104–105
application forms, 119–120
articles, avoiding, 136, 315–316
ASCII resume
  alignment, 64
  cover note, 64
  creating, 63, 141
  defined, 61
  example, 62
  page numbers, 64
  submission requirements, 318
  tabs, 64
  typefaces/fonts, 63–64
  word wrap, 64
assessment tests
  behavioral assessment, 71
  managerial assessment, 71
  personality assessment, 70–71
assisted with, avoiding the term, 139
associate editor, example resume, 233
ATS (applicant tracking system), 104–105
attachments, 66
Audacity audio editor, 57
automated resume builders, 121
automatic response to application, 290–291
avoidance dodge, common tactic of
    references, 282
awards, 118

• *B* •

baby boomers
  age discrimination, 159–162
  career changes, 162–163
  education dates, 162
  example resumes, 227–229, 232
  experience, 162
  gaffes, 163–165
  objective statement, 160–161, 164
  overqualified objection, 162–163, 177–178
  strengths, 158–159, 161
  weaknesses, 159–160
background checks, 330
Bank of America, 42
banking industry
  example resume, 208
  keywords, 133
Barrington, Linda (research director at The
    Conference Board), 40
basic evaluation in online screening
    programs, 70
behavioral assessment, 71
behavior-based competencies, 113
being verbs, 137
BEKS Data Services, Inc., 66
Bell South, 42
Beshara, Tony (*The Job Search Solution*),
    298–299
Best Resumes and Letters for Ex-Offenders
    (Enelow and Krannich), 195
blasting services, 67–68
B-list candidates, 26
BlogEasy blog host site, 53
Blogger blog host site, 53
blogs
  Joel Cheesman's blog, 31, 52
  using as a job search tool, 51–53
Blogs with Jobs Web site, 53
'bots, 30
Boutell.com Web site, 57
breaking up text, 143–144
bulleted style, 315
business, example resume, 216–217
Business.com Web site, 136

• *C* •

C. H. Robinson, 42
candidate management system, 104–105
Capital One, 42
career change
  baby boomers, 162–163
  example resumes, 240, 266–269
Career Directors International, 323

Career Success: A Step-By-Step Workbook for Students, Job Seekers and Lifelong Learners (Whitaker), 112
CareerBuilder.com Web site, 37
CareerXroads, 10, 14–15
caregiving, 129–130
case studies, 71
certifications for professional resume writers, 323
Certified Advanced Resume Writer (CARW), 323
Certified Expert Resume Writer (CERW), 323
Certified Federal Resume Writer (CFRW), 323
Certified Master Resume Writer (CMRW), 323
Certified Professional Resume Writer (CPRW), 323
checklist for targeted resumes
  achievements, 332, 335
  appearance, 336
  common sense, 333
  content, 332, 336–337
  customizing requirement, 331
  digital version, 333, 336
  focus, 332, 334–335
  format, 331, 334
  image, 332
  keywords, 332
  language (word choice), 332
  length, 333, 335
  omissions, 332
  paper version, 333, 336
  problem areas, 333
  proofreading, 337
  skills, 332, 335
  style, 331
Cheesman, Joe (head of HRSEO and blogger), 31, 35, 52
choosing references, 283–284
Christian, Jeffrey E. (CEO of Christian & Timers), 292, 297–298
chronological resume format, 80
civic affiliations, 118
classified print ads in newspapers, 39–41
Classmates.com Web site, 49
clerical services, 320
CMRW (Certified Master Resume Writer), 323

college experience, 154–155
college graduates (recent)
  example resumes, 220–221, 236
  experience, 153–155
  gaffes, 155–158
  GPA (grade point average), 152–153
  objective, 154
  strengths, 152
  useless information, 154
  weaknesses, 152–153
combination (hybrid) resume format
  creating, 87
  defined, 80, 87
  example, 88
  strengths, 87
  who should use it, 87
  who shouldn't use it, 87
common gaffes
  of baby boomers, 163–165
  of recent graduates, 155–158
common sense, 333
communications wow words, 125
company resources, 105
competencies, 113–117
Competency-Based Interviews (Keesler and Strasburg), 116
Competency-Based Resumes (Keesler and Strasburg), 116
conditions covered by the Americans with Disabilities Act, 183
The Conference Board, 40
confidential resumes, 329
consultants, 188
consumer reports, 193–194
contact information
  e-mail address, 105
  importance of, 103
  incomplete or missing information, 329
  mailing address, 104–105
  name, 104
  telephone number, 105–106
  using company resources, 105–106
  Web page address, 105
content
  achievements, 112, 121
  activities, 117–118
  awards, 118
  checklist, 332, 336–337
  competencies, 113–117

content *(continued)*
  contact information, 103–106, 329
  dates of employment, 328–329
  education, 103, 110–111
  executive summary, 91
  experience, 111
  honors, 118
  licenses, 118
  objective statement, 106–108
  organizations, 118
  salary history and requirements,
      120–121, 139
  samples of your work, 118
  skills, 111–112
  summary statement, 106–110
  testimonials, 119, 284–285
  too much information, 328
  useless information, 154, 330
contract employment, 105
converting resume to plain text, 63
core competencies, 114–116
core resume
  example of, 18–19
  keywords, 135
core resume, example of, 17
Corporate Gray Web site, 170
corporate Web sites, 41–43
costs
  for professional resume writer, 321–322, 324
  for traveling to a job interview, 307–308
cover letter, 99
cover note, 64
co-workers, choosing as references, 284
CPRW (Certified Professional Resume
    Writer), 323
creating
  academic curriculum vitae resume, 94
  ASCII resume, 63, 141
  hybrid (combination) resume, 87
  reverse chronological (RC) resume, 84
  skills-based functional resume, 85
creative fields
  graphic artist, example resume, 226
  portfolios, 99–101
  resume paper selection, 142
  wow words, 125
credit history, 193–194

Crispin, Gerry (co-founder and principal of
    CareerXroads), 14–15
Crunchboard Web site, 52
culinary career, example resume, 270–272
current address, 105
customer service keywords, 133
customizing requirement, 331
CV (curriculum vitae)
  academic, 80, 91–94
  international, 80, 94–97

● *D* ●

dates
  education dates, 162
  employment dates, 328–329
demonstrating enthusiasm at job
    interview, 307
demotions, 185–187
design
  breaking up text, 143–144
  digital version, 141, 333, 336
  fonts, 145
  footer, 146
  groupings, 143
  header, 146
  importance of, 323
  layout, 146–150
  paper selection, 142
  paper version, 141, 333, 336
  placement of information, 146
  printing, 142
  readability, 150
  style consistency, 143
  theme papers, 142
  typefaces, 145
  white space, 145
  word processing, 142
  word wrap, 64
designed versus plain text resumes, 66–67
Dictionary of Occupational Titles, 135
digital version
  ASCII text, 141, 318
  design, 141, 333, 336
  scannable resume, 60–61
Dikel, Margaret F. (*The Guide to Internet Job
    Searching, 2006–2007 edition*), 38

disabilities
  accommodations employers must
    make, 184
  adaptive equipment requests, 185
  conditions defined as disabilities, 183
  Illness and Recovery statement, 184–185,
    193
  substance abuse, 192–193
disclosing
  disabilities, 184–185, 192–193
  salary history or requirements, 120
discrimination
  ADA (Americans with Disabilities Act),
    183–184, 192–193
  age discrimination, 159–162, 176, 178
Dixon, Pam (privacy expert), 67–68
Dodd, Mike (executive search consultant),
  165
Doyle, Alison, *The About.com Guide to Job
  Searching: Tools and Tactics to Help You
  Get the Job You Want*, 32

● *E* ●

Ecademy Web site, 48
education
  dates, 162
  GPA (grade point average), 152–153
  what information to include, 110–111
EEOC (Equal Employment Opportunity
  Commission), 15, 65
e-forms, 64–65
e-mail
  attachments, 66
  follow-up via e-mail, 292
  spam filters, 68
  subject line of e-mail messages, 65
e-mail address (contact information), 105
employee referral services, 46–48
employment dates, 328–329
employment gaps
  disabilities, 184–185
  example resume, 252–253
  family obligations, 187
  unemployment, 187–188
endorsements from references, 284–285

Enelow, Wendy S.
  Best Resumes and Letters for Ex-Offenders,
    195
  *Expert Resumes for Military-to-Civilian
    Transitions*, 168
enthusiasm, demonstrating at job
  interview, 307
entrepreneurs, 188
Eons Web site, 49
e-portfolios, 101
Equal Employment Opportunity
  Commission (EEOC), 15, 65
e-stalking, 326–327
example resumes
  academic curriculum vitae, 92–93
  accounting, 205
  ASCII resume, 62
  baby boomers, 227–229, 232
  banking, 208
  business, 216–217
  career change, 240, 266–269
  core resume, 17–19
  culinary career, 270–272
  employment gap, 252–253
  food service, 213
  healthcare, 201, 214–215
  hybrid (combination) format, 88
  information technology, 210–211
  international curriculum vitae, 95–96
  law enforcement/security, 273–277
  layoffs, 250–251
  mid-career professionals, project
    manager, 237–238
  mid-career professionals, teacher, 224–225
  mid-career professionals, vice president,
    234–235
  mid-career trades, 222
  military spouse, 248–249
  military to civilian, 242–243, 254–255
  military to federal government, 260–262
  mother/homemaker, 241
  new graduates, 220–221, 236
  nursing, 204
  office workers, 209
  overqualified, 244–245
  plain text resume, 62
  professional format, 90

example resumes *(continued)*
  project management, 202–203
  retailing, 212
  reverse chronological (RC) format, 83
  sales, 200
  sales to administration, 263–265
  skills-based functional format, 86
  spin-off resumes, 17–25
  supply chain, 206–207
  temp jobs, 246–247
  too many jobs, 256–257
  young professionals, 223, 226, 230–231, 233
EXE files, 66
ExecuNet Web site, 48
Executive Job-Changing Workbook (Lucht), 173
executive jobs, 173
executive summary, 91
Executive's Pocket Guide to ROI Resumes and Job Search (Kursmark and Melnik), 173
ex-offenders, 194–195
The Ex-Offenders' Job Hunting Guide (Krannich and Krannich), 195
The Ex-Offender's Quick Job Hunting Guide (Krannich and Krannich), 195
experience
  baby boomers, 162
  overqualified objection, 176–177
  recent graduate, 153
  reentering mother/homemaker, 180–181
  too little experience, 180
  too much experience in one job, 178–179
  what information to include, 111
Expert Resumes for Military-to-Civilian Transitions (Enelow and Kursmark), 168

• F •

face-to-face job interviews, 306
Fair Credit Reporting Act, 193
family obligations, 187
faxing a resume, 61
federal contractors, 12–15, 167
federal jobs, 167–169
Federal Resume Guidebook, Fourth Edition (Troutman), 169
federal resumes, 169
Federated, 42

Feedburner Web site, 57
feeds
  how they work, 53–54
  vertical job search engines (VJSEs), 30, 32
filters
  job software filters, 315
  spam filters, 68
financial management, 130
finding keywords, 135
fired, avoiding the term, 139
first person "I," 136, 316
focus, 77–79, 332, 334–335
folders
  presentation folder, 146
  reference folder, 284–285
follow-up efforts
  automatic response to application, 290–291
  e-mail, 292
  gatekeepers, 294–296
  importance of, 290
  information freeze, 294–295
  opening statements, 293
  Resume Follow-Up Matrix, 299–304
  screeners, 294–296
  telephone calls, 292–298
  time management, 304
  voicemail messages, 296–298
  when to give up, 298–299
fonts
  ACSII resume, 63
  defined, 145
  design guidelines, 145
food service example resume, 213
footer, 146
Ford, 42
formats
  academic curriculum vitae, 80, 91–94
  accomplishment, 98
  ASCII resume, 61–64, 141, 318
  checklist, 331, 334
  chronological, 80
  hybrid (combination), 80, 87–88
  international curriculum vitae, 80, 94–97
  keyword, 98
  linear, 98
  multimedia resumes, 101
  narrative, 80

plain text resume, 61–64, 141, 318
professional, 80, 89–90
reverse chronological (RC), 80–84
scannable resume, 60–61
skills-based functional, 80, 84–86
suggested formats for various situations, 80–81
video podcasts, 100
Web resumes, 101
forms
application forms, 119–120
e-forms, 64–65
resume writing services, 321
functional resume format
creating, 85
defined, 80, 84
example, 85
strengths, 84–85
weaknesses, 85
who should use it, 85
who shouldn't use it, 85

• *G* •

gaffes
of baby boomers, 163–165
of recent graduates, 155–158
Gaim Web site, 56
gaps in employment
disabilities, 184–185
example resume, 252–253
family obligations, 187
unemployment, 187–188
gatekeepers, 294–296
GE, 43
gender bias, 182
General Mills, 43
GetTheJob.com Web site, 35–36
Gill, John S., creator of the Resume Follow-Up Matrix, 299
globalization of job market, 25
Goldman Sachs, 43
Google Talk, 56
Google Web site, 112
government contractors, 167
government rules and regulations
ADA (Americans with Disabilities Act), 183–184, 192–193

Equal Employment Opportunity Commission (EEOC), 15
Fair Credit Reporting Act, 193
Office of Federal Contract Compliance Programs (OFCCP), 12–15
GPA (grade point average), 152–153
grammar, 136–137
graphic artist, example resume, 226
groupings, 143
The Guide to Internet Job Searching, 2006–2007 edition (Dikel and Roehm), 38

• *H* •

H3 Web site, 47
Hay, Mary T. (*Military Transition to Civilian Success*), 168
HCA, 43
header, 146
healthcare fields
example resumes, 201, 214–215
wow words, 129–130
Heat Up Your Cold Calls (Walther), 297
helped with, avoiding the term, 139
helping verbs, 136
helping wow words, 129–130
Henderson, David G. (*Job Search: Marketing Your Military Experience*), 168
hiring a professional resume writer
certifications, 323
costs, 321–322, 324
forms, 321
free consultation, 321
pros and cons, 319–320
referrals, 320
samples of work, 322
targeted resumes, 322–323
homemaker/mother returning to work
example resume, 241
experience, 180–181
gender bias, 182
skills, 180–183
honors, 118
HTML resumes, 101
human resources keywords, 134–135
hybrid (combination) resume format
creating, 87
defined, 80, 87

hybrid *(continued)*
  example, 88
  strengths, 87
  weaknesses, 87
  who should use it, 87
  who shouldn't use it, 87

● *I* ●

ICQ, 56
identity theft, 67–68, 168
Illness and Recovery statement, 184–185, 193
IM (instant messaging), 54–56
image, 332
in-basket exercises, 71
Indeed.com Web site, 33–34, 46
information freeze, 294–295
information technology
  example resume, 210–211
  keywords, 134
information to leave out, 318
instant messaging (IM), 54–56
integrity tests, 71
Intel, 43
Intelligence Careers Web site, 170
interaction simulations, 71
intern, example resume, 223
international curriculum vitae resume
    format, 80, 95–97
Internet applicants, 12–15
Internet Relay Chat, 56
interviews
  enthusiasm, demonstrating, 307
  face-to-face, 306
  job conflicts with interview date, 305–306
  portfolios, 100
  resume–interview connection, 25
  strategies, 308
  telephone, 306
  travel costs, 307–308

● *J* ●

James, Mark (career coach), 43
JibberJobber job tracking program, 298
Job Accommodation Network Web site,
    184–185

job ads
  classified print ads in newspapers, 39–41
  corporate Web sites, 41–43
  job boards, 36–39
  mirroring language of, 14
job boards
  *AIRS Job Board and Recruiting Technology
      Directory*, 38
  black holes, 39
  CareerBuilder.com, 37
  defined, 36
  general, 37
  listing of, 37
  Monster.com, 37
  specialty, 37–38
Job Central National Labor Exchange Web
    site, 39, 46
job descriptions and keywords, 135–136
job fairs, 168
job hoppers, 190–192
job interviews
  enthusiasm, demonstrating, 307
  face-to-face, 306
  job conflicts with interview date, 305–306
  portfolios, 100
  resume–job interview connection, 25
  strategies, 308
  telephone, 306
  travel costs, 307–308
job market
  A-list candidates, 26
  B-list candidates, 26
  globalization, 25
job requirements
  matching, 72, 315, 317
  researching, 16
Job Search Engine Guide Web site, 31
job search engines
  GetTheJob.com, 35–36
  how they work, 30–32
  Indeed.com, 33–34, 46
  Jobster.com, 34–35, 46–48
  Searchjobs.com, 35
  Simply Hired, 33, 46
  targeted resumes, 43
  Yahoo! HotJobs, 36
job search information, organizing, 298

Job Search: Marketing Your Military Experience (Henderson), 168
The Job Search Solution (Beshara), 298–299
"Job Seeker's Guide to Resumes: Twelve Resume Posting Truths" report, 67
job software filters, 315
Job-Hunt.org, 68
JobStar Web site, 120
Jobster.com Web site, 34–35, 46–48
Joyce, Susan (CEO of Job-Hunt.org), 68

• *K* •

Kaputa, Catherine (*U R a Brand!: How Smart People Brand Themselves for Business Success*), 57
Keesler, Robin
  Competency-Based Interviews, 116
  Competency-Based Resumes, 116
keyword resume format, 98
keywords
  administration, 132–133
  banking, 133
  checklist, 332
  competencies, 114
  core resume, 135
  customer service, 133
  defined, 131–132
  Dictionary of Occupational Titles, 135
  finding, 135
  human resources, 134–135
  information technology, 134
  job descriptions, 135–136
  management, 132–133
  manufacturing, 134
  Occupational Outlook Handbook, 135
  trade magazines, 135
Kodak, 43
Krannich, Caryl
  The Ex-Offenders' Job Hunting Guide, 195
  The Ex-Offender's Quick Job Hunting Guide, 195
Krannich, Ronald L.
  Best Resumes and Letters for Ex-Offenders, 195
  The Ex-Offenders' Job Hunting Guide, 195

The Ex-Offender's Quick Job Hunting Guide, 195
Military Resumes and Cover Letters, 168
Kursmark, Louise M.
  Executive's Pocket Guide to ROI Resumes and Job Search, 173
  Expert Resumes for Military-to-Civilian Transitions, 168

• *L* •

The Landmark Destiny Group Web site, 170
language (word choice). *See also* keywords; wow words
  checklist, 332
  nouns and verbs, 316–317
law enforcement/security, example resume, 273–277
layoffs, 189, 250–251
layout, 146–150
Lemke, James M., creator of the Resume Follow-Up Matrix, 299
length of resume
  academic curriculum vitae resume format, 91
  general guidelines, 333, 335
letters
  cover letter, 99
  recommendation letters, 285
  reference letters, 283–285
licenses, 118
Lilly, 43
linear resume format, 98
LinkedIn Web site, 48
listing references in a separate document, 282
Lucht, John
  Executive Job-Changing Workbook, 173
  Rites of Passage at $100,000 to $1 Million+, 173
  RiteSite.com, 173
lying, 330

• *M* •

magic formula for writing a targeted resume, 26
mailing address, 104–105

management
  keywords, 132–133
  managerial assessment, 71
  middle managers, 173
  wow words, 124
manufacturing keywords, 134
market forces, 12
matching resume to job requirements, 72, 315, 317
medical history, 184–185
Mehler, Mark (co-founder and principal of CareerXroads), 10
Melnik, Jan (*Executive's Pocket Guide to ROI Resumes and Job Search*), 173
Merck, 43
mergers, 189–190
Microsoft, 43
mid-career professionals
  project manager, example resume, 237–238
  teacher, example resume, 224–225
  vice president, example resume, 234–235
mid-career trades, example resume, 222
middle managers, 173
Military Officers Association of America Web site, 170
Military Resumes and Cover Letters (Savino and Krannich), 168
military spouse, example resume, 248–249
military to civilian
  example resumes, 242–243, 254–255
  government contractors, 167
  identity theft, 168
  job fairs, 168
  milspeak, 166, 170–172
  resources, 168–170
  strengths, 166
  Transition Assistance Program (TAP), 165
  weaknesses, 166–167
Military to Federal Career Guide (Troutman), 168
military to federal government, 167–169, 260–262
Military Transition to Civilian Success (Hay), 168
MilitaryStars.com Web site, 170
milspeak, 166, 170–172
mirroring ad language, 14
mismatches, 325–326
missing contact information, 329

misspelled words, 137–138, 146, 328, 337
Monster.com Web site, 37
Morgan Stanley, 43
mother returning to work
  example resume, 241
  experience, 180–181
  gender bias, 182
  skills, 180–183
MSN Messenger, 56
multimedia resumes, 101
myths about older workers, 159–160

• *N* •

name (contact information), 104
narrative resume format, 80
National Resume Writers' Association, 323
Nationally Certified Resume Writer (NCRW), 323
negotiating a salary, 72, 120
networking, 48–50
neutralizing damaging references, 286–287
new graduates
  college experience, 154–155
  example resumes, 220–221, 236
  experience, 153
  gaffes, 155–158
  GPA (grade point average), 152–153
  objective, 154
  strengths, 152
  useless information, 154
  weaknesses, 152–153
newspaper classified print ads, 39–41
Non Commissioned Officers Association Web site, 170
numbering pages, 64
nursing
  example resume, 204
  wow words, 129–130

• *O* •

objective statement
  advantages of using, 107
  baby boomers, 160–161, 164
  defined, 106–107
  disadvantages of using, 108
  recent graduates, 154

tips for writing, 317–318
when to use, 107
obtaining permission from references, 284
Occupational Outlook Handbook, 135, 161
Office of Federal Contract Compliance
	Programs (OFCCP), 12–15, 167
office support staff
	example resume, 209
	wow words, 127
omissions, 332
online employee referral services, 46–48
online feeds
	how they work, 53–54
	vertical job search engines (VJSEs), 30, 32
online profiles, 50
online screening programs, 69–72
online social networking, 48–50
OnTarget resumes. *See also* example
	resumes; writing a targeted resume
	abbreviations, 98, 137
	achievements, 311–314, 316, 332, 335
	articles, avoiding, 136, 315–316
	ASCII, 318
	being verbs, 137
	bulleted style, 315
	checklist, 331–337
	defined, 10
	examples, 16–25
	features of, 10
	first person "I," 136, 316
	focus, 77–79, 332, 334–335
	government rules and regulations, 12–15
	helping verbs, 136
	information to leave out, 318
	job software filters, 315
	market forces, 11–12
	matching job requirements, 315, 317
	objective, 317–318
	resume writing services, 322–323
	sell, don't tell, 76–77
	skills, 311–314, 317, 332, 335
	value proposition, 27
	word choice (language), 316–317, 332
opening statements for follow-up efforts, 293
organizations, listing professional and civic
	affiliations, 118
organizing job search information, 298
overexposure to recruiters, 69

overqualified objection
	age discrimination, 176–177
	baby boomers, 162–163, 176–177
	example resumes, 244–245

• *P* •

page numbers, 64
paper version
	design, 141, 333, 336
	groupings, 143
	paper selection, 142
	printing, 142
	scannable resume, 60–61
	style consistency, 143
	word processing, 142
parts of a resume
	achievements, 112, 121
	activities, 117–118
	awards, 118
	competencies, 113–117
	contact information, 103–106, 329
	education, 110–111
	executive summary, 91
	experience, 111
	honors, 118
	licenses, 118
	objective statement, 106–108
	organizations, 118
	salary history and requirements, 120–121,
		139
	samples of your work, 118
	skills, 111–112
	summary statement, 106–110
	testimonials, 119, 284–285
PayScale Web site, 72, 120
permanent address, 105
personality assessment, 70–71
pet peeves of recruiters
	confidential resumes, 329
	dates of employment for jobs, 328–329
	e-stalking, 326–327
	lying on a resume, 330
	mismatches, 325–326
	missing contact information, 329
	resume-free pitches, 325
	too much information, 328
	typos, 328

pet peeves of recruiters *(continued)*
  useless information, 330
  zip files, 329
P&G, 43
phone calls
  for follow-up, 292–298
  for job interviews, 306
phone number (contact information),
    105–106
plain text resume
  alignment, 64
  cover note, 64
  creating, 63, 141
  defined, 61
  example, 62
  page numbers, 64
  submission requirements, 318
  tabs, 64
  typefaces/fonts, 63–64
  word wrap, 64
planning case studies, 71
plastic inserts, 146
podcasts, 56–58, 100
poison words, 139
political correctness, 161
portfolios, 99–101
posting resumes, 67–68
pre-employment programs, 69–72
prescreening programs, 69–72
presentation exercises, 71
presentation folder, 146
pretexting, 295
printing, 142
prisoners, 194–195
privacy issues, 67–68
problem areas
  acquisitions, 189–190
  checklist, 333
  credit history, 193–194
  dates of education, 162
  demotions, 185–187
  disabilities, 183–185, 192–193
  family obligations, 187
  gaps in employment, 184–185, 187–188,
    252–253
  layoffs, 189, 250–251
  mergers, 189–190

overqualified objection, 162–163, 176–178,
    244–245
  prison term, 194–195
  reentering mother/homemaker, 180–182
  substance abuse, 192–193
  temp jobs, 79, 164, 246–247
  too little experience, 180
  too many jobs, 191–192, 256–257
  too much experience in one job, 178–179
  unemployment, 187–188
professional and civic affiliations, 118
Professional Association of Resume
    Writers & Career Counselors, 323
professional resume format, 80, 89–90
professional resume writer
  certifications, 323
  costs, 321–322, 324
  forms, 321
  free consultation, 321
  pros and cons of hiring, 319–320
  referrals, 320
  samples of work, 322
  targeted resumes, 322–323
project managers, example resumes,
    202–203, 237–238
proofreading, 137–138, 146, 328, 337
proportional typefaces, 64
proving achievements and skills, 311–314

• R •

RC (reverse chronological) resume format
  creating, 84
  defined, 80–81
  example, 83
  strengths, 81
  weaknesses, 81–82
  who should use it, 82
  who shouldn't use it, 82
readability, 150
Really Simple Syndication (RSS), 53
recent graduates
  college experience, 154–155
  example resumes, 220–221, 236
  experience, 153
  gaffes, 155–158
  GPA (grade point average), 152–153

objective, 154
strengths, 152
useless information, 154
weaknesses, 152–153
recommendation letters, 285
recruiters
overexposure, 69
pet peeves, 325–330
pretexting, 295
rusing, 295
salary history and requirements, 121
reentering mother/homemaker
example resume, 241
experience, 180–181
gender bias, 182
skills, 180–183
reference folder, 284–285
references
avoidance dodge, 282
choosing, 283–284
co-workers, 284
letters, 283–285
listing in a separate document, 282
neutralizing damaging references, 286–287
obtaining permission from, 284
potential damage they can cause, 281–282
references available upon request, 139
staying in touch with, 284, 288
testing, 284
thanking, 287
tips for finding references when job
search is secret, 287–288
work history, 283
referral services, 46–48
requesting adaptive equipment, 185
research and analysis wow words, 128–129
researching job requirements, 16
responsibilities versus achievements, 139
resume blasting services, 67–68
resume builders, 121
resume examples
academic curriculum vitae, 92–93
accounting, 205
ASCII resume, 62
baby boomers, 227–229, 232
banking, 208
business, 216–217

career change, 240, 266–269
core resume, 17–19
culinary career, 270–272
employment gap, 252–253
food service, 213
healthcare, 201, 214–215
hybrid (combination) format, 88
information technology, 210–211
international curriculum vitae, 95–96
law enforcement/security, 273–277
layoffs, 250–251
mid-career professionals, project
manager, 237–238
mid-career professionals, teacher, 224–225
mid-career professionals, vice president,
234–235
mid-career trades, 222
military spouse, 248–249
military to civilian, 242–243, 254–255
military to federal government, 260–262
mother/homemaker, 241
new graduates, 220–221, 236
nursing, 204
office workers, 209
overqualified, 244–245
plain text resume, 62
professional format, 90
project management, 202–203
retailing, 212
reverse chronological (RC) format, 83
sales, 200
sales to administration, 263–265
skills-based functional format, 86
spin-off resumes, 17–25
supply chain, 206–207
temp jobs, 246–247
too many jobs, 256–257
young professionals, 223, 226, 230–231, 233
Resume Follow-Up Matrix, 299–304
resume formats
academic curriculum vitae, 80, 91–94
accomplishment, 98
ASCII resume, 61–64, 141, 318
checklist, 331
chronological, 80
hybrid (combination), 80, 87–88
international curriculum vitae, 80, 94–97

resume formats *(continued)*
  keyword, 98
  linear, 98
  multimedia resumes, 101
  narrative, 80
  plain text resume, 61–64, 141, 318
  professional, 80, 89–90
  reverse chronological (RC), 80–84
  scannable resume, 60–61
  skills-based functional, 80, 84–86
  suggested formats for various situations,
    80–81
  video podcasts, 100
  Web resumes, 101
resume letters, 99
*Resume Magic: Trade Secrets of a
  Professional Resume Writer*
  (Whitcomb), 145
resume posting, 67–68
resume spamming, 11, 67–68
resume writing services
  certifications for resume writers, 323
  costs, 321–322, 324
  forms, 321
  free consultation, 321
  pros and cons, 319–320
  referrals, 320
  samples of work, 322
  targeted resumes, 322–323
resume-free pitches, 325
resume–job interview connection, 25
retailing example resume, 212
reverse chronological (RC) resume format
  creating, 84
  defined, 80–81
  example, 83
  strengths, 81
  weaknesses, 81–82
  who should use it, 82
  who shouldn't use it, 82
Rites of Passage at $100,000 to $1 Million+
  (Lucht), 173
RiteSite.com Web site, 173
robots, 30
Roehm, Frances E. (*The Guide to Internet
  Job Searching, 2006–2007 edition*), 38
role competencies, 114

Roxio Easy Media Creator, 57
RSS feeds
  how they work, 53–54
  vertical job search engines (VJSEs), 30, 32
RSS (Really Simple Syndication), 53
rusing, 295
Ryze Web site, 48

• S •

salary
  calculator services, 72
  history and requirements, 120–121, 139
  negotiating, 72, 120
Salary Expert Web site, 72
Salary.com Web site, 72, 120
sales
  example resume, 200
  wow words, 125–126
sales and marketing manager, example
  resume, 230
sales to administration, example resume,
  263–265
sample resumes
  academic curriculum vitae, 92–93
  accounting, 205
  ASCII resume, 62
  baby boomers, 227–229, 232
  banking, 208
  business, 216–217
  career change, 240, 266–269
  core resume, 17–19
  culinary career, 270–272
  employment gap, 252–253
  food service, 213
  healthcare, 201, 214–215
  hybrid (combination) format, 88
  information technology, 210–211
  international curriculum vitae, 95–96
  law enforcement/security, 273–277
  layoffs, 250–251
  mid-career professionals, project
    manager, 237–238
  mid-career professionals, teacher,
    224–225
  mid-career professionals, vice president,
    234–235

mid-career trades, 222
military spouse, 248–249
military to civilian, 242–243, 254–255
military to federal government, 260–262
mother/homemaker, 241
new graduates, 220–221, 236
nursing, 204
office workers, 209
overqualified, 244–245
plain text resume, 62
professional format, 90
project management, 202–203
retailing, 212
reverse chronological (RC) format, 83
sales, 200
sales to administration, 263–265
skills-based functional format, 86
spin-off resumes, 17–25
supply chain, 206–207
temp jobs, 246–247
too many jobs, 256–257
young professionals, 223, 226, 230–231, 233
samples of work, 118
Savino, Carl S. (*Military Resumes and Cover Letters*), 168
scannable resume, 60–61
screeners, 294–296
screening programs, 69–72
search engines for jobs
  GetTheJob.com, 35–36
  how they work, 30–32
  Indeed.com, 33–34, 46
  Jobster.com, 34–35, 46–48
  Searchjobs.com, 35
  Simply Hired, 33, 46
  targeted resumes, 43
  Yahoo! HotJobs, 36
Searchjobs.com Web site, 35
sections of a resume
  achievements, 112, 121
  activities, 117–118
  awards, 118
  competencies, 113–117
  contact information, 103–106, 329
  education, 110–111
  executive summary, 91
  experience, 111

honors, 118
licenses, 118
objective statement, 106–108
organizations, 118
salary history and requirements, 120–121, 139
samples of your work, 118
skills, 111–112
summary statement, 106–110
testimonials, 119, 284–285
sell, don't tell, 76–77, 138–139, 316
Sherwin Williams, 43
short-term work, 79, 164, 246–247
Simply Fired Web site, 33
Simply Hired Web site, 33, 46
skills
  checklist, 332, 335
  matching to job requirements, 317
  mother/homemaker returning to work, 180–183
  proving, 311–314
  skills and knowledge testing, 70
  what to include, 111–112
  wow words, 131
skills-based functional resume format
  creating, 85
  defined, 80, 84
  example, 85
  strengths, 84–85
  weaknesses, 85
  who should use it, 85
  who shouldn't use it, 85
social networking, 48–50
Social Security number, 139
Society for Human Resource Management, 330
sources of keywords, 135
Southwest Airlines, 43
spam filters, 68
spamming, 11, 67–68
special equipment requests, 185
spelling errors, 137–138, 146, 328, 337
spiders, 30
spin-off resumes, 17–25
stapling, 146
Starbucks, 43
staying in touch with references, 284, 288

Strasburg, Linda
  Competency-Based Interviews, 116
  Competency-Based Resumes, 116
strategies for job interviews, 308
strengths
  of baby boomers, 158–159, 161
  of military candidates, 166
  of recent graduates, 152
Struzik, Ed (president of BEKS Data
    Services, Inc.), 66
Student's Federal Career Guide (Troutman),
    169
style checklist, 331
style consistency, 143
subject line of e-mail messages, 65
submission requirements for ASCII
    resumes, 318
substance abuse, 192–193
suggested formats for various situations,
    80–81
summary statement
  advantages of using, 110
  baby boomers, 160–161, 164
  defined, 106–107
  disadvantages of using, 110
  example, 109
  recent graduates, 154
  tips for writing, 317–318
  when to use, 108–109
supply chain, example resume, 206–207

● *T* ●

tabs in ASCII resume, 64
TAOnline Web site, 170
TAP (Transition Assistance Program), 165
Target, 43
targeted resumes. *See also* example
    resumes; writing a targeted resume
  abbreviations, 98, 137
  achievements, 311–314, 316, 332, 335
  articles, avoiding, 136, 315–316
  ASCII, 318
  being verbs, 137
  bulleted style, 315
  checklist, 331–337
  defined, 10

features of, 10
first person "I," 136, 316
focus, 77–79, 332, 334–335
government rules and regulations, 12–15
helping verbs, 136
information to leave out, 318
job software filters, 315
market forces, 11–12
matching job requirements, 315, 317
objective, 317–318
resume writing services, 322–323
sell, don't tell, 76–77
skills, 311–314, 317, 332, 335
value proposition, 27
vertical job search engines (VJSEs), 43
word choice (language), 316–317, 332
teachers
  example resume, 224–225
  wow words, 128
technical ability wow words, 126–127
telephone calls
  for follow-up, 292–298
  for job interviews, 306
telephone number (contact information),
    105–106
temp jobs, 79, 164, 246–247
testimonials, 119, 284–285
testing references, 284
Texas Instruments, 43
thanking references, 287
theme papers, 142
37Signals Web site, 52
too little experience, 180
too many jobs, 190–192, 256–257
too much experience in one job, 178–179
too much information, 328
TopJobSites.com Web site, 37
trade magazines, 135
trades, example resume, 222
Transition Assistance Program (TAP), 165
travel costs for job interviews, 307–308
Trillian Web site, 56
Troutman, Kathryn
  *Federal Resume Guidebook, Fourth
    Edition*, 169
  Military to Federal Career Guide, 168
  Student's Federal Career Guide, 169

typefaces
  ACSII resume, 63–64
  defined, 145
  design guidelines, 145
  proportional, 64
Typepad blog host site, 53
typos, 137–138, 146, 328, 337

• *U* •

U R a Brand!: How Smart People Brand Themselves for Business Success (Kaputa), 57
undue hardship provision of the Americans with Disabilities Act (ADA), 184
unemployment, 187–188
U.S. Department of Labor
  Dictionary of Occupational Titles, 135
  Occupational Outlook Handbook, 135, 161
USA Web site, 169
useless information
  as pet peeve of recruiters, 330
  on resumes of recent graduates, 154

• *V* •

value proposition, 27
verbs
  being verbs, 137
  helping verbs, 136
  word choice (language), 316–317
vertical job search engines (VJSEs)
  GetTheJob.com, 35–36
  how they work, 30–32
  Indeed.com, 33, 46
  Jobster.com, 34–35, 46–48
  Searchjobs.com, 35
  Simply Hired, 33, 46
  targeted resumes, 43
  Yahoo! HotJobs, 36
VetJobs.com Web site, 170
vice president, example resume, 234–235
video resumes, 100
virus filters, 68
VJSEs (vertical job search engines). *See* vertical job search engines (VJSEs)
voicemail messages, 296–298

• *W* •

Walther, George R. (*Heat Up Your Cold Calls*), 297
weaknesses
  of baby boomers, 159–160
  of military candidates, 166–167
  of recent graduates, 152–153
Web 1.0, 1–2, 11
Web 2.0, 1–2, 12, 45–46, 58
Web page address (contact information), 105
Web resumes, 101
Web sites
  Americans with Disabilities Act (ADA), 184
  BEKS Data Services, Inc., 66
  BlogEasy, 53
  Blogger, 53
  Blogs with Jobs, 53
  Boutell.com, 57
  Business.com, 136
  Career Directors International, 323
  CareerBuilder.com, 37
  Classmates.com, 49
  Corporate Gray, 170
  Crunchboard, 52
  Ecademy, 48
  Eons, 49
  ExecuNet, 48
  Feedburner, 57
  Gaim, 56
  GetTheJob.com, 35–36
  Google, 112
  H3, 47
  Indeed.com, 33–34, 46
  Intelligence Careers, 170
  JibberJobber job tracking program, 298
  Job Accommodation Network, 184–185
  Job Central National Labor Exchange, 39, 46
  Job Search Engine Guide, 31
  Job-Hunt.org, 68
  JobStar, 120
  Jobster.com, 34–35, 46–48
  The Landmark Destiny Group, 170
  LinkedIn, 48
  Military Officers Association of America, 170

Web sites *(continued)*
MilitaryStars.com, 170
Monster.com, 37
National Resume Writers' Association, 323
Non Commissioned Officers Association, 170
PayScale, 72, 120
Professional Association of Resume Writers & Career Counselors, 323
RiteSite.com, 173
Ryze, 48
Salary Expert, 72
Salary.com, 72, 120
Searchjobs.com, 35
Simply Fired, 33
Simply Hired, 33, 46
TAOnline, 170
37Signals, 52
TopJobSites.com, 37
Trillian, 56
Typepad, 53
USA, 169
VetJobs.com, 170
World Privacy Forum, 67
Yahoo! HotJobs, 36
Zoominfo, 49
Whirlpool, 43
Whitaker, Urban *(Career Success: A Step-By-Step Workbook for Students, Job Seekers and Lifelong Learners)*, 112
Whitcomb, Susan Britton *(Resume Magic: Trade Secrets of a Professional Resume Writer)*, 145
white space, 145
Williams, Dr. Wendell (personality testing expert), 70–71
word choice (language). *See also* keywords; wow words
  checklist, 332
  nouns and verbs, 316–317
word processing, 142
word wrap, 64
work experience
  baby boomers, 162
  overqualified objection, 176–177

recent graduate, 153
reentering mother/homemaker, 180–181
too little experience, 180
too much experience in one job, 178–179
what to include, 111
work history
  demotions, 185–187
  gaps in employment, 185, 187–188, 252–253
  layoffs, 189, 250–251
  references, 283
  temp jobs, 164, 246–247
  too many jobs, 190–192
  unemployment, 187–188
work samples, 118
work-based competencies, 113
worked with, avoiding the term, 139
World Privacy Forum, 67
wow words
  for administration and management, 124
  for caregiving, 129–130
  for communications and creativity, 125
  for financial management, 130
  for helping, 129–130
  for office support staff, 127
  for research and analysis, 128–129
  for sales, 125–126
  for skills, 131
  for teachers, 128
  for technical ability, 126–127
writing a targeted resume. *See also* resume writing services
  abbreviations, 98, 137
  achievements, 316, 332, 335
  articles, avoiding, 136, 315–316
  being verbs, 137
  bulleted style, 315
  first person "I," 136, 316
  grammar, 136–137
  helping verbs, 136
  information to leave out, 318
  magic formula, 26
  matching job requirements, 315, 317
  mirroring ad language, 14
  mission statement, 239
  objective, 317–318

sell, don't tell, 76–77, 138–139, 316
step-by-step directions, 15–16
word choice (language), 316–317, 332
writing recommendation letters, 285

• *X* •

Xerox, 43

• *Y* •

Yahoo! HotJobs Web site, 36
Yahoo! Messenger, 56

young professionals, example resumes
associate editor, 233
graphic artist, 226
intern, 223
sales and marketing manager, 230–231

• *Z* •

ZIP files, 66, 329
Zoominfo Web site, 49

Notes

BUSINESS, CAREERS & PERSONAL FINANCE

0-7645-9847-3

0-7645-2431-3

Also available:

- Business Plans Kit For Dummies
  0-7645-9794-9
- Economics For Dummies
  0-7645-5726-2
- Grant Writing For Dummies
  0-7645-8416-2
- Home Buying For Dummies
  0-7645-5331-3
- Managing For Dummies
  0-7645-1771-6
- Marketing For Dummies
  0-7645-5600-2

- Personal Finance For Dummies
  0-7645-2590-5*
- Resumes For Dummies
  0-7645-5471-9
- Selling For Dummies
  0-7645-5363-1
- Six Sigma For Dummies
  0-7645-6798-5
- Small Business Kit For Dummies
  0-7645-5984-2
- Starting an eBay Business For Dummies
  0-7645-6924-4
- Your Dream Career For Dummies
  0-7645-9795-7

HOME & BUSINESS COMPUTER BASICS

0-470-05432-8

0-471-75421-8

Also available:

- Cleaning Windows Vista For Dummies
  0-471-78293-9
- Excel 2007 For Dummies
  0-470-03737-7
- Mac OS X Tiger For Dummies
  0-7645-7675-5
- MacBook For Dummies
  0-470-04859-X
- Macs For Dummies
  0-470-04849-2
- Office 2007 For Dummies
  0-470-00923-3

- Outlook 2007 For Dummies
  0-470-03830-6
- PCs For Dummies
  0-7645-8958-X
- Salesforce.com For Dummies
  0-470-04893-X
- Upgrading & Fixing Laptops For Dummies
  0-7645-8959-8
- Word 2007 For Dummies
  0-470-03658-3
- Quicken 2007 For Dummies
  0-470-04600-7

FOOD, HOME, GARDEN, HOBBIES, MUSIC & PETS

0-7645-8404-9

0-7645-9904-6

Also available:

- Candy Making For Dummies
  0-7645-9734-5
- Card Games For Dummies
  0-7645-9910-0
- Crocheting For Dummies
  0-7645-4151-X
- Dog Training For Dummies
  0-7645-8418-9
- Healthy Carb Cookbook For Dummies
  0-7645-8476-6
- Home Maintenance For Dummies
  0-7645-5215-5

- Horses For Dummies
  0-7645-9797-3
- Jewelry Making & Beading For Dummies
  0-7645-2571-9
- Orchids For Dummies
  0-7645-6759-4
- Puppies For Dummies
  0-7645-5255-4
- Rock Guitar For Dummies
  0-7645-5356-9
- Sewing For Dummies
  0-7645-6847-7
- Singing For Dummies
  0-7645-2475-5

INTERNET & DIGITAL MEDIA

0-470-04529-9

0-470-04894-8

Also available:

- Blogging For Dummies
  0-471-77084-1
- Digital Photography For Dummies
  0-7645-9802-3
- Digital Photography All-in-One Desk Reference For Dummies
  0-470-03743-1
- Digital SLR Cameras and Photography For Dummies
  0-7645-9803-1
- eBay Business All-in-One Desk Reference For Dummies
  0-7645-8438-3
- HDTV For Dummies
  0-470-09673-X

- Home Entertainment PCs For Dummies
  0-470-05523-5
- MySpace For Dummies
  0-470-09529-6
- Search Engine Optimization For Dummies
  0-471-97998-8
- Skype For Dummies
  0-470-04891-3
- The Internet For Dummies
  0-7645-8996-2
- Wiring Your Digital Home For Dummies
  0-471-91830-X

* Separate Canadian edition also available
† Separate U.K. edition also available

Available wherever books are sold. For more information or to order direct: U.S. customers visit www.dummies.com or call 1-877-762-2974.
U.K. customers visit www.wileyeurope.com or call 0800 243407. Canadian customers visit www.wiley.ca or call 1-800-567-4797.

SPORTS, FITNESS, PARENTING, RELIGION & SPIRITUALITY

0-471-76871-5

0-7645-7841-3

Also available:

- Catholicism For Dummies
  0-7645-5391-7
- Exercise Balls For Dummies
  0-7645-5623-1
- Fitness For Dummies
  0-7645-7851-0
- Football For Dummies
  0-7645-3936-1
- Judaism For Dummies
  0-7645-5299-6
- Potty Training For Dummies
  0-7645-5417-4
- Buddhism For Dummies
  0-7645-5359-3

- Pregnancy For Dummies
  0-7645-4483-7 †
- Ten Minute Tone-Ups For Dummies
  0-7645-7207-5
- NASCAR For Dummies
  0-7645-7681-X
- Religion For Dummies
  0-7645-5264-3
- Soccer For Dummies
  0-7645-5229-5
- Women in the Bible For Dummies
  0-7645-8475-8

TRAVEL

0-7645-7749-2

0-7645-6945-7

Also available:

- Alaska For Dummies
  0-7645-7746-8
- Cruise Vacations For Dummies
  0-7645-6941-4
- England For Dummies
  0-7645-4276-1
- Europe For Dummies
  0-7645-7529-5
- Germany For Dummies
  0-7645-7823-5
- Hawaii For Dummies
  0-7645-7402-7

- Italy For Dummies
  0-7645-7386-1
- Las Vegas For Dummies
  0-7645-7382-9
- London For Dummies
  0-7645-4277-X
- Paris For Dummies
  0-7645-7630-5
- RV Vacations For Dummies
  0-7645-4442-X
- Walt Disney World & Orlando
  For Dummies
  0-7645-9660-8

GRAPHICS, DESIGN & WEB DEVELOPMENT

0-7645-8815-X

0-7645-9571-7

Also available:

- 3D Game Animation For Dummies
  0-7645-8789-7
- AutoCAD 2006 For Dummies
  0-7645-8925-3
- Building a Web Site For Dummies
  0-7645-7144-3
- Creating Web Pages For Dummies
  0-470-08030-2
- Creating Web Pages All-in-One Desk
  Reference For Dummies
  0-7645-4345-8
- Dreamweaver 8 For Dummies
  0-7645-9649-7

- InDesign CS2 For Dummies
  0-7645-9572-5
- Macromedia Flash 8 For Dummies
  0-7645-9691-8
- Photoshop CS2 and Digital
  Photography For Dummies
  0-7645-9580-6
- Photoshop Elements 4 For Dummies
  0-471-77483-9
- Syndicating Web Sites with RSS Feeds
  For Dummies
  0-7645-8848-6
- Yahoo! SiteBuilder For Dummies
  0-7645-9800-7

NETWORKING, SECURITY, PROGRAMMING & DATABASES

0-7645-7728-X

0-471-74940-0

Also available:

- Access 2007 For Dummies
  0-470-04612-0
- ASP.NET 2 For Dummies
  0-7645-7907-X
- C# 2005 For Dummies
  0-7645-9704-3
- Hacking For Dummies
  0-470-05235-X
- Hacking Wireless Networks
  For Dummies
  0-7645-9730-2
- Java For Dummies
  0-470-08716-1

- Microsoft SQL Server 2005 For Dummies
  0-7645-7755-7
- Networking All-in-One Desk Reference
  For Dummies
  0-7645-9939-9
- Preventing Identity Theft For Dummies
  0-7645-7336-5
- Telecom For Dummies
  0-471-77085-X
- Visual Studio 2005 All-in-One Desk
  Reference For Dummies
  0-7645-9775-2
- XML For Dummies
  0-7645-8845-1

HEALTH & SELF-HELP

0-7645-8450-2   0-7645-4149-8

Also available:
- Bipolar Disorder For Dummies
  0-7645-8451-0
- Chemotherapy and Radiation
  For Dummies
  0-7645-7832-4
- Controlling Cholesterol For Dummies
  0-7645-5440-9
- Diabetes For Dummies
  0-7645-6820-5* †
- Divorce For Dummies
  0-7645-8417-0 †

- Fibromyalgia For Dummies
  0-7645-5441-7
- Low-Calorie Dieting For Dummies
  0-7645-9905-4
- Meditation For Dummies
  0-471-77774-9
- Osteoporosis For Dummies
  0-7645-7621-6
- Overcoming Anxiety For Dummies
  0-7645-5447-6
- Reiki For Dummies
  0-7645-9907-0
- Stress Management For Dummies
  0-7645-5144-2

EDUCATION, HISTORY, REFERENCE & TEST PREPARATION

0-7645-8381-6   0-7645-9554-7

Also available:
- The ACT For Dummies
  0-7645-9652-7
- Algebra For Dummies
  0-7645-5325-9
- Algebra Workbook For Dummies
  0-7645-8467-7
- Astronomy For Dummies
  0-7645-8465-0
- Calculus For Dummies
  0-7645-2498-4
- Chemistry For Dummies
  0-7645-5430-1
- Forensics For Dummies
  0-7645-5580-4

- Freemasons For Dummies
  0-7645-9796-5
- French For Dummies
  0-7645-5193-0
- Geometry For Dummies
  0-7645-5324-0
- Organic Chemistry I For Dummies
  0-7645-6902-3
- The SAT I For Dummies
  0-7645-7193-1
- Spanish For Dummies
  0-7645-5194-9
- Statistics For Dummies
  0-7645-5423-9

Get smart @ dummies.com®

- **Find a full list of Dummies titles**
- **Look into loads of FREE on-site articles**
- **Sign up for FREE eTips e-mailed to you weekly**
- **See what other products carry the Dummies name**
- **Shop directly from the Dummies bookstore**
- **Enter to win new prizes every month!**

* Separate Canadian edition also available

† Separate U.K. edition also available

Available wherever books are sold. For more information or to order direct: U.S. customers visit www.dummies.com or call 1-877-762-2974.
U.K. customers visit www.wileyeurope.com or call 0800 243407. Canadian customers visit www.wiley.ca or call 1-800-567-4797.